ADVERTISING WORK

Richmond

Egert

ADVERTISING WORKS 10

Cases from the IPA Advertising Effectiveness Awards

Institute of Practitioners in Advertising, 1998

Edited and introduced by

Nick Kendall

NTC PUBLICATIONS LIMITED

First published 1999 by **NTC Publications Limited**
Farm Road, Henley-on-Thames, Oxfordshire RG9 1EJ, United Kingdom
Telephone: 01491 411000
Fax: 01491 571188
E-mail: info@ntc.co.uk

A CIP catalogue record for this book is available from the British Library

ISBN 1 84116 028 8

Typeset by NTC Publications Ltd
Printed and bound in Great Britain
by Biddles Ltd, Guildford and King's Lynn

Contents

IPA
Advertising Effectiveness Awards 1998

A call for new learning

'Learning is the only true competitive advantage.'

Aries de Gues, Head of Strategy, Shell

BACKGROUND

The IPA Advertising Effectiveness Awards have created the finest collection of advertising case histories in the world, now meticulously indexed in the IPA Effectiveness Data Bank and available to the world through the Web (http://www.ipa.co.uk).

It was from this position of strength, and with the 10th Anniversary approaching, that the IPA decided to review the Awards and consider their future development.

Advertising Works 10 therefore represents:

- a record of the changes made to the Awards' criteria and the judging process;
- a record of all the 1998 prize winners, with 17 full case histories and 13 abstracts. This is the first time all winners have appeared in this book
- first learnings from the cases, both in the form of these introductory observations and commentaries from judges who took part in the process and wished to record their observations. These commentaries, placed at the beginning of each prize section, are again new and welcome additions to the *Advertising Works* series and allow general lessons to be drawn.

THE REVIEW PROCESS

The steering group that carried out the review saw their job, first and foremost, as soliciting the views of the industry on how they wished to shape their Awards. Therefore the major parts of the changes below were based on the points of view of a wide variety of people interviewed – Agency CEO's and management, planning directors, previous authors and convenors of judges, researchers, academics and journalists, and, importantly, clients (gathered through questionnaires, a full-scale qualitative project, and industry bodies).

THE AWARDS – A PILLAR BRAND

It is worth pausing to note the extremely high regard all parties had for the Awards. The Client community indeed regarded the Awards, in many ways, as the 'finest hour' of the industry, focusing as they do on the key issues of how advertising can:

'add value to my business?'

'provide a vote of confidence to internal audiences that our advertising strategy is sound.'

'help top management to have a greater understanding of effective advertising.'

'provide excellent PR for the company and the brand.'

Source: Good Thinking Qualitative Research, 1997

This respect has been confirmed in quantitative surveys carried out with the support of the ISBA most notably:

'The IPA Advertising Effectiveness Awards scheme has highest awareness of any advertising communication award scheme at 76%.'

'66% of marketers believe the Awards reflected achievement.'

'68% would like to see 'my company/brand written.'

'52% of UK advertisers who are knowledgeable about the awards find the IPA Advertising Effectiveness Awards Cases "helpful in justifying marketing and advertising expenditure".'

Source: IPA Survey of ISBA membership 1994

The industry itself was also justly proud of the achievements of the Awards. For many, the Awards, and the industry commitment to them represented a moral foundation on which we could truly claim to be interested in accountability and, indeed, willing and able to take on its challenges. As one interviewee rightly pointed out 'imagine where we would be without them'.

It was clear that the Awards were a brand in their own right and, as such, needed to be managed like any great brand in order to preserve the relationship of respect it had with its users, namely:

- preserve the core purpose and vision of the brand;
- maintain the core quality of the brand;
- ensure a sense of contemporary relevance.

The review considered each of these areas in turn.

THE CORE PURPOSE AND VISION OF THE AWARDS

Therefore, what has not changed in 1998 is the founding principle on which the original brand was created. The objectives of the Awards remain:

'to demonstrate that advertising can be proven to work against measurable criteria for example, sales measures, and show that it is both a serious commercial investment and a contributor to profit, not just a cost.'

'though this demonstration to improve understanding, particularly outside the industry, of the crucial role advertising plays in marketing generally as well as in specific applications.'

'to achieve a closer analysis of advertising effectiveness and improved methods of evaluation and therefore to inculcate ever-improving professional standards among those within the advertising industry.'

Source: Guide to Entrants 1998

Back in 1980 these exact same objectives in effect set the industry two challenges – first, to prove that advertising could add value and demonstrably contribute to profit and, second, in doing so to develop and spread best practice.

Demonstrating that Advertising can be Proven to Contribute to Profit

In truth, 18 years ago (remarkably in retrospect and testament to how far we have travelled) not everyone believed one could isolate or prove the effectiveness of advertising:

'the idea of defining exactly, or even approximately, how effective an ad is must be self-evidently nonsense.'

'the awards attempt the impossible: to quantify one element in a marketing mix.'

'it is a delusion that the results of advertising can be isolated and assessed.'

'it is a dangerous myth that all or at least most advertisements are capable of being tried and tested.'

Source: Comments on the Award scheme in 1980
names of authors of quotes withheld to protect the guilty

It is fair to say now that there are few who do not recognise that advertising's value can be demonstrably measured. Even Lord Leverhulme could find out which half of his budget worked if he truly wanted to. The only requirement is resource, mainly in terms of time and research, intelligence in approach, and the will to do it. Certainly, there is enough expertise both inside and outside agencies.

Whether everyone does isolate advertising value and why they do not is a different question and one worthy of a separate debate, but these Awards have proved it can be done over the last 20 years.

Personally, my belief is that the biggest barrier over the next 20 years to making effectiveness a true part of the Agency/Client process is culture not understanding.

In today's business environment there seems to be general impetus not to look back, and a specific fear of learning from our past in case we are proven wrong.

This is a culture not just of Agencies – though the added chance of being 'fired' by a Client suddenly not involved in the initial agreements adds piquancy – but also of Clients' organisations unwilling to admit anything other than 100% success to their colleagues and their boardroom.

If we are to overcome these cultural issues a number of things need to happen relating to goal setting and culture creation.

- First, the upside of success for both parties has to be emphasised and increased. If we are asking the relationship to be more accountable we have to create the incentive for it to be so (and conversely of course a suitable downside if success is not achieved!).

- Second, the upsides have to be mutually aligned, so that, as a team (Client and Agency) we have shared objectives. It is a ridiculous situation if a Client's success criteria is different from an Agency's. We have all worked with enough sales forces to know the dangers of such a situation!

- Third, Client and Agency senior management have to create an atmosphere where learning about our success becomes obligatory but in a non-threatening way. Visible and vocal support can create the right culture just as silence can create a negative one.

- Finally, following on from this point, there must be investment in this area, either in resources to do the job properly, or in training. Again this investment is required both on the Client and the Agency side.

All these factors point, in my view, to some form of PRP, profit or performance related pay, becoming a permanent feature of the Agency/Client landscape. These awards have given us the tools and experience to be able to consider such an option with a confidence which would surely have been sorely lacking back in 1980.

Developing and Spreading Best Practice

Graham Hinton, IPA President, described the Awards as 'a treasure house of learning'.

His point was clear: though framed as a competition and allowing, in the short term, both individual writers and agencies a moment of deserved glory, the long term and residual benefit of the brand must be the concentrated and in-depth lessons in best practice they offer:

- Lessons to the individuals who wrote them; I have never met one author, successful or not, who did not admit (after the event usually!) that writing a paper gave them the best crash training course in measuring advertising and the principles behind it.

- Lessons to the agencies who support them year in and year out and through them strive to improve their understanding of effectiveness and create a meaningful culture of accountability.
- Lessons to the industry as a whole who digest their insights and best practice examples either directly through reading, or indirectly from the osmotic transfer of ideas and techniques.
- Lessons to academics who increasingly access the IPA Databank of specific cases to create general proofs and guidelines.
- And of course, lessons to Clients who benefit from an industry constantly investing in that learning to supply better and more accountable advice.

The Awards are, in effect, our investment in industry-wide training – a massive act of altruism, and at the same time, a hard-headed investment in our future competitive advantage.

MAINTAINING THE CORE QUALITY OF THE BRAND

Such lessons in best practice can only, of course, come from the best, not the OK, not the mediocre, and therefore, I am sorry to say, not the easily and glibly written. The purpose of these Awards is quality not simply quantity.

So, the review group resisted the temptation to 'dumb down' the Awards and suggestions to cut the words required, tinker with the criteria for proof or adapt a 'ready-made set of questions' format were rejected. Such moves, it was argued, may secure a short-term increase in numbers (the equivalent of a ruling that any athlete could go to the Olympics) but potentially destroy the long-term credibility and respect of the competition.

The changes in this year's Awards therefore were designed not to encourage more, but less, valuable gems to be added to the treasure house, to encourage a wider variety of precious lessons.

MAINTAINING THE AWARDS' CONTEMPORARY RELEVANCE

The review process made clear that any changes should preserve the core purpose and the core quality and therefore preserve the learning potential of the Awards.

However, the review process also indicated that there was some growing concern that the cases were in danger of 'repeating' themselves year on year, *refining* our understanding and methodologies rather than breaking fresh ground and opening new debates. In this context, the opening comments in the introduction of *Advertising Works 1* became particularly pertinent;

'Waiting for the response from agencies was an anxious time. Would enough advertisers agree to release details of strategy and perhaps sales? Did agencies in fact believe sufficiently seriously in these high standards of campaign evaluation? Were they confident enough that their work produced measurable results? Would the authors give the required time to write satisfactory papers?'

'Although there was no precedent to work to, would the papers prove convincing?'

Simon Broadbent, First Convenor of Judges, *Advertising Works 1*

The quote reminded us how exciting and, in many ways, how scary, the original Awards were. Authors were creating in space, on a blank canvas.

With this spirit of discovery in mind we resolved that any key changes in the Awards should represent and facilitate *a call for new learning*.

Our intention was to disrupt and so, we hoped, to create a step change in the nature and the content of the papers entered.

So, at the core of this year's changes we set the industry a new challenge. We called for cases which looked not only at advertising's effect on consumer demand – though sales would remain the cornerstone on which a case would be built – but also at advertising's ability to add value to a brand's other key stakeholders.

The industry has long talked of the *manifold effects* of advertising on these targets but, as in 1980, there is a vacuum of specific and rigorous case material. Our proofs have tended to the anecdotal. With this call for new learning in mind the guide to new entrants was issued.

The following extract is taken from this guide.

THE GUIDE TO NEW ENTRANTS

The Parameters of the Cases

- *The objectives for the Awards remain the same.*
- *Cases are invited that look beyond the sample of sales and investigate the manifold effects which advertising can contribute to profitability.*

Awards Structure and Prizes

All category definitions have been removed in order to ensure no limiting effects on the exploration of the benefits advertising can achieve.

Only one special prize will be awarded, the Charles Chanon prize, for the case that contributes most to new learning on how to isolate advertising effect overall or in the form of a new methodology or approach.

The 1998 Awards will move away from the restrictive and competitively framed pyramid structure of one Gold, two Silvers, three Bronzes, to a flatter structure of allocation of 'star ratings', which will denote the relative quality of each case. The intention is to create a 5-star system where there will be no limitation on the number of papers that can be awarded in each category and where shortlisted papers will merit at least one star. The belief is that such a system reflects the increase in quality over the years and will allow us to highlight the status of a case as appropriate to its worth (in its skill in exploring effects, on its contribution to our understanding, in its bravery in exploring manifold ways in which advertising works, and in its value, therefore, in creating new learning for any future reader).

The Grand Prix will be retained and awarded to the most outstanding paper and will be selected from those papers that achieve five stars in the judges' eyes.

For those cases that extend their argument beyond sales a maximum of 5,000 words will be allowed, if required. All other cases should remain at 4,000 words or less.

The Judging Process

The aim is to maintain and indeed, improve the quality of the judging process. There will therefore be a slightly modified two-stage judging process.

At the first stage a panel of industry specialist advisors (comprising the convenor, the deputy convenor, experts in econometrics and brand valuation, two researchers and two further industry experts) will be asked to shortlist papers and provide analysis of their technical qualities and a commentary on the validity and quality of the case and the proof contained in the paper.

The second stage of the process will consist of a jury comprising the convenor and a deputy convenor, six leading business people including disciplines outside of marketing, and a chairman of judges, who will be a senior member of the business community. This jury will be asked to judge the cases and award stars according to the impressiveness of the case based both in their 'real world' business experience and informed by the comments of the specialist panel.

THE 1998 ADVERTISING EFFECTIVENESS AWARDS ENTRIES

The challenge of 1998 was a tough one and maybe in part intimidating. Certainly, the number of entries was down versus previous years and more in line with the number of entries received at the beginning of the Awards.

However, this decline is part of a long term trend first noted by Gary Duckworth in *Advertising Works 9* and though changes in 1998 might not have helped matters they cannot be seen as the core issue.

Year	90	92	94	96	98
Entries	87	80	73	70	54

The papers do take time to construct – time that the industry, since its 20% cutbacks in 1990 when the decline first set in, has much less of to focus on important but non-urgent issues, such as these Awards.

More critically in my view, the number of Agencies entering has increased with an all-time record of agencies, suggesting an approach where Agencies are increasingly choosing only to enter their best and to thereby limit their focus and investment.

Nonetheless, the question of how to encourage more entries – there are still many notable Agencies and Clients who do not enter – is definitely a pertinent one for the next round of Awards.

However, one thing that did not decline was the quality of entries. This is not simply a personal view but one that represents the views of all the judges. As a result a total of 30 papers received star awards with the Client judges feeling it possible to award a number of five stars, and thus avoid the pyramid structure as planned.

Profile of Stars Awarded

5 stars	7
4 stars	4
3 stars	6
2 stars	6
1 star	7

Sixty per cent of these awards were to non-traditional advertisers, that is, non FMCG, continuing the trend of recent Awards. All three key prizes highlighted this trend – the Charles Channon, the Grand Prix and the ISBA award went to a telecoms campaign (Orange), a government campaign (HEA Drugs Education) and a telecoms campaign (One2One) respectively.

All three cases also argued for advertising's effect *across multiple targets* (see below) and as such all offered new learning.

NEW LEARNING FROM THE KEY PRIZE WINNERS

New Learning from the Drugs Education Case

The judges felt that the HEA paper represented a touchstone for the power of advertising. Working on what must be one of the most intractable problems, against one of the most cynical of targets, in an overwhelmingly hostile (pro-drugs) environment, the paper illustrates how advertising was able to 'infiltrate fortress youth' and actually change behaviour by educating with empathy (no scare stories, no lectures, no moral outrage!). Furthermore the paper offers proof of how advertising's public message was able to co-ordinate the whole education process, from lessons in schools through counselling at drug advisory centres, and even how the press discussed the issue. Advertising created a focused and informed debate. As a result the judges were impressed by the paper's argument for multiple payback; £28 million diverted from the black market, a saving of £11 million per year in lost working days and a saving of approximately £3 million as a result of the avoidance of producing extra or alternative education material.

New Learning from the Orange Case

The case picks up where the Gold paper of two years ago left off – with Orange's launch in the City. In doing so it adds a fresh dimension to thinking about advertising ROI by concentrating exclusively on arguing a case for the brand's/advertising's effect on Orange's share price since that launch.   This completely innovative approach culminates in a piece of City (Lehman Brothers) analysis which the judges felt was the equivalent to the first paper using econometric analysis. There is no doubt therefore that this paper should encourage more conversations, crossovers and alliances between Soho and the City to prove, beyond a doubt, that creativity pays not only against consumers but also against shareholders and their advisors.

New Learning from the One2One Case

In October 1996, One2One was suffering most in an increasingly competitive market. Prospective customers were going elsewhere for their first mobile network, employees had declining confidence in their ability to compete, and city commentators questioned One2One's future.

A new campaign re-defined mobile phones as conduits for rewarding 'fantasy' conversations. 'Who would you most like to have a One 2 One with?' passed into the vernacular, bringing the brand much-needed stature and 'brand fame'. As a result, over just a year, One2One's acquisition grew by more than any of the other three networks producing a 'remarkable' increase of 150%. The case goes on to argue the effectiveness of the advertising across all stakeholders.

Customer satisfaction research also showed the advertising fame was related to an increase in customer retention.

In the annual employee survey 'pride' rose and the number of staff who felt One2One's advertising was better than that of its competitors went from 17 to 71%.

Research with financial analysts and journalists showed that they fundamentally believed that the change in One2One's fortunes was related to the turn-around in the company's maketing.

Overall, the campaign gave everyone – internally and externally – something to be proud of.

NEW LEARNING OVERALL

As hoped, therefore, cases began to look at advertising's effect both on external and internal audiences. Against what might be considered a brand's most crucial external audience (apart from consumers of course) – the City – Orange and One2One stood out most clearly as attempts to measure advertising's effect, but the HEA's investigation of advertising's internal effect was mirrored across the piece with nearly a third of papers looking at the area, whether in terms of:

- Employees sense of pride in general as measured in employee satisfaction surveys, for example, North West Water and the Army.
- The benefits to a brand's front-line ambassadors, for example, people selling Pools or those collecting on behalf of Christian Aid.

- The financial effects on the intermediary or trade target, for example, the dealers working to sell Volkswagen or Audi, or the meat trade recovering from the BSE crisis.
- The managerial team and their sense of purpose and confidence, for example, Bacardi Breezers' decision to build on Breezer's success in the long spirit drink market with more vigorous npd, a re-structured company and a new factory.

NEW LEARNING ON THE IMPORTANCE OF PUBLIC FAME

The Awards therefore begin to define how, maybe uniquely, advertising has the ability to talk to multiple targets simultaneously and thereby align and influence those groups in a common understanding of the brand's purpose, and a common pursuit.

We have heard much in the last few years of a 'one to one' future. Interestingly the learnings from these papers suggest a crucial and valuable role for a continuing 'one to many' future; private conversations are powerful but so too are public 'fame' broadcasts.

Indeed the more fragmented and cynical the world becomes, advertising's ability to distil a brand's vision and build emotion into a communication might actually become more important, not less.

In this context it becomes clear that advertising can become the CEO's voice – a powerful, clear and inspirational voice – that can be directed at a brand's consumers and 'overheard' by other key targets.

In line with this thought many of this year's cases demonstrate a kind of *multiple effectiveness* where the investment is paid back not only in sales but then also in employee buy in, and then in city understanding and belief and so on and so on. Advertising investment achieves an accumulator return and so becomes efficient not only in a sales per pound sense but in a wider, holistic sense also.

Such an ability argues strongly for a CEO's (re)involvement in the creation and sign off of such advertising. After all would a CEO expect a speech or press release to go out to the City or to all employees without his sign off.

NEW LEARNING IN MEASURING CONSUMER DEMAND AND ADVERTISING EFFICIENCY

In the above concept of a ripple effect of success the starting point of sales success becomes more, not less, important and therefore it was notable that new learning was also in evidence in this area, in particular in *how to measure the efficiency of the advertising.*

Many papers took on the task of trying to establish not just whether the advertising was successful, but the deeper question of how successful and how its effects compared to competitors.

Several papers therefore looked at the success of their advertising on awareness and image scores versus others in the market (for example, Bud Ice) or looked at their success versus competitors whereas Pizza Hut considered the present campaign versus their own previous campaigns. Both of these I would expect to become commonplace measures in the future, and part of everyday effectiveness practice.

Most interesting was the use of the previous IPA papers themselves as norms against which to consider just how good the return on investment was, for example, MLC's analysis of payback versus other generic commodity advertisers, or Ford Galaxy's comparisons vs other IPA car cases. Again I would argue that, with more than 650 cases available this becomes an obvious use for the IPA Databank.

Finally, First Direct took the concept of efficiency measurement to an innovative new level by considering advertising's magnifier effect on other communications.

I would suggest that all these approaches are well worth pursuing in the future, particularly comparisons of return on investment. Is it too fanciful to imagine in years to come a pulling together of these above learnings in the shape of comparisons of advertising ROI's versus other investment tools, for example, training and change management?

NEW LEARNING ON RESEARCH METHODOLOGY

Many of the papers use new forms of research in order to measure manifold effects, for example, HEA's use of social academia data, Orange and One2One's research of City analysts and, of course, numerous uses of employee satisfaction data. My belief is that these examples will multiply in future years as research tools that allow us to link effects to groups of stakeholders beyond consumers.

Many of us found, when investigating employee attitudes, for example, that there were no questions on advertising. There is evidence already that this lack of connectivity will disappear. Already I have heard of brand equity tools that look at different stakeholders, and qualitative research companies that specialise in strategic and advertising development workshops with employees. These Awards, I hope, have played some part in encouraging these developments and will act as a focus for further new learnings in this area.

NEW LEARNING ON THE GROUND

Perhaps the most exciting and potentially longest-lasting lessons from this year's Awards are not within the papers in this volume but in the actual lessons learnt on the ground. One of my greatest pleasures, as convenor of judges, was in hearing of authors and their agencies knocking on the doors of disciplines they had never previously come into contact with: contacting human resource directors to look at employee issues, and of course, contacting finance directors, in order to consider City effects. Thus, in practice as well as in management theory, we began to see a real breakdown of the barriers between disciplines.

This was reflected in the judging process itself with a veritable boardroom of disciplines finding a common interest and a common exercise over which they could share their experience and their views.

I hope that these doors will remain open both in daily practise in Agency/Client relationships and in the general relationships between the IPA and the Client community.

Certainly one of the greater successes for me of this year's Awards was the increased involvement of the Client community, both in the general association of the Marketing Council and the Chartered Institute of Marketing, the specific sponsorship of a new award by the ISBA to encourage new Client entries, and in the very real support and involvement of many senior and respected Clients in the judging process. Long may this partnership continue, for the learning of these Awards, though created by the hard work of one group, is surely to the benefit of both parties.

CONCLUSION

Much discussion on integration centres around the concept of communications and yet, arguably, the core issue is delivery of a brand across all its parts. In today's hypercritical media environment and with today's hypersensitive consumer it is clear that a brand can be 'pressure tested' at all its many junctions any time, anywhere. In this context IMC (integrated marketing communications) becomes more a challenge of creating an IMCo (integrated marketing company). The key issue, therefore, becomes common brand understanding and common brand passion not standardised message. Advertising has a potentially unique role in driving, leading, and creating that passion, that is to say, a multiple role for advertising that stretches beyond consumers in its targeting, and beyond sales in its value. Such a role, however, does require new concepts of effectiveness and measurement.

Our hope in creating the changes to this year's Awards was that in ten years time the industry will be able to congratulate itself again on how far it has travelled in understanding how advertising works in this new marketing context to add value across the company and the brand.

This year's cases make for a strong first stride in that journey and I would like to thank all those people – the Client and specialist juries, the Effectiveness team at the IPA, the Agency and Client teams and, of course, the writers – who helped create this tenth book of cases: a book that shows not just that advertising works but that advertising works in many splendid ways.

Nick Kendall
1998 Convenor of Judges

The Judges

STAGE 1: SPECIALIST ADVISORS

Nick Kendall
Convenor of Judges
Group Planning Director
Bartle Bogle Hegarty

Tim Broadbent
Deputy Convenor
Managing Partner and Head of Planning
Young & Rubicam

Jackie Boulter
AMV.BBDO

Louise Cook
Holmes & Cook

Andy Farr
Millward Brown

Peter Field
Consultant

David Haigh
Brand Finance

Mike Hall
Hall & Partners

STAGE 2: CLIENT JURY

Lord Marshall
Chairman of Judges
Chairman
British Airways

David Bell
Chairman
Financial Times

Adrian Hosford
Director
Talk 21st Century, BT

John Lee
Group Personnel & Services Director
Halifax plc

Tim Mason
Marketing Director
Tesco plc

Guy Walker, CBE
Chairman
Van den Bergh Foods Ltd

Steve Williamson
Director, Finance & Business Planning
SmithKline Beecham Consumer Healthcare

Acknowledgments

The IPA Value of Advertising Executive Committee

Marilyn Baxter	(Chairman) Saatchi & Saatchi
James Best	BMP DDB
Tim Broadbent	Young & Rubicam
Leslie Butterfield	Partners BDDH
Andrew Crosthwaite	Consultant
Peter Field	Consultant
Nick Kendall	Bartle Bogle Hegarty
John Stubbings	Bates UK
Adrian Vickers	Abbott Mead Vickers.BBDO
Stephen Woodford	WCRS

Many people worked hard to make the awards a success, especially Stephen Woodford, Chairman of the Advertising Effectiveness Awards Committee, Marilyn Baxter, Chairman of the Value of Advertising Committee and Nick Kendall, Convenor of Judges.

From the IPA, particular thanks are due to Janet Hull, Tessa Gooding, Lesley Scott, Linda Calderwood-Lea and Jill Bentley.

Further thanks are due to Jenny Andersson of Andersson Whitehill and Paul Edney, Tony Cadman and Derek Tuke-Hastings of Park Avenue Productions.

Sponsors

The success of the 1998 IPA Advertising Effectiveness Awards owes a great debt to our sponsors. The IPA would like to thank the following companies whose support made the presentation possible.

OVERALL SPONSORS

SPONSORS OF THE PRESIDENT'S DINNER

Prizes

GRAND PRIX

Health Education Authority Drugs Education Campaign – How advertising turned the tide
Lori Gould and Rachel Walker
  Duckworth Finn Grubb Waters for the Health Education Authority

CHARLES CHANNON AWARD

Orange – The FSTE's bright, the FTSE's Orange
Dan Izbicki and Cameron Saunders
  WCRS for Orange

ISBA AWARD FOR BEST NEW ENTRANT

One2Many – How advertising affected a brand's stakeholders
Nick Barham
  Bartle Bogle Hegarty for One2One

FIVE-STAR AWARDS

The Army – Putting the Army back in business
Andrew Davies
  Saatchi & Saatchi for the Army

Colgate – The science behind the smile
Kathy Wood and Tim Broadbent
  Young & Rubicam for Colgate Palmolive

First Direct – Advertising as a communications magnifier
George Bryant and Brian Birkhead
  WCRS for First Direct

Marmite – How 'the growing up spread' just carried on growing
Lucy Jameson and Les Binet
  BMP DDB for Bestfoods UK

Volkswagen – How advertising helped Volkswagen and its dealers recover their profitabililty
Richard Butterworth, Les Binet and Cathy Reid
  BMP DDB for Volkswagen UK

FOUR-STAR AWARDS

Christian Aid – Strengthening the poor
David Simeos-Brown
  Partners BDDH for Christian Aid

La Dolce Vita – How Olivio learned to enjoy life with retailer brands
Dylan Willams
  Bartle Bogle Hegarty for Van den Bergh Foods Ltd

One2Many – How advertising affected a brand's stakeholders
Nick Barham
  Bartle Bogle Hegarty for One2One

Meat & Livestock Commission – Pulling round the red meat market
Sarah Carter and Sam Dias
  BMP DDB for the Meat and Livestock Commission

THREE-STAR AWARDS

Audi – Members only: how advertising hepled Audi join the prestige car club
Richard Exon
  Bartle Bogle Hegarty for Audi UK Ltd

Batchelor's SuperNoodles – Leading from the front
Justin Kent and Stef Calcroft
  Mother for Van den Bergh Foods Ltd

Johnson's Clean & Clear – Global advertising in a local market
Polly Evelegh and Sam Dias
  BMP DDB for Johnson & Johnson

Ford Galaxy – Building brand value for Ford
John Howkins
  Young & Rubicam for Ford Motor Company Ltd

Pizza Hut – Turning around the way you look at Pizza Hut
Jeremy Poole
  Abbott Mead Vickers.BBDO for Pizza Hut UK Ltd

Polaroid – How living for a moment gave Polaroid a future
Matthew Gladstone
  Bartle Bogle Hegarty for Polaroid Europe

TWO-STAR AWARDS

Bacardi Breezer
Jeremy Diamond
  McCann-Erickson for Bacardi-Martini Ltd

Bud Ice
Matt Willifer and Les Binet
  BMP DDB for Anheuser-Busch European Trade Ltd

The Famous Grouse
Lucy Edge and Ian Pearman
  Abbott Mead Vickers.BBDO for Highland Distillers

Imodium
Bhanita Mistry and Craig Mawdsley
  Saatchi & Saatchi for Johnson & Johnson MSD Consumer Pharmaceuticals

North West Water
Belinda Miller and Katherine Dinwoodie
  BDH-TBWA

Wallis
Shazia Brawley
  Bartle Bogle Hegarty for Wallis

ONE-STAR AWARDS

Boots Advantage Card
Merry Baskin
  J Walter Thompson

The Chicago Town Pizza
Nick Brookes and Nicole Ten Thij
  BDH-TBWA for Schwan's Europe

Direct Debit
Sue Pedley (Euro RSCG) and Ken Brown (BACS)
  Euro RSCG Wnek Gosper for BACS Ltd

Impulse
Simeon Duckworth and Jason Chebib
  Ogilvy & Mather for Elida Fabergé Ltd

Littlewoods Pools
Stuart Smith and Charlie Snow
  DNB&B for Littlewoods Leisure

Marmoleum
Diane Lurie and Alan Clarke
  The Morgan Partnership for Forbo-Nairn

Physical Activity
Brian Cook
  The Bridge for the Health Education Board for Scotland

Section 1

Five-Star Winners

1

Health Education Authority Drugs Education Campaign

How advertising turned the tide

EDITOR'S SUMMARY

This case represents a touchstone for the power of advertising. Working on what must be one of the most intractable of problems against one of the most cynical of targets, the paper illustrates how advertising was able to change behaviour by education with empathy.

Infiltrating Fortress Youth

Drug use, fuelled by the 'love drug' Ecstasy, had exploded at the turn of the decade, becoming increasingly prevalent and young. Crisis point came in 1995 – drug use had become a majority activity.

The problem was that millions of young people knew of no health risks whatsoever associated with recreational drugs. This was ironic, as the one thing that young people said would deter them from taking drugs was damage to health.

What we needed to tell young people became clear. If we informed them about the health risks drugs carried, more of them would conclude for themselves that taking drugs was not worth the risk.

Results and Payback

After years of acceleration, drug use has started to decline: Fewer people are starting to use, the number of users who have given up has doubled, even those who continue to use are better able to limit the risks.

Advertising took the lead role in these behavioural changes. Young people themselves say that our advertising has affected them – as one user put it *'They make me think at the end of the day do I need this shit?'*.

Advertising turned the tide. It also affected other, indirect audiences, such as teachers, advisory centres, drugs helplines and the press.

This campaign was designed to address a pressing social problem, not to generate revenue. Not only have we achieved that, we have also achieved financial payback.

ADVERTISING WORKS 10

SETTING THE SCENE

What do you imagine is the largest internationally traded commodity in the world? Oil? Tourism?

No, it's drugs, and it accounts for 8% of world trade.

Drugs represent an enormous problem, touching many lives – young people, their families and communities, teachers, medical professionals and law enforcers. The social costs of this problem run to £4 billion per year in the UK alone.

More under 25s engage in drug use than in any other illegal activity. An estimated £13 billion of drugs circulate on Britain's streets each year. That makes our illegal drugs market as big as the total beer market, larger than tobacco, and three times the size of confectionery or soft drinks.

This is the story of a battle against huge odds. The story of Goliath, £13 billion of drugs trade, being attacked by little David, our £2.3 million per year advertising budget.

David struck home against the odds. Goliath has started to lose his footing. The tide of drug use in England has finally started to turn.

THE YEAR 1995 WAS CRISIS POINT

Our story begins in the mid 1990s, a time when the drugs problem had reached epidemic proportions (Figure 1).

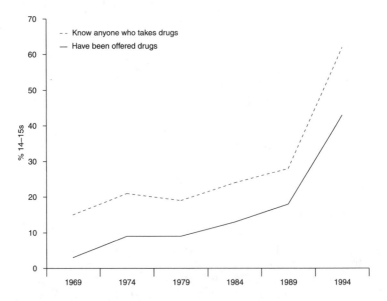

Figure 1: *Percentage of 14 to 15-year-olds in contact with drugs*
Source: Wright and Pearl in *British Medical Journal*, 1995

The 1990s had seen an explosion of drug use among young people. In just five years the proportion of 14 to 15-year-olds in contact with drugs had doubled.[1]

Not only was young people's drug use accelerating out of control, it had also changed beyond recognition.

Typically the word 'drugs' conjures up images of heroin or crack addicts in inner-city no-go areas, strung-out junkies desperate for their next fix. While these drugs are a continuing part of the picture, they represent a serious but isolated problem, the practice of a tiny minority. According to the National Drugs Survey (NDS), in 1995 penetration of both heroin and crack was only 1% of 11 to 25-year-olds.[2]

The new problem we faced in 1995 was a much wider one – huge numbers of young people using illegal and dangerous drugs such as Speed, Ecstasy and LSD for recreational purposes.

NDS found that 56% of 16 to 25-year-olds had tried drugs at some point, nearly half of them (47%) starting before they turned 15. Recreational drug use was no longer a counter-culture, it was a majority activity.

Even at the tender age of 12, many knew someone who used drugs, and their exposure increased rapidly with age (Figure 2).[3]

What had happened to get us to this state?

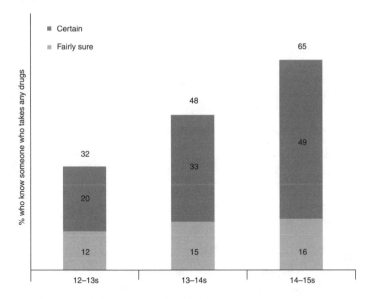

Figure 2: *Percentage of teenagers who know someone that takes drugs*
Source: Balding, J. Exeter University, 1994

1. Only age group available – sample 400–600 fourth-year students per year of fieldwork.
2. NDS ran between September and October 1995 and again between September and November 1996. Each sample is 5,000 11–35s in England. CAPI was used to aid data collection in this sensitive area.
3. Only age groups available. John Balding at Exeter University has conducted an annual national study asking young people about their drug use. Sample sizes are 24,597, 20,861, 29,074, 48,799, 19,819, 22,067 and 27,317 in the years 1991 to 1997 respectively.

ECSTASY OPENED THE FLOODGATES

It was the arrival, in the late 1980s, of the 'wonder drug' Ecstasy that changed the UK drugs scene beyond recognition.

Its users experienced a wide range of pleasures (Figure 3).[4]

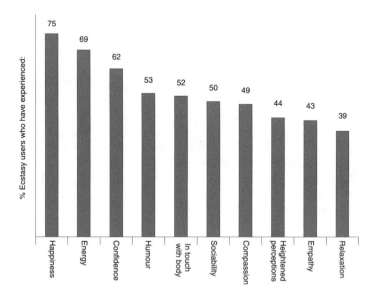

Figure 3: *Percentage of Ecstasy users experiencing the following emotions:*
Source: Release Dance and Drugs survey

Ecstasy's effects seemed to be heaven-sent. Users were evangelical in their enthusiasm.

'You just know everyone in the world is your friend, that's what I feel. Everything's amazing, it's like, yes, this is what life's all about.'

18 to 25-year-old Ecstasy user
Source: Festival Radio interviews[5]

Users could dance until morning, 'loved up' and happy with the world. Ecstasy soon became an entrenched feature of the clubbing scene: 84% of clubbers had used it, over half doing so that very evening (see Figure 4).

4. Release drugs advice agency interviewed 520 clubbers at a broad range of venues and events throughout London and the Southeast. Fieldwork dates from March to November 1996.
5. Festival Radio reporters have interviewed over 616 18 to 25-year-olds about their drugs knowledge, attitudes and experiences. Throughout the course of the campaign they have conducted six sets of fieldwork in London, Manchester and Liverpool.

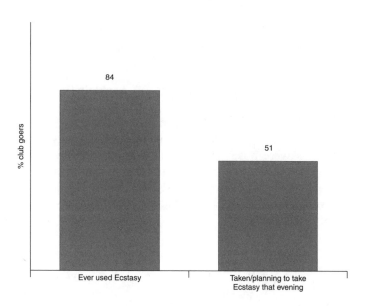

Figure 4: *Percentage of club goers who have ever used Ecstasy or are planning to take Ecstasy*
Source: Release dance and drugs survey, March 1996

This new drug, and the dance culture that surrounded it, had an impact on recreational drug use as a whole:

'I believe that E [Ecstasy] was the catalyst. It made drug-taking acceptable. If they couldn't afford E, they'd take trips [LSD] or smoke cannabis instead.'

Source: Worker at Lifeline[6]

Users of other drugs became equally evangelical:

'Acid opens up your mind to new colours, new sounds, new smells, new experiences.'

18 to 25-year-old LSD user

'Speed makes you go faster, it gives you a real rush, keeps you going for hours – really happy and smiling again.'

18 to 25-year-old Speed user
Source: Festival Radio, April 1995

6. Lifeline is a Manchester-based drugs advisory centre.

Style magazines, music and literature fuelled this normalisation of drugs, endorsing and celebrating dance drug culture.[7]

YOU'RE EITHER WITH US OR AGAINST US

The adult world, fuelled by the media, was in a state of panic. But this perspective contrasted sharply with young people's view of recreational drugs.[8]

These two worlds were poles apart, living side by side but with no common ground. Young people dismissed parents and other authority figures as ignorant, out of touch and incapable of offering unbiased advice.

Drugs were entrenched and defended inside a youth culture fortress which was impenetrable to outsiders (Figure 5).

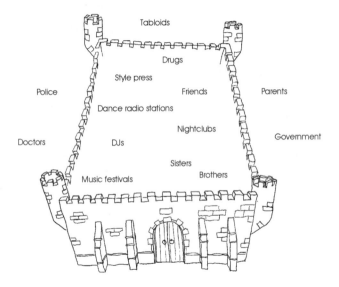

Figure 5: *Youth Culture Fortress*

---

7. Examples of headlines and lyrics in the style press, music or literature in 1995: 'drugged-up hedonism'; 'Ecstasy, sorted and on one'; 'pills 'n' thrills'; 'Cheeba 95 – I like to smoke marijuana'; 'Generation Ecstasy'; 'E's are good, E's are good. He's Ebenezer Goode'.
8. Examples of headlines in the national press in 1995: 'Ecstasy victim's parents back clubs clampdown'; 'Cage ordeal of drug-trial holiday girl'; 'Police smash drugs ring'; 'Nail E pushers who killed my brilliant boy'; 'Drugs menace'; 'Drug-fed slide of girl who died alone at 14'.

SOMETHING HAD TO BE DONE – BUT WHAT?

Evidently, nothing that teachers, the police, parents or the authorities had said or done had stemmed the tide of drug use. Successive governments had been attempting to suppress drugs supply for decades, but had been unable to stamp it out.

The government now acknowledged that a change of emphasis was needed. The only way to impact on the accelerating drugs problem was to tackle demand. It made this challenge public in the 1995 White Paper *'Tackling Drugs Together'* which had all-party support.[9]

This document defined our task as simply to 'reduce demand for drugs'.

EASIER SAID THAN DONE

Understanding the depth of the problem as we now did, the task appeared enormous and complex.

The brief gave us a degree of freedom that was liberating and daunting in equal measure. We could tackle the problem in whatever way we saw fit, but we were wary of being pulled in different directions.

We had to create an integrated campaign that could address the entire 11 to 25 age range, from children just starting secondary school to young adults with their own home, income and independence. And whereas talking to rejectors or users alone would have simplified our task, we had to target the full spectrum of drug experience.

To complicate matters further, we had to find a way of talking to young people that would not cause problems for the government, our ultimate client.

We had some decisions to take. If we were to stand any chance of winning this fight, we had to pick our battleground carefully. Our understanding of the use of heroin and crack suggested that advertising was an inappropriate weapon against these particular drugs, being inextricably bound up with social and personal problems. Only personal and ongoing help could begin to address that web of difficulties.

Recreational drug use became our target. No precedent existed for what advertising could achieve, but we were confident that this was a battle in which we stood a chance. We then had to define what we hoped to achieve.

---

9. In 1995, the Department of Health awarded responsibility for public education about illegal drugs to the Health Education Authority, a special health authority within the NHS established in 1987. One of their first actions at the start of their three year contract was to appoint ad agency DFGW to work with them to develop a communications strategy.

THE PROBLEM WAS TWO-FOLD

Currently the flow into drug use was too great, and the out flow not great enough (Figure 6).

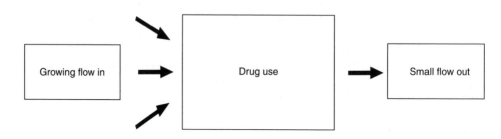

Figure 6: *A two-fold problem*

We could tackle the problem at either end – stop people starting, or get more people to stop (Figure 7).

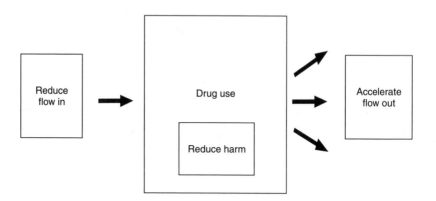

Figure 7: *Tackling the problem*

The easier task seemed to be to stem the flow of people into drugs use. Adopted exclusively, however, this would be a long-term solution. We did not have the luxury of time. There were already too many young people using drugs, and our contract only ran for three years. If we were to make an impact within that time, we had to accelerate the out flow of drug use as well.

Although our primary objective was to reduce the number of people using drugs, we had to acknowledge that there would always be some who continued to use. We therefore had a responsibility to ensure that while they continued to take drugs, these people harmed themselves as little as possible.

A UNIFYING INSIGHT

It occurred to us that the adult world, fuelled by tabloid hysteria, had got it wrong. Adults assumed that young drug users are victims of pressure from wayward friends or evil pushers at the school gates.

Our investigations with young people found this to be simply untrue – young people decide for themselves whether or not to take drugs.

This insight held true, regardless of individuals' backgrounds, attitudes and drugs experience. Young people weigh up the pros and cons and come to an active decision about whether or not to use drugs.[10]

The vast majority of users (91% in a Mixmag survey[11]) are introduced to drugs by a friend. Those who do use dealers see them as suppliers, not pushers – they fulfil a demand, they don't force people to try. Neither do friends pressurise people to join in. As two drug users explained:

'I've always hung around with people who were one step ahead of me. It's not like they've been trying to push me into it or anything like that. They've just sort of sprung my curiosity. They've said "Yeah, I was out the other night tripping my nuts off" and I'd be like "Wow can I try that?" '

Male, 20 to 22, October 1996
Source: Cragg, Ross, Dawson

'When you talk to people who've done it, you hear their stories, and you think "yeah". You just want to experiment.'

Male, 20 to 22, October 1996
Source: CRD[12]

The fortress of youth culture was full of tales of the excitement drugs could offer, with young people as enthusiastic advocates of the drugs experience. The problem was not one of pressure. It was that when young people weighed up the pros and cons to make their active choice, the balance of evidence within their world was overwhelmingly in favour of drugs.

It was no wonder that so many people chose to experience drugs for themselves. Nor was it any wonder that the 'Just say no' messages of the past had failed to impress. Why should young people say no when they were surrounded by so many compelling reasons to say yes?

---

10. Later we discovered academic support for this view: Ajzen & Fishbein's *Theory of Reasoned Action*.
11. *Mixmag*, a leading style press title, developed a questionnaire about drug usage and attitudes in conjunction with Lifeline. Over 3,000 readers from all over the country responded. Results were published in July 1996.
12. Independent qualitative researchers Cragg, Ross, Dawson have carried out near-constant research over the course of the campaign. They have talked to over 700 11 to 25-year-olds in groups across the country.

WHAT COULD TIP THE BALANCE?

We needed to let young people conclude for themselves that taking drugs was not a good idea, and to do that we needed to find new and compelling reasons that would make them think again.

There was little point telling them things that they already knew and had dismissed – 'it's illegal', 'your parents would kill you if they found out'. Not only were these messages evidently incapable of outweighing the benefits of drugs but they would position us as outsiders, rendering us powerless to affect what went on inside the youth culture fortress.

We then discovered one thing that had the power to change their minds. It was an ironic discovery. The one thing with the power to demotivate was the one thing they knew little about.

When drug users were asked what would make them stop using drugs, by far the biggest concern (63% agreement) was 'worries about my health' (Source: NDS, 1995).

And yet too many were blissfully and dangerously unaware of the health risks that recreational drugs carried. Millions knew of no health risks whatsoever associated with the most commonly used recreational drugs (Figure 8).[13]

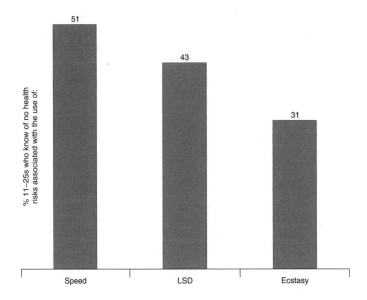

Figure 8: *Percentage of 11 to 25 year-olds who know of the health risks associated with the use of recreational drugs*
Source: NDS, 1995

---

13. According to NDS in 1995 4.6 million 11 to 25-year-olds knew of no risks associated with Speed, 3.9 million knew of none for LSD and 2.8 million knew of none associated with Ecstasy.

Even when they thought they knew of negative effects, they were often myths that experience (personal or vicarious) could easily disprove:

'LSD burns a hole through your hand.'

'Ecstasy eats your brain away.'

'Speed makes your teeth fall out.'

Source: DFGW qual, June 1995

THE POWER OF THE TRUTH

Our investigation revealed a host of health risks carried by recreational drugs (Table 1).[14]

In addition scientists had found worrying evidence that Ecstasy could permanently damage serotonin-releasing chemicals in the brain. This could potentially lead to severe depression later in life. The 'wonder drug' might not seem so wonderful in a few years' time.

TABLE 1: RISKS OF RECREATIONAL DRUGS

Ecstasy	LSD	Speed
Depression	Flashbacks	Heart arrhythmia
Paranoia	Bad trips	Heart damage/strain
Kidney damage	Can't escape once started	Unpredictable
Liver damage	Lasts up to 12 hours	Come-down/fatigue
Brain damage	Unpredictable reaction	Paranoia
Dehydration	Long-term mental illness	Psychological addiction
Come-down/fatigue		Need more each time
Anxiety		Tiredness
Heart damage/arrhythmia		Depression
Unpredictable reaction		Inability to sleep
Mental illness		
Stroke		
Paralysis		
Coma		

Source: Department of Health

We had found the key to demotivation in this market – by giving facts about health risks, we could help young people to make their own better-informed decisions about drugs. Better-informed people are less likely to engage in risky behaviour,[15] as health education work in the fields of HIV and contraception testifies.

Now we just had to find a way to get people to listen to us.

---

14. Our client, the HEA, was also keen to take drugs out of the political arena and make it a health issue. Basing our communication around health risks would enable HEA to do so effectively.
15. For further discussion of how this works in theory see Ajzen and Fishbein's *Theory of Reasoned Action*.

INFILTRATING THE FORTRESS OF YOUTH CULTURE

In our view, it would not matter how much we had to spend – our cynical audience would refuse to listen to us if they suspected that the government (ultimately our client) was responsible. We had to find a way past the defences of the youth culture fortress.

Because our audience made their own decisions, primarily trusting one another for advice, adopting a parent–child attitude would be counter-productive. We could not patronise, bully or cajole. We decided to treat them as equals.

We adopted an open, honest tone that allowed people to make up their own minds, and admitted that, in this untested market, doctors do not yet have all the facts. We recommended that the government take the bold and unprecedented step of letting us acknowledge the positive effects of drugs, to demonstrate our insider knowledge. This was crucial to the campaign's credibility. Happily they agreed.

Media choice also helped us to infiltrate youth culture. Our media partners, New PHD, recommended using teen magazines to reach 11 to 15-year-olds and dance radio stations to reach the 16 to 25-year-olds. These media are integral to youth culture – private, trusted sources of information, and environments where talk of drugs is appropriate.

This media choice also enabled us to put our limited budget of £6.8 million over three years to great effect. Over three years our radio coverage was high and press coverage almost universal, both with high frequency.[16] All this cost just 26 pence per 11 to 25-year-old each year – less than the cost of a bag of crisps.

It was also important to talk about specific drugs, not 'drugs' as a generic – only poorly informed outsiders make that mistake.

In an ideal world we would have featured every drug in advertising. But we had to be selective, in order to give each drug sufficient weight to educate effectively. We used the following criteria to ensure that our advertising addressed the most widespread and pressing problems:

— Drugs that people were likely to come across (ie be offered);

— Drugs they were likely to use, or consider using;

— Drugs that carried lots of health risks, about which people knew very little.

We therefore focused on Ecstasy, Speed and LSD, and briefly featured Magic Mushrooms and mixing drugs.

True to our aim of infiltrating the youth culture fortress, this activity was supplemented by a host of PR initiatives by Red Rooster. They placed materials containing facts about the whole spectrum of drugs in places where conversations about drugs often occur – for instance, in clubs and cafés, in record shops and in carnival and festival guides.

---

16. The entire radio campaign gave us 72% coverage of 15–24-year-olds at a rate of 50 OTH. Press gave us 92% coverage of 11 to 19-year-olds at 33 OTS.

OPENING UP A DIALOGUE

Once inside the fortress, there was more that we could do. Having encouraged people to question their current levels of knowledge and given them reasons to think twice, our plan was to establish a dialogue with young people, answering any further questions one-to-one.

A resource that we could use already existed. National Drugs Helpline (NDH)[17] had been operating since April 1995, but in England it had virtually no awareness and no brand image.

We decided to feature the NDH number on all our materials, allowing us an even bigger interactive role within the youth culture fortress.

IN SUMMARY

We aimed to get inside youth culture, and to give people the facts about drugs so that they could make their own better-informed decisions, reappraise their attitudes about drugs and so moderate their behaviour.

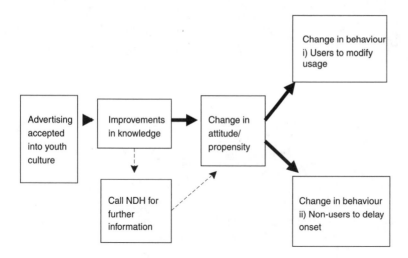

THE CREATIVE SOLUTION

Working to the brief of communicating facts about drugs from within youth culture, our press ads feature young people in drug-taking situations, with a biology textbook 'cutaway' revealing medical facts. These ads carry detailed information in an easily-digestible form.

---

17. NDH is a 24-hour telephone helpline funded by the Department of Health. It is staffed by trained counsellors who give factual information and advice in a non-judgmental way. Its service is free and confidential.

PRESS ADS

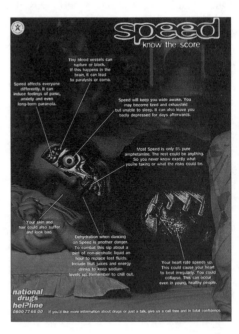

In radio, scripted ads illustrate health risks, and voxpops feature people talking about their real-life drugs experiences to a credible young man who delivers facts about drugs. These ads contribute to and mimic the way people learn from their peers.

Both radio and press advertising carry an end-line, 'Know the Score', that encapsulates our approach of encouraging young people to become better informed.

MEDIA PLAN[18]

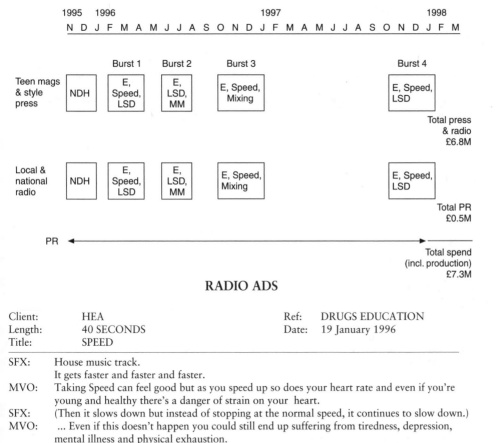

RADIO ADS

Client:	HEA	Ref:	DRUGS EDUCATION
Length:	40 SECONDS	Date:	19 January 1996
Title:	SPEED		

SFX: House music track.
       It gets faster and faster and faster.
MVO: Taking Speed can feel good but as you speed up so does your heart rate and even if you're young and healthy there's a danger of strain on your heart.
SFX: (Then it slows down but instead of stopping at the normal speed, it continues to slow down.)
MVO: ... Even if this doesn't happen you could still end up suffering from tiredness, depression, mental illness and physical exhaustion.

If you'd like more information or a talk, call the National Drugs Helpline free and in confidence on 0800 77 66 00.

Speed – know the score.

---

18. In November/December 1995 we ran advertising to purely raise awareness of the NDH number.

Client:	HEA	Ref:	DRUGS EDUCATION
Length:	40 SECONDS	Date:	25 January 1996
Title:	LSD VOXPO		

MVO:	How much do you really know about LSD ... or how much do you think you know?
KID 1:	Paranoia, that's the bad thing, it does affect your mind 'cos you're looking over your shoulder all the time ...
MVO:	True.
KID 2:	You could feel animosity, even fear, blind fear and panic.
MVO:	True.
KID 3:	You can get serious flashbacks ...
MVO:	True.
KID 4:	Doesn't have any side effects.
MVO:	False.
KID 5:	You have to take loads of it before anything really happens.
MVO:	False.
KID 6:	It's really addictive.
MVO:	False.
KID 7:	It's not sort o' like a drug you do on your own or in sort or risky situations.
MVO:	True – LSD changes your perception of things, this could be fun or it could be a nightmare.

If you want to know more facts and less fiction or you'd like ta lk call the National Drugs Helpline free and in confidence on 0800 77 66 00. Your call won't show on the bill.

LSD – know the score.

Client:	HEA	Product: DRUGS EDUCATION
Length:	50 SECONDS	Date: 10 December 1996
Title:	ECSTASY/WATER	

MVO:	What do you think happens when you take Ecstasy?
GIRL 1:	Short term you get a buzz an' you get dehydrated ...
MVO:	You only dehydrate when you're dancing on E because you sweat.
GIRL2:	... It dehydrates you which can be dangerous if you don't drink enough water ...
MVO:	She's right. You need to drink water to replace lost fluids from sweating. But you also need to keep your sodium levels up. Water doesn't do this.
BOY 1:	... You gotta drink orange juice or coke or something with sugar to keep your blood sugar level up ...
MVO:	It's sodium you need to replace, not sugar. Fruit juice or energy drinks'll do this.
BOY2:	You need to drink lots ...
MVO:	Not lots, about a pint an hour. But even this isn't an antidote to Ecstasy. There are always risks.

If you want to know more about Ecstasy and its effects, call the National Drugs Helpline free and in confidence on 0800 77 66 00.

Ecastasy – know the score.

GOOD NEWS

There is evidence from lots of different sources that, since the start of the campaign, instead of the inexorable rise, drug use has declined.

One can hardly claim that it is the end of the drugs problem, but drugs do appear to have receded from their high watermark. Even Jack Straw, Home Secretary, was recently moved to say 'There is evidence that drug use is now stabilising and might even be going down' (*Today* Programme, Radio 4, May 1998).

We will present evidence which shows, beyond reasonable doubt, that the advertising has played the lead role in turning the tide.

But first, the evidence that the tide has turned.

Fewer Young People are Trying Drugs

The only long-term trend data available for trial of drugs are for 12 to 15-year-olds (Figure 9). This shows, after several years of steady growth, two years of downturn.

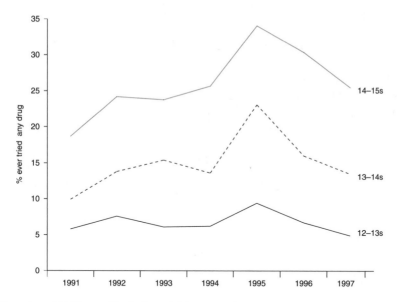

Figure 9: *Percentage of 11–25-year-olds who have tried drugs*
Source: Balding, J. Exeter University

And, as you'd expect, if fewer people are using drugs, fewer people know someone who uses drugs (Figure 10).

This is good news, since hearing users' positive feedback often encourages others to experiment. Fewer users means fewer advocates.

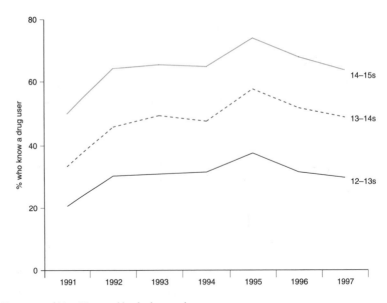

Figure 10: *Percentage of 11 to 25-year-olds who know a drug user*
Source: Balding, J. Exeter University

Fewer People are Planning to Use Drugs

Looking at a broader age spectrum, NDS found that between 1995 and 1996 the proportion of 11 to 25-year-olds who claim they would definitely or possibly consider using drugs in the future went down by 14%.[19]

More Drug Users are Quitting

At the other end of the drugs life-cycle, NDS also found the proportion of drug users who claimed to have quit doubled between 1995 and 1996 (Figure 11).

Drug Users are Better Able to Limit the Risks

Our last behavioural objective was to encourage those who continued to use drugs to minimise potential harm. Unfortunately there are no hard data to tell us how many drug users now do so. But the HEA-commissioned qualitative research, almost continuous over the course of the campaign and amounting to some 700 interviews, has shown that many drug users are now better able to reduce the risks they face.

---

19. Only two years' data available.

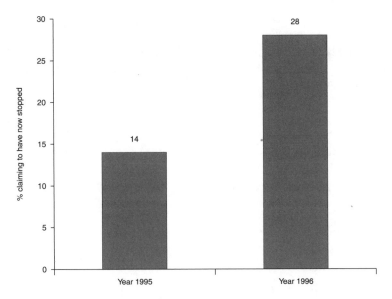

Figure 11: *Percentage who used any drug within the last 12 months claiming to have now stopped*
Source: NDS

'All users were aware of harm minimisation messages (especially regarding Ecstasy) and felt able to minimise immediate risks.'

Source: CRD, March 1997

'Detailed awareness of harm minimisation messages – "drink a pint of water an hour, keep salt levels up by drinking isotonic drinks".'

Source: CRD, August 1996

So our behavioural objectives had been met. The question is whether it was the advertising that was behind this success.

There is evidence on a number of fronts that this was indeed the case.

ADVERTISING PLAYED THE LEAD ROLE IN BEHAVIOURAL CHANGES

Advertising can be shown to have impacted on our audience in ways that strongly suggests it has brought about the reduction in drug use that we have seen.

Advertising was Noticed[20]

We know that over our first two bursts of prompted press awareness grew to 55% and prompted radio awareness had reached 62%.[21] Two years later a remarkable 90% of 15 to 19-year-olds in a test in Anglia recognised our press ads when prompted.[22]

Calls to NDH Rise when We Advertise

Calls to NDH provide us with clear evidence of a direct link between advertising and behaviour changes (see Figure 12). When we advertise, calls rise steeply, and when we stop advertising, calls decline.[23]

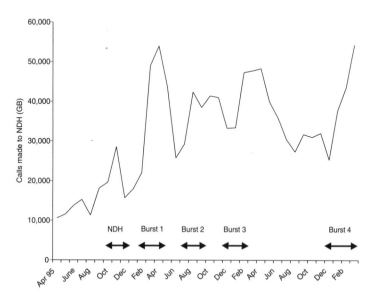

Figure 12: *Number of calls made to NDH (Britain)*
Source: Network Scotland (Operators of NDH)

Awareness of Risks has Risen

Festival Radio reporters interviewed over 600 18 to 25-year-olds over the course of our campaign[24] to collect material for our radio creative work. Respondents were asked what they knew about Ecstasy, Speed and LSD.

Comparing the responses across time, the proportion of people knowing at least one of the health facts we feature has grown to double that of the pre-campaign level (Figure 13).

20. To keep up with our fast-changing audience, the HEA relied on near continuous qualitative research. This was supplemented with tracking mid-way and at the end of the three-year campaign.
21. Source: BMRB, May 1996. Base: 111 15 to 19-year-olds in England.
22. Source: Conquest Research, May 1996, base: 180 15 to 19-year-olds. This test was set up to monitor changes before and after a one-month burst of radio activity in Anglia, following additions of new stations to our schedule.
23. A total of 1,048,838 calls were made between November 1995 and March 1998.
24. Interviews were spread evenly across the six sets of fieldwork.

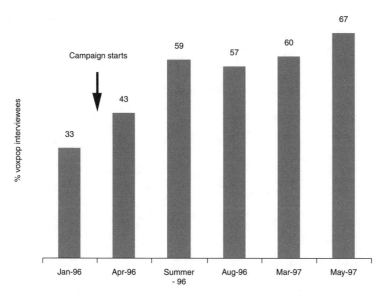

Figure 13: *Percentage of voxpop interviewees mentioning facts featured in HEA advertising campaign*
Source: Festival Radio voxpop research

Qualitative research reinforces this finding:

'Drugs messages are being absorbed and recycled within the culture. Respondents unconsciously parrot wording from press and radio ads – for example, "kidney and liver damage", "drink about a pint an hour".'

Source: CRD, September 1997

People are Less Interested in Using Drugs

Perhaps most interesting of all, our Anglia test[25] showed a 29% reduction in those who were certain or fairly sure they would use drugs in the future.[26]

Taken together, these findings suggest that advertising created attitudinal changes which brought about the reduction in drug use.

There is one more set of findings, however, that adds even more weight to this argument.

Young People Themselves say our Advertising has Influenced Them

A variety of qualitative research projects have found our target audience claiming that advertising has affected them. This goes for those who have not yet used drugs.

---

25. Sample sizes: 190 15 to 25-year-olds at pre-stage, and 358 at post-stage.
26. Shift significant to 90% level.

'Rejectors and those at risk usually found that the ads reinforced their personal conviction not to take drugs.'

Source: CRD May 1996

And those who are already using drugs:

'A typical response was "it makes you think".'

Source: CRD Nov 1996

'They [the ads] make me think at the end of the day "do I need this shit?" '

18 to 24 user
Source: Murmur May 1996

'There's a little voice at the back of your head saying "it's not safe. There's a risk".'

18 to 22 user
Source: DFGW October 1996

This picture is backed up by our Anglia test which found that 50% of 15 to 19-year-olds and 23% of 20 to 25-year-olds agreed that our one-month radio advertising burst made them think twice about drugs or taught them new things (Figure 14).

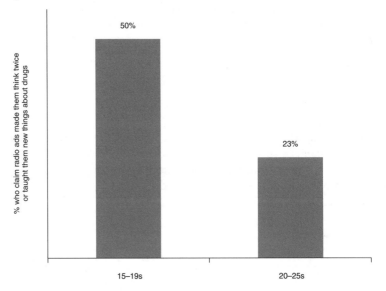

Figure 14: *Percentage aware of radio ads who claim they made them think twice or taught them new things about drugs*
Base: 285 respondents who were aware of the radio ads
Source: Conquest, May 1998

How could a Government campaign have had such an influence on people? Again our respondents have told us why we have succeeded.

Young people appreciate the approach we have taken:

'Whole approach generally well-liked as sympathetic: telling you the facts, not telling you what to do; straightforward and honest, trustworthy, believable, interesting, true to real life. Serious but not preaching and not patronising; looking at the subject from the point of view of young people rather than authorities; encouraging people to find out more.'

Source: CRD January 1996

They understand what the campaign is trying to achieve:

'They're saying be careful of messing with your body ... the dangers of long-term damage ... make you aware of the facts.'

18–25
Source: Murmur May 96

They recognise that we are doing things differently:

This [HEA campaign] was in sharp contrast to their views on drugs education as a whole, which were usually fairly negative. Most associated drugs education with prescriptive messages against drug taking and authority figures with little credibility.

Source: CRD October 1996

Consequently they have overwhelmingly positive impressions of the campaign's originators:

'These ads have been created by people who are young, know what it's like to go to clubs and (probably) know what it's like to take drugs.'

Source: CRD December 1995

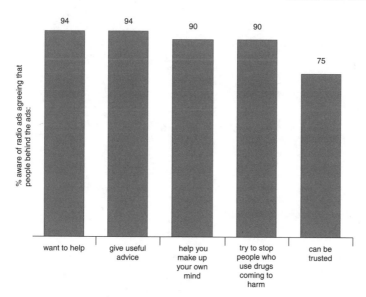

Figure 15: *15 to 25-year-olds aware of radio ads – impression of campaign originators*
Base: 285 15 to 25-year-olds in Anglia aware of HEA radio ads
Source: Conquest, May 1998

Clearly we have succeeded in gaining credibility with this cynical and defensive audience. Quantitative research, as shown in Figure 15 (previous page), supports this.

To summarise, evidence strongly suggests that it was advertising that created the attitudinal changes, which in turn led to behavioural shifts.

WHAT ELSE COULD HAVE CREATED THESE EFFECTS?

One might suspect that there are factors other than advertising that could have impacted on drug use. While we do not claim that none of them have had any effect, we demonstrate that only advertising could have accounted for the widespread and sudden changes that we see.

Activities Linked to Drug Use

People who go to clubs[27] and who smoke[28] are also more likely to use drugs. If either had declined since 1995, this might account for the change we have seen in drug use. However, clubbing has not changed significantly and teenage smoking is actually rising.

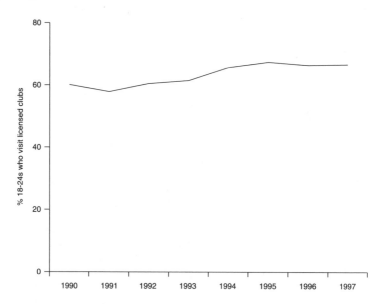

Figure 16: *18 to 24-year-olds who visit licensed clubs*
Source: TGI

---

27. Source: National Drugs Survey 1995.
28. Source: Tomorrow's Young Adults, HEA, 1992: 50% of regular smokers versus 2% of non-smokers aged 13–15 years have ever used any drugs. This suggests a correlation of risk-taking behaviour rather than a causal link.

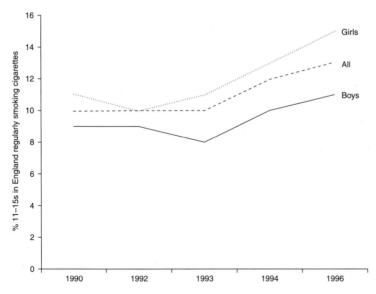

Figure 17: *11 to 15-year-olds in England regularly smoking cigarettes*
Source: ONS 1997. Smoking among secondary school age children in England in 1996, London HMSO

Market Forces

There are market forces acting on drug use. However, none of them can account for the decline in drug use that we have seen since 1995.

Prices of drugs have fallen and drugs have become easier to get hold of:

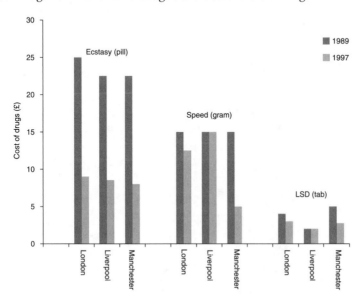

Figure 18: *Cost of drugs in London, Liverpool and Manchester in 1989 and 1997*
Source: London Release/ISDD; Liverpool HIT; Manchester Lifeline

'It's a lot easier to get drugs today than ten years, even five or six years ago. They're so widely available. You can get them anywhere. You don't even need to travel far. They're on your doorstep.'

Lifeline drugs advisory service, Manchester

Furthermore, the quality has not changed significantly since 1995.

'... in 1988 one tablet of Ecstasy contained an average of 100mg of MDMA, today the figure is closer to 70mg.'

The Face, June 1998

If we are to believe that the quality of Ecstasy drives the market, we would expect a gradual ten-year decline in quality to produce a correlated decline in usage. This is not the case, as drug usage was accelerating until 1995.

OTHER SOURCES OF INFORMATION

There have been other sources of information that could have influenced young people's decisions to use drugs.

However, local agencies' level of activity has not changed significantly. Schools' health education teaches about smoking and illegal drugs within the same lessons, but these behavioural trends are going in opposite directions; the PR element of the HEA campaign focuses on the over-18s. Media coverage of the death of Leah Betts was limited in its educational value and credibility among our target audience, (Figure 19) and cannot explain the shift in likelihood to use drugs seen in our Anglia test.

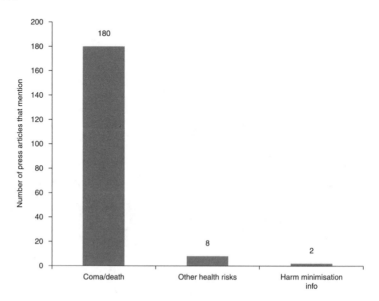

Figure 19: *Number of press articles that mention coma/death, other health risks and harm minimisation information*
Source: Network Scotland

General Decline in Interest in Drugs

One might say that the decline in interest in drugs would have happened without our intervention. However, this was not suggested by the preceding trends in drug use, which were still rising sharply, rather than plateauing. Further, it would seem unlikely that we would see a reduction in interest across all ages and for all drugs purely by coincidence.

To summarise, our campaign is the sole remaining factor which could account for the effects seen among our target audience.

We can also show that it has influenced young people in indirect ways, by empowering other people who educate about drugs to do so more effectively.

BEYOND THE EXPECTED

Teachers

Our campaign has helped some teachers to teach this potentially difficult subject.

Although we did not intend our materials to be used in classrooms, in fact they were. As a by-product of young people's trust and acceptance of our campaign, they have introduced it into their drugs education lessons themselves.

> 'The kids brought them [HEA ads] in. I was quite surprised that they were willing to hunt to find them all. Then we stuck them up on the walls and used them in a fact-finding context. It's more effective than discussing and watching videos because when it comes from them it's got to have more of an impact. If it's teacher-directed their response tends to be "you're just saying that".'

> Bristol secondary school teacher

> 'The kids brought in the [HEA] ads, from Sugar and that. It got them hooked in. Those ads mean more than dry leaflets, they got a lot of information from them. I'm out of touch and "old hat". The ads introduce things and then they ask each other. The stuff's everywhere, so they've seen it before. It gets their interest and we can pick up on that, so they can have a debate about it with the teacher there to guide it. It makes my job easier.'

> London secondary school teacher

Drugs Educators

There are many professionals working at a local level to tackle the drugs problem, such as those who work at drugs advisory centres and those who train the advisers. The HEA has had requests for approximately 150,000 copies of our ads from 15,000 organisations.

As a result our campaign has indirectly impacted on young people, by informing those who deal with them on a day-to-day basis:

> 'We've used the HEA advertising on two training courses aimed at professionals in the field – drugs workers and others. We use them to help people learn about various messages, target groups, and design.'

> Andrew Bennett, HIT[29]

Counsellors at NDH

NDH counsellors have a very important role within the campaign, giving more detailed and personally tailored information than a press or radio ad ever could.

The more information they can get across within a call, the more effective the education.

We know that the vast majority of calls are for information, as intended, and not for help in a crisis (Figure 20).

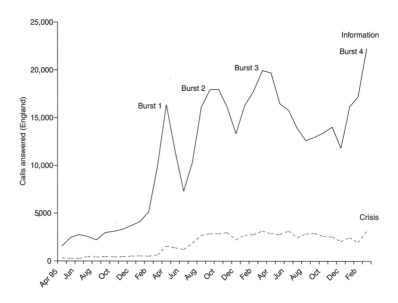

Figure 20: *Number of calls answered (England)*
Source: Network Scotland

NDH counsellors[30] say that because young people are better informed about risks, and call to find out more, the quality of the conversation has improved.

> 'Older teenagers are becoming more aware of the specific dangers. This makes it a lot easier for us – we can focus in and talk in detail about the long and short-term risks.'

> NDH counsellor

Callers have accurate expectations of the approach counsellors will take:

> 'The advertising's good because we're here to dispel myths too.'

> NDH counsellor

As a result of these changes, job satisfaction has improved.

---

29. Liverpool drugs advisory centre.
30. Source: DFGW, May 1998. All NDH counsellors questioned in the DFGW project had worked at the helpline since its inception.

'I get more job satisfaction, because we're getting more education over.'

NDH counsellor

Style Press Journalists

We demonstrated that by 1995 pro-drug articles were rife in style magazines.[31] This kind of coverage was fuelling demand for drugs.

We cannot pretend that we intended to directly influence journalists working on these magazines. In fact, we were not sure at the outset that we could even get them to carry our ads. It took at least one burst of advertising for some editors to overcome their suspicions of a Government campaign, and decide that our advertising would be acceptable to their readers.

We were delighted to find style press editorial covering drugs in an increasingly balanced or even negative way over the course of the campaign. Our analysis of *The Face* and *Mixmag*'s[32] content found that by 1997 only 18% of their articles about drugs took a pro-drug stance.

The style press now runs articles about drugs that would have seemed completely at odds with the prevailing climate back in 1995.[33]

They can now do this without adversely affecting their circulation, because young people's attitudes have changed. This is something that advertising has created.

We achieved our behavioural objectives and beyond. One final question remains.

HAS THE CAMPAIGN BEEN A FINANCIAL SUCCESS?

Although this campaign was not intended to generate revenue, we can show that it has been a financial success.

Diverting Money from Black to White Market Economy

By reducing numbers of young people who use drugs, we calculate that our annual £2.3 million adspend has diverted £28 million from the criminal fraternity into legal markets such as food, clothing, drink, even savings. This also generates incremental tax revenue.

---

1. By a pro-drug article, we mean one which glamorises or puts only the positive side of the drugs story, leaving the reader with the impression that using drugs is a good thing.
2. Two of the style mags with highest circulation.
3. Cover stories of style press titles included 'Comedown in Clubland' (*The Big Issue*,); 'Drugs Overload' (*The Face*, June 1998); 'Are drugs driving you mad?' (*Mixmag*, February 1997).

Reduction in Lost Working Days

Users of Ecstasy often report that a weekend's clubbing can result in serious exhaustion (come-down) on Mondays. They sometimes miss work as a result.

We have calculated that by reducing numbers of Ecstasy users, our annual £2.3 million advertising budget has saved British industry £11 million per year of lost working days.

Reduced Numbers Exposed to Potential Long-term Effects of Ecstasy

Scientists believe that Ecstasy may lead to serious depression later in life. This has substantial social, health and industry costs.

By encouraging young people to quit Ecstasy, thereby reducing the numbers exposed to this health risk, the campaign has created potential savings.

In order for these savings to be equivalent to the advertising spend, serious depression would need to be a future outcome experienced by one in 1,000 of today's Ecstasy users. This seems within the realms of possibility, since 68%[34] of Ecstasy users already claim that they feel depressed afterwards.

Savings to Other Drugs Education Professionals

The HEA received approximately 15,000 requests for sets of our ads from professionals in drug education. If they had not received our materials, they would have had to originate, research and produce materials of their own. If each would otherwise have spent just £200, we saved them a total of £3 million.

The campaign has therefore added value to the field of drug education beyond our original intentions.

SUMMARY

We have demonstrated, beyond reasonable doubt, that the HEA campaign played the lead role in turning the tide of drug use. It also empowered several indirect audiences to educate more effectively. Although the campaign was not designed to create revenue, it has been a financial success.

---

34. Source: *Mixmag*, July 1996.

2

The FTSE's bright, the FTSE's Orange

How advertising enhanced Orange plc shareholder value

EDITOR'S SUMMARY

This paper will demonstrate how advertising has been a key factor in Orange plc's success as a FTSE 100 plc, uniquely demonstrating the effect of advertising on Orange plc's share price.

Pursuing Value not just Volume

Between April 1996 and April 1998 Orange pursued a three-pronged strategy, with advertising contributing across every element, all designed to achieve value growth.

Results and Payback

By creating a positive predisposition towards Orange prior to the purchase decision, modelling has shown that advertising was responsible for at least 15.27% of additional subscribers since flotation, equivalent to a lifetime value of £144.34 million.

In addition, advertising contributed to a higher subscriber revenue by attracting high usage customers and by exploiting the tendency of customers to be more aware of their own brand's advertising, thus encouraging customers to increase their usage. By educating customers about Orange's improved coverage and value added features, advertising improved customer loyalty by 3.43 months helping to give Orange the highest customer lifetime in the market.

Finally, advertising's role in risk diversification can be highlighted in the area of foreign license bids and potential brand strength.

With the help of Lehman Brothers we have been able to calculate advertising's capacity to increase Orange plc's implied shareholder value per share by £2.49. This is equivalent to an increased market capitalisation of £3.0 billion.

INTRODUCTION

This paper covers the period from April 1996 to April 1998, the first two years of Orange in its new guise as a FTSE 100 plc. As a plc, the *raison d'être* of Orange fundamentally changed; the sole rationale for its existence was now to provide its shareholders with a profit, to create shareholder value.

The imperative of shareholder value resulted in a very different corporate strategy for Orange plc, as opposed to Orange in its launch years. Prior to flotation the focus had been on *volume share* in order to gain critical mass. Following flotation, Orange plc's business plan resolved that value share would be the key determinant of success. Unlike its competitors, Orange could not sacrifice margin for the sake of volume. It could not trade quality for quantity.

'Customer loyalty and usage breeds shareholder value. This means we do not chase market share at any cost.'

Source: Hans Snook, Group Managing Director, 1997

In light of its business plan, Orange plc was precluded from the two hard-hitting strategies pursued by the competition, namely price cuts and distribution growth. The former would compromise both short and long-term subscriber values. The latter would either involve high fixed costs (building or buying a national network of wholly owned shops), or would endanger short and long-term revenues (increased dealer incentives).

Instead, to achieve value share, Orange plc had three core objectives:

— Earnings growth – evidence that income is growing at an acceptable rate, given macro-economic and market conditions.

— Earnings security – providing investors with the confidence that the plc's revenue is secure, usually for a period ten years hence.

— Risk diversification – spreading the risk for the investor. An analyst would look for a plc's capacity to spread its investments over a number of areas of potential growth. For Orange this would directly relate to its ability to create a strong and transferable brand.

In order to achieve these objectives, Orange committed itself to an unequivocally brand-led strategy. If Orange could exert enough brand pull, this would prove to be the most value-enhancing insulation against its relative weakness in terms of price and distribution. Heightened brand desirability would prove to be Orange plc's core competitive advantage.

In this context, as the public face of the brand, advertising played a central role. It is consequently unnecessary to make technical distinctions between advertising/media strategies and the brand-led business strategy. Instead we will treat both strategies as indivisible, showing how, since April 1996 despite an increasingly ferocious competitive context, advertising has made a unique contribution across every element of the business. Through a variety of new methodologies we will demonstrate how advertising has delivered against the five core drivers of the Orange plc business strategy (Figure 1).

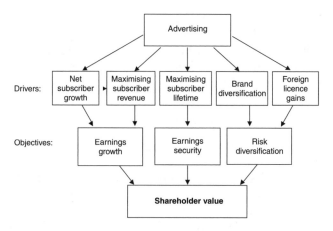

Figure 1: *Advertising's contribution to shareholder value*

We will thus demonstrate advertising's substantial contribution to a share price that has gone from strength to strength, rising 2.45p[1] since flotation, from £2.05 to £4.50, equating to an additional £2.9 billion in shareholder value. This is despite a period when Orange's volume share of the market has been under ever-increasing pressure, further confirming investor confidence in the brand-led, value-based strategy.

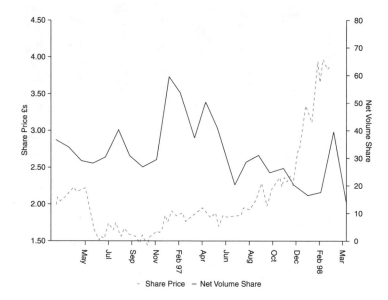

Figure 2: *Orange share price – April 1996 to March 1998*

.. As at the end of April 1998.

MARKET CONTEXT

It is important that Orange plc's business objectives are appreciated in the context of the overall marketplace. Over the last two years there have been three key trends in UK mobile telecoms: competitive price cuts, tied distribution and increasing advertising spend.

Competitive Price Cuts

Since 1996 the average cost of using a mobile phone has fallen by 25%. This fall is solely attributable to tariff changes among Cellnet, Vodafone and One2One. Instead of price-cutting in line with the market, Orange's core tariff proposition has remained unchanged.[2] The result is that Orange is now approximately 5% more expensive than Vodafone and Cellnet and 20–35% more expensive than One2One. This analysis is confirmed by Merril Lynch:

'We conclude that the Orange and Vodafone tariffs are broadly similar, with Orange around 6% more expensive for low-users and around 3%more expensive for high users. One2One are the cheapest of the bunch offering discounts of approximately 17% and 28% to Orange for low to high users repectively'

Merril Lynch, 14 January 1998

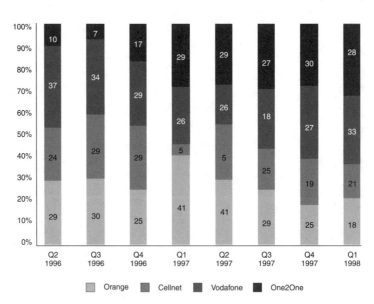

Figure 3: *Net volume share of connections*
Source: FT Mobile Telecoms

---

2.   New tariffs have been added to the Orange portfolio. However, these have been about trading up usage to group talk plans.

This price premium inevitably impacted on volume share, as shown in Figure 3 on the previous page. But as we will demonstrate below, it did not impact on Orange plc's value share of the market, the key driver for shareholder value.

Tied Distribution

The last two years have seen significant changes in the distribution strategies of Orange's rivals. In advance of their October 1997 brand relaunch, Vodafone spent millions buying up distribution channels. Talkland, Peoples Phone (purchased at a cost of £77 million), London Car Telephones, Vodacom, Vodacall and Vodac were all converted into Vodafone branded outlets exclusively selling Vodafone. By the third quarter of 1997, Vodafone had by far the strongest distribution of any of the four mobile networks, with over 250 wholly owned shops – one on nearly every high street in the country.

One2One's distribution has grown at a speed to mirror its network expansion. Between April 1996 and April 1998 the One2One network grew from 45% to 95% population coverage[3] (compared to equivalent figures for Orange of 90% to 96%). It has also adopted a similar, though less expansive, strategy to Vodafone, rebranding a significant number of dealers across the country as One2One outlets selling only One2One. Cellnet has taken ownership of The Link group throughout the UK, and leading mobile phone retailer DX Communications in Scotland.[4] This significantly improved Cellnet's distribution strength adding to its nationwide chain of BT Shops.

In contrast, between April 1996 and April 1998 Orange opened 13 own-branded shops. There were no other changes to its distribution strategy.

Further compounding the competitor's breadth of distribution was its quality. For the networks this quality equated to the likelihood of a dealer recommending their networks to customers. This likelihood is driven by two factors. First an assessment of customers' needs and future satisfaction with a network, second, the dealer incentives being offered by all four networks. In a context where price and coverage were converging, the latter was of growing importance:

'We estimate that other operators (than Orange) increased their dealer incentive payments in Q4 (1997), thus encouraging some dealers to recommend other networks above Orange, even if Orange was the customer's initially favoured network.'

Source: Dresdner Kleinwort Benson Analysts Report, March 1998

These distribution changes once again highlighted the strong challenges Orange faced in volume terms, and the importance of a strong brand to create the necessary predisposition and attract quality subscribers.

---

3. Network quoted figures.
4. While The Link and DX Communications continue to sell Orange, both retailers obviously have a strong interest in pushing Cellnet, especially given the pricing changes detailed above.

Increasing Advertising Spend

The success of the Orange advertising campaign during its first two years did not go unnoticed.[5] It would be fair to say that all four networks have now appreciated the power of a strong brand within a traditionally commoditised market. The result has been heavy investment by all the competitive networks in brand advertising, with significant media support (Figure 4).

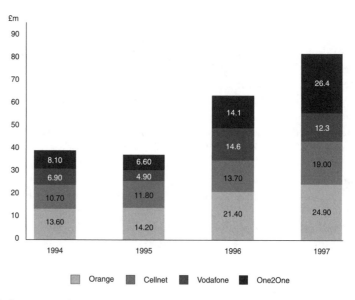

Figure 4: *Total advertising spends 1994 to 1997*
Source: AC Nielsen MEAL

The result of these increases in spend has been a curtailment in Orange's share of voice (Figure 5).

The Impact of the Market Context

The effect of this ferocious competitive activity is neatly summarised in our econometric models for each network's market share (Table 1).

---

5.   Orange won a gold at the IPA Advertising Effectiveness awards for the advertising from 1994 to 1996.

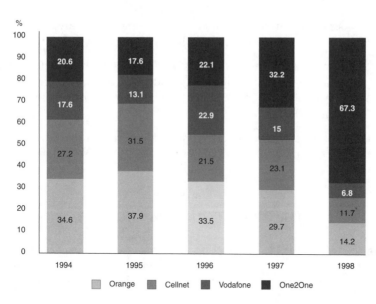

Figure 5: *Share of voice 1994 to 1998*
Source: AC Nielsen MEAL

The figures in Table 1 give the percentage of each operator's market share attributable to the key sales drivers within the marketplace.

TABLE 1: SHORT-TERM MARKET SHARE SALES DRIVERS

	Orange %	Cellnet %	Vodafone %	One2One %
Distribution	5.26	7.09	16.17	11.61
Pricing	12.29	0.03	9.26	0.01
Previous sales[6]	16.55	51.20	16.68	35.14
Seasonality	13.59	11.97	11.93	25.79
Other features[7]	37.03	26.43	42.40	19.07
Short-term advertising	15.27	3.30	3.57	8.38

Source: Independent Data Analysis Ltd

Our model mirrors expectation in several respects:

— With their expansion of branded retail outlets, Vodafone and One2One's market share is the most sensitive to distribution.

— One2One, as the most consumer-orientated brand, is the most seasonal, specifically in relation to fourth-quarter Christmas purchases.

. This is a measure of the underlying growth of the market and the relative momentum (compared to the four other factors) of individual brands.

. These include handset advertising, handset choice, co-funded advertising, coverage, macro-economic factors and long-term effects, as well as the multitude of promotional offers which are a constant element of the marketplace. The complexity of the mobile phone market makes it difficult to disentangle these individual variables, hence they have been grouped together.

— The most desirable brand in the marketplace – namely Orange – would see the biggest benefit by reducing its prices in line with the market.

— Cellnet, the worst performing network in terms of both volume and value, is reliant on its familiarity and the residual effect of the past. One2One, with its renewed momentum since its relaunch in late 1996, is also benefiting from an inbuilt sales momentum.

— All networks are responsive to advertising. However, as the most brand-driven operators in the marketplace, Orange and One2One are the most advertising sensitive.[8]

THE ORANGE BUSINESS STRATEGY

As we can see from Table 1, by lowering its prices Orange would have increased its market share. However, this would have been fundamentally opposed to the Orange plc business strategy of 'always looking at the long term with an eye on the short term'.[9] Moreover, lower cost tariffs would be likely to attract lower value customers. This is clearly a key consideration as high acquisition costs and low contributing customers can result in an actual loss for the network.

Instead, as outlined above, Orange plc has pursued a brand-led, shareholder value-enhancing strategy with three core objectives. We will now assess advertising's contribution against these measures.

Earnings Growth

Earnings growth is enhanced by two key factors. First, an increase in the net number of subscribers, essential in an expanding marketplace. Second, an increase in the revenue from those subscribers, a combination of quantity and quality. We will examine each of these contributory factors in turn.

Increasing the net subscriber base
Orange has been the third biggest UK network operator since it overtook One2One in January 1996 (see Table 2).

---

8. Using the same model, an attempt has been made to gauge the longer term effects. The results serve to highlight further the advertising responsiveness of the market. The advertising effect for individual brands is 24.58% for Orange, 25.06% for One2One, 10.09% for Cellnet and 5.91% for Vodafone. However, by definition it is harder to quantify long-term effects and IDA have less confidence in the robustness of this analysis. Hence it will not be used to analyse advertising payback.
9. Hans Snook, Orange plc Group Managing Director.

TABLE 2: NETWORK SUBSCRIBER BASES, 1 APRIL 1998[10]

One2One	1,198,000
Cellnet	3,077,000
Vodafone	3,431,000
Orange	**1,318,000**

Source: FT Mobile Telecoms

Across the period April 1996 to April 1998 Orange was neither the cheapest, nor the most readily available of the four network operators. Consequently, the business strategy required advertising to produce a brand pull to attract new subscribers, that is, to create a positive predisposition towards Orange before purchase. The success of this strategy is illustrated from a number of research sources (see Figures 6 and 7). This brand pull is also shown by the high purchase consideration of Orange[11] (see Figure 8).

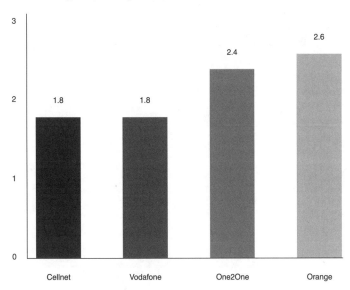

Figure 6: *Importance of advertising in cellular acquisition. Mean score by network*
Source: GfK Home Audit (April 1998)

The role of advertising on this measure can be demonstrated by analysing the correlation between Orange advertising ratings and consideration. Figure 9 shows how an increase or decrease of 100 ratings relates to an equivalent increase or decrease consideration to purchase by +/- 1.8%.[12]

---

10. These were the most recent data at time of print. Cellnet and Vodafone figures include both digital and analogue subscribers.
11. The Millward Brown tracking survey ended in February 1998.
12. The consideration score is based on percentage of non-Orange customers agreeing to the statement 'Would seriously consider [Orange] if purchasing a mobile phone'.

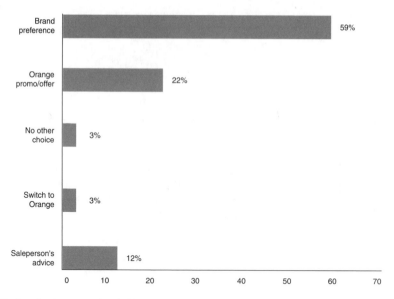

Figure 7: *The best descriptor regarding decision to connect to Orange*
Source: Orange New Customer Survey.

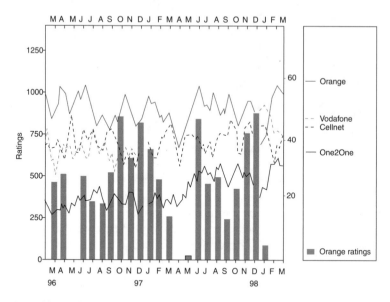

Figure 8: *Would seriously consider if purchasing a mobile phone (based on non-users of relevant brand)*
Source: Millward Brown

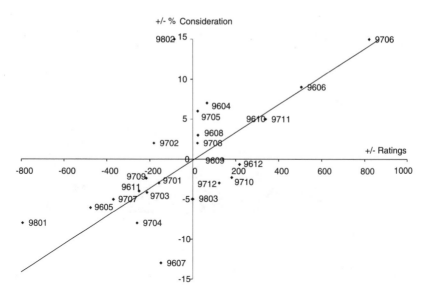

Figure 9: *Month-on-month change in consideration to purchase versus month-on-month change in Orange TVRs*
Source: Millward Brown/Mediapolis

Quantifying advertising's contribution to subscriber growth

The mobile phone market is inherently complex and a model must look to address not only the behind-the-scene issues such as dealer incentives, but also the extremely complex consumer decision-making process (see Figure 10).

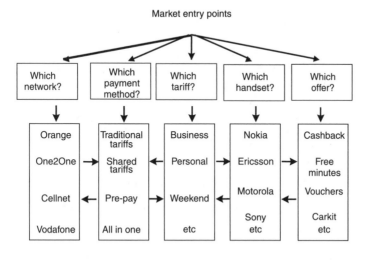

Figure 10: *Cellular decision options*

Accordingly, a huge number of variables were trialed before a satisfactory model was developed exhibiting sufficient levels of statistical confidence. As a result of these trials, we were able to isolate four key drivers within the mobile network marketplace: pricing, distribution, the market trend and seasonality (Figure 11).

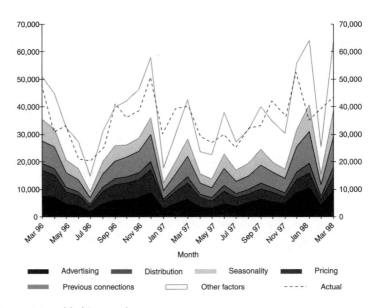

Figure 11: *Econometric model of Orange sales*
Source: Independent Data Analysis Ltd

The results of this model show that, at the very minimum (excluding long-term effects), advertising has contributed 15.28%[13] of Orange sales since its flotation.

Given that Orange has connected an additional 722,000 subscribers since flotation, this equates to a contribution of 110,320 connections.

The lifetime value of a network customer is calculated as follows:

(annual average revenue per subscriber – acquisition cost) x customer lifetime

Advertising's contribution from April 1996 to April 1998 therefore represents £144.34 million (110,320 x (£497 - £225) x 4.83 years[14]), more than three times the payback on this one measure alone.

However, the Orange business plan requires that earnings growth comes from not only attracting a volume of subscribers, but by maximising the revenue obtained from each customer.

Maximising subscriber revenue
Advertising has had the opportunity to maximise subscriber revenue in two ways:

— by attracting high revenue customers at the outset,

— by encouraging all subscribers to increase their usage.

---

13. Our confidence in the model is further enhanced by its correlation with the Millward Brown version developed for the 1996 IPA Effectiveness paper.
14. All figures taken from Dresdner Kleinwort Benson report, March 1998.

It is a combination of these two factors, as well as the company's ability to retain its customers, that has enabled Orange plc to increase its net share of market value, despite a declining net market volume (Figure 12).

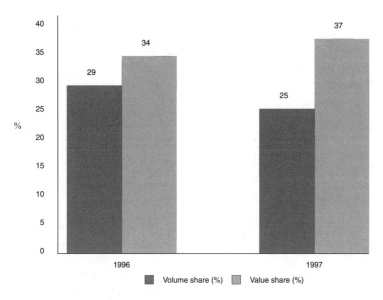

Figure 12: *Orange share of market value*
Source: Dresdner Kleinwort Benson

Attracting high revenue customers

As Table 3 shows,[15] Orange plc has achieved the highest revenue per customer of the four networks:

TABLE 3 : AVERAGE REVENUE PER CUSTOMER

One2One	£480
Cellnet	£355
Vodafone	£427
Orange	£498

Source: Annual reports/Orange Market Planning Department.

Advertising's role in this success has been to attract appropriate customers through its distinctive style and the communication of specific messages.

The success of this strategy can be quantified by analysing the value of customers attracted through advertising, compared to the whole customer base (Table 4).

---

15. Post-service provider payments.

TABLE 4: VALUE OF AVERAGE ADVERTISING CONNECTION VERSUS TOTAL AVERAGE CONNECTION

Tariff	Annual Talk plan value to Orange	Talk plan profile per 100 advertising attributable connections	Revenue per 100 advertising attributable connections	Talk plan profile per 100 average Orange connections	Revenue per 100 average Orange connections
Talk 15	£280	48.56	£13,597	51.30	£14,364
Talk 60	£572	44.52	£25,465	41.70	£23,852
Talk 200	£1,032	5.13	£5,294	5.00	£5,160
Talk 360	£1,483	0.97	£1,439	1.00	£1,483
Talk 540	£1,755	0.82	£1,439	1.00	£1,755
Average talk plan revenue (total revenue from 100 subscribers ÷100)		£472.34		£466.14	
Connection charge		£31.00		£31.00	
Average revenue/subscriber		£503.34 (ad related)		£497.14 (total base)	

Source: LVB Draft Worldwide/Orange Market Planning Department

Orange plc's response handling system is capable of linking all advertising-driven telephone enquiries through to a subsequent talk plan connection.[16]

Advertising generated sales are worth, on average, an incremental £6.20 per annum (£503.34 - £497.14). We can therefore calculate an additional contribution to earnings growth of:

Advertising-generated connections x incremental revenue per year x customer lifetime

This gives us a figure of £3.30 million.

Increasing usage

In sharp contrast to the competition, Orange advertising is information-rich. Over the last two years Orange advertising has communicated 17 different services on TV alone; the closest competitor has communicated eight.

This strategy of continually communicating Orange's *value-added* services has exploited the tendency of customers to be more aware of their own brand's advertising. In Orange customers this disposition is significantly more pronounced than in Cellnet and Vodafone customers, and ahead of the customers of the fast improving One2One.

This high awareness, coupled with the communication of new product and service messages, serves to remind and encourage customer usage.

Figure 13 demonstrates the correlation between month-on-month increases in Orange TVRs, and subsequent changes in the average number of outgoing minutes made by the average Orange customer.[17]

16. While the response analysis does not provide details of all advertising-related sales, we are confident that it gives a fair representation of sales driven through advertising.
17. This analysis is based on Orange TV advertising only, with a lag of one month between TVRs and the

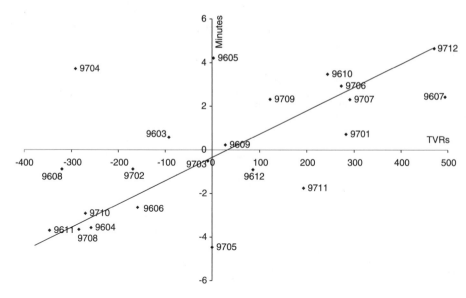

Figure 13: *Month-on-month change in Orange TVRs versus usage change* (%)
Source: Mediapolis/Orange

Taking the line of best fit illustrated above, an increase of 100 TVRs leads to an increase in outgoing usage of 1.06 minutes.

Given the average investment of 280 TVRs each month, it can be calculated that advertising had the effect of increasing outgoing usage per customer by an average of just under three minutes each month (280 x 1.06 minutes/100 TVRs).

With an average revenue per outgoing minute of 29.6 pence,[18] this is an incremental £0.88 per customer per month. Multiplying this figure by Orange's subscriber base over the period covered by this paper leads to a figure of £18.70 million in revenue generated by advertising's effect on increasing usage.

Quantifying advertising's contribution to earnings growth

Advertising can thus be seen to have not only attracted a finite number of subscribers, but also to have maximised subscriber revenue by attracting quality connections and by prompting the base to use their phones more. The net effect of advertising on annual earnings growth is thus shown in Figure 14.

---

resultant increase in seasonally adjusted usage.
8. This figure is provided by the Orange market planning department and takes into account inclusive minutes. City analysts all use similar figures.

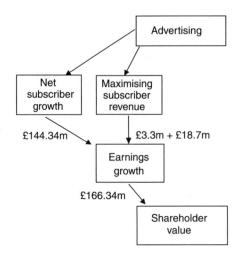

Figure 14: *Advertising payback via earnings growth*

Earnings Security

Mobile communications is a growth market throughout the world, with the promise of significant long-term return for shareholders. However, it is characterised by a conflict between short-term earnings growth and long-term earnings security.

At the heart of this conflict are the heavy subsidies that networks are willing to offer in order to attract new customers. In the UK these subsidies mean that each new customer will typically cost the networks anywhere between £200 and £300. If a customer then leaves at the end of their contract, the network is in danger of making a minimal profit or even a loss.

For Orange plc to be confident of maximising shareholder value it must not only attract and cultivate quality customers (delivering earnings growth), but maintain them (delivering earnings security).

Maximising subscriber lifetime

The marketplace's measure of loyalty is 'churn' – the percentage of the base that leaves the network each year. Orange has the lowest churn levels in the UK (see Table 5).

TABLE 5: NETWORK CHURN LEVELS

	Churn %	Customer Lifetime[19] years
One2One	25.0	4.0
Cellnet	32.0	3.1
Vodafone	28.0	3.5
Orange	20.7	4.8

Source: Dresdner Kleinwort Benson

Orange's enviable level is primarily influenced by the overall service and product quality of the Orange network. However, in contributing to this low churn level Orange plc has capitalised on its customers' sensitivity to Orange advertising.

Among the numerous advertised products and services, there are two that research has identified as being of particular relevance to the subscriber base in minimising churn. These were, unsurprisingly, network coverage and price (Table 6).

TABLE 6: REASONS FOR LEAVING THE ORANGE NETWORK[20]

Coverage related	58%
Cost	21%
Other	21%

Source: Harris Research Centre

Advertising was identified as a means of changing long-term customer perceptions of Orange coverage and value.

Communicating improved coverage

Orange's network roll-out has been consistent over the past two years, the net effect of which has been an overall upward trend in coverage perceptions. The advertising strategy has been to boost these perceptions by highlighting key milestones in network expansion, such as 90% GB population coverage in February 1996 and 92% UK population coverage in February 1997.

Both campaigns have specifically targeted Orange customers. It was felt that advertising, allied with the improved reality, would allow Orange customers to become brand evangelists, countering negative perceptions of Orange coverage among prospective users and increase Orange customer loyalty by countering their prime reason for churning off the network.

Both campaigns resulted in a step change in perceptions (Figure 15).

The February 1996 campaign falls outside the remit of this paper (having run immediately prior to the flotation); we will therefore limit ourselves to quantifying the results of the second campaign.

The long-term effect can be seen to have raised perceptions among Orange users by 9%, equivalent to reducing the number of dissatisfied customers from 49% to 40%.[21]

From March 1997 to April 1998 (the period following the campaign) annualised *voluntary* churn averaged 9.35%.[22] Given research has shown that 58% of this voluntary churn is due to coverage dissatisfaction (see Table 6), churn due to coverage has averaged 5.4% (58% of 9.35%).

---

19. The number of years required for churn to equal 100%.
20. Research among voluntary churners.
21. These are the median percentages of people disagreeing with the statement 'Orange offers wide coverage', pre and post the 'Covered' campaign.
22. The majority of churn is due to fraud, bad debts and people returning their phone within the 14-day money-back guarantee period, none of which advertising could be assumed to affect.

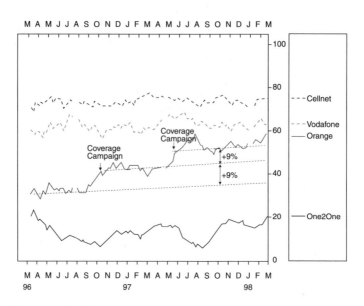

Figure 15: *Perceptions of 'Wide Coverage' among Orange users*
Source: Millward Brown

With a 40% customer dissatisfaction level being proportional to a churn of 5.4%, we can calculate that a customer dissatisfaction level of 49% (without the 'Covered' campaign) would have resulted in a churn level 1.2% higher at 6.6% (5.4% x 49%/40%).

Communicating value for money
In a highly price-sensitive marketplace it is also imperative that Orange's current customers are dissuaded from switching to a potentially cheaper alternative network, particularly given the price reductions of the key competitors.

The success of advertising in maintaining value perceptions among Orange customers can be seen in Orange's ongoing customer satisfaction survey shown in Figure 16.

In quantifying the effect of advertising on customer perceptions of value, we have looked at the months where there was little or no advertising spend. During such periods, satisfaction levels have decayed rapidly.[23] Given competitive price cuts, the degree to which satisfaction levels have declined is also falling over time. We can therefore calculate a satisfaction trend without advertising (Figure 17).

The effect of advertising has maintained customer satisfaction levels at an average of 86%, equivalent to dissatisfaction of 14% (100% – 86%). Had advertising not produced this offsetting effect, dissatisfaction over this period (reflecting cheaper competitive offerings) would have increased to 21%. On this basis the average uplift provided by advertising from March 1996 to March 1998

---

23. The exception is the rise in satisfaction in March 1997, corresponding to the particularly effective 'Covered' campaign. While the ratings shown include the press element of the campaign, there is no equivalent measure to account for the poster campaign during this period.

PRESS ADS

'COVERED' CAMPAIGN
FEBRUARY 97

'ASTERISK' CAMPAIGN
NOVEMBER 96

'GROUPS' CAMPAIGN
SUMMER 97

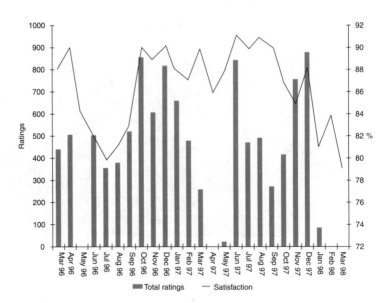

Figure 16: *Customer satisfaction with value-for-money against Orange advertising*
Source: Research Business/Mediapolis

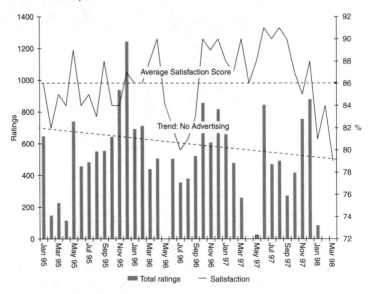

Figure 17: *Customer satisfaction with value-for-money against Orange advertising*
Source: Research Business/Mediapolis

can be calculated as 6%. This is a long-term and growing contribution of advertising.

Churn due to value dissatisfaction is 1.45% (6.9% voluntary churn[24] x the 21% of churn due to cost dissatisfaction, see Table 6).

Given that a 14% customer dissatisfaction level is directly proportional to a churn of 1.45%, we can calculate that a customer dissatisfaction level 6% higher at

20% (without advertising) would have resulted in a churn level 0.6% higher at 2.07% (1.45% x 20%/14%).

Quantifying advertising's contribution to earnings security

The combined effect of advertising has thus been to reduce churn by 0.6% over the period April 1996 to February 1997, and 1.8% (0.6% + 1.2%) from March 1997 to April 1998. Averaging out over the period gives a churn decrease due to advertising of 1.3%, equivalent to an additional customer lifespan of 3.43 months.[25]

The average revenue per subscriber is £497.14 per year (see Table 3), or £41.42 per month. Advertising can therefore lay claim to £142.07 (3.43 months x £41.42) of the lifetime value of an average Orange customer connected during this period.

The total number of new subscribers between April 1996 and April 1998 is 722,000. We can therefore calculate advertising's contribution to earnings security as follows:

$$722{,}000 \times £142.07 = £102{,}600{,}000$$

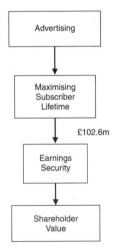

Figure 18: *Advertising payback via maximising subscriber lifetime*

Risk Diversification

While Orange is a proven success in the UK mobile telecoms marketplace, it has an obligation to create further shareholder value through the diversification of its interests so that it is not reliant on one finite market.

24. This figure is the average for the period in April 1996 to April 1998 and is therefore different from the figure of 9.35% quoted for the 'Covered' campaign, which represents voluntary churn for the second of the two years.
25. The number of years required for churn to equal 100%, based on a 20.7% churn rate, is 4.83 years. The number of years required for churn to equal 100%, based on a 22% (20.7% + 1.3%) churn rate, is 4.54 years, a difference of 0.28 years or 3.43 months.

Foreign licence bids

In the particular case of Orange plc, investors and analysts have remained concerned about the rate of growth of the UK mobile telecoms market, which has lagged behind other European markets. Thus, the opportunity for foreign licence acquisition has formed a core element of Orange plc's risk diversification.

The situation internationally is strikingly similar to the circumstances in the UK over the past 15 years. Government-owned telecommunication monopolies are being opened up to competition from both fixed and mobile companies, creating plenty of opportunity for Orange plc if it could successfully convert bids into awarded licences.

Many of the bid situations are ongoing (for example, Sri Lanka, Ireland and Austria). But where Orange has won (as part of a consortium), the brand has been shown to play a pivotal role:

> 'Orange's experience in the UK mobile phone market, where it was a late entrant but now has one of the best recognised brand names, is understood to have counted heavily with the Swiss authorities.'

> Source: Financial Times, 21 April 1998

> 'Orange is strong in marketing and advertising, and brings a new aggressive style to the telecoms market.'

> Source: Dr Georg Obermeier, Viag CEO (Orange plc's partner in Switzerland)
> *Mail on Sunday*, 8 February 1998

This international success has been driven by the inherent transferability of the brand. In a worldwide telecoms market, which is plagued by the familiar problems of nationalised monopolies and consumer confusion, Orange advertising has been designed to have an international appeal. It has been successfully researched in countries as diverse as Greece, Belgium, Sri Lanka, The Netherlands, Israel and Switzerland .

The advertising has thus significantly contributed to the global potential of the Orange brand:

> 'Given that Orange has created one of the strongest worldwide cellular brands, we feel it is an extremely attractive partner for those looking to bid for and run PCN licences in Europe.'

> Source: SBC Warburg, Orange Analysts Report, March 1998

In lieu of the fact that much of Orange plc's international potential is latent (Orange has the scope to capitalise on dozens of foreign licences in the future), it is difficult to place a full value on advertising's role in foreign licence bids. However, it is possible to have a rule-of-thumb quantification of advertising's contribution to one of the successful bids to date using the judgment criteria for the Swiss licence (Table 7).

Capability	20%
Network roll out	20%
Coverage	20%
Innovations	20%
Marketing	20%

Source: Swiss Government's Invitation to Bid Document

Given that advertising represented 37% of the marketing investment for Switzerland, we can attribute on a pro-rata basis the same proportion to its contribution to the marketing section. We therefore have an advertising contribution of 7.4%. The current value of the Swiss licence has been estimated at £100 million;[26] the contribution of advertising to this bid alone amounts to £7.4 million. This example clearly shows the enormous potential value of Orange advertising worldwide, with the implication being that advertising has similarly contributed to Orange's other foreign success in Belgium. Indeed, such is the power of the Orange name that Hutchison Whampoa, the huge Hong Kong based backer of Orange, is considering rebranding all its worldwide operations as Orange.

Brand diversification

Another feature of Orange plc's risk diversification is the ability of the brand to enter new markets, a capacity that is even more latent than its potential as a worldwide telecoms brand. This capacity is recognised within Orange plc:

'There is more in the brand than in the business.'

Source: Orange employee, Corr Research, March 1997

In exploratory research consumers enthusiastically endorsed the idea of Orange operating in new markets:

'Orange's consumer champion image allows consumers to accept that Orange could move into the financial arena and expect a similar high-quality service offering to the mobile phone offering. The brand appears to have an elasticity, similar to Virgin and Sainsbury.'

'Orange is perceived as capable and credible in developing the Orange bank.'

Source: The Research Business International Ltd, August 1997

It is hard to dispute the fact that brands will play an increasingly important role in the world of technology. As we are faced with an ever more confusing array of formats and systems, companies will need to be able to package this bewildering choice. It is therefore the brands with the greatest potential for transferability that will survive. Just as Orange has the opportunity to be a worldwide telecoms brand, so it has the potential to be a utility provider, a bank or an internet provider.

26. Dresdner Kleinwort Benson.

Quantifying Advertising Contribution to Risk Diversification

As we have seen, most of advertising's contribution to risk diversification remains latent. In the case of Orange plc's brand transferability, while a clear inherent strength resides within the brand, it has yet to deliver shareholder value. It would therefore be inappropriate to give this transferability a value. We will therefore only include the contribution of advertising to one of Orange plc's successful foreign licence bids.

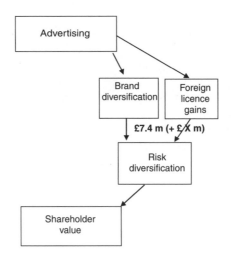

Figure 19: *Advertising's payback via risk diversification*

MAKING IT EASIER FOR ORANGE PLC TO DO BUSINESS

A plc's share price is a measure of investor faith in the future potential of that company. This faith can be driven by a huge number of factors, many of them beyond the control of an individual company. However, analysts will naturally evaluate a company on its own performance. This analysis is based on a detailed evaluation of the company's current and predicted balance sheet, as well as its belief in the strength and desirability of the brand or brands managed by a given company.

In surveys among City financial media and fund managers, marketing and advertising consistently come out as Orange's single most powerful inherent strength.

This confidence and admiration is reflected in the following quotes taken from these surveys[27]:

---

27. Dewe Rogerson City Scan Reports, 1996 and 1998.

'Its major strength is the marketing nous that it has demonstrated – a product rapidly becoming a commodity by very clever advertising and support.'

Source: Fund Manager, shareholder

'They have developed a strong brand image in the UK market via advertising and clear tariff structure.'

Source: Fund Manager, non-shareholder

'One hell of a marketing campaign ... they are seen as young, vibrant, exciting, more secure and generally a fashionable thing to have around.'

Source: Analyst

'The marketing is excellent, it's well thought out and they've used the right agencies and put a lot of resources into it.'

Source: Fund Manager, shareholder

'I think the brand is the main strength they have. Everything else they've got has been able to be copied and therefore it's not a sustainable strength.'

Source: Analyst

'It's developed a very strong brand image in the UK through very innovative advertising.'

Source: Financial Media

'The UK is perceived to be its market strength and it has good advertising.'

Source: Fund Manager, non-shareholder

'It has established itself strongly as a brand and that could be used elsewhere.'

Source: Analyst

Advertising's impact can be also seen in the analyst reports themselves. In summarising their faith in the future of Orange plc, SBC Warburg Read lists a number of key factors. These include:

'Orange is likely to launch a new advertising campaign at the end of April.'

and

'Recent figures from advertising agency Millward Brown [sic] suggest that Orange still ranks highest amongst the cellular operators for spontaneous awareness.'

Source: SBC Warburg Dillon Read report on Orange, March 1998

VALUING ADVERTISING'S CONTRIBUTION

So far, the advertising payback figures we have provided show the impact of advertising on earnings. In our view this is a robust but somewhat conventional assessment of advertising's overall contribution. Throughout this paper we have sought to emphasise how advertising performance was inextricably linked to Orange plc's performance in terms of shareholder value.

Accordingly, we would prefer to advance a more radical calculation of advertising's contribution based on the actual working practices used by City analysts to determine the value of UK stocks. To this end we have enlisted Lehman Brothers to apply the sophisticated spreadsheet methodology by which it calculates an implied value per share. The difference between this implied value and the real value is the basis on which it bases its notices to buy, sell or hold.

Currently, Lehman Brothers' equity market valuation shows Orange to be a buy stock with an implied value per share of 528p, compared to the current market value of 443p (Table 8).[28]

TABLE 8: LEHMAN BROTHER'S CURRENT EQUITY MARKET VALUATION

Discount rate	9%
NPV cash flows	1035
PV terminal value (£m)	6396
Enterprise value Orange PCS	7432
Other business	459
Asset/enterprise value	7891
Net debt (projected end 1998)	(1571)
Equity value	6320
Implied value per share	**528**
Current share price	443
Current discount premium	**16%**
Implied in perp growth rate	4%

We then asked Lehman Brothers to rework the valuation on the assumption that advertising's effects on net subscriber growth, customer revenue and churn had not applied over the course of the plc's history (Table 9).[29]

---

28. These equity market valuations are based on standard net present value formulae, whereby future cashflows are discounted against the opportunity cost of capital for investments of comparable risk (the 'discount rate' of 9%). The asset value is comprised of two components, the first of which is the NPV of cash flows within the planning period. This is the period in which the analyst believes cash flows can be meaningfully forecasted (generally in the region of 5–8 years). Following this period cash flow is assumed to grow in line with the market – in this case at the implied in perpetuity growth rate of 4%. The second component of asset value is the PV terminal value, which is the present value of all cash flows falling beyond the planning horizon.

29. Given that foreign bids either result in success or failure (as opposed to the variable levels of the other measures), it was not possible to include advertising's contribution to Orange's success abroad.

TABLE 9: LEHMAN BROTHERS' EQUITY MARKET VALUATION
REMOVING ADVERTISING CONTRIBUTION

Discount rate	9%
NPV cash flows	328
PV terminal value (£m)	4172
Enterprise value Orange PCS	4500
Other business	459
Asset/enterprise value	4959
Net debt (projected end 98)	(1,616)
Equity Value	3,343
Implied value per share	279
Current share price	443
Current discount premium	(59%)
Implied in perp growth rate	4.0%

In this way it was able to arrive at a surrogate for Orange's implied value per share, excluding advertising. The results are an emphatic confirmation of advertising's contribution.

The implied value per share plummets from 528p to 279p, suggesting that without advertising Orange plc would have underperformed the FTSE 100 index by 19%.

CONCLUSION

Although Orange plc is now the sixtieth largest company in the UK, it is still a minor player in the game of global telecommunications. Within the UK mobile market it is up against the might of Vodafone, BT (50% shareholders of Cellnet) and Cable and Wireless (owners of One2One). Yet it is a company that has continued to flourish through its commitment to a brand-led, value-based strategy.

Most importantly from the advertising industry's perspective, it is a company that believes in the manifold power of advertising. It is this power that has enabled Orange plc, on a budget of £43.6 million[30] to create a conventional payback in excess of £276.34 million – over six times the advertising investment (Figure 20).

However, as we stated in the introduction to this paper, Orange plc's objective is to create shareholder value. For shareholders the effect of advertising on the bottom line is in itself neither here nor there; rather their sole concern is the manifold contribution of advertising to the share price. For this reason, our objective has been to demonstrate advertising's contribution by ways that would be meaningful beyond the parochial world of marketing and advertising.

---

30. Advertising expenditure April 1996 to April 1998. Source: Mediapolis.

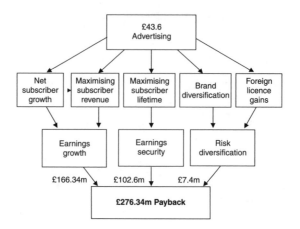

Figure 20: *Advertising's conventional payback*

In proving advertising's effect across a range of business drivers, we have been able to provide Lehman Brothers with the information by which they have calculated advertising's capacity to increase Orange plc's implied value per share by £2.49. This is equivalent to an increased market capitalisation of £3 billion.

3

The Army

How advertising rose to the Army's challenge to 'Be the Best'

EDITOR'S SUMMARY

This paper shows how the 'Be the Best' advertising for the Army simultaneously improved recruitment and saved money by redefining the role of advertising to one of improving the quality not simply the quantity of applications.

The Problem – Bridging the Shortfall

In 1994 the Army faced a manning shortage. Recruitment targets were raised by 63%, to 15,000 soldiers a year. Using the historical ratio of enquiries to enlistments of 6.7:1, this implied generating around 100,000 enquiries.

Part of the reason for the high ratio of enquiries to enlistment was that many of the enquirers were of poor quality. The Army was attracting the wrong people.

The role of the advertising had to be to attract young men with the right mental attitude in order to improve the conversion ratio.

Our message focused on the fact that the Army brings out the best in its people, and therefore challenges potential recruits to be the best they could be.

Results and Payback

Since 1994, the number of enlistments has steadily increased, and this year we will exceed the target. This has been achieved by reducing the conversion ratio from 6.7:1 in 1994 to 3.4:1 now.

We estimate that the increase in the efficiency of recruitment has saved the Army £16.4 million after deducting the advertising spend.

Other savings have also accrued. Better quality applicants are less likely to fall out of basic training, and we have seen the fall-out rate reduce over the period.

Furthermore, it has led to something of a culture shift. The 'Be the Best' line has also been widely adopted by the Army as an internal mission statement, and is used above and below the line, in all media.

INTRODUCTION: AN ORGANISATIONAL TURNAROUND

This case is about the British Army, which has succeeded in achieving a dramatic turnaround in recruitment after years of decline, and despite a very negative social and demographic environment.

Recruitment has increased by over 60%, and is now twice as efficient as prior to the campaign (saving money for the Army and ultimately the UK taxpayer).

Perhaps more significantly, the attitude and culture of the Army has started to shift. The Army is not known as an organisation that embraces change, which makes this effect all the more striking.

This case will show how the 'Be the Best' strategy and advertising has been the catalyst for this substantial turnaround. It has been an investment in the long term and has involved a total rebranding of the Army. The advertising issued a challenge to potential recruits and to the Army itself: 'Be the Best.' The evidence shows that both audiences have risen to this challenge.

THE SCOPE OF THIS PAPER

Limitations on the length of this paper mean that it will focus on soldier rather than officer recruitment. In terms of numbers of recruits, the soldier is where the greatest recruitment challenge lies (20 soldiers are required for every one officer). The strategy development section will make reference to how the strategy works against both soldier and officer targets.

The paper will also only look at enquiries via Army recruiting offices. A minority of enquiries come via phone or coupon, but these ultimately end up as referrals to the recruiting offices.

BACKGROUND ON SOLDIER RECRUITING

The Army needs to recruit a set number of new soldiers each year. This is essential in order to achieve manning at levels which are capable of meeting UN and NATO commitments, and are able to defend our interests at home and abroad.

Meeting the Recruitment Targets is No Easy Task

Joining the Army is a big decision. 'Signing up' is a rather more significant step than accepting any 'normal' job. It requires moving away from friends and family and adopting a life of structure and discipline probably unlike anything experienced before. There is a minimum commitment of three years, which is a long time if you do not enjoy it. This is not a decision to be rushed or taken lightly.

Broadly, enquirers fall into one of the following categories:

— Those with an interest in or contact with the Army over a long period.

— Those who approach the Army as a career choice.

— Those who see the Army as a 'last resort' career.

Source: Counterpoint Qualitative Research

The attitudes of parents, careers advisers and the general public all affect these groups, as do many social and economic factors.

The Environment in the Early 1990s made the Recruiting Task Even Harder

The ending of the Cold War with the USSR raised questions about the future role of the Army and led to calls for the Army to be more cost-effective. In 1992 the 'Options for Change' white paper instigated a reduction in the overall strength of the Army from 145,000 to around 116,000. Not only did this affect the morale of serving soldiers, the widespread headlines about redundancies also damaged public confidence in the Army as a secure employer. People were leaving faster than the natural attrition rate, some through redundancy, others through poor morale. In addition, the flow of recruits coming in was reduced because people assumed that the Army was not recruiting. The Army was caught in a vicious downward spiral.

A DRAMATIC INCREASE IN RECRUITING TARGETS WAS ESSENTIAL

If the Army could not start recruiting more soldiers, it was calculated that it would face a catastrophic manning shortage of 20,000 by the year 2000. This would result in a serious failure to meet international obligations. Therefore, during 1994 and 1995 soldier recruiting targets (paradoxically) had to be increased and the new levels were set at 15,000 soldiers per year – a huge 63% increase from 9,200 the previous year.

But Where Were the New Recruits Going to Come From?

Aside from the consequences of the ending of the Cold War, virtually all social and demographic trends were working against Army recruitment:

— a demographic trough among 15 to 19-year-olds, reducing the overall pool of potential recruits;

— an increase in the number of people going into further education, taking aspirations beyond what they believed the Army could offer (and beyond the key recruiting age of 16 to 18);

— unemployment falling among 16 to 24-year-olds (traditionally, high unemployment has always favoured Armed Forces recruitment);

— declining fitness levels among 16 to 24-year-olds with a minority taking part in sports (the Army has fitness thresholds);

— increase in drug usage among young people (a bar to entry).

The general publicity environment was hostile, portraying the Army as an anachronistic organisation failing to come to terms with the 1990s. Over a two-month period in 1995 there were 120,000 negative column inches of news coverage, equating to an annual equivalent of £42 million of media expenditure at ratecard.

In addition to this, the visibility of the Army was reducing:

— the number of Army Careers Information Offices, a main source of visibility and information, fell from 170 in 1990 to 152 in 1994, and to 124 today, not a good sign of job security in the Army;

— issues of security prevented soldiers from wearing uniform outside military installations, thus adding to the lower 'military presence'.

The effect of these trends and the consequences of 'Options for Change' were seen in enquiry levels, which had fallen from over 144,000 during 1986 and 1987 to 58,000 during 1993 to 1994, a consistent decline of 14% year on year.

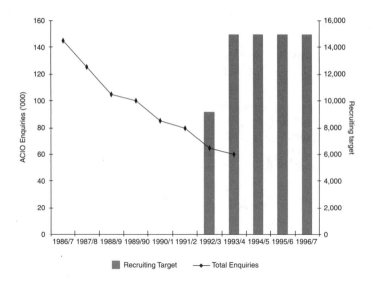

Figure 1: *Total ACIO enquiries 1986/7 to 1993/4 and recruiting targets*
Source: DAR2

RECRUITMENT HAD TO BECOME MORE EFFICIENT

First, some essential information about the recruitment process.

The majority of soldiers are recruited from men between the ages of 16 and 19 (a very small yet now growing percentage are women). An enquiry is made to an Army Careers Information Office (ACIO). An application is completed and, if successful, this applicant will go through to recruit selection. Over two days, a series of medical and physical checks are made, along with other tests, to decide whether the applicant meets the standard. If selected they become an enlistment and will pass on to do their basic training. After that they are sent to a regiment for further training (Figure 2). This terminology will be referred to throughout the case.

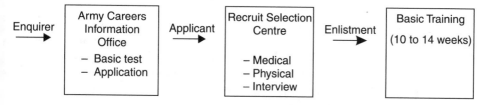

Figure 2: *The recruitment process*

The recruiting problem was twofold: there were fewer people coming forward as enquirers, and enquirers were of poor quality.

Our measure of quality of enquirer is the ratio of enquiry to enlistment. During 1993 and 1994 the ratio was 6.7:1 (6.7 enquiries required to generate one recruit). This was the accepted norm. With all that had happened, we suspected that the Army was seen more as a 'last resort' than a 'career of first choice', and perhaps the ratio reflected this.

Applying this ratio to our new target of 15,000 recruits, we calculated that we would require 100,000 enquiries. This level hadn't been reached since 1988 to 1998, since which time the number of recruiting offices and capacity of the system overall had shrunk. This level of enquiries would clog the system. Although the system could be expanded (at a high upfront cost of establishing new recruiting offices), there was a bigger problem. Due to all the factors discussed above the recruitment pool had shrunk – demographic and education trends alone reduced the pool to approximately 1.2 million men.

Even if all of the 16 to 24-year-old men who expressed a definite interest in joining the Army (6%) actually came forward, which was unlikely given the trends, it would not yield anywhere near the 100,000 enquiries.

THE KEY

The task became clear. We had to get a better conversion from enquiry to enlistment, thereby bringing down the ratio. Recruitment had to become more efficient to have a chance of reaching the target.

Although this ratio was considered the norm, we felt it was possible to improve on it.

Research had shown that the previous advertising campaign ('Frank') painted an idealised and somewhat unrealistic view of Army life. Perhaps this had brought less committed people into the system with false expectations, and this was reflected in the ratio.

ADVERTISING OBJECTIVES

The primary job for the advertising was to bring forward better quality enquirers. This meant attracting people with the 'right mental attitude' (of which more below) and bringing them forward with realistic expectations of what the Army was really about, so that they were not put off upon contact with military life.

To increase the quality and conversion, the advertising had to inspire the right type of enquirers and screen out the wrong kind.

The advertising also needed to make a statement about the Army to those who influence potential recruits – parents, careers advisers and society at large. We had to restore their confidence in the organisation, its professionalism and its future.

Finally, the internal audience needed a message to restore their faith in the Army as a long-term career (keeping motivated soldiers serving is the most cost-effective way of manning the Army).

DEVELOPING THE NEW STRATEGY

One Army Approach

Although soldier and officer careers attract very different types of people, they are both part of the same 'brand', the Army. As such, many of the issues and perceptions that these different audiences have of the brand are similar. For this reason we wanted to develop one strategy to work against both officer and soldier targets.

We also needed to stretch the budget. We needed officer and soldier advertising to work synergistically.

Understanding What the Army Does for People

The magnitude of lifestyle change and the need to improve conversion led us to focus the creative strategy on those already interested in an Army career. Recruiters talk about the 'mental attitude' of potential recruits as being the most critical determinant of their trainability and ultimately whether they will make good soldiers. We needed to understand this, and use this insight to shape our strategy and appeal to the right kind of recruits. We had to understand what the Army represented for those who were drawn to it. Rather than talk about it in theory, we were allowed to experience it firsthand.

A series of field trips was made to Army selection and training centres, and to Sandhurst, the officer training college. We spent time simply absorbing the atmosphere. We watched recruits being put through their paces and compared the intake with those about to pass. We talked to potential officers and soldiers at various points.

The most striking experience was the 'before and after' test. Arriving at basic training were unconfident 16-year-olds with concave chests and acne, who would not look you in the eye. After ten weeks, out came disciplined, confident and proud individuals. This gave us a real insight into what the Army could do for people. It seemed to be a hugely transformative experience for these young men.

We talked to some soldiers during their basic training. A couple had been rejected at recruit selection stage – one for physical fitness and one because he was dyslexic and had struggled with a written test. Both were so committed to joining that they had worked at their specific issues and tried again. A picture emerged that seemed to be consistent across both soldier and officer targets. Despite their different backgrounds, they had in common a will to succeed. They wanted to be the best they could be and they believed the Army could bring out the best in them. This mental attitude was characterised by people who were confident, down-to-earth, self-disciplined and ambitious.

The advertising proposition was:

> The British Army will bring out the best in you.

An important part of the creative brief was tone of voice. Given we were trying to attract quality enquirers with realistic expectations, the tone of voice needed to be exciting, challenging and real.

The campaign was developed in ways appropriate to the recruiting task of soldiers and officers. Officer commercials focused on the more intellectual challenges, which were in line with what they demanded from a career. Soldier commercials focused on the more physical, exciting, teamwork-based challenges.

MEDIA STRATEGY

Soldier versus Officer Messages

People's perceptions of the Army tend to be dominated by their perception of soldiers.

Previously, more media had been placed behind soldier recruiting as a reflection of the recruiting challenge. The new campaign had to affect a wider audience than recruits. Overemphasising officer messages within the mix allowed us to make a stronger quality statement about the Army. We also felt it would have a halo effect on bringing forward the more aspiring and better-quality soldier. We therefore chose a more equal split between officer and soldier advertising than the recruitment targets justified.

Media Mix

The decision to sign up is made over time and with many influences. We needed a medium capable of reaching this broad audience, and building a picture of the Army over time. We also needed the advertising to make a powerful statement about the Army and capture people's hearts and minds, in particular 16 to 19-year-olds and serving personnel. Television was the ideal medium for the tasks.

Advertising also had to deliver strongly on a specific recruiting message and provide a trigger to action. We chose to do small space 'brand' focused ads in the classified section of the tabloid press. This clearly said, 'recruiting' and the medium provided a good context for creative standout. The low cost of this medium made it possible to deliver very high frequency. Radio has also been used to extend 'brand' presence when we are not on television. Posters have been used to inform people about the number of vacancies in the Army.

Media Spend

Initially, the media budget for 1994 to 1995 was £1.6 million for soldiers. With media inflation this was an 8% decline over the previous year. The scale of the task – reversing long-term decline, reaching multiple audiences and ultimately attracting high numbers of quality enquirers – meant that the budget was increased to £6.8 million for soldier advertising during 1995 and 1996. In subsequent years it has been £6.8 million and £6.5 million. In real terms, given very high media inflation over this period, the budgets have fallen in the past two years.

THE ADVERTISING

The campaign was made up of the following executions, a selection of which appear on pages 69 to 71.

Television		Radio
Soldier 'Night Driving'	1994	Anti-tank
Soldier 'Team'	1995	Twig
Soldier 'Enemy Base'	1995	Breathe-in
Soldier 'Earthquake'	1996	
Officer 'Trust'	1995	
Ethnic Minorities 'Accident'	1998	
Equal Opportunities 'Torchlight'	1998	
(PR Footage of Equal Opportunities Launch)		

Press (Selection)	Posters
Ladder	15,000 Caretakers
Chocolate Bar	15,000 Security Guards
Surveillance Techniques	15,000 Repairmen
Your Country Needs You	
Changing of the Guard	
Six Practical Ways	
Bin	
Paint by Numbers	

'EARTHQUAKE'

Sound: location effects

'TEAM'

Sound: Location effects.
(MVO): Hello Zero.

This is alpha three zero.

Heading to your location.

On stand by, over.

Hello zero, this is alpha three two.

Crossing point is down.

Assessing situation.

PRESS ADS

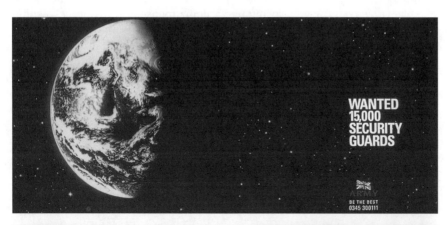

CAMPAIGN EVOLUTION

The campaign is a flexible communication vehicle for the Army. As the role of the Army has evolved, so the advertising has become focused on the peace-keeping and humanitarian role of the Army. It remains important to bring forward committed enquirers with realistic expectations. This shift in emphasis also shows a more contemporary Army playing its global peace-keeping role.

This year we are focusing on equal opportunity policy changes within the Army, specifically, women and ethnic minorities: 70% of Army jobs are now open to women (up from 40%); and the Army has a new policy on stamping out racism and a desire to reflect the ethnic diversity of modern Britain.

HOW DO PEOPLE RESPOND TO THE ADVERTISING?

Sources

The COI runs the Army tracking study through RSGB's Omnibus survey. (The study is somewhat limited in its detailed measurement of advertising effect.)

In addition, we have quantitatively pre-tested two commercials, and conducted major qualitative projects across all target groups on each new commercial and on the overall campaign.

We have found these qualitative studies especially valuable in understanding how the advertising is working. As Geoff Bond, ex-Research Director of COI, said at a recent Admap seminar:

'Often it is far easier to appreciate that the advertising is working, and how it's working, through qualitative rather then quantitative research. In my experience, if the quantitative findings are not in line with the word on the street and the qualitative feedback, people are quite likely to rubbish them – and probably rightly so.'

Firstly, the campaign is seen as impactful and involving:

'An involving, distinctive and memorable creative idea'

Source: Carne Martin, January 1998

'Spontaneous recall of current campaign is truly impressive

— precise recall of storyline and communication

— executions characterised by strong involvement via action (thrill) and/or direct request (thought).'

Source: Navigator, March 1998

Quantitatively, all target groups show very high awareness of the campaign (Figure 3).

Recall of specific soldier commercials is also high among both potential recruits and their parents (Figures 4 and 5). The campaign is also seen as highly original and involving (Figure 6).

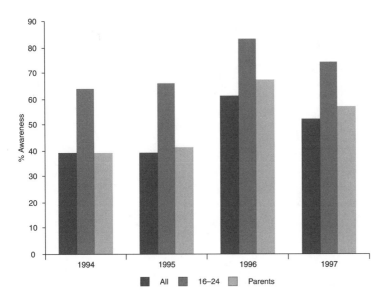

Figure 3: *Advertising awareness (prompted)*
Source: COI/RSGB

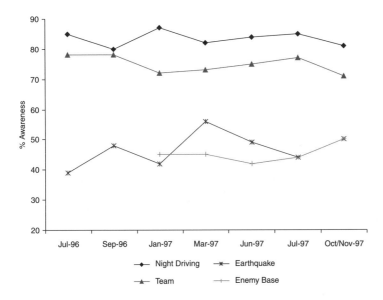

Figure 4: *Prompted recall of soldier advertising (16 to 24 year-olds)*
Source: COI/RSGB

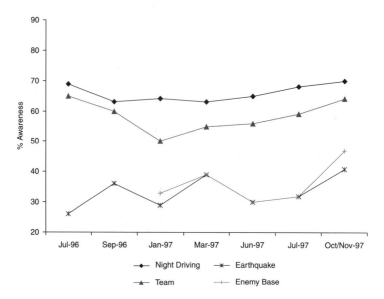

Figure 5: *Prompted recall of soldier advertising (Parents of children under 24)*
Source: COI/RSGB

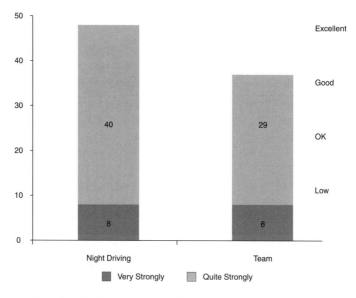

Figure 6: *'How strongly caught up in advertising were you?'*
Source: COI/HPI

The line 'Be the Best' has very high branded recall among 16 to 24-year-olds: 51% recognise it, and 73% of them correctly attribute it to the Army. Where there is mis-attribution, it is most likely to be confused with Nike. Considering 6% of 16 to 24-year-olds express a definite interest in the Army, and probably 100% express an interest in training shoes, these results are impressive.

The campaign communicates most strongly the qualities needed to be a soldier (Table 1).

TABLE 1: WHAT DO YOU THINK THESE SOLDIER ADS WERE TRYING TO SAY?

Qualities needed to be a soldier	30
Recruitment	26
Job prospects	23
Positive role of the Army	20
Exciting lifestyle	19
Base: All claim to have seen any soldier ad	1451

Source: COI/RSGB, August 1997

The campaign has established a clearer template for the type of quality person the Army wants to recruit (Table 2).

TABLE 2: WHAT TYPE OF PERSON IS MOST SUITED TO AN ARMY CAREER?

	1994 %	1997* %
Ambitious	44	54
Self-confident	39	54
Common sense	43	60
Base: Men age 16 to 24	(160)	(146)

	1994 %	1997 %
Ambitious	63	4
Self-confident	39	51
Common sense	43	52
Base: Parents with sons under age 24	(567)	(573)

Source: COI/ RSGB
* Note: Any shift shown is significant at 95% level

Qualitatively,

'It implies you have to be;

— prepared to do a responsible job;

— quick thinking;

— sure of yourself/self-confident.'

'It's about brains as well as brawn.'

'The Army isn't just about meatheads anymore.'

'I do want to be the best – and this says they won't take just anyone.'

Source: 16 to 19 year-old potential recruits

It also sets more realistic expectations among potential recruits, and they find this motivating.

'It's like trying on the uniform.'

'I'd be much more interested in the Army that showed you what it was really going to be like. It is serious. It is dangerous.'

'This is the more serious side, the real side.'

'Not trying to cover up what the Army is really about.'

Source: 16 to19-year-old potential recruits

It has painted a clearer picture of what an Army career would offer them (Table 3).

TABLE 3: WHAT DO YOU THINK A JOB IN THE ARMY COULD OFFER?

	1994 %	1997 %
Practical/rigorous/professional training	51	57
Sense of public service	45	58
Long term career opportunities	37	43
An opportunity to fulfil potential	32	41
Respect from family	28	36
Respect from friends	26	37
Chance to work with the best	22	32
Base: All 16 to 24 year-olds:	(341)	(292)

Source: COI/ RSGB

Qualitatively, it also indicates personal benefits:

'A sense of achievement, character building, self confidence, believing in yourself.'

'If you're going to join the Army you're going to be someone.'

'If you meet the challenge, that's an achievement, it makes you feel good about yourself.'

Source: 16 to 19-year-old potential recruits

Research also showed that the commercials were working as planned to filter applicants of the right calibre. Both 'Team' and 'Night Driving' encouraged greater consideration of the Army as a career amongst the predisposed, but also managed to put off a significant proportion of the sample who were less interested in an Army career – evidence that the strategy of deterring the faint-hearted was effective (Table 4).

TABLE 4: ATTITUDE TOWARDS A CAREER IN THE ARMY

	Before viewing %	Night driving %	Team %
I'm seriously keen on the idea	7	10	9
It's definitely something I'd consider	10	18	21
I'll find out more, then decide	28	17	11
I've not really thought about it, but I might	17	18	20
I've not really thought about it, but I probably won't	25	20	16
I'm not at all interested	12	18	23

Source: COI/HPI

As the role of the Army has changed, and policy changes are made to reflect modern practices, the advertising has focused people on the new realities rather than old sterotypes (Figure 7).

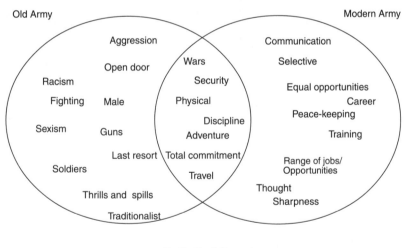

Figure 7: *Old stereotypes versus new realities*
Source: Navigator, March 1998

In summary, the 'Be the Best' campaign was highly noticeable and appeared to be working the way we had intended. Was it having the required effect on recruitment?

CAMPAIGN EFFECTIVENESS

The Results

The main measure of effectiveness is the number of enlistments achieved, and the ratio of enquiry to enlistment (an indication of the quality of the people attracted).

In the first year of the new campaign, the number of enquiries fell from 58,120 between 1993 and 1994, to 48,562 between 1994 and 1995. The media spend had also dropped in real terms by 8% over this period. However, despite this, the number of enlistments increased from 8,700 to 9,289. This meant that despite a smaller budget the efficiency ratio had increased in the first year from 6.7:1 to 5.1:1, an improvement of 24%. Given that there were no changes over the period which could have led to this, other than the change in strategy and advertising execution, it was early evidence that the filtering nature of the advertising seemed to be bringing forward better quality recruits.

Once confident in the advertising's ability to deliver the right people and reduce the ratio, it became clear that we needed greater numbers of quality enquirers to move towards the 15,000 target. The Army recognised the scale of the task and the budgets were increased as a result. In 1995 to 1996, the first year of higher budgets, the enquiry level went up by 34% and reversed the long-term decline (Figure 8).

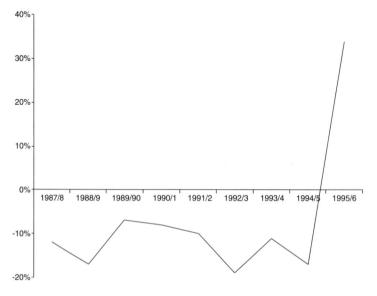

Figure 8: *ACIO Year on year change in enquiries 1986/7 to 1995/6*
Source: DAR2

In subsequent years, although the numbers of enquiries have not increased beyond the initial jump, enlistments have continued to rise consistently towards the 15,000 target (Figure 9).

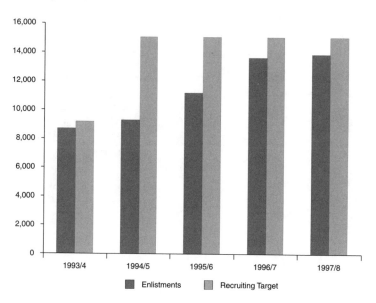

Figure 9: *Soldier targets and enlistments 1993/4 to 1997/8*
Source: DAR2

During 1997 to 1998 recruitment fell just short of target. The figures for the first quarter 1998 are for the first time in excess of what will be required to reach the target.

How has this Result been Achieved?

To understand how this has been achieved, we can look at the ratio between enquiries and enlistments. Overall, this has fallen substantially since the campaign was launched (with the exception of 1995 to 1996 when the increased spend generated a particularly high enquiry level). The ratio is now at approximately half the pre-campaign level, (from 6.7:1 to 3.4:1), thus recruitment is operating at almost twice the 1993 to 1994 efficiency (Figure 10).

The improvement in the ratio proves that higher quality enquirers have been attracted. The efficiency improving over time has been an important factor in the Army now being able to reach its targets this year. Media spend has also fallen in real terms over the period, and yet the ratio continues to fall and enlistments continue to rise (Figure 11). In summary, the main effects have been:

— An improvement in the conversion ratio of enquirers to enlistments, now achieved almost twice as efficiently.

— A dramatic growth in enlistments over the campaign period, where this year we will meet targets.

— An efficiency improving over time, while the real spend has declined.

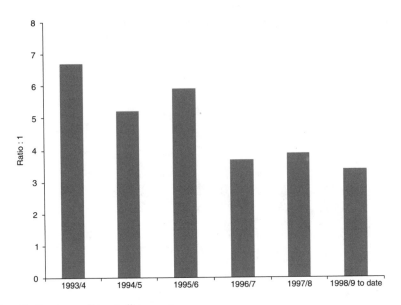

Figure 10: *Enquiry to enlistment efficiency ratio*
Source: DAR2

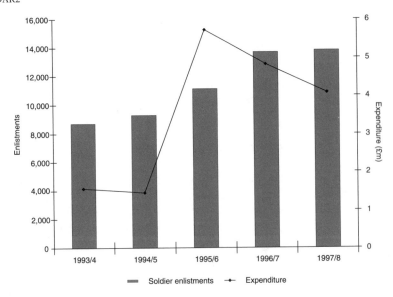

Figure 11: *Real advertising expenditure versus soldier enlistments*
Source: Saatchi & Saatchi / DAR2

THE FINANCIAL VALUE OF BETTER QUALITY APPLICANTS

Saving money was not the motivation behind this advertising – there were more important things at stake. However, there have been financial benefits from the effects we have achieved.

The processing of enquirers does not cost very much. Significant costs are incurred when the enquirer becomes an applicant.

The pre-campaign enquirer to enlistment ratio was 6.7:1. The application to enlistment ratio for that time was 3.9:1. As the enquirer to enlistment ratio has fallen over the last few years, so has the application to enlistment ratio.

Our approach to calculating the financial benefit of having better quality applicants in the system is as follows:

— Each year of the new campaign a number of enlistments were made, in each case at a lower application to efficiency ratio than 3.9:1.

— We have calculated the difference between the actual number of applications each year, and the number that would have been needed (to reach the same end point of enlistments that year), if recruitment had been working at 3.9:1.

— We have multiplied this difference by the cost of processing an application, which is £800 (variable cost).

We can therefore calculate a cost saving each year of this more efficient strategy:

Year	Actual applications	Application at 3.9:1	Difference	Saving £m
1994/5	29,286	36, 227	6,941	5.6
1995/6	41,132	43, 458	2,326	1.9
1996/7	38,102	53, 438	15,336	12.3
1997/8	9,998	54, 311	14,313	11.5

Total Savings = £31.3m

If we calculate the total additional sum invested in 'Be the Best' soldier advertising over this period (assuming that investment behind the old campaign had remained at £1.6 million per year), this is £14.9 million.

We can then deduct this from the savings of this approach, to reach a net saving overall of £16.4 million.

ADDITIONAL EFFECTS OF THE ADVERTISING

'The first step is to measure whatever can easily be measured. This is OK as far as it goes. The next step is to disregard that which cannot easily be measured, or presume it to be relatively unimportant. This can be artificial or misleading. The final step is to say that which cannot easily be measured does not exist. This can be suicide, commercial or otherwise.'

Source: Longer & Broader Effects of Advertising

A Knock-on Effect of Quality is Lower Wastage in Basic Training

If the Army is bringing people in with a better and more realistic mental attitude, it seems reasonable to assume that, apart from improving the efficiency of recruiting, the new recruits would be less shocked by what was involved when they started. It is therefore interesting that fall-out rates from basic training have been on a downward trend since 1994 to 1995 (Figure 12).

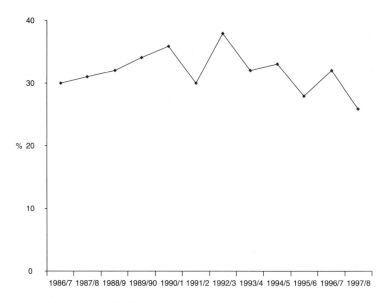

Figure 12: *Percentage fall-out rate from basic training*
Source: DAR2

Meeting Global Commitments

The ultimate global benefit of the success of this strategy has been our ability to fulfil our UN and NATO commitments. Had we been unable to achieve this, the negative effect on both our international standing and on those countries where the Army is deployed in a peace-keeping role would have been dramatic.

A Cultural Shift from 'Break Them Down' to 'Build Them Up'

'Be the Best' has raised the quality of recruits. This has in turn effected a subtle yet important cultural shift within Army recruitment and training. As people came forward with a different attitude from before – one that the Army identifies as being more 'trainable' – selection shifted to become about *selecting* the good rather than *weeding out* the bad. The advertising set a clear and high standard and screened out those who were not serious, thereby providing better 'raw material'. This allowed selectors to shift their focus. They had more time to assess people properly. The standards were higher, and therefore selectors became better at spotting and nurturing potential, all further evidence of improved efficency.

The effect of bringing quality people forward with realistic expectations also affected changes in the relationship between the recruiting and training organisations.

Historically the view had been that training was there to 'break people' because the quality and attitude was not there in the first place. As the mental make-up of the recruit improved, trainers felt less need to 'break' people. The culture started to shift to 'build them up'.

'Be the Best', as the New Mission Statement

The Army has applied 'Be the Best' to many areas of their own operations. It is used on all recruiting group stationery and literature. Having offered that challenge to the potential recruit, they have now challenged themselves to live up to it.

Recent equal opportunity policy changes, more jobs open to women, the Army owning up to racism and making a public statement about stamping it out, the desire to recruit more ethnic minorities are all part of 'Being the Best'. They reflect a more modern organisation that is prepared to admit the errors of the past and take positive action.

It would be foolish to argue that this is a direct consequence of the campaign. However, the campaign did publicly set standards for the Army to live up to. Racism and sexism for which the Army have been known have no place in a modern Army committed to 'Being the Best'. These policy changes were not made while previous campaigns were running, and yet the civilian currency of these topics was great at the time. We and the Army feel that the campaign played a role in creating an environment where these changes could be made public. The campaign has provided a credible platform for talking about these issues.

Campaign materials and national media coverage which the Ethnic Minorities campaign generated are used as part of Army training courses on race issues (see press ads).

Effect on Other Advertisers

The Army campaign has set a new standard in recruitment advertising and created a powerful new property in the world of advertising *per se*. Its use of small sizes in press with potent messages have now been adopted by the other Armed Forces advertisers. The way the audience is drawn into interacting with the advertising and issued with a challenge has been imitated by many other advertisers; for example, Audi, Adidas (television and radio), Dr. Pepper, Jag (a Special Forces programme on Sky), Flora and Kwikfit have all 'borrowed' from the powerful equity of the Army campaign in their advertising.

In the 1996 to 1997 IPA Recruitment Advertising Awards, the Army won in every category in which it was entered. In 1996 to 1997 the Army won Best Poster Campaign at the Campaign Poster Awards, Direct Campaign of the Year in 'Campaign' 1997 and was overall winner in Campaign Press Awards 1996.

Clearly this has been a highly influential campaign in both recruitment and advertising circles.

Through the Line

The campaign has totally rebranded the Army to the external audience. The thought, look and tone of the campaign have gone through everything the recruiting group does. It also extends to the Army's award-winning Website, which brings the challenge of the Army to life (see http://www.army.mod.uk).

ISOLATING ADVERTISING'S EFFECT

The trends that were working against Army recruitment in 1994 largely continued over the life of the campaign.

A positive change that could have affected the numbers was candidates being told about fitness requirements ahead of time. This is likely to have meant more people getting through selection first time (the Army does not collect this data). Most of those who fail on the physical fitness requirements retry and succeed the second time.

The significant advertising effects have come from a combination of a change in advertising approach and increased media spend. The change of advertising was necessary to attract higher quality enquirers, thereby bringing down the efficiency ratio. This was critical to having any chance of reaching the targets, given the limited numbers in the recruiting pool.

The increase in spend allowed the message to penetrate multiple audiences with significant weight. The combined effect was to increase the number of quality enquirers to the level where we have achieved targets in a very difficult market.

The financial efficiencies were also a consequence of this combined change, as were the cultural shifts within the Army. All the evidence suggests that had we put more money behind the old campaign, the depth and breadth of effects would not have been achieved.

Could the Money have been Spent more Effectively?

We could have tried to get a bigger group of people interested in the Army. However, this would have inevitably meant less committed people in the system. Therefore the ratio would not have improved, and the limited numbers in the actual recruiting pool would have prevented us from reaching the targets.

We could have invested the media budgets in opening new recruiting offices. Their mere presence would generate enquiries, but not high-quality ones. Increasing volume of enquiries was not going to meet targets, or have any longer term image effect. The increased budget could have been spent on incentives to join, but again, this would not have attracted the right quality of recruit.

In summary, the 'Be the Best' campaign has totally rebranded and refocused the Army in recruitment and many other areas of operation. An air of optimism surrounds it, which would have been difficult to envisage four years ago. As Dr John Reid states;

'The Army is back in business'

Dr John Reid
Armed Forces Minister
3 April 1998

4

Colgate

The science behind the smile

EDITOR'S SUMMARY

This case history shows how advertising helped Colgate achieve its highest-ever share of the UK toothpaste market, with the introduction of brand advertising together with product advertising.

Recognising the Need to Make Colgate Important Again

In 1994 Colgate learned that Sainsbury's planned to launch a new oral care range.

Colgate was potentially vulnerable. Housewives believed that all toothpastes are much the same.

Mums had to be made more aware of the importance of choosing the best toothpaste to protect their family's teeth, and of Colgate's history of innovations which makes it the doyen of dental care.

Results and Payback

The evaluative challenge is to estimate what the brand campaign added to the sales that would have been created anyway by product advertising and the new products launched since it began. The evidence rests on hard data based on two in-market 'area tests': the first a UK comparison with other European countries (where no brand advertising was used), the second a regional comparison within the UK, where brand advertising ran at heavier weights in one area.

These comparisons show that:

— Colgate has become a stronger brand only in the UK: Colgate's market share has increased in the UK to its highest-ever level while it has declined in other countries, and other UK brands have also declined.

— Colgate's margins have improved by 15%; higher than the European average.

— Colgate's sales through Sainsbury's have increased after their own label launch!

INTRODUCTION

This case history shows how advertising helped Colgate achieve its highest-ever share of the UK toothpaste market. The decisive factor was the introduction of Colgate brand advertising in 1995. Brand advertising together with product advertising has been more sales-effective than product advertising alone.

This is potentially a useful piece of learning about how different kinds of advertising work, which is a primary objective of these Awards.[1] Brand advertising budgets are under threat because of an increasing tendency to evaluate advertising in terms of its immediate sales effects. There is of course nothing wrong with short-term gains, but they are not necessarily the most profitable advertising effects.

In this case, it has been possible to show that the introduction of brand advertising accelerated Colgate's market share growth. The advertising did not only create a short-term blip in the sales graph, as do promotions, it also changed the shape of the sales curve, moving the trend more steeply upwards. The evidence rests on hard data based on two in-market 'area tests':

— A regional comparison of Colgate's market performance in the UK versus its performance in other European countries. While Colgate products and product advertising are much the same everywhere, the brand campaign runs only in the UK.

— A regional comparison of Colgate's market performance within the UK. Brand advertising has run at a heavier weight in one area, London, than in the rest of the country.

Taken together, these two 'tests' make it possible to estimate what strengthening the Colgate brand via brand advertising has contributed to the business, over and above what would be expected from product advertising alone.

BACKGROUND

The Need for a Brand Campaign

Colgate was founded in 1806 and has been selling toothpaste ('dental cream') since 1877. It competes against some of the world's leading marketing companies, including Lever, Beecham, and Procter & Gamble. Colgate is more focused on oral care, and is the market leader in toothpaste across Europe as a whole (Table 1).

Most Colgate ads are product-specific. They dramatise that product's benefit. There is no overall Colgate brand theme or house style.

---

1. 'We should never forget that though framed as a competition, the major contribution of the awards has been to create a "treasure house of learning"' (Graham Hinton, Guide to Entrants, 1998).

TABLE 1: TOOTHPASTE SHARES BY VALUE ACROSS EUROPE (%)

Colgate branded	21
Colgate other	4
Lever	14
Beecham	13
Procter & Gamble	10
Henkel	6
Others	32
	100

Source: Colgate, FY 1995

Colgate is becoming increasingly international in approach. The same ad is used to support the same product across Europe. However, the UK is a special marketing case because of the greater threat posed by retail brands (Table 2).

TABLE 2: OWN LABEL TOOTHPASTE SHARES BY VALUE (%)

UK	Average of France, Germany, Italy and Spain*
9	3

Source: Colgate 1994
*Together with the UK, these markets account for approximately three-quarters of Colgate's European sales

In 1994 Colgate learned that Sainsbury's planned to launch a new oral care range. As the bestselling brand it had the most to lose. Sainsbury's policy was to tackle leading brands head-on. It has been estimated that JS Classic Cola initially increased its share from 20% to 65% (within JS), and that JS Novon detergent cost P&G/Lever 12% share, worth £45 million at RSP.

Internal calculations suggested that Colgate might lose up to 5% of total UK sales a year to Sainsbury's. Moreover, there was the risk that other retailers might follow suit if consumer loyalty to Colgate was seen to be 'soft'.

Accordingly, Colgate and Young & Rubicam developed a campaign to strengthen the brand. The objective was ambitious: to *increase* Colgate's market share, despite inevitable own label growth, by diverting share losses to other brands.

THE COMMUNICATIONS STRATEGY WHICH MET COLGATE'S OBJECTIVES

Colgate's Potential Vulnerability

Qualitative research among mothers indicated they had become complacent about dental health. The feeling was that 'the fight against cavities has been won'.[2]

---

2.   Felicity Randolph Research, December 1994.

There has indeed been a dramatic improvement in the nation's dental health, particularly among the young: 74% of children under age 12 have never had a filling (versus 42% in 1983).[3]

But toothpaste manufacturers were not given much credit. Improvements were put down to such things as fluoride in tap water and a better diet. In fact, only 12% of the population receive fluoridated water, and consumption of crisps, sweets and sweet drinks has increased.

Experts claim that the major cause of fewer fillings was the introduction of fluoride into toothpaste.[4] This was a Colgate innovation. Nevertheless, prevailing beliefs were such that any suggestion that some of this success was due to Colgate was met with incredulity.

Housewives' relationship with the Colgate brand had become largely emotional. It had become a little old-fashioned. It was well liked, but more from memories of maternal care and the toothpaste's pleasant taste than because it was believed to make a material difference to their families' dental health.

Colgate was therefore vulnerable. Consumers were likely to give the new Sainsbury's products a try, as 'all toothpastes are pretty much the same', and the core benefit of better dental protection was seen as due to things other than toothpaste.

However, even committed Sainsbury's shoppers were more likely to buy manufacturer brands than own labels in certain categories, for example, medical products. The research explored the reasons for this.

Such categories were seen as a greater personal or family priority. There was then a greater risk in buying a retailer's own brand. It might have lower product quality, due to lack of expertise when compared to a manufacturer's brand. This insight into own labels' Achilles heel guided the development of the Colgate brand campaign.

Making Colgate Toothpaste More Important

The requirement was to raise the stakes in the toothpaste market: to position Colgate more as a brand with 'medical-like' benefits, and to increase Colgate's dental expertise beyond competitors' reach.

It was also crucial to maintain and strengthen consumers' emotional relationship with Colgate as a warm, trusted, family brand. More people have grown up with Colgate than with any other toothpaste; it is an old friend.

Thus the strategy was to increase the importance of the oral care category as a personal priority and to build on Colgate's heritage. The message was timely because of consumer concerns over reduced NHS dental provision.

3. British Dental Association, 1993.
4. 'Fluoride is the best thing that has happened to us in dentistry' (Sally Goss, Chairman of British Dental Health Foundation).

The role of advertising was to make mothers more aware of the importance of choosing the best toothpaste in order to protect their families' teeth. The target audience was thus defined as all housewives between the ages of 25 and 44, especially mothers and shoppers who might be tempted by the new own label range.

The creative proposition was that 'Colgate is the better protector'. This was supported by three facts:

— Colgate has specialised in making the best possible toothpaste for 120 years.

— Colgate does not make toothpaste for anyone else.

— More dentists choose Colgate for their families than any other toothpaste.

The communications plan was phased as follows:

1. A PR campaign to challenge consumer complacency, in particular regarding children's dental health, the priority for mothers ('It may be too late for *my* teeth, but ... ').

2. A TV campaign to establish Colgate's leadership in oral care expertise via its history of innovations.

3. A poster campaign initially based on dentists' endorsements of Colgate. Dentists are seen as experts, and while they are unlikely to recommend any particular brand to their patients, the fact that most use Colgate at home carried real weight.

Campaign Development

The campaign was launched in 1995 (see Table 3). Consumer response was so positive that the campaign is still running today. What was originally conceived as a response to a particular threat has become a consistent element in Colgate's advertising planning.

TABLE 3: MEDIA WEIGHTS

	Brand support		Product support	Total spends
	TVRs	Poster sites*	TVRs	£m
1994	–	–	2,550	5.1
1995	542	1,982	1,810	7.1
1996	938	3,266	1,173	10.0
1997	297	9,426	1,778	10.4
Total Spends	£9.9m		£22.1m†	£32.1m

*48 sheet equivalent
† includes £1.7 million press

The poster campaign house style, having been established as a Colgate property, has also been used to support products that evidence the brand proposition, and for recruitment ads and so on.

THE CREATIVE IDEAS

Television

The 60-second TV commercial 'Through the Years' was made up of snippets from Colgate commercials old and new.

The theme was that parents and children have trusted Colgate through the years. During this time Colgate has worked incessantly to improve its products. Colgate was presented as the original and still the best. Humour and a lightness of touch defused what could have been a rather self-congratulatory ad. It is hard to watch it without smiling.

By using the power of emotions – such as trust and likeability – viewers were led to accept the rational message of real product worth. The warmth which people feel towards Colgate was rekindled, and with it came greater awareness that Colgate is an innovative and progressive manufacturer of up-to-date products.

'The science behind the smile' endline brought together modern technological competence and a simple human benefit.

Posters

The 'Red' campaign is derived from Colgate's ubiquitous red packaging.

Huge expanses of red on 48 and 96 sheets with 'toothpaste' typeface make the posters strongly branded (they could *only* be for Colgate) and unmissable. The executions feature snappy headlines, mostly about dental health, supported by surprising facts that demonstrate Colgate's credentials.

The stance is confident and assumptive: Colgate is presented as the doyen of dental care. The ads have been welcomed by dental professionals because their message resembles public service announcements about the importance of dental health, though the tone is less worthy as befits Colgate's status as a family friend.

ISOLATING THE EFFECTS OF THE BRAND CAMPAIGN

The evaluative challenge is to estimate what would have happened to Colgate's sales if the brand campaign had never existed. What did the brand campaign add to the sales that would have been created anyway by product advertising and by the new products launched since it began?

The following evaluative approach is believed to be new to the IPA competition. It is in two parts. Together they create a body of evidence which allows for many of the other influences on Colgate sales besides the brand campaign.

'THROUGH THE YEARS' TV AD

Old woman: Well carrying on like that, just look!
(MVO) We've been making toothpaste for a long time. But we're still not bored, because we've never stopped improving it to help make your teeth healthier, your breath fresher ...
Dancing man: Lucky man, she's a honey!

(MVO) ... and your mouth go, well sort of ping. And over the last few years, we've really pulled out the stops, with dual fluoride with calcium, tartar control, bicarbonate of soda, strawberry cheesecake flavour ...
Man: I like that Colgate flavour!
(MVO) Okay, not strawberry cheesecake flavour, but we do have a formula so advanced that it actually works between brushings.

TV announcer: Yes, everyone in the family loves Colgate.
(MVO) And we'll carry on improving because we reckon as long as we keep changing our toothpaste, it means you won't have to.

Song: Brush your teeth with Colgate, Colgate Dental Cream, it cleans your breath (what a toothpaste) while it cleans your teeth.

POSTER ADS

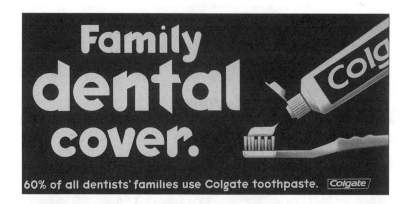

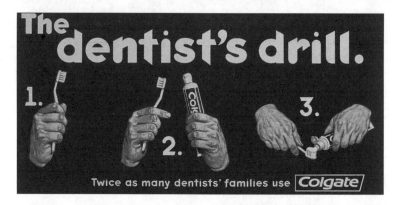

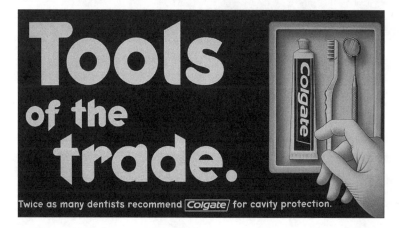

Part 1 : European comparisons

The principle that other countries can serve as surrogate 'test areas' in order to isolate the effect of UK advertising has been established in previous IPA case histories, most notably perhaps by the 1994 Grand Prix winner (BMW).

All these countries sell similar Colgate products.[5] The same creative is also used across Europe, but Colgate's share of advertising voice increased substantially in the UK (Figure 1).

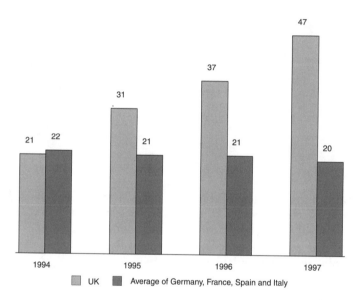

Figure 1: *Colgate's share of advertising voice (%)*
Source: Y&R media

The effect of this increased advertising on consumer perceptions of the brand is shown by Young & Rubicam's proprietary Brand Asset™ Valuator research. The BAV™ includes a database of the brand strength of over 10,000 brands in Europe, all ranked on 32 consistent measures of brand equity. Each brand is ranked against every other brand. Sample sizes were between 2,000 and 4,000 respondents per country for each of the 1993 and 1997 waves of research.

Figure 2 shows that Colgate's brand strength increased significantly in the UK, while it declined in the other countries.

The key to the improvement in Colgate's brand strength in the UK was that it became perceived as more highly differentiated. Highly differentiated brands are at less risk from competitive inroads, because consumers believe they offer something that other brands do not. Brands that are perceived as low in differentiation, on the other hand, are more easily substituted.

---

5. There is only one purely local Colgate brand among them: Chlorophylle in France, which has less than 2% share.

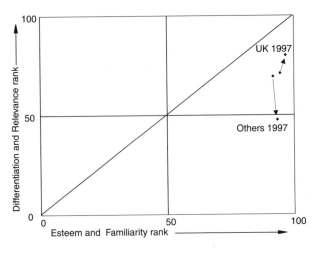

Others = Average of Spain,
Italy, Germany and France

Figure 2: *Colgate's brand strength, 1993 to 1997*
Source: BAV™

Relevant differentiation is crucial to brand strength as it is the prerequisite of consumer preference, which is the ultimate source of brand value. Preference creates the loyalty which secures sustainable long-term revenues, and also allows premium prices to be charged. The improved differentiation of the brand in the UK has been of major commercial benefit to Colgate, as will be shown below.

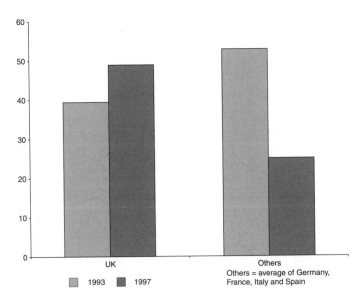

Others = average of Germany,
France, Italy and Spain

Figure 3: *Colgate's differentiation ranking, 1993 to 1997*
Source: BAV™

Improvements in Colgate's UK brand imagery, on scores relevant to the brand advertising content, indicate how the brand was strengthened in consumer perception (Figure 4). Colgate in the UK is much more likely to be perceived as 'innovative', 'up-to-date', 'progressive' and 'authentic', while its ranking in the other countries has declined.

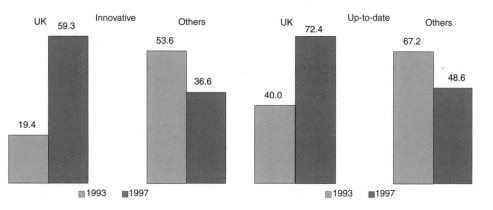

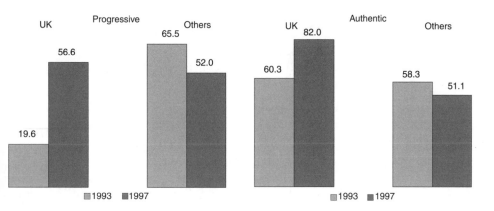

Figure 4: *Colgate's brand imagery in Europe (%)*
Source: Y&R BAV™
Other = average of Germany, France, Italy and Spain

Higher consumer preference for Colgate in the UK, indicated by these higher BAV™ rankings fed through into higher market shares (Figure 5).

Over this period, Colgate's volume share rose by 13% in the UK, while in the other countries it fell by 8%. These share increases for Colgate in the UK are even more remarkable as own labels continued to grow in the UK (from 9% to 12%), while they remain at 3% in the other countries.

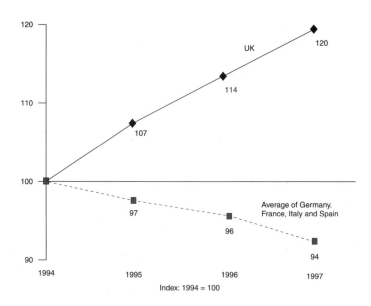

Figure 5: *Colgate's share of European toothpaste markets by value*
Index: 1994 = 100
Source: Colgate

To summarise, it has been shown that:

— Colgate's share of advertising voice increased substantially in the UK following the introduction of the brand campaign, but was static in the other countries.

— Colgate has become a stronger brand in the UK, while its brand strength has declined in the other countries. In particular, its perceived differentiation, essential for greater customer loyalty, has increased.

— Colgate's rankings on desired brand attributes such as 'innovative', 'up-to-date', 'progressive' and 'authentic' have only increased in the UK.

— Colgate's share of the toothpaste market has increased by 20% in the UK despite own label growth, while it has declined by 6% in the other countries.

An inference would be that the brand campaign increased consumer predisposition towards Colgate in the UK, which then resulted in higher product sales. This inference can be tested by examining Colgate's performance within the UK on a regional basis. The area 'test' within the UK removes the possible biases of differing cultural and marketplace circumstances in other European countries.

Part 2: UK Performance

Intermediate measures
The TV brand ad was highly visible. It achieved an Awareness Index of 12 (the category average is 5). More significantly, Colgate's Base Level (which represents residual advertising memories) rose from 20 to 33, a 65% increase (Figure 6).

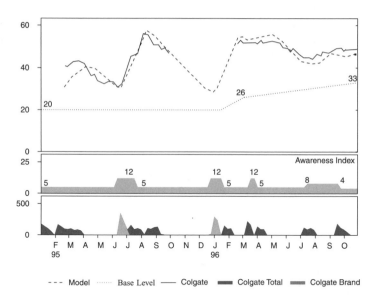

Figure 6: *UK performance*
Source: Millward Brown rolling data

The effect of the brand advertising (rather than just increased weights of product advertising) is suggested in research that shows that before the campaign began, 26% of housewives considered it 'extremely important' to choose a reliable brand of toothpaste for their children's dental health, but after the first burst the figure rose to 35%.[6] Viewers were reminded of Colgate's heritage but in the context of continuous improvement (Table 4).

TABLE 4: MAIN COMMUNICATIONS

	%
Old and new	75
Colgate through the years	53
Been going a long time	37
Always improving	28

Source: Millward Brown

Qualitative research suggested that the commercial had 'reinforced and articulated the positive emotional values at the heart of the brand: tradition and evolution'.[7] Consumers were surprised at the extent of Colgate's heritage, and its innovations and expertise also increased the brand's differentiation.

This ad increased consumers' emotional commitment to the brand: 'Bolsters perceptions of Colgate as "our brand"; one we want to identify with.'

6. BMRB, 1995.
7. Diagnostics, 1995.

The poster campaign achieved recognition scores of 49%, an exceptionally high figure. Correct attribution was 81% (the category average is 33%).[8] Research suggests that posters have communicated strategic brand messages (not just increased saliency) (Table 5).

TABLE 5: COLGATE BRAND IMAGERY

	Recognise TV only %	Recognise TV and posters %
Modern and up-to-date brand	57	71
Most advanced toothpaste available	51	65
For all the family	68	75

Source: Research International 1998

Dentists have also been enthusiastic about the advertising:

'Red now means Colgate. The messages are simple and the posters grab your attention. The message is obviously getting home because oral health has improved in this area.'

Dentist, North London

'The Red Colgate posters are full of impact and certainly noticed. "Dental Practice" had a message that was not about drilling teeth but helping to prevent cavities, and that is the future of dentistry.'

Dentist, Winchester

Market performance

Sainsburys launched its TOPS range ('Total Oral Protection System') in Autumn 1995. It comprised over 80 SKUs including toothpastes. However, by then shoppers had seen the Colgate brand campaign, which began in June 1995, and they were less likely to try the new products (Table 6).

TABLE 6: ATTITUDES TO TOOTHPASTE BRANDS, % AGREEING

	May 1995 %	November 1995 %
Shops' own label toothpastes are as good as brand names	73	62
Extremely likely to buy supermarket own label toothpaste	21	13
Colgate is a significantly advanced toothpaste	65	76
Colgate is modern and up-to-date	85	91

Base: Shop at Sainsburys
Source: BMRB

Sales of Colgate through Sainsbury's actually rose after the TOPS launch. For the first time, Colgate's sales through Sainsbury's exceeded £1 million a month. Share losses from own label growth were diverted to other brands.

---

8.   RSL Signpost, 1995

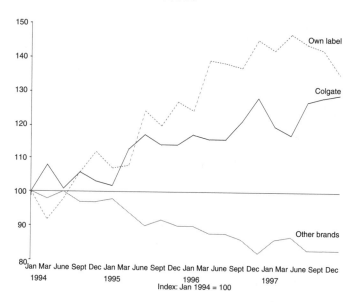

Figure 7: *Brand versus own label shares*
Source: Colgate

Colgate's market share has increased to its highest-ever level, rising above 30% of market volume for the first time.

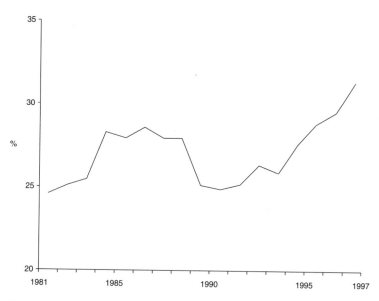

Figure 8: *Colgate UK market share by volume*
Source: Colgate

Colgate has not 'bought' volume through lower prices. Relative unit prices increased, as is shown in the comparison between value share and volume share (Figure 9).

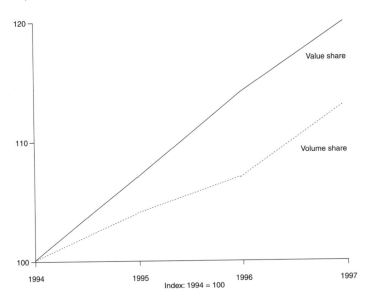

Figure 9: *Colgate's value share verus volume share*
Source: Colgate

Linking market performance to weight of brand advertising
The brand poster campaign has run at a heavier weight in one region, London, than in the rest of the country (Table 7).

TABLE 7: REGIONAL ADVERTISING WEIGHTS

	London	Rest of country
Number of posters per '000 of population*	5.1	1.4

Source: Concorde, 48-sheet equivalent, 1995–97
* Housewives with children

Heavier exposure led to stronger Colgate brand imagery in London, as is shown in Figure 10.

Consumer penetration grew at a slightly faster rate in London (7% against 4%), but loyalty grew much more, as is shown in Figure 11.

In keeping with these image and behavioural improvements, sales and share grew more strongly in London (Figure 12). Own label growth has been slower in London (Figure 13).

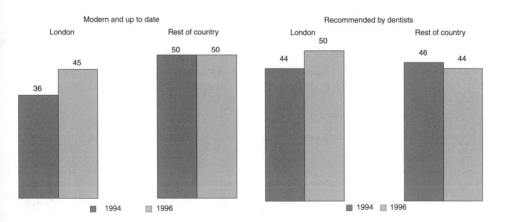

Figure 10: *Comparison of Colgate brand imagery by region %*
Source: Millward Brown

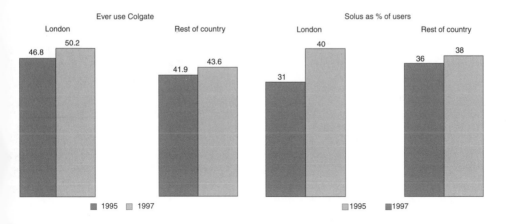

Figure 11: *Consumer penetration and loyalty by region (%)*
Source: TGI

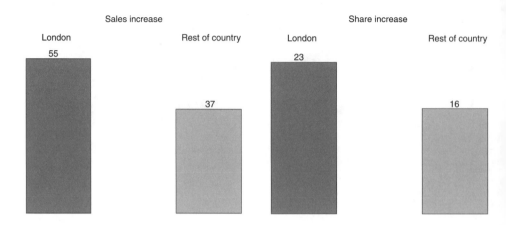

Figure 12: *Sales and share increase by region (%)*
Source: Colgate/IRI Infoscan 1997/8 vs 1994/5

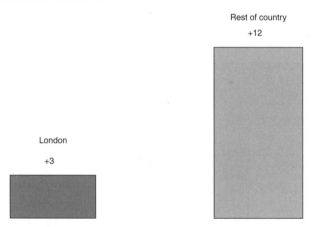

Figure 13: *Own label volume growth by region (%)*
Source: Colgate/IRI Infoscan 1997/1998 vs 1995/1996

Allowing for other factors

A number of other factors were taken into account when evaluating the effect of the advertising:

— Promotions

Colgate has stated that regional variations in promotions do not exceed 15%, but that if anything, 'Lower proportions of volume appear to have been on deal in London compared to other areas'. The extra sales in London therefore cannot be due to heavier promotions.

— Distribution

Colgate has stated that 'distribution on the principal Colgate brands has remained consistently around 100%'. The extra sales in London therefore cannot be due to improved distribution.

— PR

Colgate's PR agency Cohn & Wolfe has stated that the campaigns have been entirely national, but that if anything 'northern papers took up the stories more than the rest of the country'. The extra sales in London therefore cannot be due to increased PR.

— Price

Colgate average unit prices have been consistently 11p higher in London than in the rest of the country. The extra sales in London therefore cannot be due to lower prices.

— Competitive activity

Colgate's share of TV voice was slightly higher in London (50%) than in the rest of the country (46%), even though London received fewer TVRs (8,400 versus 9,400) over the period.

The Effects of the Brand Campaign: Conclusions

It has been shown that Colgate's share has risen in the UK but fallen in other European markets which sell similar products, supported by much the same advertising, except that the brand campaign ran only in the UK.

It has also been shown that Colgate's share has risen more in London than in the rest of the UK, even though exactly the same products are sold nationally, against exactly the same competitors, supported by exactly the same advertising, except that the brand campaign ran at a heavier weight in London.

Research suggests that consumer preference for Colgate has increased in the UK because the brand is seen in a more positive light, and that greater weights of brand advertising led to greater preference.

It seems reasonable to conclude that the brand campaign has had a decisive influence. What remains is to quantify the value of this effect and relate it to the cost of the advertising.

PAYBACK ESTIMATES

Two payback methods have been used:

1. Suppose that Colgate in the UK *had grown at the same rate as all other brands;* in other words, that its growth was the same as the UK brand average (excluding own labels).

This seems a reasonable assumption. Colgate is the largest UK brand, and it is likely that its sales performance would be close to the market average.

2. Suppose that Colgate in the UK had grown at the same rate as Colgate in other
European markets; in other words, that its growth was the same as Colgate's
European average.

This also seems a reasonable assumption. Colgate sells similar products across
Europe, supported by much the same advertising. (These calculations assume actual
UK market growth. In fact, Colgate's success accounted for a substantial amount of
market growth. Therefore they are *minimum* estimates of incremental growth.)
    Colgate's actual value share in 1994 was 28.5%. On these two assumptions, it
would have fallen to 24.8% by 1997 if Colgate had shown the same market
performance as other UK brands, or to 26.8% if it had shown the same
performance as Colgate in other European countries. In fact Colgate's 1997 share
was 32.9%. Adding sales for the years 1995, 1996 and 1997 gives the following:

	Colgate sales £m		
	Actual	If same as other countries	If same as other UK brand
	244.6	213.4	202.2
Actual higher by	n/a	31.2	42.4

These two methods give a range of between £31 million and £42 million
incremental sales. However, these sales estimates do not allow for the increased
profitability of Colgate in the UK.
    While Colgate's actual margins must remain confidential, it is possible to
indicate how they have grown in the UK compared to the European average
(Figure 14).

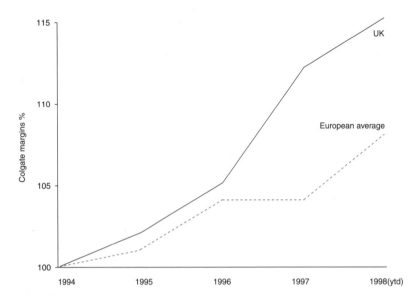

Figure 14: *Colgate European toothpaste margins* *
*Net margins allowing for costs of product, packaging, depreciation and so on.

UK margins were already four percentage points higher than the European average in 1994. Achieving a 15% relative improvement on a higher base is impressive and indicates a substantial improvement to the bottom line. The brand campaign has generated approximately three times more profit than it cost.

In conclusion, it has been shown that despite own label growth in the UK, strengthening the Colgate brand has helped to:

— Increase value sales by 20%.

— Increase volume sales by 13%.

— Increase profit.

— Increase margins by 7% above Colgate's European average.

★★★★★

5

First Direct

Advertising as a communications magnifier

EDITOR'S SUMMARY

This paper looks at the role television advertising plays within a multi-media campaign that has effectively re-launched First Direct. Ground-breaking modelling is used to demonstrate the manifold effects of television advertising.

The Need to Re-launch First Direct

When WCRS won the First Direct account in 1995 all was not well. Essentially, First Direct's successful formula had been copied by the big banks. The net result was a declining rate of annual growth for the first time in First Direct's history, in both 1994 and 1995.

A two-stage approach was taken to re-launching First Direct. The first stage – 'Tell Me One Good Thing' – was developed to exploit the perceptual negatives surrounding traditional banks, and force separation between them and First Direct.

The second stage built on the process of separation using the Bob 'I hate bank ads' Mortimer campaign to promote First Direct's own positives.

Television has been used as a communications magnifier, increasing the effectiveness of parallel media within a truly integrated campaign.

Results and Payback

Millward Brown's tracking study demonstrates the success of the re-launch in dramatically increasing people's understanding of First Direct. Today, almost 4 in 5 people know that it is a bank, almost twice as many as two years ago.

First Direct's rate of growth has increased in line with this growth in potential customers, enabling the bank to take on one in four of those customers switching banks. A bank with a share of less than 2% acquired over 25% of the available market – 15 times more than its size alone would dictate.

Overall, taking into account its magnifying effects on parallel media, television advertising has contributed in excess of £220 million, a remarkable payback of almost 30 times in initial investment.

INTRODUCTION

The advertising industry is increasingly coming to terms with the fact that advertising alone is not enough to build strong brands. Today's marketeers are well aware that advertising does not work in isolation – it is but one point of contact between consumers and brands – and strong brands will be consistent across each point of contact. In the words of Robin Wight, 'It's all advertising', be it brochures, point of sale or a conversation with a customer. The multi-media approach is slowly being accepted by our industry as a necessity, not an afterthought.

Why then has almost every previous entrant to these awards sought to discount the effects of so-called 'secondary media'?

If an objective of these awards is to provide a 'better understanding of how advertising works', surely we must explain how advertising works with other media.

Taking this further, as response directly attributable to advertising becomes an ever-increasing means of measuring its effectiveness, is there not a need to show that advertising does have an effect on parallel media? Without this proof, the danger is that short-term response rates alone will be used to judge advertising's worth.

Although First Direct has experimented with a range of media since its high-profile launch, the last two-and-a-half years of activity have been the closest yet to a fully orchestrated multi-media approach, building on the same message at the same time in different media.

The bank underwent a step change during this period, acquiring one in four customers who changed their bank (at the peak of activity this figure rose to approximately one in two), putting the bank on course to pass the million customers mark by the new millennium, three years ahead of its original target. It is important to understand that First Direct competes primarily for those switching their current account, not simply for those buying an additional financial package. Getting people to change banks is a far greater task than getting them to take out a Sainsbury's savings account or a Virgin PEP.

This paper will demonstrate the effectiveness of the bank's multi-media approach. Ground-breaking modelling will be used to demonstrate the manifold effects of television advertising and the inadequacy of unifold (narrow, media specific) evaluation.

Specifically, modelling will show that in the two-and-a-half years since WCRS won the First Direct business with a television-led strategy, television activity has been almost three times as effective as direct response data would suggest, repaying the initial investment a remarkable 30 times over.

More broadly, this paper will show how the right advertising helped to double the bank's universe of potential customers, successfully relaunching the brand, helping it to nearly double its customer base, and enabling it to win 15 times more customers than its market share alone would predict. All this was achieved despite the complete equalisation of First Direct's main functional advantage.

THE LAUNCH OF FIRST DIRECT

First Direct, the UK's first 24-hour telephone bank, was launched in 1989. At the time of launch, banks were among the most disliked, distrusted organisations in the commercial world. Customers hated dealing with them, finding that they actually complicated, rather than simplified, their increasingly busy lives.

First Direct was born out of the recognition that banks were increasingly out of touch and ill-equipped to deal with the commercial realities of the time. It was designed to be a 'better bank' built on the principle of all good service industries: *the customer comes first.*

At its heart, First Direct was the first bank to recognise whose money it really was. A highly tuned data management system ensured that the bank could anticipate and satisfy its customers' individual needs, while First Direct's culture was driven by a desire to give customers more control of their money.

In practical terms, this led to two key initiatives.

— The act of banking itself was radically simplified through the harnessing of technology, specifically branchless banking. Many of the points of traditional inefficiency were removed at a stroke. No queues, no forms, no branches, no arcane opening hours.

— Functionality apart, the traditional 'us and them' customer service ethos was abolished. Telephone operators were recruited on the basis of their interpersonal skills (not banking experience). They were briefed to treat customers as they themselves would like to be treated: as individuals, not just account numbers.

THE EARLY YEARS

Launched with unconventional, esoteric advertising, First Direct got off to a positive start. Within three years of launch the bank had acquired a quarter of a million customers, although as we shall see this was far from realising its full potential.

It attracted those early adopters independently-minded enough to do something different with their money – and those who joined were rewarded with the highest levels of customer service, as Figure 1 (overleaf) clearly demonstrates.

First Direct had clearly succeeded in being the first customer-focused bank. The danger for First Direct was that it would become a victim of its own success.

Essentially, First Direct's success forced its high street rivals to follow suit:

'First Direct changed the way people bank, this has led to change in other organisations.'

Steven Day, The *Express*, 1994

First Direct was the first successful launch in its sector since the last of the 'Big Five' was launched in 1975. It showed that even in a category with as much inbuilt inertia as banking (the last thing anyone wants to do is to change banks), doing something better will ultimately reap rewards.

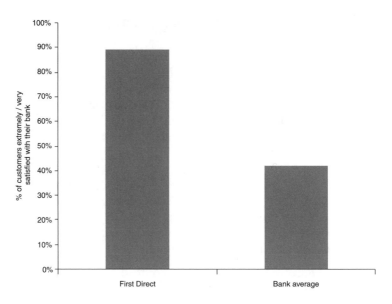

Figure 1: *First Direct customers are twice as happy as those of other banks*
Source: MORI, 1992

Others were quick to catch on and, with launches galore, the financial sector became a dynamic category. By 1995, 75% of banks had launched a direct telephone service. This reached 100% two years later.

First Direct's most basic functional advantage was rapidly disappearing. And not just its functional advantage: high street banks were beginning to realise that they could no longer afford to treat their customers as an unwanted distraction.

While First Direct continued to deliver an extraordinary level of service, banks made every effort to close the gap. It is no coincidence that service levels, having undergone gradual decline, began to increase throughout the industry only three years after First Direct was launched.

First Direct faced the most damaging of all threats: the erosion of its two key points of difference; functionality and service.

These disadvantages were compounded by the esoteric nature of the bank's launch which had left fewer than two in five adults even realising that First Direct was a bank, clearly limiting its potential growth.

The bank's increasingly pressured position is clearly illustrated by its decline in annual growth after 1993 (Figure 2).

The bank needed a step change before it was too late, before being submerged by the high street banks' direct alternatives or suffering from increasing customer satisfaction with the competition.

When WCRS was asked to pitch for the First Direct account in the summer of 1995, we collectively recognised that the central challenge was to address the fact that the bank had never been properly established as a mainstream option. Our task was to relaunch First Direct in a convincing manner, capitalising on its six-year USP before it had completely disappeared.

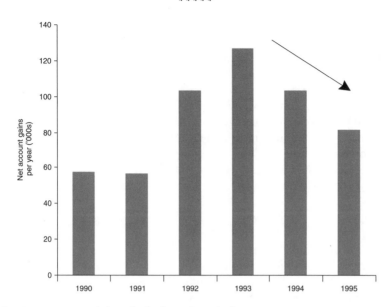

Figure 2: *First Direct experiences declining levels of annual growth after 1993*
Source: First Direct data

RELAUNCHING FIRST DIRECT: A TWO-STAGE APPROACH

The first stage in relaunching First Direct was to force a reappraisal of the competition while there was still time. Although in reality the big banks offered a direct option, in perception they were dogged by many of the traditional negatives. First Direct had a window of opportunity to exploit these negatives, destabilising the market in its favour and forcing clear separation between itself and the competition.

The second stage would build on this process of separation, providing more evidence of what made First Direct so different.

We made one further requirement for both stages.

Since launch, television had played an increasingly small part in First Direct's communications mix, not least because it generated responses less cost-effectively than more discrete response media such as press and direct mail.

Although television does not generate responses with the same efficiency as other media, we believed that its presence would be necessary in helping to step change First Direct's performance. A television-led strategy would give us the opportunity to raise awareness rapidly and give the bank a much needed outerface, countering its somewhat ill-defined identity.

Moreover, by taking a genuinely integrated approach, we believed television could act as a *communications magnifier,* increasing the efficiency of parallel media.

As a result, both stages of activity involved a powerful and leading role for television advertising. Given this role for television, its effectiveness could not be measured simply by gauging the corresponding level of unifold response. Modelling would have to be used to measure the manifold response generated by its magnifying effect on other media.

We will look at the results later in this paper, but the headline finding is that in terms of unifold response the advertising delivered £82 million, while the manifold response was in excess of £220 million (an overall payback of 30 times the advertising investment), marking the onset of a period of prolific growth. First Direct's customer base had built to 500,000 in its first six years and in 1995, the bank's stated business objective was to grow to a million customers by 2003. However, after two years of reinvigorated advertising, First Direct has now grown to more than 800,000, doubling its annual rate of acquisition and putting it firmly on track to surpass the million customers mark by the new millennium (a significant result for the bank and its shareholders).

Stage One: Tell Me One Good Thing

The first stage of relaunch was to position First Direct as a mainstream player, while marking it out as pre-eminent in its category.

One of the principal objectives was simply to get the public to understand First Direct's basic function; ie, that it was a bank.

In order to gauge the successful achievement of this objective we set up a tracking study measure known as Spontaneous Bank Awareness (SBA). This is more than spontaneous awareness. To be classed as SBA, respondents must have heard of First Direct and know that it is a bank.

As outlined in the introduction, pre-advertising tracking found a lowly SBA of around 40% among the sample of ABC1 21 to 54 year-olds with a bank account, highlighting First Direct's recessive identity.

By growing the bank's level of SBA, we would effectively grow the universe of customers who might consider First Direct, if they were to switch banks.

The best means of reviving First Direct's fortunes was to leverage the public's dissatisfaction with conventional banks. People do not like banks, but they do tolerate them. The task of the first stage of advertising was to challenge this tolerance.

The hassle of changing banks fills most people with dread, particularly when historically banks have been as bad as each other. The 'better the devil you know' mentality tends to prevail:

'I'd rather change my wife than my bank.'

Source: Corr Research, 1995

The 'Tell Me One Good Thing' (TMOGT) campaign was developed to overcome this high degree of inertia, by challenging the public to name even one good thing about their bank, the most immediate means of destabilising the market in First Direct's favour.

The campaign worked across all media. A series of short television films contrasted the TMOGT thought with a number of First Direct's benefits, while poster, press and direct mail activity served to feed off and substantiate the claims, hitting the right people at the right time, dependent upon their relationship with the brand.

The campaign was launched in January 1996 and, over the following five months, First Direct's level of SBA grew by 50% (more of which later).

Stage Two: Bob 'I Hate Bank Ads' Mortimer

Having successfully exploited competitor negatives and forced separation for First Direct, it was time to promote the bank's own positives.

From one perspective, conventional banks can be viewed as an absurd anachronism. They were launched in a bygone era – at a time when banks believed they were actually doing customers a favour by keeping their money safe for them. Built in the days of the cash economy, long before the widespread usage of telecommunications, banks are ill-equipped to deal with the realities of the modern financial world.

The direct result is an industry built around outdated business practices: organisations that seem to complicate rather than simplify their customers' increasingly busy, time-pressured lives.

By taking an independently minded approach to banking, First Direct removed the absurd complications keeping customers from their money, allowing them more control over their financial lives.

Our core brand and advertising proposition became;

> First Direct allows you to sort your finances by removing the
> absurd complications of conventional banking.

Support for this proposition was provided by the list of simplifications:

— No queues.

— No closing.

— No charging.

Each benefit would be the basis of a concerted phase of integrated activity.

However, the brief did not stop there. Bank advertising over the years has been as outmoded as banks themselves.

The opinion among consumers is that banks are among the worst advertised brands in the commercial world, with campaigns that not only ignore the realities of most banking relationships, but actually magnify consumers' underlying resentments. They ask for your trust one minute, and overcharge you the next. They show the happy faces of employees the very week you receive a patronising letter from your bank manager. They tell you 'we're listening' and then do not return your calls.

'There is a genuine gulf between the "open arms" of bank advertising and the reality of the customers' experience.'

Source: Corr Research, 1996

'TELL ME ONE GOOD THING' CAMPAIGN

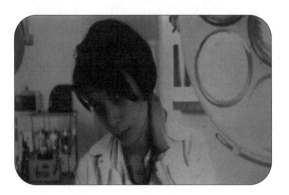

THE 'BOB' CAMPAIGN

The result is advertising which is disparaged on the one hand, and ignored on the other.

The solution was a brief that called for 'unbank' advertising. If bank advertising was seen as over-promising and unlikeable, First Direct required work based on indisputable, tangible claims delivered in a likeable, entertaining manner.

The creative solution was truly 'unbank'.

The campaign built on the premise of an absurd world – the absurd world of banks. A world in which things close at random and unhelpful times. A place where people are left stranded in pointless queues. Where charging extortionately on the flimsiest pretext, is the norm.

The ads involved Bob Mortimer highlighting the absurdity of queuing, closing and charging by interacting with the public, filmed using hidden cameras.

If conventional wisdom holds true and people will not buy from a clown, what chance did we have of getting them to bank with one?

But conventional wisdom is there to be challenged, and research confirmed that Bob was the ideal brand personality:

> 'Bob Mortimer is perceived as an extremely likeable, quick-witted "man of the people" with a friendly, approachable quality.'

> Source: Corr Research, 1996

Dramatising tangible product points in an entertaining and engaging manner, the campaign talked to adults as adults. Never patronising, never over promising, the advertising had the potential to be as radical and as likeable as the bank itself.

THE MEDIA STRATEGY

The media plan was designed around increasing television's magnifying effect on parallel media. 'Tell Me One Good Thing' was launched in January 1996 using a burst strategy to maximise the potential disruption it could inflict upon the financial category as a whole.

The campaign ran for five months, backed by a budget of £5 million, and encompassed heavyweight television, poster, press and direct mail activity (Figure 3).

The more gradual second stage adopted a slower build drip strategy.

In a series of six-monthly periods, Bob television commercials set up one overriding principle that parallel media built upon.

Importantly, the campaign is synergistic through message, not executional vehicle, with each medium being used to bring the message to life in a manner wholly appropriate to that medium. In this way, no executional straitjacket is imposed on parallel communications.

For example, in the first six months of 1998 the television campaign set up the 'No Charges' principle. In tandem with this, direct mail, press, posters and a range of other media spelt out the advantages of free banking.

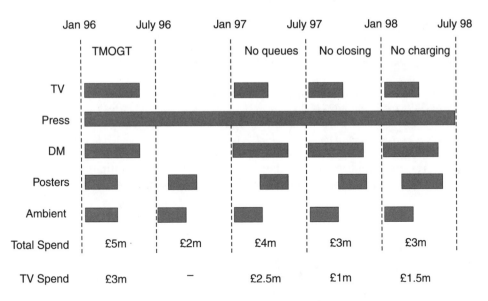

Figure 3: *The re-launch media plan*

INDICATORS OF SUCCESS

Stage One: 'Tell Me One Good Thing'

Pitch research conducted by First Direct clearly confirmed the strength of the TMOGT strategy. The following quote demonstrates the power of the campaign to undermine customers' relationship with their existing bank:

'The campaign is able to convert even the more inert respondents into doubting whether their own bank is serving them adequately. That alone is a significant achievement.'

Source: Douce Research, 1995

The key objective of the activity was to build awareness and understanding of First Direct's bank status as gauged by the SBA tracking study measure. In the four months of advertising, SBA built by over 50%.

Increasing SBA naturally translated into a bigger source of potential business for First Direct. According to NOP, there are 33 million current account holders in the UK. A shift in SBA from 43% to 63% equates to an increase of more than six-and-a-half million potential customers.

After building awareness of First Direct as a mainstream player, we had the opportunity to demonstrate what made the bank so much better than the rest.

Stage Two: Bob 'I Hate Bank Ads' Mortimer

Before airing, Bob had to pass through rounds of qualitative development and quantitative pre-testing.

The qualitative survey, conducted among customers and prospects alike, drew three main conclusions:

1. 'It clearly communicates that First Direct is a 24-hour telephone bank and that the benefit of this is convenience.'
2. 'It has the potential to be extremely funny ... laugh out loud rather than just smiley.'
3. 'It is seen as a radically different approach for financial advertising.'

Source: Corr Research, 1996

The results could not have been more 'unbank'. Quantitative pre-testing confirmed the exceptional enjoyability of the campaign (Figure 4).

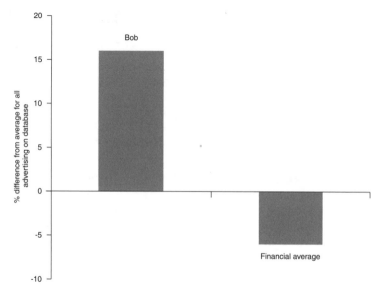

Figure 4: *Bob's superior level of enjoyability*
Base: 312 ads
Source: Millward Brown Link Test

The ads were not only enjoyable relative to those of other banks; according to Millward Brown they fell into the top 10% of all ads tested in all fields.

Unsurprisingly, quantitative research confirmed the campaign's potential to achieve a high level of cut-through (Figure 5).

An Awareness Index of 12 is the highest ever for the first ad in a new financial campaign.

Building on the success of TMOGT, Bob served to further increase First Direct's level of SBA. As can be seen from Figure 6 the tracking study was carried out bi-monthly from June 1996 onwards, but the data are still comparable.

Obviously First Direct's growth in customers will have contributed partially to the uplift in SBA. However, the bank's customer base still consists of less than 2% of the UK's population, clearly lacking the potential to explain an increase of around 40%.

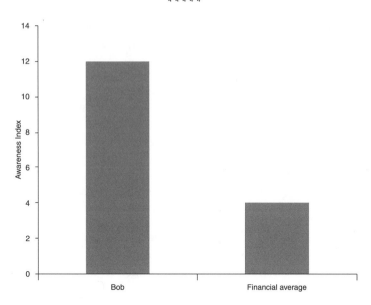

Figure 5: *Bob's superior Awareness Index*
Source: Millward Brown Link Test, 1997

Through increasing First Direct's SBA from 42% to 80%, the brand has virtually doubled its potential customer universe – that is, an increased potential of almost 13 million customers (16 times the bank's existing size) in little more than two years.

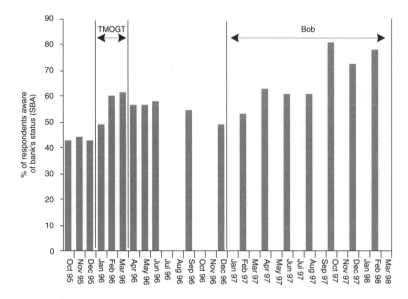

Figure 6: *Doubling First Direct's level of SBA*
Base: ABC1, 21 to 54-year-old banked adults
Source: Millward Brown, 4-weekly rolling data

However, the truly 'unbank' nature of the work only becomes apparent by considering the feedback from two different groups – advertising critics and First Direct stakeholders.

The campaign is, uniquely, bank advertising which is also creative advertising:

> 'First Direct (with Bob Mortimer) cut through the otherwise abysmal standard of advertising in its category. It looks like the beginning of a very promising, long running campaign.'

> Source: *Campaign*, 'Campaign of the year' article, 1997

As well as being voted one of the top ten campaigns of the year by *Campaign* and the *Sunday Times*', Bob has received a number of creative accolades. Most notably, at the 1997 British Television Advertising Awards, Bob picked up the first silver award given to a bank in the last decade – a true sign of the campaign's populist appeal given the broad-based nature of the BTA jury.

Staff and customers alike have been particularly supportive of the campaign, feeling that it is the closest advertising has ever got to capturing a sense of First Direct's unique culture:

> 'Response to Bob has been fantastic. Numerous customers have telephoned us simply to praise the campaign, feeling that it genuinely conveys a sense of "First Directness".'

> Source: Mike Phillipson, Brand Communications Manager, First Direct

GROWING THE FIRST DIRECT BUSINESS

The indicators of success outlined in the previous section have been borne out in hard financial terms by the successful growth of First Direct's business.

A simple correlation demonstrates the face value case that growth in First Direct's universe of understanding has resulted in an increase in the bank's sales opportunity (Figure 7).

The three peak advertising periods which have driven growth in First Direct's SBA correspond to the highest increases in enquiries from prospective customers, hereafter described as responses.

At the peak of activity, First Direct achieved higher monthly rates of response than ever, for the first time exceeding the record response generated during the bank's first full month in existence, a time when it had benefited from the natural momentum of an all-new proposition.

Record levels of brand response have in turn translated into record levels of new customer acquisition.

As outlined above, two years of advertising have played an instrumental role in helping to virtually double the bank's size in a third of the original time.

Although general market data are scarce, given the confidential nature of the category, it is important to put the significance of this achievement in a broader context.

A NOP study estimates that 600,000 customers switch their bank (ie, main current account) annually.

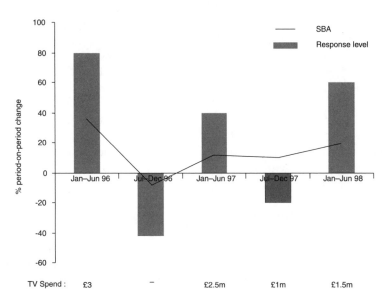

Figure 7: *Increases in SBA correspond to increases in levels of response from prospective customers*
Source: Millward Brown/First Direct

Over the course of 1996 and 1997, First Direct took on over 300,000 new customers. Therefore;

Total number of customers switching banks 1996/97   1,200,000

Total number of customers switching to First Direct in 1996/97   300,000

Percentage of customers switching banks to First Direct in 1996/97   25%

One in four of those switching banks in the last two years came to First Direct – at the peak of activity this figure was closer to one in two.

In other words, a bank with a market share of less than 2% has taken on 25% of customers switching banks – more than 15 times as many as market share alone would dictate, a proportion almost identical to the 16-fold expansion in First Direct's universe of knowledge relative to its actual size, a similarity which suggests a strong correlation.

First Direct has clearly undergone a step change in performance since the two-stage relaunch process began.

While we are not claiming that this level of brand success is due solely to advertising (the contribution of which is isolated in the following sections), it is worth stressing that change to the bank's communications over the period was the only advantageous variable.

First Direct underwent no significant product change in the period. Nor did it alter its pricing policy or its rates relative to other banks. The effects of seasonality are the same every year – customers tend to switch their bank accounts in January and September. The weather has no relevance. Distribution is obviously unchanging for a telephone bank, and the number of customers switching their bank annually has remained unchanged for the past decade.

In fact, the only non-communication variables which did change were ones having a potentially negative impact on First Direct's growth.

Banks improved their service levels. More 'direct' alternatives were launched. Brands with non-financial backgrounds became competitors, and First Direct lost the 'new news' potential it once had.

We must now consider the concrete contribution of television advertising to this period of outstanding growth and communications success.

THE UNIFOLD RESPONSE TO TELEVISION ADVERTISING

Television's role is by no means centred around response generation – direct mail, press and recommendation are the dominant response channels. That said, response levels are an important measure of television's overall contribution to brand success.

The manifold response to television is modelled in the next section.

Here we look at the unifold levels of response directly attributable to television (recorded at source when potential customers contact First Direct).

For the purpose of Figure 8, the data for 1998 is annualised, although calculations of advertising's contribution are based on actual figures to March 1998.

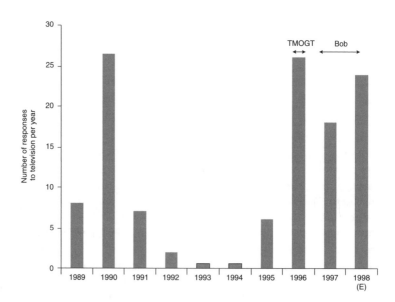

Figure 8: *Unifold levels of response to television advertising*
Source: First Direct data

In the two-and-a-half years of relaunch activity, television advertising, supported by a budget of £8 million, has delivered 18,630 new customers (based on actual, not estimated values for 1998).

This equates to a return on investment of £82 million given industry levels of customer turnover and value:

TV acquisition	18,630
Customer annual value	£220
Average duration of customer current account	20 years

Therefore,

Customer lifetime value	220 x 20 = £4400
Value of TV acquisition	4400 x 18630 = £82m

Thus, based on unifold evaluation, television investment has been paid back more than ten times.

But the television advertising was never meant to work in isolation. Television was the lead element in a brand campaign. Therefore unifold response to television is an inadequate means of judging its effect on overall brand response.

To assess television's manifold effect in magnifying the effectiveness of other more responsive media, we brought in the database marketing consultancy, Macon Consulting Limited.

THE MANIFOLD RESPONSE TO TELEVISION ADVERTISING

Methodology

The main objective of the Macon modelling was to measure the total response effect of television advertising.

This effect consists of the direct response to the television itself, and the uplift in response to other media caused by the 'magnifying effect' of the television presence.

The direct response is simply to quantify from the marketing source code captured at the time of enquiry. This has already been covered in the previous section.

Quantifying the 'Magnifying effect' required a new methodology.

Three periods were selected:

— A period of 'TMOGT' between January and March 1996.

— A period of 'Bob' between January and March 1996.

— A 'control' period of no television advertising between September and November 1996.

The periods were selected to ensure that the marketing mix was similar (with the exception of television), and the effect of seasonality was reduced to a minimum – January and September are both peak acquisition times.

Response levels to all non-television media were then assessed for both periods. Modelling was able to isolate the incremental effect that television advertising had on parallel media during the periods of TMOGT and Bob. The 'magnifying effect' of television can then be calculated as the difference between the level of response and the reduced level projected by the Macon model based on no television presence.

Results

All results are based on converted response, ie levels of new customer acquisition rather than response alone.

The modelling identified an incremental uplift of 19% to customer acquisition via non-television media during the period of TMOGT and an uplift of 11% during the period of Bob.

The modelling also demonstrated that the campaigns worked optimally against relatively affluent responders, the ideal audience for First Direct, given their superior levels of profit potential and the fact that they are the basis of the bank's direct mail targeting.

During the modelled period of TMOGT, television generated 4,089 customers directly and 8,047 as a result of the 19% uplift to parallel media. Thus, in acquisition terms, television's magnifying effect produced twice as many customers via parallel media as it did in terms of direct, channel-specific response. Overall, the manifold contribution of television advertising was 12,136 customers, three times the level of unifold response.

In the same way, Bob generated 3,966 customers directly in the modelled period, and 6,122 as a result of the 11% incremental uplift. The manifold contribution in this case was 10,088 customers, more than two-and-a-half times the level of unifold response.

The Manifold Payback

We have demonstrated that the unifold contribution of advertising was approximately ten times in excess of payback.

We must now consider the payback in terms of manifold response.

Following the letter of the law, we can only evaluate the incremental effects of television advertising during the two modelled periods. Including the overall unifold response to television advertising, this totals 32,799 customers, equating to a total payback of £144 million (18 times the original investment of £8 million).

However, if we allow ourselves to extrapolate from the model, applying the magnifying effects of television advertising throughout the relaunch activity, the number of customers generated is 50,619. This results in a remarkable 30-fold payback of £223 million, confirming the fundamental contribution of television advertising to First Direct's business success.

CONCLUSION

This paper has sought to demonstrate advertising's manifold contribution to overall communications and the development of a strong brand.

Rather than belittle or discount parallel media, we are proud to have been able to build them in as an integral part of advertising's overall success, not rivals or obstacles to it.

Coming back to the original observation that 'It's all advertising', we also hope to have demonstrated the ability of television advertising to make a unique and vital contribution to the growth and vitality of a brand that could otherwise have languished.

We have seen how, without television advertising, First Direct was gradually losing ground. By reasserting itself in the most public and intrusive of all media it was not only able to flourish, but it did so in conditions that were more hostile and disadvantageous than at any time in its history.

We are not claiming that television advertising is a panacea for all brand ills, but this paper should represent a strong exemplification of the extraordinary potential that this 40-year-old medium still offers to advertisers.

6

Marmite

How 'The growing up spread'
just carried on growing

EDITOR'S SUMMARY

By looking at the benefits of advertising investment over a 23-year period (1975–1998) this paper demonstrates the importance of thinking long term in a world where demand for instant results is becoming increasingly prevalent.

Marmite's Early History

From 1903 to 1975, Marmite consumption had its roots in the sampling and recommendation of Marmite by health professionals. This created a mother-and-baby life cycle, where mothers were persuaded to feed their babies Marmite and in turn these Marmite babies became Marmite mothers.

However, by 1975, where our paper starts, the future was looking bleak: the endorsement of health professionals had been lost, the declining birth rate threatened the mother-and-baby life cycle, the threat from Own Label was increasing and finally, increasing levels of concern about salt in the diet threatened Marmite's health position.

Results and Payback

Advertising (and in particular two campaigns – Ogilvy & Mather's 'Soldiers' and BMP's 'I Hate Marmite') successfully created higher levels of adult consumption of Marmite, meanwhile maintaining the core mother and baby life cycle.

Volume sales increased by over 50% over the period, which is remarkable given that Marmite was a mature brand.

As a consequence of their exposure to lower levels of advertising (nearly three time less over 23 years), the paper shows that the northern regions' share of sales has significantly declined since 1975 while those in the south grew. Penetration, consumption and levels of competition also responded to these regional patterns in advertising. Marmite advertising has also created extremely high financial rates of return. Without disclosing sensitive information, we can reveal that the average annual return on investing in Marmite advertising is 27%.

INTRODUCTION

This story begins in 1902, when a strange black substance, called Marmite, was launched on the unsuspecting British public. As the brand matured, it was supported by the endorsement of health professionals and became a firm family favourite.

By the 1970s, however, the brand was facing a mid-life crisis. This paper will show how Marmite coped with the crisis and has flourished as a result, experiencing two particularly sharp periods of growth from 1987 to 1989 and 1995 to 1998.

We will look at the contribution of advertising from 1975 onwards, and focus particularly on the two campaigns which drove those two periods of sharp growth: the Ogilvy & Mather 'Soldiers' campaign, and BMP's recent 'I Hate Marmite'/'My Mate Marmite' campaign.

WHAT IS MARMITE?

Origins

The first records of yeast show that it was used in the production of an acid beer called 'boozah' in Egypt in 6000 BC. People have enjoyed the effects of beer ever since and by the eighteenth century breweries in England were producing roughly 200,000 barrels of yeast a year as a by-product of brewing. As a result, new uses for yeast were sought, and during the late nineteenth century the German chemist Liebig discovered how to produce a yeast extract suitable for human consumption. In 1902, yeast extract was first manufactured in England under the name of Marmite, which refers to the French cooking pot which gave its shape to the Marmite jar.

Health Properties

Marmite received instant acclaim as a healthy and delicious product. Interest in Marmite, however, increased further early in the century, when the function of vitamins was discovered, as Marmite contains all five B-complex vitamins.[1] It is also 100% vegetarian, and contains virtually no fat and no sugar.

---

1.   The B-complex vitamins are Thiamin (B1), Riboflavin (B2), Niacin, Folic acid and B12. These are crucial
     for the healthy growth and functioning of blood, as well as helping the body convert sugar and starches
     into energy.

Usage

Marmite is very versatile and can be used as a spread, a drink and a cooking ingredient. Marmite is, however, used almost exclusively as a spread (96%), and generally at breakfast time (52%). It therefore competes most directly against other spreads, and other breakfast foods such as cereals.

INTRODUCING PEOPLE TO MARMITE

The Barriers to Creating Adult Usage

Marmite is a unique product which looks quite unlike most foodstuffs. Non-users tend to find its smell, appearance and ingredients rather off-putting.

'Looks like tar', 'horrible black sticky stuff', 'smells disgusting'.

'It doesn't sound very nice', 'it looks like a brown stain on toast'.

Source: BMP Qualitative Research

Indeed, unfortunately for Marmite, it is often active prejudice against the brand, rather than apathy or lack of awareness, which stops many non-users trying Marmite (Figure 1).

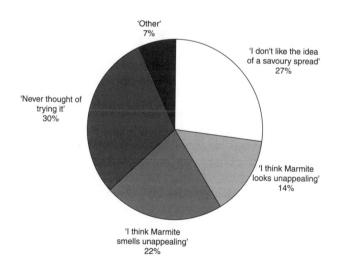

Figure 1: *Reasons for not trying Marmite*
Base: All adults who gave reasons why they had not tried Marmite
Source: Audience Selection Omnibus 1997

Marmite also has a very polarising taste and, compared to most foods, it evinces strong views (Figure 2).

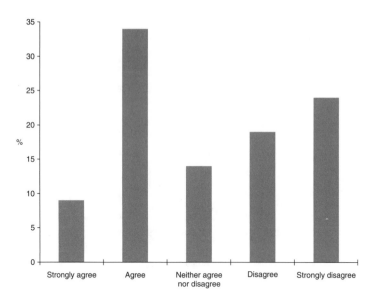

Figure 2: *Marmite has a delicious savoury taste*
Source: PPCR Non-User Taste Tests 1998

Gaining growth for the brand by targeting adult non-users is therefore exceptionally difficult. This consumer comment illustrates the point:

'If you don't like it by the time you're an adult, it's no good.'

Source: BMP Qualitative Research

Feeding Marmite to Babies

Fortunately for Marmite, there is another way to recruit new users. If mothers can be persuaded to feed their babies Marmite, then these children acquire a taste for Marmite, which frequently stays with them, on and off, for life. In fact, the vast majority of users (78%) are introduced to the brand as children.

When these 'Marmite babies' grow up and have their own children, they tend to feed them Marmite too (Figure 3).

This, in turn, creates a new generation of loyal Marmite users, and the life cycle is perpetuated.

Consumers' comments illustrate the way the life cycle works:

'I was always given it as a youngster, and if we have kids it will always be there.'

'Having the children myself, I'd go around the supermarket, and back to all the things I used to have as a kid. Marmite is probably the one that has stuck again.'

'I used to have it a lot when I was little, now I just have it when I give it to the children.'

Source: Leading Edge Qualitative Research, KGB Research

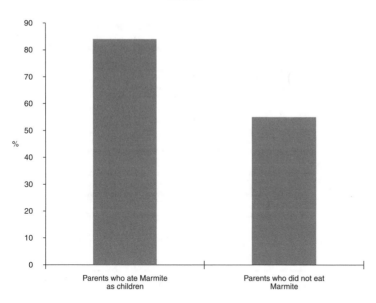

Figure 3: *The percentage of adults who feed their children Marmite*
Source: Audience Selection Omnibus 1998.

Finally, looking at the household penetration of Marmite by life stage, we can see exactly how the life cycle works. Marmite is much more likely to be present in households with young children, demonstrating that the mother-and-baby life cycle is key to penetration (Figure 4).[2]

THE MARMITE LIFE CYCLE, 1903 TO 1975

From 1903 to 1975, Marmite was highly recommended for children by numerous articles in newspapers and medical journals. It was distributed through the school meals programme and through traditional 'village hall' health clinics and child health clinics, which had shops attached selling Marmite. Up until the 1960s, there was even a dedicated Marmite medical sales force which called exclusively on clinics and health visitors. The Marmite cycle of consumption therefore had its roots in the authoritative sampling and recommendation of Marmite by health professionals.

Maintaining Broader Adult Usage

The medical profession also recommended Marmite as a dietary supplement for adults in order to combat various illnesses, which were seen as relating to vitamin B deficiency. (Constipation and consequent colitis, chronic appendicitis and innumerable other digestive troubles were all prevalent among the adult British

---

2. The earliest year in which Nielsen analysed penetration by life stage was 1993.

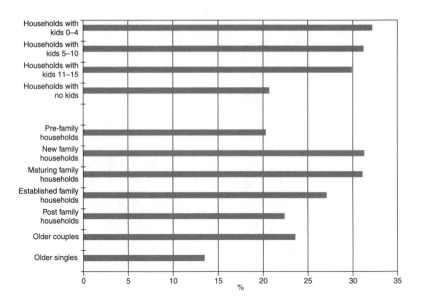

Figure 4: *Household penetration by lifestage*
Source: Nielsen Homescan 1993

population, and at the time were seen as directly related to lack of vitamin B in the diet.) Marmite was therefore also distributed to adults through health clinics and welfare associations. It was given to pregnant mothers and featured in hospital meals. Marmite was even used in the First World War to prevent outbreaks of beri-beri among English soldiers in Gallipoli, and it was sent to prisoners of the Second World War in Germany in Red Cross parcels.

MARMITE'S MID-LIFE CRISIS – THE SITUATION IN 1975

Marmite entered the 1970s, with a future that looked less clear.

Losing Endorsement/Distribution via NHS

First and most significantly, the reorganisation of the National Health Service in 1974, meant that traditional 'village hall' clinics were replaced by custom-built welfare centres where retail sales were forbidden. This meant that a vital prompt, which had encouraged Marmite usage among adults and children, had been removed.

The Falling Birth Rate

By the 1970s, demographics were also turning against Marmite. Birth rates were dropping, as women both had their children later and had fewer children. The larger gap between childhood and parenthood which women experienced and the increase in adult-only households were extremely worrying for Marmite, given its dependence on a mother-and-baby life cycle.

Own Label/Competition

With the growth of grocery multiples, all products, including Marmite, were facing increasing threats from own label brands.

Increasing Levels of Concern about Salt in the Diet

Finally, during the 1970s, people became increasingly concerned about salt and its link with heart disease. Although a serving of Marmite actually contains less salt than the bread it is served on, Marmite does contain salt. It was therefore prey to sensationalist articles in the media which, while unfounded, could have dented its position as a healthy product.

MARKETING OBJECTIVES – 1975 ONWARDS

Given the threatening situation, the marketing of Marmite was crucial, and focused on the following issues:

— Compensating for the loss of the NHS prompt to childhood usage, by maintaining Marmite's position as a healthy, vitamin-rich spread for children.

— Combating concerns over salt by focusing on Marmite's positive aspects; that is, Marmite's overall healthy image.

— Combatting the demographic trends against Marmite and the loss of the NHS prompt to adult usage, by broadening Marmite's positioning to support adult usage.

— Defending its territory against competition, by consistently supporting the brand.

THE IMPLICATIONS

Looking back at these objectives, one might question whether Marmite had been over-ambitious, attempting to increase adult usage and maintain the core mother-and-baby life cycle.

Figure 5, however, demonstrates that this was not the case. It shows that children whose parents continue to eat Marmite are more likely to eat Marmite than children whose parents are lapsed users. Hence increasing adult usage actually reinforces the mother-and-baby life cycle.

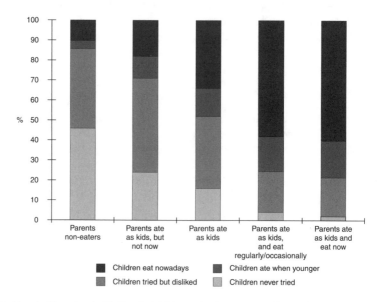

Figure 5: *The Marmite life cycle* – the likelihood of children eating Marmite according to their parents' Marmite habits
Source: Audience Selection Omnibus 1998

Intuitively this makes sense. Women are not likely to forget Marmite prior to parenthood if it remains relevant to them as adults. Furthermore, given the way children mimic adults, they are more likely to eat something that their parents enjoy rather than something which is forced upon them as 'good for children'.

The decision to encourage adult usage was therefore not only brave, but astute.

ADVERTISING OBJECTIVES – 1975 ONWARDS

The brand had always been advertised, but advertising now became critical. In 1975 the advertising spend was doubled, and it has remained at higher levels ever since (Figure 6).[3]

New advertising also needed to answer the new marketing objectives. In advertising terms, these can be summarised as follows:

1. Maintaining the mother-and-baby life cycle.

2. Making Marmite more relevant to adults.

---

3. Marmite advertising has primarily been on TV, and has consisted of at least one heavyweight burst per year, usually in wintertime.

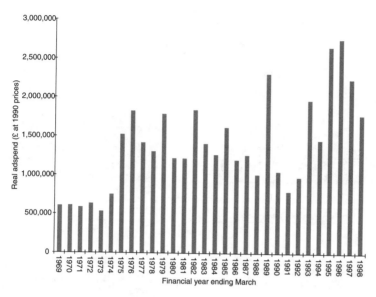

Figure 6: *Total Marmite adspend*
Source: MEAL

THE ADVERTISING: 1975 TO 1997

Theme 1: Maintaining the Mother-and-Baby Life Cycle

In the 1970s, advertising focused on Marmite's role at the heart of the family. Out of this emerged the famous and long-running 'The Growing Up Spread' campaign.[4] As the campaign continued, it gradually became less formal and didactic, and humour was introduced to ensure that the brand remained appealing.

By the 1980s, the mother-and-baby life cycle was supported by using more tightly targeted mother-and-baby executions and media selection.[5]

Theme 2: Making Marmite More Relevant to Adults

During the mid-1980s, there was concern that Marmite was being pushed too far into a mother and baby niche. As a result, Ogilvy & Mather launched the famous 'Soldiers' campaign in December 1987 and with it the enduring slogan, 'My Mate Marmite'.[6]

The campaign positioned Marmite as a spread which would help your children grow up healthy and strong, and featured various happy and healthy Marmite families.

The mother and baby TV executions usually ran on daytime and breakfast TV. Press campaigns also ran in specialist mother and baby magazines, and highlighted Marmite's health position as a savoury spread, rich in vitamin B.

The campaign was intended to update Marmite's image and raise its profile among adults in general by showing the product used by men and with a healthy outdoor appeal.

'SOLDIERS'

Sergeant: 1 2, 1 2. Move your feet, we're nearly there.
Men: Ten more miles and we don't care.

Sergeant: Feeling great and that's no lie.
Men: I'm so hungry I could die.

Sergeant: Let's get back to my mate.
Men: Whose mate?
Sergeant: Your mate.
Men: My mate.

Sergeant: Marmite.
Men: Marmite.
Sergeant: Want some?
Men: Want some?

Sergeant: Feed me.
Men: Feed me.

Sergeant: Good stuff.
Men: Good stuff.

Sergeant: My mate.
Men: Marmite.

'I HATE MARMITE'

Low Rider music throughout.

Singer: I hate Marmite.

Singer: I hate Marmite.

'MY MATE MARMITE'

Low Rider music throughout.

My mate, Marmite.

My mate, Marmite.

In 1996, BMP DDB and Best Foods again felt the need to focus on adult usage. This time, the response was to reinterpret the 'My Mate' theme in a more radical way, to target a younger adult audience who had become far more cynical and advertising literate.[7]

WHAT HAS HAPPENED TO MARMITE SINCE 1975?

Sales

Since 1975 sales have increased by 51%, with particularly strong growth between 1987 and 1989, and 1995 and 1998 (Figure 7).

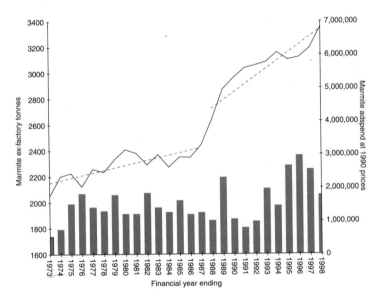

Figure 7: *Marmite sales versus advertising 1973 to 1998*
Sources: CPC, Register-MEAL

Moreover, since 1995, price has moved slightly ahead of inflation and therefore value growth has outstripped volume growth. In fact, between 1995 and 1998, Marmite has experienced its fastest value growth rate in a decade.

---

7. BMP's current 'I Hate Marmite/My Mate Marmite' campaign forced adult lapsed users to reappraise the brand. It also forced current users to reconsider Marmite as a modern and personal choice, rather than something which was merely a hangover from childhood.

Penetration

Household penetration has not, however, grown as much as sales. Unfortunately, household penetration can only tell us half the story, as it does not tell us who was eating Marmite within households.[8]

	1985	1997	
Household penetration	29.5	32.9	(+11.5%)

Source: TGI

Scrutinising household penetration further did, however, give us a clue about what had actually happened to produce the sales uplifts.

While household penetration had increased among all household types, the biggest increases had been among adult-only households and households with older children. This suggested that, in line with the marketing objectives, more adult usage was responsible for the extra sales growth, while the mother-and-baby life cycle had been maintained (and, in fact, had grown slightly).

Consumption

However, a breakthrough in understanding came when we examined a Usage & Attitude study from 1982.[9] This showed definitively that household penetration figures were masking increased levels of adult consumption within households. The marketing objectives of broadening out the life cycle had been successful.

	1982	1997
Housewives eating Marmite themselves (indexed against 1982)	100	124

Source: U&A 1982, Audience Selection Omnibus 1997

A Famous Brand

Marmite had also become something of a household icon and is now extremely well known and well loved.

8. NB. We are considering TGI household penetration figures from 1985 onwards as, prior to that, the question about Marmite was located at a different place within the questionnaire. This affected the levels of response to questions about Marmite, and thus prevents comparisons with earlier years.
9. Ideally, we would have liked to have looked at consumption data from the 1970s rather than from the 1980s. Since the 1970s, however, Marmite had changed hands twice, first from the Cavenham group to Beechams in 1980, and then more recently to Best Foods (formerly known as CPC UK Ltd). During this period, much data has inevitably been lost.

Brand awareness and image	
Prompted brand awareness	100%
Spontaneous brand awareness	70%
One of the nation's favourite brands	63% agreed with this statement

Base: Adults 20–60
Source: Research International Tracking, January 1998

Consumer Comments:

'I don't know of anyone who doesn't know what it is, it's like cornflakes.'

'Everybody has a jar of Marmite.'

'It's a classic', 'It's like an old friend.'

Source: Quotes from RDS Research and BMP Qualitative Research

Obsessive Marmite Users

Marmite has also created a peculiarly loyal following. Many users religiously take their Marmite on holiday and the Internet is clogged with messages from expats searching for Marmite abroad. Others even create websites to declare their love of Marmite. Even more extreme are those, such as Daniel Parkes, who exist on a diet of almost pure Marmite.

THE CONTRIBUTION OF ADVERTISING SINCE 1975

So far we have shown that Marmite has emerged from its mid-life crisis, not only intact but actually stronger. Sales have grown, the mother and baby life cycle has been maintained, and adult usage of the brand, as desired, has increased. Next, we intend to show that advertising has been crucial to this success.

It is immediately obvious that the two periods of particular growth between 1987 and 1989 and 1995 and 1998, coincided with two particularly famous advertising campaigns which were intended to increase adult usage. Putting these campaigns under the microscope was therefore our focus.

FAMOUS, IMPACTFUL ADVERTISING

'Soldiers'

During our search through the archives at Best Foods, we found the Millward Brown documents from the period of the 'Soldiers' campaign. These demonstrated that it was clearly impactful, communicative advertising.

OBSESSIVE MARMITE USE

Boy's Marmite diet 'perfectly healthy'

BY A CORRESPONDENT

AN 11-year-old boy who has eaten only Marmite sandwiches since he was weaned has been given a clean bill of health by a nutritionist.

Daniel Parkes said: "I've tried chips and burgers and pizzas. Maybe I will eat other things when I get older but I don't think so. I just don't like

Daniel Parkes: "I don't like anything else"

anything else." His mother Lynne said: "We thought he'd grow out of it, but he never has. Then we worried about his health but a nutritionist says he's perfectly healthy. So now we just let him get on with it."

Daniel, of Newton Abbot, Devon, takes Marmite sandwiches when he eats out with his family. They also take jars of the yeast and vegetable extract spread on holiday. Mrs Parkes said: "It comes as second nature to us now — just like checking we've got our passports."

Daniel eats at least one loaf a day and supplements his diet with milk, orange juice — and Marmite on toast.

Lyndel Costain of the British Dietetic Association said: "This isn't a diet I'd recommend for all kids but as long as he drinks plenty of milk and orange juice, he should be fine."

MARMY BARMY

Danny, 11, eats nothing but Marmite sandwiches

| | 1988/1989 |
	%
Claimed TV advertising awareness	50
Communication (unprompted)	
'Good for you/healthy/wholesome/nourishing'	35
'Makes you strong/keeps you fit, etc.'	14
Image **of Marmite (prompted)**	
Suitable for children	83
Suitable for women	84
Suitable for men	81
Up-to-date product	57

NB. All figures are averages taken from the period of 'Soldiers' advertising, 1988–1989.

Example verbatims
'Lots of hunky soldiers eating Marmite.'

'Men love Marmite too – anyone can eat it.'

'It's for tough people and it helps to build you up.'

'The one with soldiers, and they were on a run shouting and chanting about Marmite. It's so good everyone wants to come home to it.'

Source: Millward Brown International

'I Hate Marmite'/'My Mate Marmite'

Meanwhile, at BMP, there was plentiful evidence that the 'I Hate Marmite/My Mate Marmite' campaign was particularly successful. According to Research International, it was one of the most impactful campaigns they had ever tested. It achieved particularly high levels of awareness among adults (Figure 8 – 'pre' refers to opinions of the previous Marmite campaign). Tracking also showed that people were not merely aware of the campaign, but that most could also recall detail from the specific executions (Figure 9). In addition, the campaign was clearly a powerful and original piece of communication (Figure 10). As a result of this, claimed likelihood to eat Marmite increased (Figure 11).

Consumers' comments demonstrate how 'Hate/Mate' worked:

'It's going to make people sit up and talk about it.'

'It really did make me think, I don't hate it, I love it.'

'Puts you in mind to try it again.'

'It's the sort of humour people of our generation appreciate.'

'Original', 'Unique', 'It's true, isn't it?'

Sources: BMP Qualitative Research, RDS Open Mind

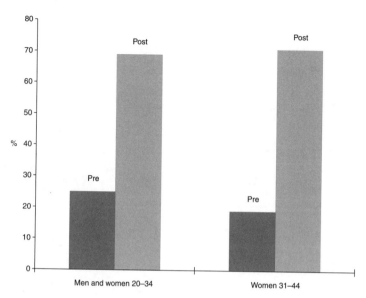

Figure 8: *Prompted TV ad awareness*
Source: Research International 1997

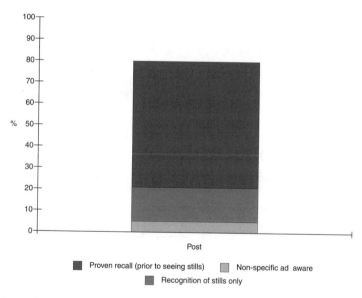

Figure 9: *Level/type of ad awareness*
Source: Research International 1997

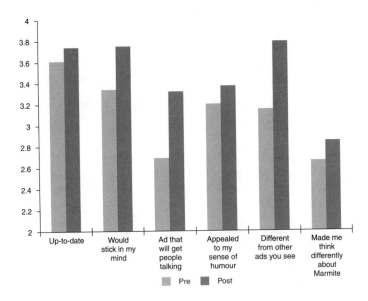

Figure 10: *Advertising descriptors*
Source: Research International 1997

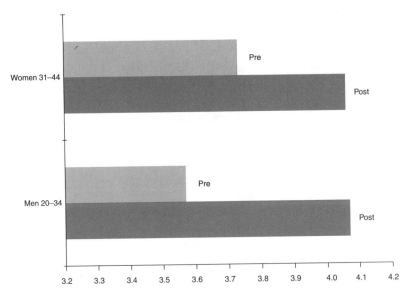

Figure 11: *Likelihood of eating Marmite*
Source: Research International 1997

THE CORRELATION BETWEEN ADS AND BEHAVIOURAL TRENDS

Consumption of Marmite

'Soldiers' and 'I Hate Marmite/My Mate Marmite' were intended to increase adult consumption of Marmite. There is strong evidence to show that both campaigns worked as expected. Consumption data from the 1980s confirmed that the 'Soldiers' campaign had coincided precisely with a significant increase in the proportion of Marmite which was consumed by adult households (Figure 12).[10]

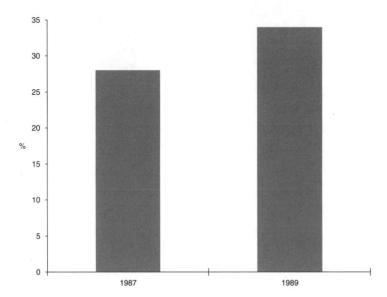

Figure 12: *The effect of 'Soldiers'*
Source: AGB

Meanwhile, consumption data from the time of the 'Hate/Mate' campaign also showed that adults, and men in particular (see Figure 13), consumed a higher proportion of the total Marmite eaten during the period of advertising than they did in the period prior to advertising.

Sales and Advertising

Furthermore, annual data also show that there is a long-term relationship between sales performance and levels of advertising support (Figure 14).

---

0. Two-person households are primarily two-adult households.

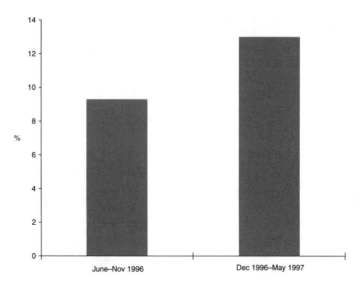

Figure 13: *The effect of 'I Hate Marmite/My Mate Marmite'; the increase of Marmite consumption by men aged 17–34*
Source: Family Food Panel

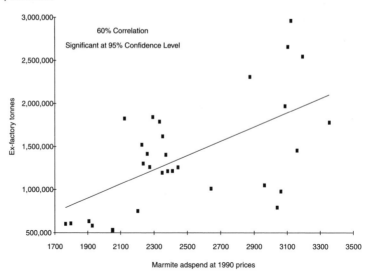

Figure 14: *The relationship between Marmite sales and advertising annual data, 1969–1998*
Source: CPC, Register-MEAL

REGIONAL EVIDENCE

Our search for evidence did not stop there however. More definitive proof that advertising was crucial to the Marmite life cycle and to Marmite's growth comes out of yet another peculiarity in Marmite's idiosyncratic history. Interestingly for us, an accident of history means that Marmite has been subjected to what must be one of the longest-lasting regional tests in marketing history.

Marmite's base of loyal users has historically been located in the southern areas.[11] Not surprisingly, advertising support was therefore concentrated in those areas. Hence, for over 25 years, they have been exposed to approximately three times as many TVRs as the northern regions.

Claimed Usage

Given the south's exposure to higher levels of advertising, one would expect the life cycle to have grown more in the south than in the north. Referring back to the 1982 U&A study, but this time dissecting the figures regionally, we can see that this was indeed the case.

Since 1982, the percentage of children eating Marmite has slightly increased in the south, whereas it has declined in the north. Meanwhile, the life cycle has also broadened out further to include more adults eating Marmite. Again, this trend is particularly marked in the south, but was also present in the north, which is not surprising given that most of the admittedly low-level advertising support which the north received focused on increasing adult usage.

	South		North	
	1982	1998	1982	1998
Children eating Marmite (1998 percentage indexed against 1982 percentage)	100	109	100	95
	1982	1997	1982	1997
Housewives eating Marmite (1997 percentage, indexed against 1982 percentage)	100	125	100	119

Source: U&A Study 1982, Audience Selection Omnibus 1997 and 1998

Meanwhile, heavier advertising support in the south has ensured that, today, a far higher percentage of southern 'Marmite babies' versus northern 'Marmite babies' feed their children Marmite and continue to eat Marmite themselves.

1. During Marmite's early history, its distribution through welfare clinics and associations was limited to the southern areas. Meanwhile, in Scotland, Marmite was only handled through an agent up until 1962. This therefore meant that most of Marmite's loyal users were primarily located in the southern areas. CPC and previous owners of Marmite have occasionally attempted to rectify this regional imbalance, but the relative sizes of the user bases in the different regions always meant that the largest short-term returns came from advertising in the south.

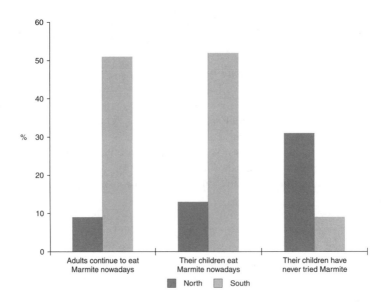

Figure 15: *Commitment to the Marmite lifecycle – adults who ate Marmite as children*
Source: Audience Selection Omnibus 1998

Penetration

Given the differences in advertising support, it was also unsurprising to see that household penetration had grown faster in the south than in the north.

Sales

If advertising has really driven growth, then one would expect the northern sales growth to have been poorer than that in the south, given that it has been exposed to far less advertising. This has indeed been the case, and the north's share of GB sales has steadily declined since 1979 (see Figure 16).[12]

Advertising Tests in the North

Moreover, we can also show that when the north has been supported by advertising, sales have responded to that support. In 1995 three regions (Scotland, the Midlands and the north west) received extra advertising support, and their performance immediately improved compared with that of the rest of the country. Figure 17 shows that there is a statistically significant relationship between the changes in advertising support and regional sales performance.

---

12. Unfortunately, 1979, rather than 1975, is the earliest year for which we have regional sales data.

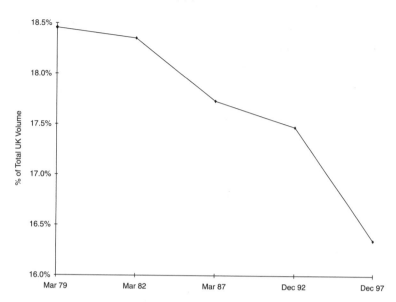

Figure 16: *The northern regions' share of Marmite sales*
Source: Nielsen, BARB, CPC

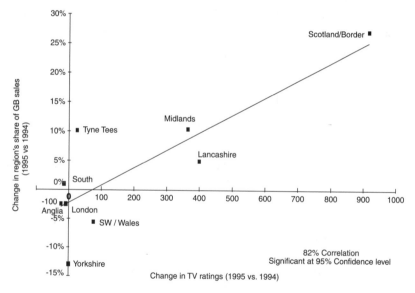

Figure 17: *The effect of the regional upweight test 1995*
Source: Nielsen, BARB

Furthermore, we can see from Figure 18 that when advertising support was withdrawn again, sales responded negatively. Advertising support was withdrawn from Scotland and the north west, while the Midlands only received a lower level of support. The sales performance slumped in the two non-advertised regions, while the Midlands saw a more moderate decline. Once again, the relationship is statistically significant.

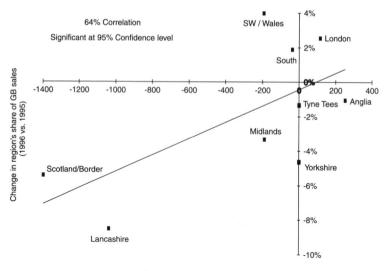

Figure 18: *The effect of withdrawing advertising from the northern test regions, 1996*
Sources: Nielsen, BARB

Figure 19 goes further, as it shows that the change in sales' performance matches the point at which the ads went off air to within a month.

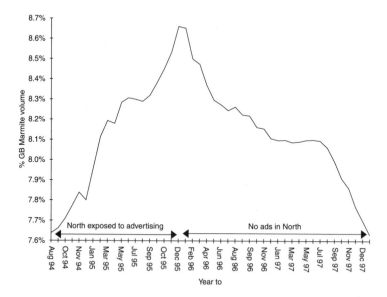

Figure 19: *The northern regions' share of Marmite sales during the test period*
Source: Nielsen

SUMMARY

We have shown that the life cycle is now functioning better in the advertised southern regions than in the north. We have also shown that sales have grown more in the southern regions, and that this is in direct response to advertising support.

We have also shown that bursts of advertising activity in the north do produce direct and positive results. The weight of this evidence clearly indicates that Marmite sales growth is intimately linked to advertising.

ELIMINATING OTHER FACTORS

Before we accept these compelling pieces of evidence, however, we should ask whether there are any other factors which could explain Marmite's growth as a whole and, in particular, the regional differences we have observed.

Product Changes

Overall, there have been no significant launches or new pack sizes which could have driven Marmite's growth. New introductions, such as Marmite cubes, are not the main drivers of growth and, in total, actually contribute less than 5% of the brand's volume sales.[13]

Meanwhile, there have been no significant changes to the product formulation or packaging.[14]

Promotions

Consumer promotions, meanwhile, have generally been on a relatively small scale. More importantly, however, these promotions have also been national, and therefore could not be responsible for Marmite's increased success in the southern regions.

---

13. Two pack sizes (8g and 600g) have been experimented with since 1975, but never contributed significantly to growth. Marmite cubes were launched in 1996, but again have not created any significant new growth. Meanwhile, at the time of metrication in 1987, the 113g jar was replaced by the 125g jar and the 227g jar was replaced by the 250g jar. Again there were no significant changes to growth.
14. The packaging was changed in 1984, when the original metal lids were exchanged for plastic lids. This change did not increase Marmite's growth, however, and was, in fact, initially met with an outcry of disapproval from Marmite loyalists.

PR

PR has perhaps played a more important role than promotions, as it has attempted to raise Marmite's profile and maintain its image as a healthy product. However, PR activities have again been national, and therefore can have had no role in generating the extra growth in the south.

Mother and Baby Distribution

When the original distribution of Marmite through health clinics and welfare associations stopped, Marmite tried to compensate with new distribution via bounty packs.[15]

While the introduction of bounty packs might have led to an initial step change in Marmite's growth rate, it could not have increased Marmite's growth rate continually from 1975, given that its distribution levels have not increased significantly since its introduction.

Finally, given that the bounty pack enjoys national distribution, if it is a powerful motivator to sales we would have expected it to even out the regional growth differences rather than exaggerating them.

Grocery Distribution

Distribution over the past ten years has been virtually static at 90%, and has been far eclipsed by growth in rate of sale (Figure 20). Any grocery distribution gains have also been almost entirely in the north, and so could have played no part in the growth of Marmite in the southern regions.

Price

Meanwhile, Marmite's real price did fall a little between 1987 and 1989, but since then the price has risen marginally faster than inflation. Yet, despite these price rises, the brand has managed to grow particularly fast.

We also know that price can have played no role in the regional divergence, as there have been no significant regional price differences.

---

15. Bounty packs are distributed nationally to mothers when they have children. Bounty packs contain samples of various products relevant to mothers, such as nappies and baby food. The packs also contain accompanying literature which gives guidance to new mothers. Tokens for Bounty packs are distributed to mothers, and can be redeemed for the actual packs at retail outlets, such as Boots.

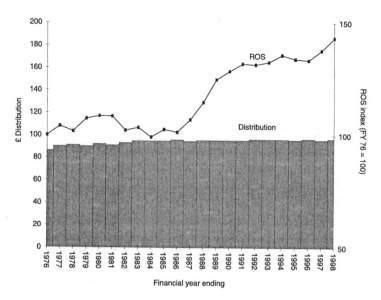

Figure 20: *Marmite distribution and ROS*
Source: Nielsen, CPC

Demographics

Overall, population trends have not been a significant factor in Marmite's growth, as sales of Marmite have risen much faster than the growth in population. In fact, as Figure 21 shows, sales of Marmite per head of the population have grown significantly, both nationally and also particularly in the south.

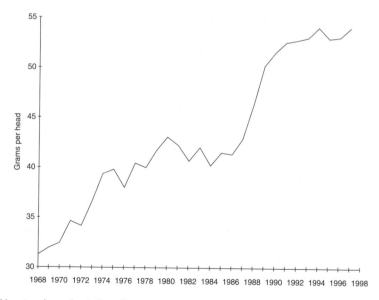

Figure 21: *Marmite sales per head of population*
Source: CPC Ex-factory, ONS

A more subtle criticism might be to suggest that the increase in the child population is responsible for Marmite's growth. As we have already pointed out, however, the birth rate has been declining through most of the period. Again, this decline has occurred in the south as well as nationally (Figure 22).

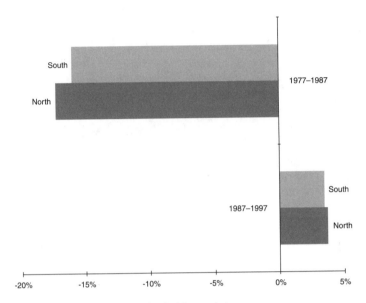

Figure 22: *Change in number of children per head of the population*
Source: ONS

We can therefore conclude that demographics cannot have been responsible for Marmite's growth, either nationally or in the south.

Economic Factors

It might seem plausible to suggest that Marmite's growth has been related to economic growth, since Britons have become much more affluent in the last 30 years. Intuitively, however, one would expect economic growth to benefit luxury items far more than a product like Marmite. It seems implausible to believe that economic growth could result in Marmite growing much faster than total consumer spending on foods.

Looking at this issue in more detail, we explored whether economic changes could explain the regional differential. It is true that, during the late 1970s and for much of the 1980s, incomes did rise much faster in the south than the north, but the actual effect on general consumption was more modest, perhaps because unemployment and the cost of living rose faster in the south (Figure 23).

Nevertheless, this might have helped to explain Marmite's relatively poor northern performance from 1979 to 1987.

During 1987 to 1997, however, the north–south economic divide narrowed, with the south hit harder by the last recession. Despite this, it is during this period that we see Marmite's southern growth surging ahead (Figure 24).

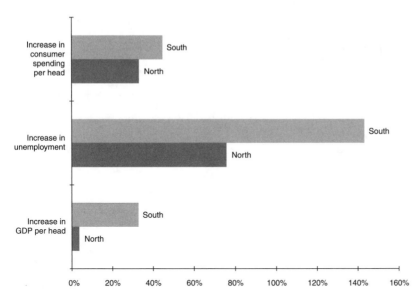

Figure 23: *The north–south divide 1977–1987*
Source: ONS

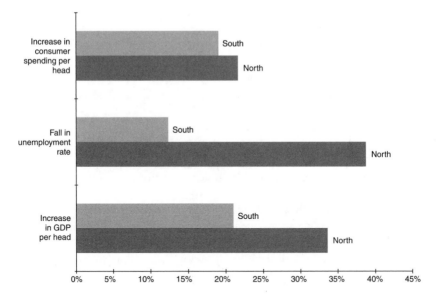

Figure 24: *The north–south divide narrows further, 1987–1996*
Source: ONS

We must therefore conclude that although increasing affluence is undoubtedly a factor in Marmite's success, it is only a minor one.

Food and Health Trends

Marmite, as we know, operates primarily as a spread, and at breakfast. So could changes in attitudes and behaviour, particularly a trend towards more health-conscious eating, have accounted for its growth?

It is certainly true that there has been a decline in the great British breakfast, and one might guess that this would benefit Marmite as a quicker, healthier alternative. Yet Figure 25 shows that cereals, not spreads, have been the main beneficiary of this trend.

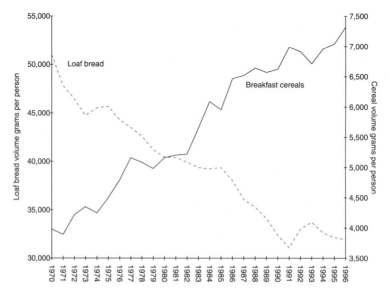

Figure 25: *Average consumption of loaf bread and breakfast cereals*
Source: National Food Survey

In fact, Marmite's growth has been achieved in the context of a massive decline in spreads overall.

The cynical might, however, leap to the conclusion that this decline in spreads was driven by a decline in less healthy sweet spreads, rather than savoury spreads like Marmite. Yet looking at the figures, we can see that Marmite's growth must be considered in the context of declines in savoury as well as sweet spreads.

The decline of spreads 1980–1996	
Sweet	-27%
Savoury	-9%

Source: National Food Survey

Dietary trends cannot therefore explain Marmite's growth.

Competition

Marmite has few significant competitors. While this might be used as a reason to explain why Marmite sales have not declined, it can by no means explain Marmite's growth, particularly as competitive presence has actually increased slightly over the period (Figure 26).

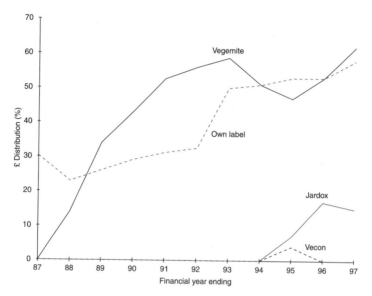

Figure 26: *Distribution of other yeast extracts*
Source: Nielsen

SUMMARY

The above analysis has clearly demonstrated that, although a number of factors such as income and price have undoubtedly contributed to Marmite's success over the last 25 years, they cannot explain the extent of the growth nor the regional sales patterns we have observed. In particular, we have shown that during the period of strongest growth (1987 to 1997) there were no factors, other than advertising, which could explain why sales grew so much faster in the south than in the north.

QUANTIFYING THE CONTRIBUTION OF ADVERTISING

The Contribution of Advertising to Revenue Since 1975

Since 1987, the south has been exposed to 6025 TVRs more than the north. As a result, the total growth rate (from 1987 to 1997) has been 38% in the south, compared to 25% in the north. This therefore suggests that 100 TVRs of advertising contributes around 0.2 percentage points to growth.[16]

Hence, if both north and south had had no TV advertising, then the national growth since 1987 would have been only about 17%.

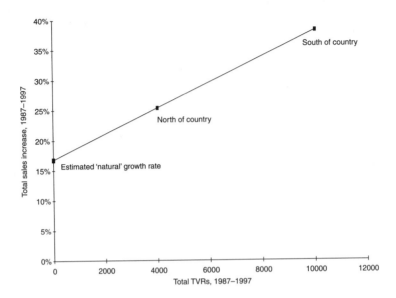

Figure 27: *Marmite sales growth versus advertising*
Source: CPC, BMP DDB

However, the national growth rate since 1987 is in fact 32%. Hence, advertising appears to account for around half of the sales growth seen since 1987.

Without disclosing sensitive information, we can confirm that the profit generated by this growth is greater than the advertising investment. Discounted cashflow analysis reveals that the average annual return on investing in advertising is, in fact, around 27%. This compares extremely favourably with the returns obtained on alternative investments (Table 1).

TABLE 1: AVERAGE ANNUAL RATES OF RETURN 1987–1998 (%)

Marmite advertising	27
Unit trusts	11–18
FTSE	14
Bonds	8
Bank/Building society deposits	5

Source: BMP Estimates

Furthermore, this figure is almost certainly an underestimate because:

1. It ignores the fact that there were several non-advertising factors that buoyed up the north in the period in question, and hence it underestimates the advertising's contribution to generating extra growth in the south versus the north.

---

16. $(100 \times (38 - 25)/6025) = 0.2$.

2. It ignores the contribution of national non-TV advertising (yet we have included all non-TV advertising costs in our calculations).

3. It ignores the future consequences of the advertising on sales, particularly with regard to the mother-and-baby life cycle.

4. It does not attempt to quantify the effect of advertising creating a barrier to entry to the yeast extract market.

This last point is probably very significant, as the following section will show.

Advertising as a Barrier to Competition

Looking at Marmite since 1975, one is struck by how little competition Marmite faces, even though it is clearly profitable and the process of manufacturing yeast extract is by no means inimitable.[17] The presence of own labels seems particularly low when compared to the rest of the spreads market.

Perhaps more interestingly, though, levels of own label and Vegemite growth have been lower in the southern regions where Marmite advertising has been focused (Figure 28).

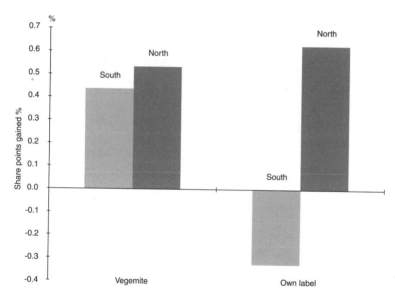

Figure 28: *Changes in competitors' shares of the yeast extract market 1995–1997*
Source: Nielsen

---

7. The process of regulating the texture of yeast extract is difficult, but by no means impossible to copy. Other competitors could also easily have secured yeast from other breweries to manufacture yeast extract, as Marmite by no means has a monopoly on purchasing the necessary yeast to make its yeast extract.

This indicates that Marmite advertising has indeed created barriers to entry to the yeast extract market, and this has in turn facilitated Marmite's past growth and its future growth potential.

CONCLUSION

Since Marmite's mid-life crisis in 1975, advertising has played a crucial role in preventing the collapse of the mother-and-baby life cycle and has also grown the brand among adults. Advertising has therefore clearly made a huge contribution to Marmite's growth and has also been extremely profitable.

Within the period, two campaigns have been particularly effective. These campaigns were Ogilvy & Mather's 'Soldiers' campaign and BMP's 'I Hate Marmite/My Mate Marmite'. Both campaigns were intended to increase adult usage and did so extremely successfully.

Furthermore, it is interesting to contemplate the potential effects of this Marmite advertising in the future. Given the Marmite life cycle, by which the Marmite 'habit' is passed on from generation to generation, the effect of current advertising may well have repercussions far into the twenty-first century, ensuring that Marmite's second century is as profitable as its first.

Overall, this paper demonstrates the importance of thinking long term in a world where demand for instant results is becoming increasingly prevalent.

★★★★★

7

Volkswagen

How advertising helped Volkswagen
and its dealers recover their profitability

EDITOR'S SUMMARY

This case highlights the broad benefits to a business of keeping demand ahead of supply and the power of advertising as a tool to achieve this.

Results and Payback

Since autumn 1995, Volkswagen and its dealers have enjoyed unprecedented success. They have sold 61 per cent more cars and achieved their highest ever share of the UK car market.

The evidence for advertising's part in this success is considerable. First, the paper demonstrates a statistical relationship between advertising communication and short listing of Volkswagen cars. Second, the paper demonstrates a correspondence between advertising and short-term growth in the UK. Third, it demonstrates that the different performance between the UK and other European markets can be related to different levels of advertising investment. Finally, the paper shows that other non-advertising factors, although vital to growth, can explain neither the pattern or the magnitude of this growth.

Advertising has enabled Volkswagen to keep demand for its products consistently ahead of supply. Short-term revenue gains are dramatic and the high lifetime value of a customer in the car market means that these benefits extend significantly into the long term.

Furthermore, the costs of doing business have decreased. In a market typified by surplus stock, Volkswagen has been selling cars as soon as they have left the factory. This has reduced storage costs and enabled Volkswagen to sell cars without the need for costly give-aways. It has also enabled Volkswagen to meet specific customer demands and therefore sell a richer mix of product. Economies of scale have further reduced unit costs.

Consumers too have benefited. In becoming more demand driven in the way it does business, Volkswagen is now more able to meet consumers' specific requirements. Moreover, by fuelling demand for its product in the new car market, resale values have increased, enabling customers to retain a higher proportion of their initial outlay when they come to sell their car.

INTRODUCTION

Since autumn 1995, Volkswagen UK and its dealers have enjoyed unprecedented business success. Making excellent products available at the right price was a necessary precondition for this success, but advertising – in bringing these developments to the notice of prospective car buyers – unlocked their full market potential and fuelled extraordinary levels of demand. In so doing, advertising has benefited three interested parties: Volkswagen UK (as an importer and wholesaler of cars), the Volkswagen dealer network, and Volkswagen's customers.[1]

MARKET BACKGROUND

Most of the UK car market falls into three volume sectors dominated by the three domestic marques: Ford, Vauxhall and Rover (Figures 1 and 2).

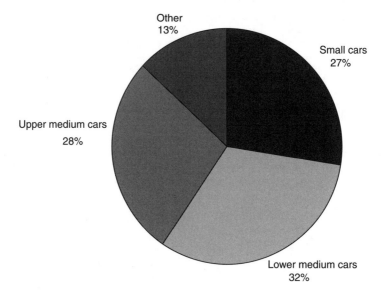

Figure 1: *The UK car market by sector (1994)*
Source: SMMT

Historically, Volkswagen has competed in all three sectors with its Polo, Golf and Passat models. Throughout the 1980s it was one of the best performing importer marques, but, in the early 1990s, demand for its cars fell and it began to lose market share for the following reasons:

---

1.   Throughout this paper the following terminology will be used: Volkswagen = 'marque', Polo/Golf/Passat = 'model', Polo L/Golf GTi = 'variant'.

Price

Following Britain's withdrawl from the ERM, the value of sterling fell relative to the deutschmark, making Volkswagen's price position less competitive. Indeed, for a short period in Spring 1993, people had to pay an 18% premium for Volkswagens.

Competitive growth offensives

The French marques, Peugeot, Citroen and Renault, began to market themselves aggressively, advertising at a share of voice disproportionate to their market size, and (as the recession began to bite) offering more and more tactical sales incentives. For example, 0% finance deals or free insurance in the first year of ownership.

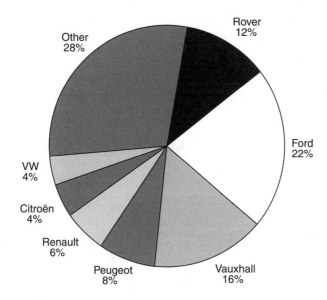

Figure 2: *The UK car market by manufacturer (1994)*
Source: SMMT

This had serious consequences for Volkswagen and its dealers. Costs increased as unsold cars languished in storage areas and showrooms. In addition, margins were sacrificed as Volkswagen offered more tactical incentives at both importer level and discounts at dealer level[2] in order to reverse declining share. Although decline was arrested in 1994, the long-term profitability of this 'holding strategy' was questionable.

The tactical sales incentives budget increased by a massive 350% between 1991 and 1994.

A STRATEGY FOR PROFITABLE GROWTH

In 1994 Volkswagen set itself two objectives:

— To increase its volume share in the UK not just to the point where the previous years' losses had been recovered, but beyond that, to achieve an unprecedented share level of 5.4% by 1996 and to continue to grow at a similar rate until the year 2000.

— To reduce the cost of doing business both as an importer and for its dealers, thereby increasing profitability at both levels.

Achieving improvements in both importer and dealer profitability was vital because their fates were mutually interlinked; without a significant improvement in profitability the dealers could not reinvest in their business. Without such reinvestment, they would not be able to gear up their operations to support a higher market share for Volkswagen in the long term.

To achieve these objectives Volkswagen needed to reverse the mismatch between supply and demand by fuelling demand for its cars.

CREATING DEMAND FOR VOLKSWAGENS

Good products at competitive prices were essential prerequisites for Volkswagen's subsequent growth:

Good products
Volkswagen was confident that it had, or would soon have, excellent products: a new and improved Polo was launched in late 1994 and a new Passat was expected in 1997.

Competitive pricing
Prices had been progressively realigned since their high point of early 1993. The last phase of realignment was completed in Autumn 1994, making Volkswagens competitive.

However, Volkswagen's market performance in late 1994 and early 1995 made it clear that product and pricing alone were not sufficient to fuel the demand necessary for profitable growth. Volkswagen therefore worked closely with BMP DDB to identify how demand could best be stimulated.

Key to subsequent strategy was a revised understanding of the car-buying process and the point at which marketing resources could be used most efficiently within it.

HOW PEOPLE MAKE DECISIONS IN THE CAR MARKET

Research indicated that the car-buying process typically divided into two phases: the passive phase and the active phase.

The 'Passive' Phase of the New Car-Buying Process

During the first phase, typically lasting two-and-a-half years, people were not consciously deciding which new car to buy but, by the end of it, most had actually formed a shortlist of the one or two models that most interested them. This shortlist was arrived at as a result of a continual – almost unconscious – review process, influenced by seeing cars around, or hearing good things about them via colleagues, friends, relations, or mass media (usually TV) advertising. To achieve a position on it, a car had to be deemed desirable and, just as crucially, affordable: if a car was assumed to be 'beyond my pocket' it would be rejected during this phase, no matter how desirable it was thought to be.[3]

> 'You know what you've got to spend so you don't bother going about looking at cars that are beyond your limits.'

> 'You've got a price range so you only look at what you think will fall within it.'

> 'I wouldn't go back to one of their dealers now unless I was really sure that I had enough money to buy the car I wanted, otherwise you feel so embarrassed.'

Source: BMP DDB, Price and Price Communication Research

However, these all-important price perceptions were rarely based on any real knowledge about what a car would cost. In research, people who openly claimed to have no idea about car prices explained that they did not think about buying certain cars because they simply felt them to be beyond their budget. These feelings about price were based on various factors which often bore little relation to current pricing realities:

— A person's last active experience of the car market – probably two or three years previously.

— Word of mouth, usually based on other peoples' last active experience of the car market, again probably out of date.

— A car's image; more desirable, 'classy' car marques were assumed to cost more.

The 'Active' Phase of the New-Car-Buying Process

The second phase, lasting anything from one week to six months, was when people consciously looked to buy a new car by investigating the two or three models which had been shortlisted during the passive phase.[4] Most people started this process

---

». The reasons for this were partly practical and partly emotional. On a practical level, people were far too busy to bother spending precious Saturday mornings traipsing round dealerships for cars they were not going to be able to buy. On an emotional level, they did not want to suffer the indignity of having to tell a dealer that they could not afford what was on offer.

». The terminology here might be somewhat misleading because, for many prospective car buyers, even this phase is not terribly active. It often simply involves paying more attention than usual to car ads in national

with a clear idea of the car they wanted, and few changed their minds as a result of their investigation – they almost never bought a car which had not been on their original shortlist.

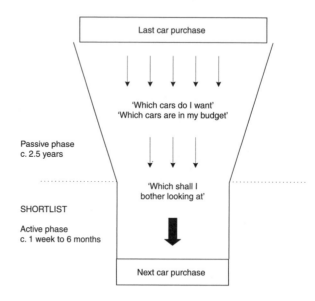

Figure 3: *The new-car-buying process*

VOLKSWAGEN'S PROBLEMS AND THEIR SOLUTIONS

This analysis of the buying process made it clear why demand for Volkswagens had declined:

— Not enough people wanted a Volkswagen car. Compared with heavily marketed 'stylish' French marques, Volkswagens were seen as much less desirable than they were in the heady boom-days of the 1980s. This was particularly true for Polo and Passat which, unlike Golf, had never really established identities in their respective market sectors.

— Not enough people realised that they could afford a Volkswagen car. People seriously overestimated the price differences between Volkswagen models and competitors. As a result, many people who clearly desired the cars were simply not bothering to shortlist them:

'I have thought about buying one, maybe a Golf, but they always come across as being more expensive, so I've always assumed that it wouldn't be a new car that I could afford.'

'I've thought about buying a Golf, but I've always associated them with being more pricey.'

---

newspapers, flicking through car magazines, picking up brochures from dealers, scanning list prices, and (perhaps) seeing what additional incentives might be on offer.

'The Polo's a nice little car ... but I wouldn't really look at one because it would be a bit more pricey.'

'The one thing that has always stopped me from looking at a Volkswagen is the cost.'

Source: BMP DDB Price and Price Communication Qualitative Research

These problems in the passive phase were exacerbated by a further problem in the active phase. Volkswagen and its dealers were spending a large amount of money on tactical purchase incentives to convert those people who had shortlisted Volkswagens. However, research into the impact of such incentives suggested that if people had got to the point of actually visiting a dealer, they were usually so committed to the idea of acquiring a Volkswagen that they were likely to buy one with or without any added incentive.[5]

Essentially, Volkswagen was spending a high proportion of its marketing budget on persuading the relatively small number of people who had shortlisted their cars to buy a car which they would probably have bought without such an incentive.

The solution was straightforward: Volkswagen needed to redirect its marketing budget if it wanted to fuel demand for its cars. Instead of offering unnecessary inducements to people in the active phase of the purchase process, it needed to focus on people when they were in the passive phase. These people needed to be persuaded that the marque and its models were both desirable and affordable; only then would Volkswagens get onto more shortlists.

IMPLICATIONS FOR ADVERTISING

The strategic implications for advertising were clear:

— We needed to move from a unified marque campaign to three model-focused campaigns.

— We needed to develop a campaign to tackle price misperceptions.

— We needed to increase the advertising budget.

Model-focused Campaigns

To ensure that all three volume models developed their own distinct and motivating identities – and, by doing so, to reinvigorate the overall marque – we needed to replace a common brand campaign, which had primarily benefited Golf, with three separate campaigns for Golf, Polo and Passat. Each campaign was designed to communicate the desirability of these models in the most appropriate way for the sector of the market in which they had to compete.[6]

BJM prices and incentives trade-off research, 1995.
Until 1995, Volkswagen's brand advertising had typically featured Golf GTi. The 'If only everything in life was as reliable as a Volkswagen' campaign was so strongly associated with Golf that even when other

— Polo advertising emphasised that Polo shared many of the benefits of a bigger car, most notably strength and safety. Two new television films ran between 1995 and 1997 which focused on this theme: 'Surprise' and 'Protection'. Press work also supported this theme.

— Passat advertising focused on the car's German design qualities. The 'Obsession' campaign ran on television, press and posters from the car's relaunch in April 1997.

— Golf advertising focused on product stories which still demonstrated class-leading qualities: direct injection diesel engineering and VR6 engine technology. 'UFO' and 'Beetle' ran on television throughout 1996 and early 1997.

A Campaign to Tackle Misperceptions about Volkswagen Prices

We needed to adopt an unconventional media and creative strategy to convince people that Volkswagens were not 'beyond their pockets' before they had finalised their new car shortlists.

Traditionally, advertising talking about car prices had appeared in the media used by people during the active phase of the new-car-buying process (such as local newspapers). However, research indicated that the ads which ran in such media were used selectively; prospective car buyers only attended to the prices of cars they had already shortlisted. We needed to talk to people while they were still in the passive phase. The implication was clear: we had to use relatively intrusive media channels.

Although people were genuinely surprised when confronted with Volkswagen's actual price levels in a research context, we found that communicating them in advertising was likely to be more tricky. People were so cynical about price points quoted in car ads that mere exposure to Volkswagen's prices would not be enough to address their misperceptions.[7] We needed to deliver that price point accompanied by some kind of overt challenge to their expectations. By doing so, we hoped that even if people had suspicions about the actual price points in the campaign, the challenging stance of the surrounding 'story' would be enough to leave people thinking 'Maybe Volkswagen's aren't beyond my pocket after all'.

A heavyweight television, poster, radio and press campaign aimed at sowing a seed of doubt in people's minds was developed called 'Letters'. This ran throughout 1996, featuring Polo and Golf models, and was refined in 1997 (evolving into 'Surprises').

---

models were featured, consumers tended to assume that it was Golf being advertised.

7.   There were two reasons for this cynicism: such prices tended to be surrounded by caveats and provisos (for example, 'excluding number plates and delivery'); or prices for bottom-of-the-range model variants were accompanied, somewhat misleadingly, by pictures of variants from the top of the range.

'AFFORDABILITY' ADS

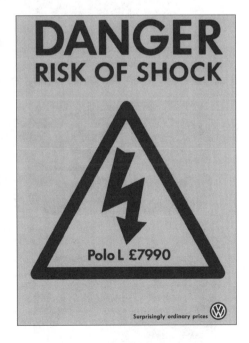

POLO 'PROTECTION'

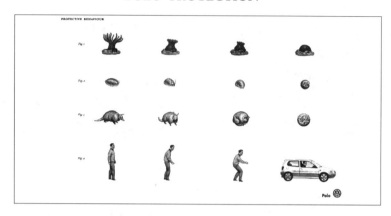

PASSAT 'OBSESSION'

GOLF 'BEETLE'

GOLF 'UFO'

Higher Level of Advertising Spend

Volkswagen could not support so many campaigns without spending more money on advertising. In 1995, following a detailed analysis of the optimum relationship between market share and share of voice in the UK car market, spend levels were increased.[8] This change took effect from September 1995.

This increase did not require a high increase in overall marketing spend. As outlined above, the strategy to boost demand for Volkswagens involved redirecting marketing resources which had previously been focused on people in the active phase of the purchase process to people who were in the passive phase. In practice, this meant that the money saved by reducing tactical incentives was spent on advertising instead.

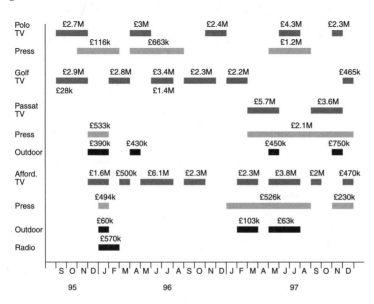

Figure 4: *Media schedule*

WHAT HAPPENED?

Between autumn 1995 and autumn 1997 Volkswagen met all its objectives. Overall sales grew by 61%, from 74,548 units in 1994 to 119,767 units in 1997.

Volume share increased. Indeed, in 1996 Volkswagen's share grew by 36%, the fastest rate of growth experienced by a top-ten car manufacturer for ten years, and far exceeding the original objectives set.[9]

. Share of voice increased from 4.1% in 1994 to 5.2% in 1996 and to 5.9% in 1997.

. In 1997 came the 'run out' year for the Mark 3 version of Golf. From September supplies were severely restricted as the factory prepared for mass production of the new (Mark 4) Golf.

The mismatch between supply and demand was addressed: demand moved ahead of supply to the point where the average time taken to sell a Volkswagen in the UK more than halved.

The amount of incentives offered to prospective Volkswagen buyers was reduced.

As sales became demand driven, Volkswagen increased its ability to predict – and then order from the factory – the model variants and specification levels which UK car buyers wanted. Since car buyers with precise needs (such as air-conditioning or blue metallic paint) were happy to pay for their needs to be met, the average price paid for Volkswagens increased between 1995 and 1997 relative to their sector averages.[10]

TABLE 1: ACTUAL PRICE PAID FOR VOLKSWAGENS
INDEXED AGAINST SECTOR AVERAGE

	Polo vs. small	Golf vs. lower medium	Passat vs. upper medium
1995	101	110	103
1996	114	111	102
1997	114	114	109

Source: NCBS

Consequently, Volkswagen's value share increased even more dramatically than its volume share.[11]

The profile of Volkswagen's customer base improved; fewer bargain-driven, potentially 'promiscuous' car buyers bought a Volkswagen.

The costs of doing business decreased[12] and Volkswagen's dealers' margins were recovered.

Thus, the strategy was tremendously successful – but what evidence is there that advertising contributed to this success?

DEMONSTRATING THE EFFECT OF ADVERTISING

It is traditional in car market IPA effectiveness case studies to observe how hard it is to demonstrate an advertising effect in this market.[13] The most convincing cases tend to evaluate relatively 'discrete' advertising tasks such as campaigns to launch new models (for example, Nissan Micra) or coherent marque advertising campaigns which concentrate on promoting values common to all its models (for example, BMW).

---

10. This was not because people were paying less for other new cars within the respective market sectors: the absolute average amount spent increased in each successive year.
11. There is no standard industry-wide measure of value share available for the UK market. We calculated value share figures by using car volume data (from SMMT) and data on the average price paid for a new Volkswagen versus the average price paid for all new cars (from NCBS).
12. For example, car storage costs were reduced and the increased 'throughput' of cars meant that cashflow could be managed more astutely – see the section on 'Business Returns Due To Advertising'
13. The most commonly cited reasons are that it is a market where purchase is infrequent and 'high investment'; and where, because of the long purchase cycle, there are opportunities for many non-advertising variables to influence the ultimate purchase decision.

Volkswagen's move from one marque campaign to three model-specific and one price-related campaign made our evaluation task even harder than usual.

Nonetheless, we can show that the advertising has been extremely effective. Our evidence for this is as follows:

— Consumers responded to all the new advertising exactly as planned.

— There was a strong correspondence between Volkswagen's market performance and its advertising activity.

— Other factors cannot explain the pattern or the extent of Volkswagen's growth.

1. CONSUMERS RESPONDED TO THE ADVERTISING EXACTLY AS PLANNED

There is strong evidence that the advertising worked exactly as planned:

— It communicated the desirable qualities of the cars and, in so doing, improved their image.

— It communicated that the cars were not beyond people's pockets and therefore persuaded more people that the cars were affordable.

— This positioned Volkswagen as a better make to own.

— This translated into greater consideration and shortlisting of Volkswagens.

a) Advertising Communicated the Desirability of the Cars

As outlined above, the model campaigns were designed to communicate those aspects of the cars that were most desirable in the sectors of the market in which they had to compete. Each of the campaigns achieved this objective.

Polo advertising communicated that it had all the benefits of a bigger car, especially in the area of safety (see Figure 5).[14]

Quotes from Polo research:

'Surprise'

'Don't be deceived by its looks – it's a lot more than you'd expect from a small car.'

'It's got all the qualities of a big car, even though it's just a tiny little Polo.'

'With your eyes closed you would believe you were in a Ferrari.'

---

14. All the quotes in this section of the paper are from research conducted after work had appeared on air.

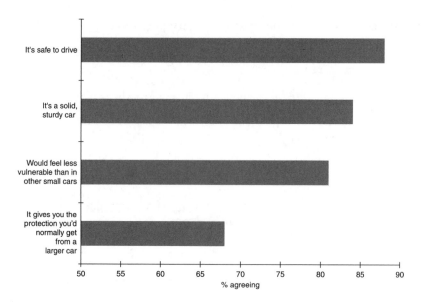

Figure 5: *Prompted impressions from the Polo 'Protection' TV ad*
Source: Millward Brown 22 September 1997 – 22 March 1998

'Protection'

'I got the impression that you feel safe when you're small.'

'Even though it's a small car, it's a safe car.'

'I think it was emphasising the compactness and safety of the car.'

'They're just trying to tell you that it's a safe car.'

Sources: Millward Brown tracking study verbatims, BMP DDB qualitative research

Golf advertising demonstrated its class-leading engineering credentials.

Quotes from Golf research:

'UFO' (TDi engine)

'It goes further on a tank of fuel than any other car.'

'It tells you that it can go so far without needing to be filled up which to someone like me who drives a long way to work is very important.'

'It's saying "look at this car, it's something out of the ordinary – it's unbelievable" '.

'Beetle' (VR6 engine)

'They've got amazing engines.'

'It's stronger, it's better, and it's super!'

'It's saying it's stronger and better and faster.'

'The difference is what's under the bonnet.'

Source: BMP DDB qualitative research

Passat advertising communicated its embodiment of the design standards and distinctive styling associated with German cars.

TABLE 2: PROMPTED IMPRESSIONS FROM PASSAT 'OBSESSION' CAMPAIGN[15]

| | Designed with attention to detail | Built to German design standards | Technically advanced for its class | It has distinctive distinctive styling |
	%	%	%	%
'Karl Schneider'	80	63	30	77
'Video Diaries'	87	72	57	53
'Wind Tunnel'	61	63	55	49
'Doors'	91	75	61	47

Base: Definite recallers
Source: Millward Brown, June 1997, December 1997

Quotes from Passat research ('Obsession' campaign):

'It's trying to tell us it's a well thought out design.'

'It was trying to give the impression it's as good as other cars in its range such as Audi and BMW.'

'It was built and designed with precision.'

'They strive for perfection, even little details are important.'

Base: Non-owners of Volkswagens
Source: Millward Brown Passat Launch Monitor Tracking, June 1997

b) Advertising Improved the Image of Volkswagen Models

Polo's reputation was established as the best made, safest and most reliable small car.[16]

---

5. Each execution was intended to highlight different things; for example, 'Karl Schneider' emphasised the new Passat's distinctive styling, 'Doors' emphasised quality of construction.
6. Tables 3, 4 and 5 are based on the total sample and so, strictly speaking, do not control for ownership of the requisite Volkswagen model. However, because owners of Polos, Golfs, and Passats only constituted 5%, 8%, and 2% of the respective samples, we don't think that the pattern of these results can be wholly explained by owner's relatively high awareness of ads for their particular car.

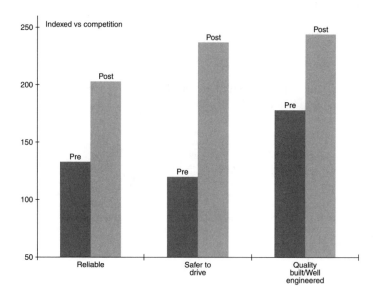

Figure 6: *Polo model image*
Base: Total sample (pre), excluding Volkswagen owners (post). Competitive set: Corsa, Peugeot 106, Clio, Micra, Punto
Source: Hall & Partners dipstick (June 1995), Millward Brown 22 September 1997 – 22 March 1998

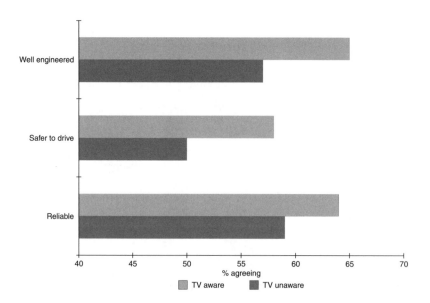

Figure 7: *Polo model image: TV ad aware versus unaware*
Base: Total sample (pre), excluding Volkswagen owners (post). Competitive set: Corsa, Peugeot 106, Clio, Micra, Punto
Source: Hall & Partners dipstick (June 1995), Millward Brown 22 September 1997 – 22 March 1998

TABLE 3: POLO'S IMAGE VS. OTHER SMALL CARS

	Well engineered %	Sturdy & solid %	Safer to drive %	Reliable %
Polo	64	62	56	61
(rank vs. comp.)	(1st)	(1st)	(1st)	(1st)
Fiesta	31	30	34	42
Peugeot 106	33	23	26	34
Corsa	28	25	27	34
Clio	26	19	24	27
Micra	28	15	24	37
Rover 100	29	25	24	29
Punto	16	13	27	18
Saxo	22	12	19	20

Base: Small car drivers who do not own a car from that marque
Source: Millward Brown 22 September 1997 to 22 March 1998

Golf's reputation for reliability, build quality and excitement was reinforced, leaving it well ahead of its competitors.

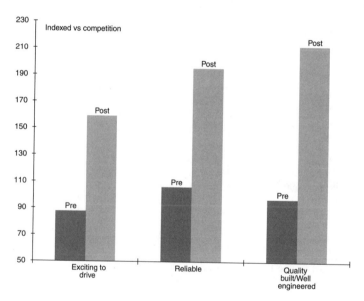

Figure 8: *Golf model image*
Base: Total sample (pre), excluding Volkswagen owners (post). Competitive set: Astra, Peugeot 306, Renault 19/Megane
Source: Hall & Partners dipstick (June 1995), Millward Brown 22 September 1997 – 22 March 1998

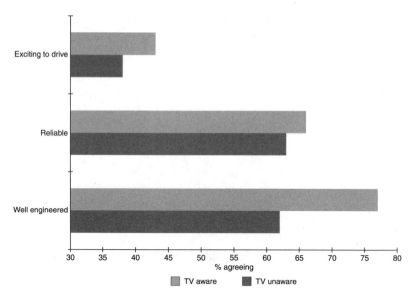

Figure 9: *Golf model image – TV ad aware versus unaware*
Base: Lower medium car drivers
Source: Millward Brown, January 1998

TABLE 4: GOLF'S IMAGE VS. OTHER LOWER MEDIUM CARS

	Reliable %	Well engineered %	Exciting to drive %
Golf	63	65	35
(rank vs. comp.)	(1st)	(1st)	(1st)
Megane	26	30	26
Rover 200	39	38	18
Peugeot 306	38	37	27
Escort	36	22	12
Astra	33	25	13
Almera	30	27	11
Xsara	20	20	13
Bravo	14	14	11

Base: Lower medium car drivers who do not own a car from that marque
Source: Millward Brown 22 September 1997 to 22 March 1998

Likewise, Passat's image was improved to the point where it was seen as the best engineered, best designed, most reliable, and least 'run of the mill' car in its sector.

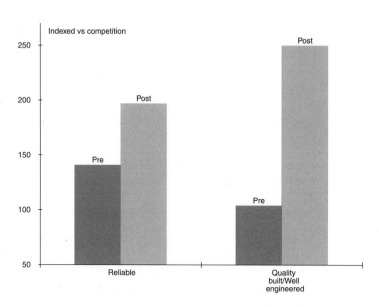

Figure 10: *Passat model image*
Base: Total sample (pre), excluding Volkswagen owner (post). Competitive set: Mondeo, Laguna
Source: Hall & Partners dipstick (June 1995), Millward Brown 22 September 1997 – 22 March 1998

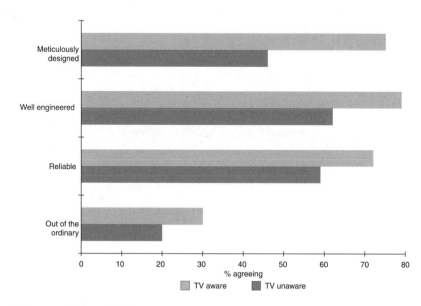

Figure 11: *Passat model image – TV ad aware versus unaware*
Base: Upper medium car drivers
Source: Millward Brown, January 1998

TABLE 5: PASSAT'S MODEL IMAGE VS. OTHER UPPER MEDIUM CARS[17]

	Meticulously designed %	Well engineered %	Reliable %	Out of the ordinary %
Passat	52	65	61	22
(rank vs. comp.)	(1st)	(1st)	(1st)	(1st)
Mondeo	26	24	32	2
Vectra	28	28	34	4
Peugeot 406	36	35	35	8
Rover 600	34	35	33	5
Laguna	31	28	30	13
Primera	26	30	37	4

Base: Upper medium car drivers who do not own a car from that marque
Source: Millward Brown 22 September 1997 to 22 March 1998

c) Advertising Communicated Volkswagens were not Beyond People's Pockets

The 'Surprisingly Ordinary Prices' campaign successfully challenged people's expectations that Volkswagens were beyond their pockets, leaving them eager to look more closely into buying one.

— Eighty-six per cent of people who recalled having seen the campaign spontaneously described the advertising message in (at least) one of the following ways: low prices, cheaper than people think, affordable, value for money, reasonable price.

— Ninety-three per cent agreed with the prompted impression 'It's saying Volkswagen make affordable cars.'

Source: Millward Brown, April 1998

Quotes from affordability research

'When you saw the advert you thought, "that's a reasonable price for a car".'

'I was surprised that they're that price because I've always thought that they're about fifteen hundred dearer than something like a ZX or 306.'

'They're telling you to get off your bum and go and have a look because you can get something that you didn't think you could afford.'

'They're saying you can have that expensive feel for not as much money as you think. I think it will work because I think people will think "But I didn't think I could afford a Golf, I think I'll just pop in and have a look." '

---

17. Other German cars such as BMW and Audi were not considered by Volkswagen to be direct competitors to Passat. The relevant competitive set in tracking terms therefore consists of mainstream marques.

'You think "Hang on, this car is supposed to be like a quality car and yet it's really cheap, so I am getting value for money, so I'll include it when I look". '

Base: Non-owners of Volkswagens
Sources: BMP DDB ongoing qualitative research. Verbatim from Millward Brown tracking study

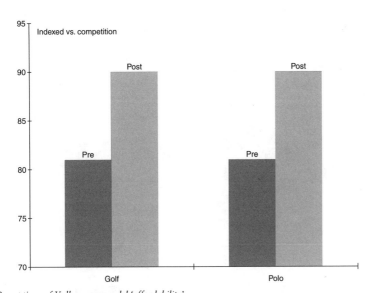

Figure 12: *Perceptions of Volkswagen model 'affordability'*
Base: Total sample (pre), excluding Volkswagen owner (post).
Competitive sets: Corsa, Peugeot 306, Clio, Micra, Punto, Astra, Renault 19/Megane
Source: Hall & Partners dipstick (June 1995), Millward Brown 22 September 1997 – 22 March 1998

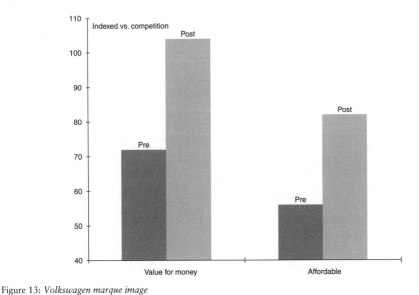

Figure 13: *Volkswagen marque image*
Base: Total sample
Competitive set: Vauxhall, Renault, Rover
Source: Hall & Partners dipstick (June 1995), Millward Brown 22 September 1997 – 22 March 1998

The perceived affordability of Polo and Golf improved dramatically. (By contrast, the perceived affordability of Passat, which was not included in the 'Surprisingly Ordinary Prices' campaign, fell.) The overall marque was also seen as more affordable and offering better value for money.

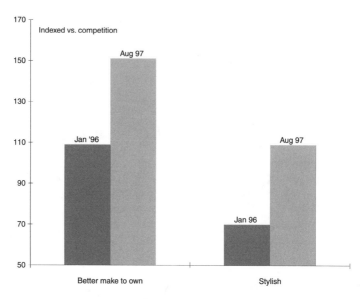

Figure 14: *Volkswagen marque image*
Base: Total sample. Competitive set: Vauxhall, Renault, Rover
Source: Hall & Partners continuous tracking (4w/e ending January 1996 versus August 1997)

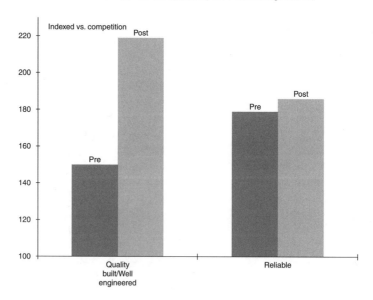

Figure 15: *Volkswagen marque image*
Base: Total sample. Competitive set: Vauxhall, Renault, Rover
Source: Hall & Partners dipstick June 1995, Millward Brown 1998

In combination, these developments fuelled the brand's reputation as a better make to own, positioned it as stylish, and reinforced its key image strengths of reliability and build quality.

TABLE 6: VOLKSWAGEN MARQUE IMAGE VS. COMPETITION

	Well engineered %	Reliable %
Volkswagen	65	62
(rank vs. comp.)	(1st)	(1st)
Ford	33	47
Vauxhall	27	38
Rover	37	35
Peugeot	29	33
Renault	25	27

Base: Total sample
Source: Millward Brown, January 1998

Not only did consideration increase by almost 100% between June 1995 and January 1998, but Volkswagen was established as the make of car that people would most want to have on their drive:

	June 95	Jan 98
'I would/might consider buying' indexed versus competition	57	110

TABLE 7: VOLKSWAGEN CONSIDERATION VS. COMPETITION

	Proud to have on my drive	Might consider buying
Volkswagen	53	47
(rank vs. comp.)	(1st)	(1st)
Ford	43	46
Vauxhall	38	47
Rover	51	45
Peugeot	38	41
Renault	33	34

Base: Total sample
Source: Millward Brown, January 1998

At both a model and marque level, the objective of getting Volkswagens on to more new car shortlists in the passive phase of the car-buying process was achieved. Within their respective market sectors Polo became the model most likely to be shortlisted, and Golf and Passat the second most likely. This was no mean achievement for the Golf, which was in the last few months of its model life cycle.

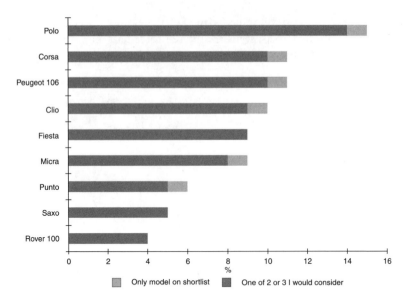

Figure 16: *Shortlisting of small cars*
Base: Drivers of small cars who do not own a car from that marque
Source: Millward Brown December 1998

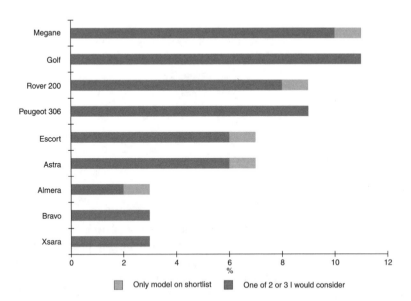

Figure 17: *Shortlisting of lower medium cars*
Base: Drivers of lower medium cars who do not own a car from that marque
Source: Millward Brown December 1998

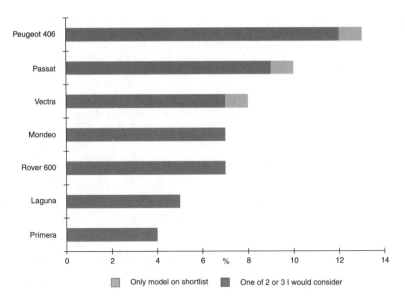

Figure 18: *Shortlisting of upper medium cars*
Base: Drivers of upper medium cars who do not own a car from that marque
Source: Millward Brown December 1998

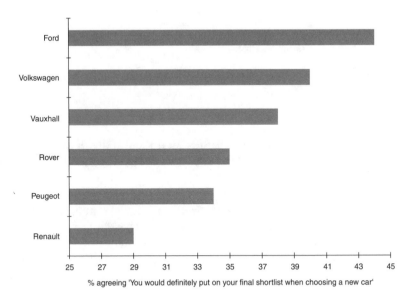

Figure 19: *Marque shortlisting – percentage agreeing 'You would definitely put on your final shortlist when choosing a new car'*
Base: Total sample
Source: Millward Brown January 1998

Marque shortlisting increased to the point where Volkswagen became the second most likely to be shortlisted.

	Jun 95	Jun 98
Shortlisting indexed vs. competition	29	112

Sources: Hall & Partners dip-stick (June 1995), Millward Brown (January 1998)
Base: Bought new car in last six months (pre), total sample (post)
Competitive: Renault, Peugeot, Vauxhall, Ford

The existence of such a 'chain of effectiveness' was confirmed when we looked in more detail at the statistical relationship between these measures.[18] But did these advertising-driven improvements in marque and model image, consideration, and shortlisting, influence Volkswagen sales? Yes, they did.

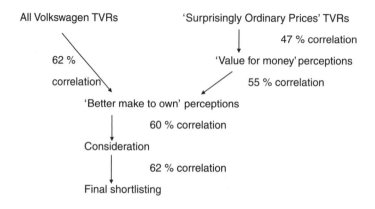

Figure 20: *The link between advertising and shortlisting*
Note: all these correlations were significant at the 95% confidence level

2. CORRESPONDENCE BETWEEN VOLKSWAGEN'S MARKET PERFORMANCE AND ITS ADVERTISING ACTIVITY

Case studies which look at the effectiveness of car advertising usually struggle to show any relationship at all between advertising activity and short-term share performance. In a market with an average inter-purchase interval of three years, where the majority of people in the target audience may not be actively 'in the market' for many months, this is hardly surprising. However, in this case we can show such a relationship.

---

18. There was a 62% correlation between Volkswagen TVRs and perceptions that the brand was 'a better make to own', there was a 60% correlation between these perceptions and consideration levels, and so on.

UK

The timing of Volkswagen's share growth, beginning in September 1995, exactly matches the time when the advertising spend increased. For many months thereafter, the two measures follow each other closely.

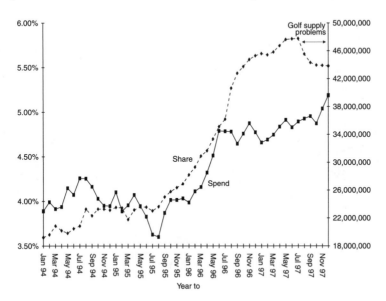

Figure 21: *Volkswagen's UK market share versus advertising*
Source: SMMT, Register-MEAL, Advertising Association

In fact, there was a statistically significant correlation between advertising spend and market share.

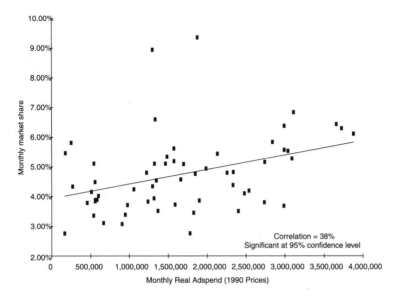

Figure 22: *Volkswagen's UK market share versus advertising*
Source: SMMT, Register-MEAL

Furthermore, there was a statistically significant correlation between advertising spend and share *gains* from month to month.

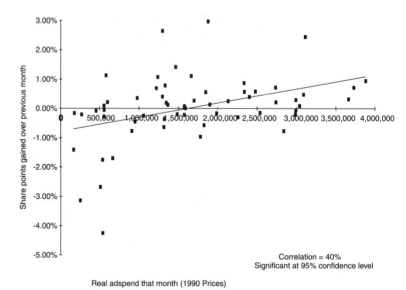

Figure 23: *Volkswagen's UK market share gains versus advertising*
Source: SMMT, Register-MEAL

Europe

There were two key differences between Volkswagen's advertising strategy in the UK and in the other major European markets: different copy was run and advertising share of voice increased more in the UK. Likewise, Volkswagen's UK share of market also saw the greatest increase (Figures 24 to 27).

Indeed, Volkswagen UK's share performance relative to Europe correlated almost directly with UK adspend levels.

Looking at annual share and advertising share-of-voice growth on a country-by-country basis, we found that there was a strong correlation between changes in the two across all the markets.

3. OTHER FACTORS CANNOT EXPLAIN THE PATTERN OR THE EXTENT OF VOLKSWAGEN'S GROWTH

As outlined in the introduction, excellent products at good prices were a vital precondition for growth. However, neither these nor other non-advertising factors can explain either the pattern or the magnitude of that growth. We shall now look at each in turn.

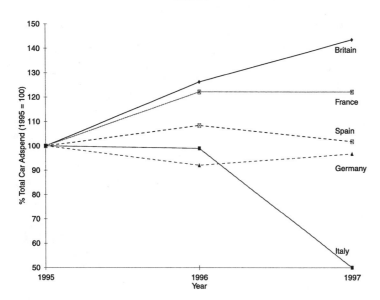

Figure 24: *Volkswagen's share of voice across Europe*
Source: BBJ

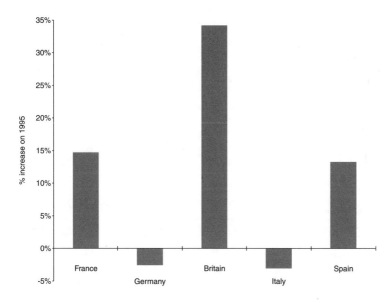

Figure 25: *Volkswagen share growth across Europe, 1996*
Source: SMMT

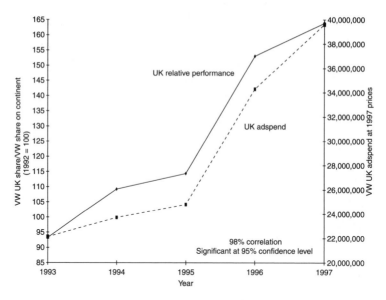

Figure 26: *Volkswagen UK performance relative to continent versus advertising*
Source: SMMT, BBJ

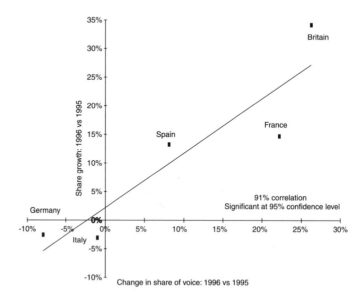

Figure 27: *Volkswagen European share growth versus advertising support*
Source: SMMT, BBJ

Better Product

The Volkswagen factory has always made excellent cars. However, excellent as these products were, the scale of Volkswagen's growth in the UK cannot be explained by the launch of upgraded models. Volkswagen Europe offered the same models in the four largest continental markets: Germany, France, Italy and Spain. Yet share growth in the UK far exceeded growth in those markets at both a marque level and at the level of individual models.

TABLE 8: % CHANGES IN VOLKSWAGEN MARKET SHARE
ACROSS EUROPE 1996 VS. 1995

	Golf %	Polo %	Passat %	Total VW %
Britain	14	84	3	34
France	-4	43	0	15
Spain	-6	57	-17	13
Germany	-14	10	-6	-3
Italy	-18	21	-50	-3
Continental average	-13	22	-11	0

Source: SMMT, Volkswagen

Furthermore, the timing of Volkswagen model upgrades did not correspond with the timing of the share growth:

— The Golf was last upgraded in March 1992, over three-and-a-half years before share began to grow.

— A new version of the Passat was launched during the time period we are looking at. However, this launch was not until April 1997, over 18 months after market share began to grow.[19]

— There was a gap of nearly a year between the launch of the much improved Polo (in December 1994) and the time when Volkswagen's share began to grow.

Better Supply

Volkswagen's UK share performance cannot be explained by supply-related factors:

— Supplies became progressively tighter as Volkswagen's share grew (Figure 28).

— Lack of availability was cited as a greater barrier to purchase during the period when Volkswagen's share was growing than before that period.

---

9. Thus, during 20 out of the 29 months covered by this paper Volkswagen was selling the old Passat, a car at the end of its product life cycle.

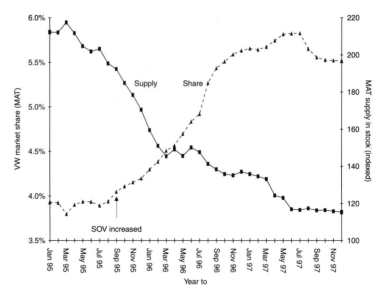

Figure 28: *Volkswagen UK market share versus supply of cars*
Source: SMMT, Volkswagen

TABLE 9: LACK OF IMMEDIATE AVAILABILITY WAS INCREASINGLY
CITED AS A REASON FOR NOT BUYING A VOLKSWAGEN[20]

	Pre-growth 1993–95	During growth 1996–97
Percentage citing 'Lack of availability' as reason for rejection of shortlisted VW	7.7%	13.2%
Index vs. market average	192	241

Base: People who shortlisted a Volkswagen but did not actually buy one
Source: NCBS[21]

More Attractive Price

The pattern and extent of Volkswagen's share growth cannot be attributed to pric
cutting. List prices were cut significantly between April 1993 and September 199
but there was only a relatively small uplift in market share. By contrast, there was
much smaller price cut between September 1995 and September 1997, yet this wa
the period when the most dramatic share growth occurred (Figures 29 and 30).

Furthermore, because Volkswagen and its dealers cut back on incentives its 'al
in' price position relative to its incentive-offering competitors became less attractiv
to prospective new car buyers.

---

20. This pattern is almost certainly due to the supply restrictions in 1996–97.
21. NCBS data is annual, covering – conveniently – the period from September through to the following
    August. For example, data from 1995 actually covers the last four months of 1994.

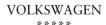

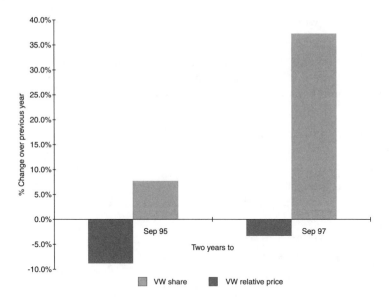

Figure 29: *Volkswagen UK share gains versus price changes*
Source: SMMT, Volkswagen

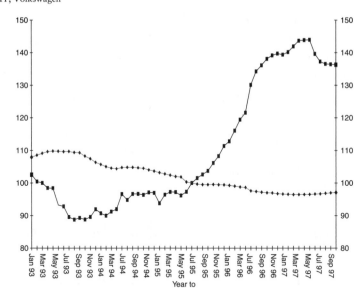

Figure 30: *Volkswagen UK share versus relative price*
Source: SMMT, Volkswagen

Better Distribution

Volkswagen's share growth was not driven by improvements in its distribution network:

— The number of dealerships decreased.

— There was no big programme to replace underperforming dealers with ones who had a greater talent for selling cars.

— The physical or working infrastructure of existing dealerships was not radicall altered.

— Customer experience of dealerships deteriorated slightly. (Given that the dealer had to cope with a massive increase in rate of sale between 1995 and 1997, thi marginal drop is hardly surprising.)

TABLE 10: UNSATISFACTORY SALES AND SERVICE QUALITY LEVELS
CITED AS A REASON FOR NOT BUYING A VOLKSWAGEN.

	Pre-growth (1993–95)	During-growth (1996–97)
Percentage citing 'Sales/Service' quality as reason for rejection of shortlisted VW	6.8%	10.5%
Index vs. market average	110	260

Base: people who shortlisted a Volkswagen but did not actually buy one
Source: NCBS

Better Fleet Marketing

In autumn 1995, Volkswagen increased its fleet marketing staff levels. However this expansion cannot explain the scale of Volkswagen's business success. Th proportion of Volkswagen's sales, which it was their primary role to deal witl (direct sales to medium-sized and large company fleets), decreased slightly an remained relatively small over the time during which Volkswagen's overall sale grew.

TABLE 11: VOLKSWAGEN DIRECT SALES TO CAR FLEETS 1995–97

	1995	1996	1997
Direct sales to fleet (units)	7245	9526	8514
Proportion of overall VW sales	8.8%	8.4%	7.1%

Source: Volkswagen

However, these figures (in isolation) underestimate their contribution. The nev staff also played an important secondary role: helping dealers to prepare for th launch of the new Passat, and helping to service those demand-driven, smaller flee accounts which were handled by the dealers rather than directly through flee marketing.

Direct Marketing

Volkswagen's direct marketing strategy changed in early 1996 and this nev strategy was demonstrably successful.[22] However, the absolute scale of this succes accounted for less than 5% of total sales. This cannot explain either the pattern o the extent of Volkswagen's share growth.[23]

Better PR

Finally, it is unlikely that Volkswagen's growth was due to the coverage it received in motoring magazines or on the motoring pages of national newspapers. We have no reason to believe that Volkswagen had any more coverage, relative to its competitors, during the last three years than in the period before share began to grow.[24]

Summary

Although it would be wholly unrealistic to suggest that these factors played no part in Volkswagen's recent business performance, none can explain either its pattern or magnitude. By contrast, the fact that the advertising worked exactly as planned, and that it corresponded with Volkswagen's market performance, suggests that it made a vital contribution to success.

But how can this contribution be disentangled from the other factors which were necessary for growth?

QUANTIFYING THE CONTRIBUTION OF ADVERTISING

There is no wholly satisfactory technique for isolating and quantifying the contribution made by advertising. Such a task is both methodologically complex and philosophically intractable – how, for example, can the effect of a particular advertising campaign be separated from the quality and attractiveness of the stories being advertised?

Nevertheless, we have employed two different methods (neither ideal) to try to assess the magnitude of the advertising effect:

— We compared the extent of Volkswagen's growth in the UK with the extent of its growth in the major continental markets during the same time period. Such a comparison led to the conclusion that 78% of UK growth was related to advertising.

---

2. Source: Barraclough Hall Woolston Gray's records of the number of Volkswagen sales attributable to their direct marketing activity.
3. The strategy changed from offering incentives to encouraging test drives at the time of model launches to targeting people who were in the active phase of the new car-buying process. Such a change makes isolating the relative effects of advertising and direct marketing a somewhat artificial exercise, as the two were intended to work synergistically: advertising increased the number of people who shortlisted Volkswagens as they entered the active phase of the new car-buying process, and then direct marketing converted a greater proportion of those shortlisters into actual buyers.
4. Unfortunately, there was no formal 'share of press' audit data to confirm this. However, we could make an inference based upon an interesting cross-cultural phenomenon: drivers on the continent are generally keener to read about cars than drivers in the UK. Accordingly, in the major European markets there are many more motoring magazines, with greater readership levels relative to population size. Thus, given that UK and continental car magazines are likely to have covered the same Volkswagen-related stories, it seems fair to assume that Volkswagen received more 'coverage per driver' in these markets than in the UK. Yet, as we have seen, share growth in the UK far exceeded share growth in these markets.

— We constructed an econometric model looking at Volkswagen's UK sale
performance. This model suggested that 70% of growth was related to
advertising.[25]

ESTIMATING THE BUSINESS RETURN OF THAT ADVERTISING

Taking the more conservative of these estimates, we have tried to gauge both the
direct and 'wider' business returns due to advertising, returns which have benefited
three key parties: Volkswagen UK, its dealer network, and its customers.

Benefits for Volkswagen UK

Assuming that 70% of Volkswagen UK's growth between September 1995 and
September 1997 can be related to its additional advertising investment, this equates
to 52,000 extra cars sold. Using NCBS data on the average price paid for a
Volkswagen over this period, this in turn equates to a revenue increase of £650
million.[26]

Volkswagen cannot publish details of its profit margins but we can assert with
the utmost confidence that it has already more than recouped the £29-million
increase in advertising investment which the strategy required.[27]

Bearing in mind that the advertising has already been profitable, it is worth
stressing that this £29-million investment will continue to generate returns for
many years to come. It is generally accepted that advertising can influence more
than short-term sales; this is certainly true in the car market where the average
purchase cycle is three years. It is therefore reasonable to assume the sales effects of
much of the advertising that ran in 1996 and 1997 won't become evident until, on
average, three years after it ran.[28]

But Volkswagen UK hasn't just benefited from extra sales; keeping demand
ahead of supply has enormous implications for the cost of doing business in the car
market:

— Storage costs have been substantially reduced.

— Additional revenue has been generated by astutely managing cash flow.

— More profitable 'up range' model variants have been sold.[29]

---

25. The similarity of the European comparison estimate to the estimate based on econometrics provides a
degree of cross-validation for the latter.
26. Estimate based on the average price paid for a new Volkswagen during this period according to NCBS
multiplied by 52,000.
27. This figure of £29 million overstates the investment made: it is based on Register-MEAL data and so does
not take account of the substantial discounts obtained by Volkswagen's media-buying agency.
28. For example, someone who last bought a new car in August 1995 might have shortlisted Polo as a
potential replacement for that car, having seen advertising which has run since then. However, because
they will not be actively 'in the market' for a new car until Summer 1998, the effect of this advertising will
not yet have had a chance to 'translate' into a sale.
29. Dealers have less financial necessity to sell existing surplus stock and therefore can order and sell cars

— Economies of scale have reduced unit costs.

— By attracting fewer incentive-hunting and potentially 'promiscuous' car buyers, it has improved the potential life-time value of its customer base.

And it has achieved much of this by re-investing, rather than simply increasing, its marketing budget.

Benefits for Volkswagen Dealers

The advertising benefits for dealers have been considerable. It has helped them to sell 52,000 more cars in the short term, and is likely to contribute to future sales. More significantly, because the increase in demand for Volkswagens allowed dealers to recover their profit margins, they have made more money on all the new Volkswagens they have sold since September 1995.

They have also benefited in two further ways:

— Many people who bought new Volkswagens did so having first traded in their old car; thus secondhand car sales have increased in value as a source of dealer income.

— After-sales and servicing revenues have increased because there are more Volkswagens on the road.

Perhaps most importantly from a long-term perspective, in helping to make the business of being a Volkswagen dealer more remunerative, advertising has helped to increase dealers' long-term enthusiasm and commitment to being holders of the Volkswagen franchise.

TABLE 12: OVERALL DEALER RATING OF THE VOLKSWAGEN FRANCHISE (SCORE OUT OF TEN)

	Winter 1995–6	Winter 1997–8
Volkswagen	6.1	8
(rank vs. comp.)	(6th)	(1st)
Competition Average	6.2	6.6

Base: Dealers who operate a franchise from that manufacturer
Competitive set: Ford, Vauxhall, Rover, Renault, Peugeot, Nissan
Source: RMI Dealer Attitude Survey

Consequently, these dealers are now willing to invest in future infrastructure changes which will be necessary to sustain Volkswagen's higher share position. Volkswagen will then be able to offer better service levels to its much expanded customer base. This is likely to translate into increased loyalty rates and, consequently, increased marketing efficiency. Thus, wholesaler gains, dealer gains and consumer gains are inextricably interlinked.

which are not already in stock.

Customer Gains

Volkswagen's customers have also benefited from advertising's contribution to demand levels for Volkswagen:

— People who bought new Volkswagens now retain a higher proportion of the money they paid when they come to sell them a few years later. This is because increased demand for new Volkswagens has reinforced (already high) resale values in the Volkswagen secondhand car market.[30]

— People are more likely to be able to obtain the exact model they want (in terms of variant and specification levels) because Volkswagen and its dealers can better predict exactly what they are likely to want.

CONCLUSION

Many marketing morals could be drawn from this case study:

— It adds weight to the view that advertising creativity and advertising effectiveness are mutually supportive objectives as the campaigns covered by this paper have, between them in the last two years, won every major creative award.

— It emphasises the importance of understanding not just purchase motivations but also purchase behaviour, and of isolating at what point in the consumer decision-making process marketing can have most effect.

— It demonstrates the wider benefits of advertising not just for the advertiser but for all its stakeholders.

However, two morals are key. First, this case highlights the wide-ranging benefits to a business of keeping demand ahead of supply and the power of advertising to do this. Second, and just as importantly, it emphasises that advertising is most effective when it has something good to say. It is only because Volkswagen had such a strong story to tell that its advertising was so effective.

---

30. For example, in November 1995 six-month-old three-door, one-litre Polos sold for 84% of their original purchase price. By March 1998 this figure, for the identical six-month-old variant, had increased to 91%. Such an increase in resale values leaves the average Volkswagen customer hundreds of pounds better off.

The Effectiveness Paradox

Adrian Hosford
British Telecom

As someone who has developed and run hundreds of different campaigns over the years, it was fascinating to analyse the 30 shortlisted campaigns. What struck me most forcefully was that it still comes down to the basics of marketing – that is, understanding customer needs and motivations; mapping the offer against the most powerful need that can be met better than the competition; coming up with a big idea that optimises the offer; putting it across with impact and empathy; aligning the best marketing mix behind the campaign; and sticking at it with determination. If these things are done well, success should follow.

Yet there is so much change happening to marketing – increasingly demanding and discerning consumers, new media and tools to reach people; increasing transparency and participation in the whole marketing process; growing fragmentation of markets and channels – that the basics have to be executed with higher and higher levels of sophistication.

Taking this paradox as a backdrop, listed below is my personal checklist of key lessons about advertising effectiveness. Each lesson is illustrated by reading the case studies. I have tried to highlight some of the most sophisticated or excellent examples in each area.

Understanding Customer Motivations

An in-depth understanding of the customer needs and motivations which make the market is required. How does it work from the consumer perceptive? Look at the whole system and how to leverage it. Volkswagen did this and moved its focus from sales incentives to getting on the buyer short list.

HEA recognised that the real need was for credible neutral information, not advice. One2One recognised that the real need in the mobile market is for 'rewarding conversations', while Imodium found that the critical customer need is confidence.

Mining where the Gold is

A causal understanding of the market system, together with an understanding of competitors' strengths, should allow you to pinpoint where the most leverage can be applied. Is there a powerful unmet or partially unmet customer need? Is there an over-concentration of activity in one part of the buying process?

Wallis spotted the unmet need for tbe 'forever 30' discerning brand in the fashion-conscious high street. Chicago Town Pizza spotted the over-concentration and reliance on Italian heritage in the pizza market, and Forbo-Nairn recognised a current need for 'good looks' which were practical in the floor-covering market.

Bacardi Breezer identified the unmet need for a 'refreshing alternative' for young beer drinkers, while the Army pinpointed the synergy between potential recruits' need for personal development and their own need for effective quality recruitment.

Finding a Human Truth with which to Align the Offer

To cut through and reach people in an overcrowded, noisy media market, it is necessary to resonate with the target audience as deeply and widely as possible. Aligning the offer to a meaningful human truth, which the target already believes in, not only makes this possible but will, in time, make it more and more effective (provided that it is credible). Aligning Marmite with the warm reassurance of a manly platoon running home plays into a real, universal human truth.

Batchelors Super Noodles used the human truth of 'how oddly men behave around food' in the home, while Littlewoods' appeal to 'our personal tendency to want to get the right football results' also hit a deep human truth.

Finding an Enduring Idea that Taps into that Human Truth

Campaigns seem to work far better if there is an enduring idea behind the presentation of the offer. If the idea is complementary to the identified human truth then it will be very effective. Olivio's big idea of taking the fun and joy epitomised by healthy Mediterranean life plays into our need for positive health. Colgate's idea of scientific reassurance plays into our sensitivity towards the issue of oral hygiene, while Ford Galaxy's was to reposition people movers as a new kind of superior luxury commensurate with the superiority enjoyed by first class travel. Finally, Polaroid's big idea of spontaneity tapped into the human truth of 'living for the moment'.

Communicating the Idea with Empathy and Impact

Time and time again these cases underlined the need for empathy at both an emotional and rational level. Johnson's Clean and Clear simply reapplied the same proposition with empathy to enjoy a major and provable uplift.

We all empathise with the absurd behaviour banks put us tbrough in order to look after our money, which was quirkily illustrated by First Direct. It is very easy for many of us to empathise with the 'successful but intelligent' buyer of an Audi particularly when contrasted with the 'successful but flash' alternative. HEA's presentation of credible neutral information connected with youth through empathic situations and language.

Keeping at it

It is so easy for the agency or client, fuelled by the ambitions of new account or brand-team changes, to want to move on. The enduring success of Marmite over ten years, while displaying most characteristics of the above checklist, is a classic example of the benefits of sticking at it. Volkswagen's track record is also starting to reap the rewards of such a policy. One2One is heading in the same direction with a consistent track record of 'rewarding conversations'. 'Ownership of the future' by Orange likewise demonstrated the clear gains of consistency.

Keeping it Fresh and Relevant

Finally, keeping at it does not mean standing still. There is ample evidence that the idea and presentation must be kept fresh and relevant. Impulse is an excellent example of how to contemporise the idea of 'acting on impulse'. The Famous Grouse took their well-established 'icon' and modernised it successfully to arrest a serious market situation.

Section 2

Four-Star Winners

★★★★★

8

Christian Aid
Strengthening the Poor

EDITOR'S SUMMARY

This case shows how advertising can break the conventional fund-raising paradigm of shocking but negative images and build a positive definition of a charity both internally and externally.

A Misunderstood Organisation Facing Compassion Fatigue

In the early 1990s Christian Aid had a low profile. Most people thought that it was a Christian missionary organisation. The collector base which Christian Aid relied upon to deliver envelopes was dwindling. More people were fed up with donating money to the Third world without the situation seeming to improve.

In response Christian Aid and Partners BDDH overturned the conventions of Third World charity advertising. The traditional fund-raising paradigm of hunger, disease and death was replaced by a call to give the Third World quality of life, summed up in the end-line: 'We believe in life before death.'

Results and Payback

The results of taking this bold stance were dramatic. The amount raised from 1991 Christian Aid Week reached a staggering £10.04 million, a 52% increase. But this was not a temporary reversal. By 1997, each TVR brought in £45,095 compared to £34,437 in 1991. At the same time there is evidence that other main sources of giving – legacies and covenants – were stimulated, turning around a long-term decline and bucking a trend in the Third World charity marketplace. Additional income, including increases in legacies, is estimated at £20 million plus.

The signs of advertising being at work include dramatic shifts in brand awareness with no other discernible source, decreases in misunderstanding of what Christian Aid actually does, and a clearer understanding of Christian Aid's real mission – working with the poor to ensure a better quality of life. Following the advertising the proportion of people who said they would donate to Christian Aid in 1997, had increased by a massive 60%. There is also evidence that the advertising built the confidence of collectors, with higher numbers of envelopes being delivered and collected.

205

INTRODUCTION

This paper shows how advertising built Christian Aid Week income to a radical new level in 1991 during a severe recession, and maintained this level despite reduced advertising budgets and a step change in competitive activity throughout the 1990s. The contributions of advertising to this success were in raising awareness, building a clear and trusted brand and giving compelling messages about the Third World and why people should give. But the Christian Aid advertising did much more than this. It encouraged Christian Aid Week collectors, the 'salesforce', to have the confidence to 'go the extra mile'.[1]

What is Christian Aid?

Christian Aid, the official agency of 40 British and Irish churches, works with the world's poorest communities primarily in the Third World. In partnership with local people and organisations, it encourages self-help and independence. Its mission statement 'To strengthen the poor' reflects a belief that the poor in the Third World should have the right to determine their own destiny, finding local solutions to local problems. Christian Aid works with 700 local partners in over 60 countries and, in accordance with Christian principles, helps the poor irrespective of their faith.

The largest proportion of the voluntary income Christian Aid raises (approximately 40%) comes from one week a year – Christian Aid Week – in May. During this week a small army of 250,000 collectors visit households across the UK with the well-known red envelopes.

Charitable Giving in the 1990s

An apparent rise in voluntary contributions from £1,185 million in 1990 to an estimated £1,520 million in 1997 evaporates when inflation is factored in. In real terms, giving in 1997 was only 1.7% ahead of the level at the beginning of the decade (Family Expenditure Survey, ONS). To make matters worse, this is being shared out among a rapidly increasing number of charities. In 1990, 171,434 charities were registered with the Charities Commission and in 1995 this figure had climbed to 181,467.

---

1. The period we will be examining is 1991 to 1997.

Why was Charitable Giving Static?

There were three main reasons which combined to thwart the development of the 'caring 1990s':

1. The recession.

2. Compassion fatigue.

3. Charity cynicism.

The recession

When times are hard, the first items of expenditure to be cut are 'unnecessary' items like trips to the cinema, premium foods and giving to charity.

In fact it has been shown (Dimensions of the Voluntary Sector, CAF 1997) that a 10% rise in income increases the probability of giving to charity by 1% and furthermore the size of donations increases by over 10%. Charitable giving thus behaves as a luxury item and is severely affected by personal economic circumstance.

There was a deep recession between 1988 and 1992 which had a profound effect on consumer spending levels. When Partners BDDH's Christian Aid campaign commenced in 1991, there was the highest recorded level of contraction in consumer spending for years (Figure 1).

Household disposable income has increased only slightly (less than 0.9% a year) between 1991 and 1996 (Office for National Statistics) and even this feeble level of growth has been largely diverted into savings and pensions, that is, self-interested expenditure rather than charity giving.

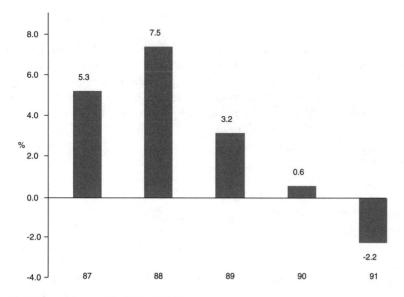

Figure 1: *Change in consumer spending 1987–1991 (%)*
Source: The Henley Centre

Compassion fatigue

Evidence of compassion fatigue began to appear after the popularisation of TV events in the early 1990s. *Comic Relief*, ITV's *Telethon* and BBC's *Children in Need* had contributed £72.6 million revenue in 1990 but only £56.8 million in 1992: a decline of 22%. ITV's decision in 1993 to end the *Telethon* reflected this trend. There was an increased familiarity with the problems portrayed. This was especially true of the Third World and gave rise to an increasing professed immunity to shocking images as portrayed in the news and in normal Third World charity advertising. Consumers in group discussions were referring to 'flies on faces' pictures. The NOP tracking study commissioned by Christian Aid in 1991 showed that 62% of adults agreed with the statement 'I am getting fed up with being asked to donate money year after year for the Third World without the situation ever seeming to improve'.

Charity cynicism

The prevailing 'look after number one' philosophy of the 1980s formed the background to a more cynical view of charities, particularly Third World charities which were getting a bad press. A number of cases of inefficiency were coming to light. War on Want, in the same sector as Christian Aid, almost collapsed in 1990. In 1991, NOP research revealed that 75% of adults were 'worried that charities spend too much on administration' and 71% believed that the 'Government needs to have greater control over what charities do and how they spend money which is donated to them'.

FACTORS AFFECTING CHRISTIAN AID MORE DIRECTLY

How was the Third World Charity Sector Faring?

Giving to International Aid as a proportion of total voluntary contributions had undergone a dramatic decline since the mid 1980s. In 1984 to 1985 this was 25.5% and by 1989 to 1990 it had shrunk to 13.2%, just over half its former figure.

Data from the NOP tracking study conducted for Christian Aid immediately prior to the Partners BDDH's advertising campaign in 1991 showed that only 10% of UK adults ranked the Third World as a first priority out of five sectors.

In addition, Partners BDDH isolated three main issues that were more specific to Christian Aid:

1. Low awareness.

2. Poor brand understanding.

3. Difficulty in collecting donations.

Low Awareness

Christian Aid was one of the smaller and less well-known Third World charities. In 1990, for example, Oxfam raised £45 million and Save the Children raised £38 million, compared to Christian Aid's £18 million).

In 1991, before the campaign commenced, awareness figures compared poorly with other leading Third World charities (Table 1).

TABLE 1: BRAND AWARENESS OF THIRD WORLD CHARITIES – 1991

	Spontaneous %	Prompted %
Oxfam	45	97
Save The Children	31	94
Red Cross	10	94
Christian Aid	5	80

Base: All Adults
Source: NOP, 1991

In 1991, 61% of adults agreed that Christian Aid is 'a charity you don't hear much about' (NOP). The wider gap between spontaneous and prompted awareness of Christian Aid highlights the difficulties of remaining salient throughout the year with only one week of major advertising support.

There was another awareness problem. Christian Aid Week itself was losing its distinctiveness. By 1997, there were 56 other national weeks promoting major charities and in May 1997 alone there were five major charity weeks other than Christian Aid's.

Poor brand understanding
A more profound and intransigent problem for Christian Aid was that it was misunderstood. Relative to such charities as Save The Children and Freedom From Hunger, with their descriptive names, Christian Aid was often thought to help only Christians or to propagate Christianity. The majority (60%) of adults questioned in 1991 believed that Christian Aid was a missionary organisation (NOP). With this misunderstanding and lack of awareness came a lack of trust: 52% agreed that 'It's a charity where you're never quite sure what happens to your money' (NOP).

Difficulty in collecting donations
Christian Aid had pioneered the use of envelopes which were delivered door-to-door, often being described in qualitative research as 'the envelope charity'. Yet this unique position was rapidly being eroded. Partners BDDH qualitative research revealed that envelopes were regularly being delivered by an increasing number of local and national charities.

The coverage of Christian Aid's collectors had shrunk to just 48% of UK homes and envelopes were only picked up at 56% of these. There were several reasons for this.

First, door-to-door collecting had become more difficult in urban areas due to the proliferation of remote entry systems. Second, the rise in women working meant that they were less likely to be at home at the key collection time (early weekday evenings). Third, there was increasing danger in walking the streets easily identifiable as someone carrying money. Collectors tend to be over 60, female and feel particularly vulnerable. Fourth, collectors are mainly recruited through mainstream churches where attendance is falling (Table 2).

As Mintel noted in 1994, 'The steady decline in ... churchgoers may result in difficulties in raising funds for religious charities such as Christian Aid.' As the

number of older people for whom giving money and their services to the Church is
an accepted practice reduces, so the religious missionary (sic) charity sector will be
affected.

TABLE 2: CHURCH OF ENGLAND MEMBERSHIP 1975–1992

	1975	1980	1992
Adult Church Members (millions)	2.30	2.18	1.81
Index 1975 = 100	100	98	79

Source: CSO/Social Trends

Furthermore, a proportion of Christian Aid week income is given by
congregations in church, thus placing a further burden on income levels.

In line with the church trend, religious-based charities were experiencing
difficulties. UK adults ranked religious/missionary charities 13th out of 15 types as
charities 'which are held to be most appealing or worthwhile' (Mintel, 1997). This
ranking was three places lower than international aid charities.

CHRISTIAN AID'S INCOME TO 1990

Christian Aid's income was therefore under long-term threat. Although in the four
years prior to the start of the Partners BDDH advertising campaign in 1991
Christian Aid Week's income had shown modest increases, these equated to a 13%
drop after inflation. Worse, compared to the total charity market, Christian Aid
Week's share fell by 25.5% over this period.

TABLE 3: CHRISTIAN AID'S MARKET SHARE 1987–1990

Year	Prompted voluntary giving*	CAW income as a % of prompted voluntary giving
1987	578.6	1.02
1988	710.7	0.87
1989	778.0	0.80
1990	866.7 (+49.8%)	0.76 (-25.5%)

Source: CAF/Christian Aid
Note: *Voluntary contributions minus legacies and covenants

If this reduction had continued, Christian Aid Week's share in 1997 would
have shrunk to approximately 0.5% (Figure 2). This dramatic reduction in share
was also visible as a proportion of Third World voluntary donations, the immediate
competitive set. Measured against major Third World charity brands, Christian Aid
Week's share had dropped by 9% over the three years before the campaign
(Table 4).

This decline is thrown into relief if you consider that if Christian Aid's income
had grown in line with the market from 1987 it would have reached £8.4 million in
1990, 27% higher than the £6.6 million actually achieved (Table 5).

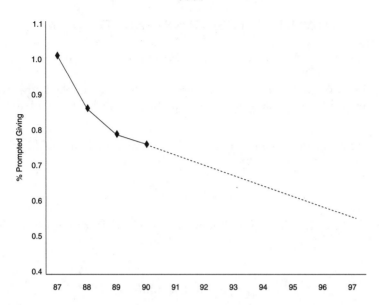

Figure 2: *Christian Aid Week income*
Source: CAF/Christian Aid

TABLE 4: CHRISTIAN AID'S DECLINING SHARE OF THIRD WORLD CONTRIBUTIONS

Calendar year	Third World voluntary income £m (excluding retail, legacies)	Christian Aid Week income £m	Christian Aid Week share %
1987	87.0	5.9	6.8
1988	105.0	6.2	5.9
1989	101.5	6.2	6.1
1990	106.4	6.6	6.2

Based on the 1987 Top 10 Third World charities
Excludes War on Want
Source: CAF

TABLE 5: CHRISTIAN AID WEEK INCOME PROJECTIONS 1987–1990

	Total charitable household contributions £m	Index 1990 = 100	Projected Christian Aid Week income £m
1987	835	100	(5.9)
1988	927	110	6.5
1989	958	115	6.8
1990	1185	142	8.4

Source: Family Expenditure Survey/ONS

In short, the early 1990s in the UK would not have been the best time or place to start a religious-based international aid charity.

ADVERTISING OBJECTIVES AND STRATEGY

Advertising Objectives

1. To make sure that when the envelope is delivered people know that it is Christian Aid Week, understand and empathise with Christian Aid and so want to give.

2. To inspire collectors to deliver to and collect from more households.

Core Proposition

'Give now to help the Third World poor exercise their right to a decent life before death.'

Target: All UK Adults

The advertising needed to reflect Christian Aid's beliefs, expressed in 'To Strengthen the Poor' in such a way as to be accessible to a broader public beyond supporters. Christian Aid stipulated the wide advertising target audience of all adults, wishing to give as many people as possible the chance to help rather than concentrating on an older, female, more up-market audience who are known to donate more to charity. The advertising was not only aimed at those who received a Christian Aid envelope but those who could respond to other campaigns throughout the year, and who might become regular donors.

It was decided to adopt a new creative strategy, changing from the launch of a new topical theme each year to one theme which could be built up and expanded over several years. Partners BDDH developed a campaign theme: 'We believe in life before death.' The idea was readily understood by respondents in research in 1991. It communicated a desire to give the poor a life which was of true quality rather than mere existence. The Christian overtones of the line were seen as uniquely appropriate to Christian Aid, thereby helping branding and memorability.

This theme broke the conventions of the Third World charity sector. It presented a radical view of the Third World which was removed from the stereotypes of traditional charity advertising, taking the issues beyond hunger and disease into dignity and purpose.

Partners BDDH produced TV executions with supporting press targeted at light TV viewers, opinion formers in Government and the media, the staff of Christian Aid and other non-governmental organisations.

THE MEDIA STRATEGY

The original media strategy was devised by CIA Billett and was developed from 1993 onwards by John Ayling Associates (JAA).

TV ADS

I have survived hunger.

I have survived cholera.

I have survived eviction.

I have survived war.

But I don't want my granddaughter to survive.

I want her to *live*.

Please help us in Christian Aid Week.

PRESS ADS

Using TV was a relatively new strategy for Christian Aid. We continued to employ a church and national press campaign (approximately 15% of expenditure) in order to communicate with Christian Aid's core constituency and increase light TV viewers' opportunities to see.

TV advertising was closely linked to the activities of collectors who deliver envelopes on Monday and Tuesday of Christian Aid Week and collect them between Wednesday and Friday. Airtime was weighted towards the five days prior to Christian Aid Week to maximise awareness build before envelope delivery. During the week itself, airtime was concentrated in the early peak period when collectors would be knocking on doors.

Real budget levels have diminished over the campaign period and so JAA have become more focused in choice of TV regions and in press titles. They now allocate TV budget broadly in line with Christian Aid's regional strengths and have added radio in London to compensate for the expense of TV in that key giving region.

THE RESULTS OF ADVERTISING

Advertising and Income

Christian Aid Week in 1991, featuring the launch of the 'We believe in Life Before Death' campaign was the most successful in Christian Aid's history (Table 6). The total level of donations increased by a record 52%, equating to an increase of £3.4 million.

'Christian Aid Week 1991 with its compelling theme "Do you believe in life before death?" challenged millions at a time when one disaster after another had its impact on public opinion and sympathy. It was the start of Christian Aid's most successful fund-raising year ever.'

Michael Taylor, Christian Aid's Director, in the annual statement, 1992

TABLE 6: CHRISTIAN AID WEEK INCOME 1987–1997

Year	CAW Income £m	Index 1987 = 100
1987	5.90	100
1988	6.15	104
1989	6.20	105
1990	6.60	111
1991	10.04	170
1992	9.08	153
1993	9.09	154
1994	9.23	156
1995	8.90	151
1996	8.84	149
1997	9.47	161

Source: Christian Aid

This step change in income levels has been maintained for the subsequent six years. The week's income for four years before the Partners BDDH advertising was £6.2 million. In subsequent years, this average was £9.2 million.

Advertising and Share of Donations

In addition to the sustained rise in Christian Aid Week income, Christian Aid's decline in share of total prompted voluntary giving was halted. From its nadir of 0.76% in 1990 it improved to an average of 0.88% in the years 1991 to 1997. The decline in Christian Aid Week relative to other Third World Charities was also arrested (Table 7).

TABLE 7: CHRISTIAN AID SHARE OF THIRD WORLD VOLUNTARY INCOME

Calendar year	Third World voluntary income £m (excluding retail, legacies)	Christian Aid Week income £m	Christian Aid Week share %
1987	87.0	5.9	6.8
1988	105.0	6.2	5.9
1989	101.5	6.2	6.1
1990	106.4	6.6	6.2
1991	138.4	10.0	7.2
1992	127.1	9.1	7.2
1993	123.2	9.1	7.4
1994	132.7	9.2	6.9
1995	123.3	8.9	7.2

Based on the 1987 Top 10 Third World charities – War on Want. Data for calendar years 1996 and 1997 unavailable
Source: CAF/Christian Aid

This share increase also tells us that Christian Aid was doing better than its closest competitors, and not merely benefiting from market growth. This share level (about 7%) has been maintained at a significantly higher level than before the advertising. The decline in share has been dramatically turned around.

Advertising and Brand Measures

Partners BDDH had defined the roles of advertising as generating brand awareness, promoting understanding, empathy and trust of the Christian Aid brand and helping to motivate collectors.

Brand awareness
Brand awareness of Christian Aid had been stable for several years before the period covered in this paper. Spontaneous brand awareness was at 5% and prompted at 80% in 1991, before the campaign commenced. During Partners BDDH's advertising campaign spontaneous brand awareness was boosted significantly each year (Table 8).

TABLE 8: CHRISTIAN AID SPONTANEOUS BRAND AWARENESS
1991–1997

	Pre %	Post %
1991	5	23
1992	7	21
1993	8	24
1994	6	21
1995	5	14
1996	10	19
1997	10	20

Base: All adults
Source: NOP

The same pattern is evident in prompted awareness. The trended awareness levels also show a steady improvement. The relatively low levels of post-brand awareness after 1995 can be explained by the reduction in the number of TVRs over this period, discussed below.

Encouragingly, the base level of prompted awareness in the pre-Christian Aid Week measure has increased steadily from its original level of 80% to 87% in 1997 – a 'ratchet effect' on brand awareness outlasting Christian Aid Week itself. The Third World charity sector as a whole was not becoming more salient and simply carrying Christian Aid with it. The levels of awareness for market leader Oxfam were also measured and found not to have moved significantly. In addition, fewer people agreed that Christian Aid is 'A charity you don't hear much about'. By 1997, the number agreeing had been dramatically reduced by over one-third, from 62% to 38% (NOP).

Brand understanding, empathy and trust

Attitudes which had been identified as important in determining propensity to support Christian Aid (Partners BDDH qualitative research, 1991) have consistently improved throughout the campaign. The misunderstanding that Christian Aid is a missionary organisation and the worry that Christian Aid is a charity where 'You are never quite sure what happens to your money' have been consistently reduced, the latter to approximately half its former level (Figure 3).

However, there is one image statement which provides direct evidence of a link between the advertising and the shift in empathy and understanding of Christian Aid. The statement 'Works to ensure the poor have a better quality of life' is related to the campaign's end line 'We believe in life before death'. This measure has improved steadily from the first time it was measured (Figure 4). This repositioning of the brand was further supported in qualitative creative development research each year among Christian Aid collectors and the general public.

Advertising and Behaviour

In addition to shifts in awareness and image, reported propensity to give was changing. In the third year of the campaign, respondents were asked which charities they would donate to if they had not already done so that year and which they would never donate to. In 1993, 5% said they would donate to Christian Aid and in 1997 this rose to 8%, the equivalent of an extra 1.1 million people being motivated. The proportion who would never give to Christian Aid dropped from 4% to 2% over the same period, down by 0.76 million.

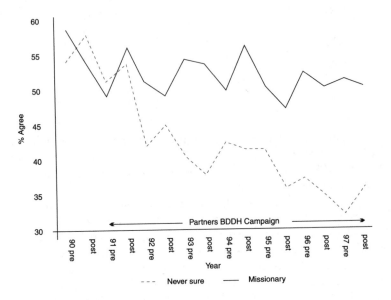

Figure 3: *Change in Christian Aid brand measures 1990–1997*
Source: NOP

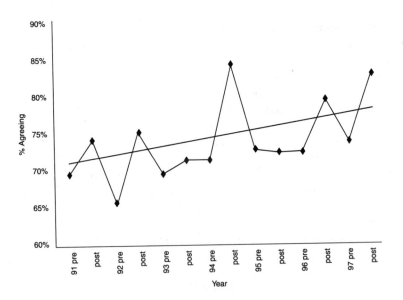

Figure 4: *Christian Aid works with the poor the ensure a better quality of life 1991–1997*
Source: NOP

DIRECT EVIDENCE OF THE EFFECTS OF ADVERTISING

We first review a regional test that was carried out in 1996 and 1997. We then examine the advertising's effect on collectors.

Regional Test

In 1996, Partners BDDH and John Ayling Associates devised a regional test plan to determine the sensitivity of income to varying advertising levels. This involved a two-year TV upweight/downweight test. For 1996 and 1997 the effects of varying the levels of advertising expenditure, on income, awareness and brand image, have been monitored.

The effects on income
Previous experience showed that regional influences on Christian Aid income are the strength of church-going (and therefore the collector network) and the predisposition of the population to support Third World charities. We measure the latter with the TGI Overseas Relief Index (Table 9).

For the test we chose two TV regions that were similar to each other in their propensity to donate to 'Overseas Relief' charities. They also had no particular strengths or weaknesses in churchgoing and in the number of collectors. This we inferred by comparing how likely each region was to give to overseas charities with the success of Christian Aid in that TV region.

We also needed to choose small areas that did not represent a great risk to income. We decided on Anglia (6.68% of net homes) for upweight, almost doubling the TVR level in 1996. West Country (2.90% of net homes) was the downweight area where we halved TVRs.

TABLE 9: REGIONAL STRENGTHS OF CHRISTIAN AID VERSUS THIRD WORLD SECTOR

ITV region	1995 Christian Aid Week income indexed on net homes	Gave to overseas relief TGI Index (100 = Average)
Grampian	162	101
Central Scotland	134	103
Wales and West	117	107
Granada/Border	110	141
Anglia	**107**	89
West Country	**102**	82
Meridian	99	93
Central	88	96
London	87	115
Yorks/Tyne Tees	78	94

Source: JAA/Christian Aid

Significant differences in brand awareness developed, as expected, but more importantly Christian Aid Week income changed. Anglia's income grew by 13.7% in the two years of upweight whereas the West Country's income remained the same.

Over this period, the rest of the UK's Christian Aid Week income grew by
5.4%. This makes the static picture in the West Country one of relative decline.
Anglia's income grew more than the rest of the UK.

TABLE 10: RELATIVE CHANGES IN CHRISTIAN AID WEEK INCOME 1995 TO 1997

ITV area	Total change in TVRs 1995 to 1997 (%)	Total income change 1995 to 1997 (%)	Net Improvement in income relative to rest of the UK 1995 to 1997
Anglia	+73.5	+13.7	+8.3
West Country	-67.2	0	-5.4

Source: Christian Aid/JAA

To ensure that these movements were not the result of a change in giving to
Third World charities in these regions, movements in their TGI Overseas Relief
indices were tracked. Anglia's index had dropped to 75 in 1997, making the
increase in income even greater, relative to overall Third World giving, in that
region. The West Country's index had remained the same, at 82.

Other factors which could have had a regional influence were also discounted:
Christian Aid informed us that there were no significant fluctuations in collector
numbers, the weather or fund-raising events in these regions.

Helping to Motivate Collectors

The other powerful effect of advertising was in motivating collectors, the
'salesforce'. Ease of recruiting collectors each year for Christian Aid was made
harder by the dwindling church congregations and their ageing profile. Yet it was
not expected that the advertising would have any direct effect on the recruitment of
new collectors, as this was the responsibility of local organisers in churches whose
persuasion skills were far more important.

It was more likely that advertising effects would be found in motivating
collectors to deliver envelopes to more households or to return more often to those
households to collect. The number of households visited in a given collector's
'patch' was reported not to change much from year to year. Collectors tend to visit
a certain number of streets they know and where they will be known. It was more
likely that any advertising effect would manifest itself in the tenacity of collectors in
returning to these streets more often. Seeing the campaign would act as a call to
action for collectors to return and reassure them that they were expected, being part
of a nationwide, high-profile event.

In fact there is evidence to suggest that the advertising was working as a call to
action, motivating collectors to pick up more envelopes (Table 11).

The proportion of envelopes collected has shown a sustained increase over the
advertised period, apart from 1997. This dip can be explained by the weather. May
1997 was a very high rainfall month: 78mm compared to the May average for the
previous ten years of 53mm (Meteorological Office).

TABLE 11: CHRISTIAN AID WEEK COLLECTION PATTERNS 1991–1997

	Envelopes delivered % UK households	Envelopes collected % UK households	Proportion collected % delivered
1991	48	27	56
1992	49	32	65
1993	52	35	67
1994	50	39	78
1995	47	34	72
1996	44	32	73
1997	49	32	65

Source: NOP

Further evidence of a direct effect on collectors can be found by analysing the data from the upweight/downweight test regions. Anglia and the West Country had been chosen for their average collector network strengths and people in both regions have similar propensities to give to Christian Aid as Table 12 shows for 1997.

What separates the regions is that by 1997, Anglia, the upweight region, had become the region with the highest recorded donor households, and the West Country, the downweight region, was joint lowest.

TABLE 12: CHRISTIAN AID REGIONAL COLLECTION PATTERNS 1997

ITV region	Propensity to give to Christian Aid (% adults, post wave 1997)	Delivery of envelope (% households 1997)	Donated in Christian Aid Week (% households 1997)
Anglia	31	54	41
STV	46	63	39
Yorks&TyneTees	38	50	35
Ulster	36	45	33
Central	31	49	33
HTV	29	52	28
Meridian	30	36	24
Carlton	29	45	24
Granada	44	57	18
West Country	29	40	18
National	32	49	28

Source: NOP

The notable difference in donating households seen can be explained by a higher number of envelopes being delivered and more being collected: 74% were collected in Anglia as opposed to 60% in the West Country. It is no surprise that local organisers in the West Country were pushing for a reinstatement of TV advertising to its former weights. This was subsequently promised for Christian Aid Week 1998.

How was the advertising motivating collectors?

Quantitative research in 1998 explained how the advertising motivated collectors. The majority reported that they considered the advertising was effective (65%), helped when collecting (59%) and motivated them (55%). As hypothesised above, fewer believed that the advertising would help with collector recruitment (33%). In addition to serving as a call to action, collectors gained a sense of confidence from knowing that advertising was being broadcast. They reported that people 'would be more receptive to their visit' (41%), were 'more aware of Christian Aid Week' (76%), that it gave collectors 'something to talk about on the doorstep' (35%) and that the advertisements 'promoted understanding of Christian Aid' (48%).

In qualitative research they told us:

'It makes one feel that I'm part of a national thing. People are expecting you.'

Collector, female, age 45–54, Carlton

'A lot of people don't know about Christian Aid. It makes people think of Christian Aid and make donations.'

Collector, male, age 65+, Meridian

ELIMINATING OTHER VARIABLES AFFECTING CHRISTIAN AID WEEK INCOME

Were there any Population and Demographic Changes Which May have Helped Christian Aid?

Although Christian Aid's target is all adults, females aged 45+ are known to give more to charity. This segment has grown by 5% between 1990 and 1997, but there is no evidence to suggest that this group is particularly generous to Third World charities. Another factor which could have helped Christian Aid is the overall increase in the number of households. However, the number of households giving to charity has decreased during the 1990s (Family Expenditure Survey).

Did Changes in the Economy Favour Giving to Christian Aid?

Although there was a relative recovery of GDP in the 1990s, spending and consumer confidence remained depressed (Henley Centre). Savings and pensions benefited, not charitable giving.

Did the Market Become Less Competitive?

No. The growth in the number of charities continued and the approximate number of new charities being registered is now running at 9,000 per year (Mintel, 1998). Advertising expenditures for the charity sector have continued to rise steeply as more organisations took advantage of the 1989 change in the law allowing charity advertising on TV. This was particularly true of aggressively successful direct response TV using the sort of portrayal of the poor that Christian Aid found undignified. Furthermore, the number of charity shops, a sector in which Christian Aid is not represented, has more than doubled since 1992 (Mintel).

Did the Public Become More Positive Towards the Third World?

The downward trend in voluntary contributions up to 1995 subsequently continued. TGI shows the proportion of UK adults giving more than £5 to Third World charities in a year decreased from 9% in 1991 to 6% in 1997.

Did any other Marketing Activity Affect Awareness?

NOP measured all sources of brand awareness during Christian Aid Week. TV advertising consistently came top and other sources such as PR and the envelope remained relatively constant.

Could the Advertising Effect be Explained by the Move to TV Advertising?

This was certainly responsible for some of the campaign's success and, of course, one part of the effect of advertising rather than an external factor. Christian Aid had conducted a regional TV test in 1990 and obtained a 6% increase in income in TV-supported regions with similar advertising weights to those later used in 1991. This effect was clearly of a lower magnitude than the 52% increase obtained in 1991, and the 1991 increase in giving in those regions that had enjoyed TV support in 1990 as part of the test was as pronounced as in the rest of the country. The change in message was more influential than the change in medium.

FURTHER CONTRIBUTIONS OF ADVERTISING TO THE BOTTOM LINE

The sustained increase in income during Christian Aid Week was obtained despite a background of a reduction in the amount of advertising. This was partly as a result of a sensitivity to public concerns about the fund-raising expenditure of charities. In fact, over the 1987 to 1997 period the proportion of income spent by Christian Aid on fund-raising remained in line with the top 200 charities (CAF).

Media inflation, in particular TV, has progressively reduced the power to reach people during Christian Aid Week.

The number of TVRs actually achieved in 1997 was 30% less than in 1991 (Table 13). Furthermore, as Christian Aid's real advertising expenditure levels were falling, the rest of the sector was rising. From 1991 to 1997 Christian Aid's share of voice of the charity sector has declined by 40% to just 2.6%.

If the level of advertising as measured by TVRs is compared to Christian Aid Week income, we see an increasing efficiency of advertising as the campaign developed from 1991. In this year, for every TVR bought, income of £34,437 was collected. By 1997 the ratio had risen to £45,095 for every TVR, a rise of 31%. If the base taken is 1992, in order to eliminate any novelty effects, the increase is even more striking at 75%.

The proportion of Christian Aid income accounted for by Christian Aid Week has risen from an average of 33.9% for the four years prior to the advertising to an average of 37.1% during the campaign.

TABLE 13: CHRISTIAN AID TV ADVERTISING WEIGHTS 1991–1997

Year	Network ABC1 adult TVRs in CAW
1991	302
1992	352
1993	252
1994	244
1995	215
1996	225
1997	210

Source: JAA/Register MEAL/MMS

Income Other than Christian Aid Week

The advertising also seems to have had an effect on covenanted giving or inclusion in a legacy. The proportion of these types of giving for Christian Aid was declining before the advertising. This was in marked contrast to the other top ten Third World charities whose proportion of legacy and covenanted income had risen from 28% in 1987 to 32% in 1990 and would go on rising until it reached 38% in 1993.

For Christian Aid in 1991 the proportion continued to decline, perhaps to be expected given that income from wills written in 1991 would not make a significant contribution in the first year. After 1992 however, the decline was reversed and Christian Aid's committed giving is now growing strongly (Figure 5).

In contrast, that of the other Third World charities is now declining from its peak in 1993. There was virtually no change in the small amount of advertising for legacies (one or two executions in legal year books) and no appreciable increase in other legacy marketing activity which would have affected income in this period.

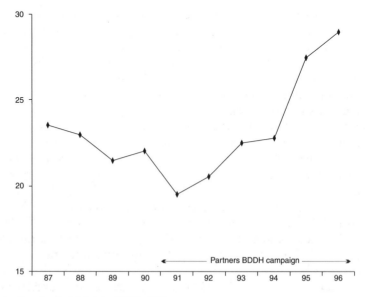

Figure 5: *Proportion of committed giving 1987 to 1996*
Source: Christian Aid

CONCLUSIONS

Despite a tough economic environment, little growth in overall charitable donations and increasing competition, Partners BDDH's campaign contributed significantly to the reversal in fortunes of Christian Aid Week, the charity's single most important source of contributions.

Not only did income rise to a new level, but the decline in Christian Aid's shares of the charity market and Third World charities was reversed. Awareness and understanding of the Christian Aid brand and a consistent and powerful advertising campaign contributed to a greater willingness to give.

Furthermore the advertising influenced another key stage in the process of raising income, in helping to motivate collectors.

Christian Aid's sources of income other than Christian Aid week were also influenced, but over the period of Partners BDDH's campaign the total extra contribution of Christian Aid Week income alone, calculated by extrapolating the income trend for the four years prior to 1991, works out at an additional £15 million. However, this is an underestimate. Even if only half of the increase in committed giving were accounted for by advertising, this would add £5.03 million to the above figure, bringing the total to just over £20 million. It is not possible to reveal the advertising expenditure, but the total incremental income is many times what was invested.

9

La Dolce Vita

*How Olivio learned to enjoy life with
retailer brands*

EDITOR'S SUMMARY

The rise of Retailers Own Brand (ROB) is one of the marketing dilemmas of the Nineties. This paper argues that, in an age of rapid technological advance, 'Future-Relevant' emotion is the principal source of sustainable competitive advantage. It goes on to argue that the concept of advertising effectiveness should be further reframed to embrace the epistemic payback that clients receive as a result of its agency's work on strategy development.

Relaunching Olivio on its Emotional Relevance

Within one month of Olivio going to test the market, Sainsbury and Tesco had produced their own brand versions and in less than a year ROB was selling more than Olivio. Based on a product truth, Olivio's launch advertising had built a category but not a brand. Consumers could see no difference between Olivio and ROB.

Research identified an emerging trend towards 'Positive Health' where people sought a stress-free approach to health and life. Being a future trend, it was one that own-label had not yet been able to spot. There was an opportunity to link this phenomenon with Olivio via olive oil's Mediterranean origins.

Results and Payback

Volumes grew from an 8% year-on-year decline in 1995 to 53% growth in 1996 and a further 63% growth in 1997. Over the same period, the price premium over ROB increased. Indeed, so complete has been Olivio's turnaround that ROB users are now trading upward into the brand.

A model was used to isolate the volume directly attributable to the advertising. This indicated that Olivio sold over 13 million more tubs of margarine and sales were 148% higher than they would have been had Van den Bergh not advertised. From the econometric model, it is estimated that total advertising expenditure will payback in November 1998.

INTRODUCTION

The inexorable rise of Retailers Own Brand (ROB) is one of the marketing dilemmas of the 1990s.

History tells us that nobody is safe:

> 'In 1994 Sainsbury launched Classic Cola directly against the giants. This proved highly successful, taking over 60% of the cola market in Sainsbury compared with only 20% for own label previously, and this share has been held.'

> Source: Dr Stephen Buck, Admap, March 1995

Conventional wisdom says that once problems set in, the situation is irreversible:

> 'It seems to be a general rule that once premium brands lose their franchise in a particular product field it is almost impossible for manufacturers to regain their former dominance.'

> Source: Dr Stephen Buck, Director Taylor Nelson, 1995

Theorists maintain that the only way to compete with ROB is via continual product innovation, focusing on each succeeding product difference in the creation of 'new news' persuasion advertising:

> 'The key to profitably competing with private label brands is through "Sales-Effective" or "Persuasive" advertising as measured by ARS persuasion metrics. [This means] ... as Bob McCann of IRI was quoted in Brandweek as stating " ... smart marketers have to create new products and new reasons to buy existing products – and then advertise those reasons".'

> Source: How to Effectively Compete Against Private-Label Brands,
> Journal of Advertising Research, February 1998

Olivio turns all this on its head:

— In two years the brand has moved from a near terminal position versus ROB derivatives to one where it now drives growth as category leader.

— Instead of losing its franchise to cheaper imitations, Olivio has ROB users trading up into it.

— It has achieved this feat without a product difference (indeed it is ROB that has pursued a new variant strategy);

— And without a series of persuasion ads that convey new, rational 'reasons to buy'.

Olivio provides an example of what can be done when faced with retailer brands so sophisticated that you cannot rely on product innovation to provide sustainable competitive advantage.

As such, this paper will suggest that we further reframe the concept of advertising effectiveness. As well as looking beyond sales at the back end of the process we should also look to acknowledge the broader effects of front-end strategic thinking; thinking which costs clients money.

We will argue that when Van den Bergh Foods (VdB) asked BBH to develop advertising for Olivio it received not one but two principal returns on its investment:

1. A step change in Olivio's market performance as a result of the *creative* work developed.

2. An increase in VdB's stock of knowledge as a result of the *strategic* work developed.

The thinking that guided Olivio's creative solution has been freshly bottled as corporate learning on how to compete against ROB in parity markets. It is now applied by VdB in training programmes, NPD, to other brands, and in the international roll-out of Olivio.

For this reason, as well as proving that advertising more than paid for itself by driving sales, this paper will detail the additional 'epistemic payback' that VdB got for its money.

THE LAUNCH OF OLIVIO

A Time of Learning

Olivio is a reduced-fat spread made with olive oil, launched in 1991 as an addition to VdB's portfolio of margarines and low-fat spreads.

Its launch represented a tactical manoeuvre by VdB. Back in 1990, polyunsaturated fats were receiving adverse publicity. This prompted the company to invest in an alternative mono-unsaturated health spread. The aim was to create a safety net for its profit hero, Flora, if things got out of hand.

Olivio was thus launched modestly – allocated less than half the adspend usually given to a new brand. Moreover, significant communication constraints were placed upon it.

Olivio has a clear rational benefit. Like Flora, it can help reduce cholesterol levels. Olivio could therefore credibly position itself as a 'heart health' spread. However, it was felt that such a route might exacerbate the problems of Flora and her 'poly-whats-her-names'. As a consequence, we had to walk past the strategic solution prescribed by the ARS school of thought. We had to launch a new health spread without overtly conveying its product benefit.

The Sophistication of ROB

Denied a product benefit, we reasoned that the task for communication was to make Olivio completely synonymous with olive oil. In this way we aimed to appropriate its inherent values and imply its benefits. Accordingly we developed clear product truth advertising.

The proposition: 'All the naturalness and goodness of olive oil – in a spread.'

Press and TV were used to introduce Olivio to its London test region in February 1991. Within a month both Sainsbury and Tesco had launched their own olive spreads, nationally. Olivio went national two months later with big four-multiple distribution and advertising. The brand's launch performance was not extraordinary. AGB did not pick up ROB sales in the launch year but, in truth, Olivio struggled from the start.

Over the next four years the brand continued to be supported at low levels, but neither this nor a package design change significantly improved its performance (Figures 1 and 2).

By 1995, Olivio's volume share of the £500-million margarine and low-fat spreads market (MLF) had tailed off to 0.6%. Moreover, ROB were growing the olive spreads sector with a 2:1 sales ratio over Olivio.

Olivio struggled to justify its premium over ROB olive spreads. Consumers saw no difference between Olivio and its derivatives, other than price. It appeared that Olivio's product truth advertising had helped to launch a category but failed to launch a distinctive brand – playing directly into the hands of ROB.

Consumers, ROB and the Age of Product Parity

Our initial feelings on why this had happened centred on launch communication constraints. It was tempting to attribute Olivio's failure to the fact that we had been unable to overtly convey its rational benefit. However, inspection of the wider MLF market and indeed FMCG markets en masse forced us to revise this opinion.

Today's consumers understand and expect product parity. They naturally transplant product benefits from an advertised brand to cheaper ROBs. Despite a clear 'heart health' product benefit, Flora's main source of volume loss is at the hands of ROB sunflower spreads.[1] Likewise 'I Can't Believe It's Not Butter', marketed on a taste benefit, has recently haemorrhaged volume to ROB taste spreads.[2]

A more overt expression of Olivio's product benefit might have invigorated the olive spreads category but it wouldn't have helped the brand reverse its sales ratio with ROB.

The real problem was not that consumers could see no difference between Olivio and ROB; it was that they didn't *feel* any difference.

The Power of Emotion Confirmed

This both corroborated and built upon our understanding of brands and the importance of emotional equity.

---

1. Twenty-five per cent of Flora switching losses (June 1997 MAT) were to ROB Sunflower, by far the greatest single source of loss.
2. Fifty-four per cent of ICBINB! switching losses (June 1997 MAT) were to ROB Taste, again by far the greatest single source of loss.

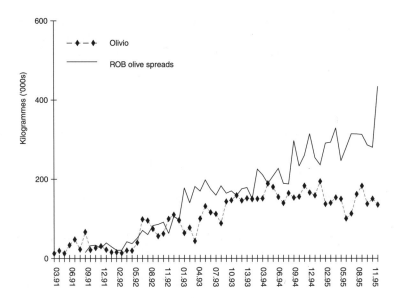

Figure 1: *Launch volume sales*
Volume measure: KG (000s)
Source: AGB

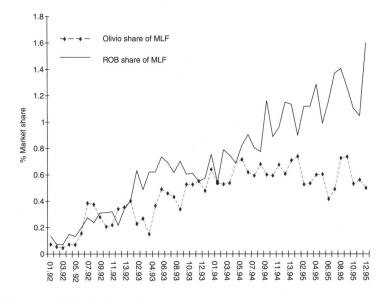

Figure 2: *Volume share of MLF: Olivio versus ROB*
Source: AGB

The industry mantra has long been that it is the extra layer of less tangible meanings and associations that differentiate brands from products. However, the case of Olivio and the market it sits within served to remind us that emotional values do more than merely differentiate. Against sophisticated ROB, they are the key means of motivating consumers and, as such, a brand's primary source of sustainable competitive advantage.

We had hoped that by focusing on olive oil we would borrow its emotional codes. However it seemed that these operated at too low a level to build a brand that stood distinct from heavily advertised competitors like Sainsbury and Tesco.

The Marketer's Paradox

Olivio reflected the paradox faced by FMCG marketers when launching new products today:

— You develop a new product.

— It is new, so your advertising needs to emphasise it and inform consumers of its benefits.

— It is increasingly difficult for brands to 'own' product benefits in the way they once could.

— Thus, in effect, you run category launch advertising that imitators can thrive on.

— And focusing on the production launch advertising leaves less opportunity to invest in the fabric of the host brand.

— So at the precise moment when additional layers of meaning are needed to provide a point of difference over derivative products you find your brand has not got any.

In relaunching Olivio we needed to provide consumers with a brand benefit: to work from a product platform to create something emotionally unique.

The way to avoid the marketer's paradox was quite simple: do not launch products with product truths and benefits or launch brands with brand truths and benefits.

A Recommitment to Olivio

In 1995 two things happened:

1. The trade indicated that Olivio was about to sleep with the fishes.

2. A decision was made by VdB to take some of its eggs out of Flora's basket; to spread the risk of market shocks across its portfolio.

The shackles were off.

Future-Relevant Emotion and the Importance of Trend-Catching

The task at relaunch, then, was to build a brand with deep-rooted emotional values. However, this in itself was not sufficient. Brut has deep-rooted emotional values. So does the *Daily Express*. The point is that those values are no longer relevant to consumers.

If emotional meaning was to provide Olivio with a long-term competitive advantage, Olivio should be associated with values that would connect with increasing numbers of people over time.

We needed to identify 'future-relevant' emotional values and appropriate them before anyone else. For this reason we looked to identify and develop values around emerging trends.

Identifying a Trend

We looked at changing attitudes towards health and diet within society. This did not involve extensive qualitative research among our volume target. We were looking to anticipate the emotional wants and needs of the broad population before they could be voiced in focus groups. Instead, we canvassed the views of the agenda-setters and influential early adopters in the health arena: 'media doctors', health farm owners, food enthusiasts and restaurateurs. We also consulted Henley Centre articles and MAFF surveys. It became apparent that society's attitudes and behaviour have shifted through two distinct waves: 'The Era of Denial' and 'The Era of Portfolio Management'.

'The Era of Denial' was characterised by a regimented 'no pain, no gain' approach to health. Healthiness was a function of what was left out of one's lifestyle and diet. Diet shakes were all the rage and cream cakes needed advertising.

'The Era of Portfolio Management' saw consumers displaying a more liberated mindset. Contradictory health reports had engendered a culture of legitimisation. Consumers chose to be selective in what they were told and sought to achieve balance over time rather than on any single occasion. Thus a Saturday night 'blow-out' was followed up with a Monday detox. People jogged to McDonald's. More importantly, an emerging third wave was identified: 'The Era of Positive Health'.

'The Era of Positive Health' appears to be born of a 1990s fixation with stress. The perceived failure of science to explain the mind–body connection has led to a devaluation of 'sciencey' brands and remedies in favour of a more holistic approach to healthiness. From the evening 'tipple' through to the growing popularity of aromatherapy and yoga, evidence of a change in attitude reveals itself. Increasingly, health is something that is attained via an overall approach to life rather than something to be invested in on certain occasions.

Positive health provided us with a new perspective with which to consider Olivio.

Third wave consumers were interested in things that were 'stress-free', 'relaxing' and 'enjoyable'. A health brand that was associated with these values would be both distinct and popular.

Developing a Positive Health Brand Benefit

We then returned to olive oil and looked at it through third-wave health lenses. We sought to understand its wider context and this led us to consider its Mediterranean origin.

World Health Organisation statistics showed that a lower incidence of coronary heart disease in the Mediterranean is combined with a longer life expectancy compared to Northern Europeans.

However, against ROB, 'Live longer' would be no more ownable a benefit than would 'Heart health'.

Returning to qualitative research, it became clear that people's attraction to the Mediterranean was based on the lifestyle that was seen to be enjoyed there. The region conjures up images of happy, relaxed, down-to-earth folk; of stress-free days eating alfresco with friends and family.

The Mediterranean was a metaphor for a way of life totally in-keeping with that aspired to by third-wave consumers. This, we realised, was the way to build Olivio's emotional values. By couching a longevity claim in such emotionally appealing terms we could create a positive health brand benefit.

We decided to sell the brand on a Mediterranean approach to life.

THE ADVERTISING

The proposition: eating Olivio as part of an olive oil-rich Mediterranean style diet can help you enjoy a longer life.

The advertising idea: characters who personify the brand proposition; old Mediterraneans living a stress-free, enjoyable, longer life.

Two films – 'Hand down' and 'Football' – and three press ads ran in 1996. Two further films – 'Doctor' and 'Tug' – ran in the autumn of 1997.

THE MEDIA PLAN

VdB reasoned that a drive to claim control of the olive spreads category would require heavy upfront investment to yield a future dividend. Olivio's relaunch plan thus comprised two parts.

In 1996 a trial run was planned. If the advertising was seen to work then heavy investment would occur the following year.

Some £3.2 million was spent on advertising in the relaunch year with TV spend split by upweighted and downweighted regions. Low-level national TV presence was attained via Channel 4 with additional spend on ITV in regions displaying high penetration of olive oil (Figure 3).[3]

Viewing 1996 as a success, VdB invested £6.4 million the following year – this time pulsed evenly across the country (Figure 4).

---

3. Initiative Media used olive oil consumers as a broad proxy for third wave wealth consumers.

		J	F	M	A	M	J	J	A	S	O	N	D
	ABC1 TVRs												
BURST 1	223			■	■								
BURST 2	167					■	■						
BURST 3	135									■	■		
	GRPs												
PRESS	538			■	■	■	■	■	■	■	■		

Figure 3: *Olivio 1996 media activity*
Source: Initiative Media London

		J	F	M	A	M	J	J	A	S	O	N	D
	ABC1 TVRs												
BURST 1	579		■	■									
BURST 2	125					■							
BURST 3	125						■						
BURST 4	125							■					
BURST 5	125								■				
BURST 6	352									■			
BURST 7	170										■		
BURST 8	152												
	GRPs												
PRESS	542	■	■	■	■	■	■	■	■	■			

Figure 4: *Olivio 1997 media activity*
Source: Initiative Media London

OLIVIO'S RELAUNCH PERFORMANCE

Upon inspection of the key performance indicators, it quickly becomes apparent that Olivio has experienced a significant upturn since its 1996 relaunch. It is also clear that the timing of this upturn coincides quite tightly with relaunch advertising. We shall seek to prove that this coincidence is causation.

Volume Growth

By the end of 1995, total annual volume sales had fallen 8% on the previous year. In the first year of relaunch total volume sales increased by 53% to 2.95 million kilogrammes. In 1997 year-on-year growth of a further 63% occurred.

'FOOTBALL'

Sound: (SFX) Italian folk music.

(MVO) One reason people live longer in the Mediterranean is their diet – fresh fish, pasta, fruit vegetables and olive oil...

(MVO) '...or maybe it's their fans that keep them going.

(MVO) Olivio spread, made with the oil of age-old olive groves.

'DOCTOR'

Sound: (SFX) Italian folk music throughout.

(MVO) One reason people live longer in the
Mediterranean is their diet. Plenty of fresh
fish, fruit, vegetables and, of course, olive oil,
help keep them healthy.

(MVO) So sometimes they visit the doctor...

(MVO) ...for other reasons.

(MVO) Olivio spread, made with the oil of
age-old olive groves.

Increased Price Premium

Volume growth was accompanied by an increase in Olivio's price premium over both ROB olive-oil spreads and the health-spread category average in the two-year period. In 1996 Olivio increased its RSP on three separate occasions. As ROB followed, Olivio's average premium over ROB fell marginally by 2p to 37p. However, in 1997 Olivio extended its premium over ROB to an average 45p.

Olivio's premium over the total health-spread category average rose consistently throughout the period, from 70p in 1995 to 91p in 1997.

Share Gain

Sales uplift was not simply a function of a sudden market upturn. Olivio's volume shares of both the olive oil spread category and the MLF market have risen markedly since January 1996. Olivio saw its annual average volume share of MLF rise from 0.6% to 1.5% over the relaunch period, breaking the 2% barrier by the end of 1997. Similarly, its volume share of the olive oil spreads category rose from 23.1% to 47.8% over the same period.

Out-competing ROB

Sales have been so bullish since relaunch that Olivio has asserted itself as the olive-oil spread category leader. Before relaunch, ROB was driving category growth with a sales ratio of 2:1 over Olivio. By 1997 this sales ratio had been reversed, peaking at 2:1 in Olivio's favour by the end of the year.

ROB Users Trading Upwards

Beyond this, switching data suggest that Olivio's source of volume gain is partly made up of ROB olive spread users trading up into the brand. Indeed, ROB olive oil spreads represent the highest single source of volume gain for Olivio.

Ranking actual volume gains against an expected figure gauged by size of brand, the extent of Olivio's incursion into ROB franchise becomes clear (Table 1).

However, Olivio's resurgence has not been detrimental to the health of ROB. An invigorated olive-spread category, captained by Olivio, has benefited the retailer brands. ROB volume sales have also increased since 1996.

Sales-driven Distribution Gain

Olivio already enjoyed a healthy 73% sterling distribution. However, this rose to 88% over the campaign period as distributors reappraised a previously stagnant brand.

TABLE 1 : GAINS RANKED ACTUAL VERSUS EXPECTED (INDEX = 100)

ROB Olive	845
Golden Churn	155
Total Vitalite	134
Flora Buttery	109
Total Low Fat Spreads	106
Flora Standard	104
I Can't Believe It's Not Butter	78
ROB Pufa	77

Source: Van den Bergh data

Rate of Sale Increase

However, it can be seen from Olivio's rate of sale performance that sales uplift cannot be attributed to distribution gains. The virtuous circle of sales growth and distribution gain was clearly kick-started by an exogenous force (Figure 5).

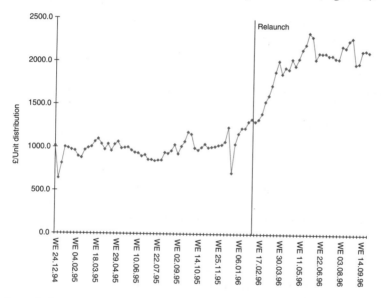

Figure 5: *Cash rate of sale*
Source: Nielsen

VdB set three business objectives for Olivio at the time of recommitment:

— To achieve a volume target of 2,600 tonnes in relaunch year.

— To increase market share to 2% of total MLF by the end of 1997.

— To reverse the ROB:Olivio sales ratio by the end of 1998.

These objectives were all met ahead of schedule, and all before the end of 1997.

THE CONTRIBUTION OF ADVERTISING

We will seek to prove advertising's contribution in three ways:

1. By showing that advertising worked as we intended.

2. By examining the part played by other variables in order to demonstrate that none could have been the catalyst for such brand growth.

3. By econometric modelling, on both a regional and national basis, to show the strong correlation between advertising and brand sales.

Advertising Worked as Intended

A model of how Olivio advertising should work was drawn up at the time of relaunch. Advertising needed to do four key things:

1. Raise brand awareness.

2. Communicate 'enjoyable longevity' benefit.

3. Drive trial.

4. Help the brand to achieve a 'kitchen currency' among housewives.

So, did we raise awareness?

The number of ABC1 housewives spontaneously aware of Olivio rose by 21% in relaunch year and doubled in 1997. Total brand awareness, although tracked discontinuously in 1997, showed an increase of 25% in relaunch year. This growth in brand awareness is consistent with the increases in TV ad awareness recorded over the same period. Higher overall awareness levels were accompanied by a high efficiency of both TV and Press[4] advertising as measured by the Awareness Index (AI).

Did we communicate the 'enjoyable longevity' brand benefit?

Tracking of the core proposition shows that the percentage of ABC1 housewives agreeing with the relevant image statement increased by 28% over the course of the campaign to December 1997.

Furthermore, splitting the sample to reflect the spread of TV spend in relaunch year reveals that this image statement scores higher in regions where the campaign is now more established.

ROB olive spreads are not tracked specifically. For this reason we have established the extent to which the new campaign has differentiated Olivio by looking at how the brand is seen in comparison to 'any retailer branded spread' among a population of olive oil spread users. The difference is immediately apparent (Figure 6).[5]

In establishing whether 'enjoyable longevity' had enabled us to catch the new positive health trend we viewed the brand image score for 'Getting more popular' as the best proxy.

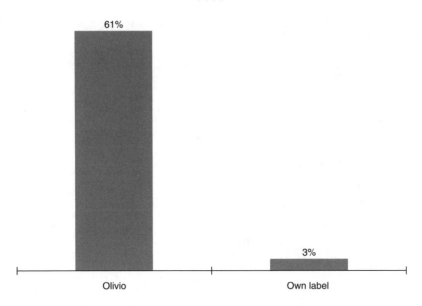

Figure 6: *Helps you enjoy a longer life (16 June to 14 December 1997)*
Base: ABC1 Housewives
Source: Millward Brown

The number of people agreeing with this statement rose markedly with the first burst of relaunch advertising and consistently with the 1997 drip (Figure 7).

Significantly, the reasons spontaneously given by Olivio users to explain purchase justified our belief that relevant emotional values would prove the key means of motivating consumers. While recall of the rational longevity benefit became evident upon prompting, people spontaneously referred to 'the feel' of the brand as the primary reason for trying it.

'I'd just like to live in a world like that. If Olivio did holidays I'd go on one.'

'It sounds stupid but it just makes my shopping basket a bit less boring.'

Source: Olivio users. Penny Beadle Research

The clear and consistent distinctions drawn between Flora and Olivio in Gestalt world projective exercises further confirmed that advertising was developing Olivio's values as we had intended:

---

4. Print Track was used to monitor press work throughout the relaunch year.
5. Unfortunately discontinuity in the tracking study means that Figure 6 has had to sit as a static measure. It is therefore impossible to prove that the 'perception gap' has widened since relaunch.

Olivio world: 'Relaxed families', 'A glass or two of wine', 'Warm, sunny', 'Rustic bread and fresh fruit', 'A nice pace to life', 'Well-being'.

Flora world: 'Individuals eating muesli', 'Dieting', 'Gyms and aerobics', 'Sciencey', 'Restrictive', 'Orange juice', 'Running', ' Fitness'.

Source: Penny Beadle Research

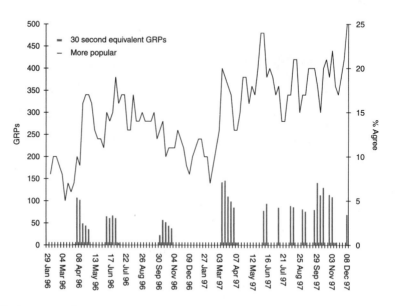

Figure 7: *Getting more popular*
Base: ABC1 Housewives
Source: Millward Brown

Did we drive trial?

In January 1996 Olivio's four-weekly penetration of housewives was a static 0.75%. By December 1997 this figure had risen to 2.75%.

Splitting purchase consideration and claimed usage measures by regions with different levels of exposure to relaunch advertising suggests that people with more advertising exposure are more likely to buy Olivio (Figure 8).

Did we help the brand achieve a 'kitchen currency'?

By developing trend-catching brand advertising, we believed that Olivio could become a bit of a 'kitchen conversation' piece. We posited that consumers might mention Olivio to friends in the context of a 'kitchen chat' about health, diet or ways of living, with the ads themselves providing neat conversational hooks and cues. In this way we hoped that new recruits to Olivio would, in effect, become brand spokespeople.

While ambitious, there seems to be evidence that this has indeed occurred. The increase in calls made to the Olivio 'Careline' since the new campaign broke suggests that the advertising has certainly caught consumers' attention.

Overlaying weekly calls with advertising activity depicts a clear relationship between the two (Figures 9 and 10).[6]

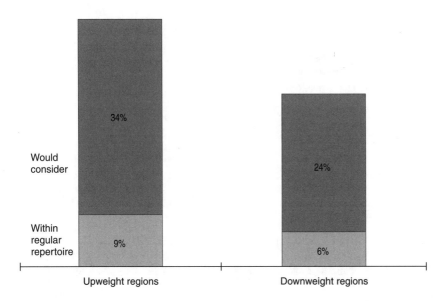

Figure 8: *Consideration of Olivio (16 June to 14 December 1997)*
Base: ABC1 Housewives
Source: Millward Brown

Beyond this, research among users informed us that many did indeed talk to friends and family about the brand, some openly admitting that they refer to the advertising and the approach to life which it captures:

'I told my sister about it, she likes that sort of thing. She's into natural health and she's always on about Italy.'

'A friend in work mentioned it. She'd teased her husband after seeing the ad about the old man's football match. She bet him he wouldn't be doing that when he was that old.'

Source: Olivio users. Penny Beadle Research

During econometric modelling an interesting phenomenon revealed itself. This again suggested that the brand had assumed a 'kitchen currency'. We observed that advertising's effect on Olivio sales exhibits zero decay.

Normally, brand sales tail off once TV advertising comes off air as a function of the advertising decay rate. Not with Olivio. Instead ad-driven sales remain at a steady level following initial uplift.

After exhaustive analysis we would postulate that this lack of decay is the result of a number of influences including high repeat purchase, an unidentifiable press effect and the achievement of a 'kitchen currency'. That is, by mentioning the brand in conversation, users help to recruit trialists once advertising comes off air.

---

5. As press advertising carried the 'Careline' number, the relationship between press and calls is particularly strong.

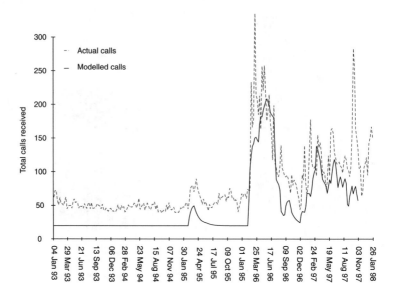

Figure 9: *Olivio Careline: Actual and Modelled*
Source: VdB Careline

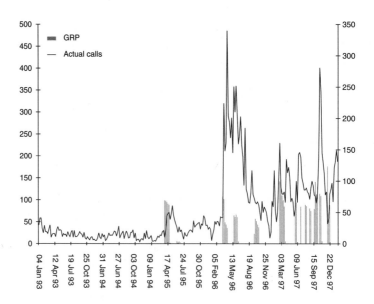

Figure 10: *Careline calls against GRPs*
Source: VdB Careline

Econometric Modelling

Olivio's key market drivers were identified and quantified using econometrics. Regression analysis of Olivio's national sales accounted for all the principal variables. Separate coefficients were provided for distribution, relative price, non-price promotions, Olivio advertising[7] and competitive advertising.[8]

Modelling shows a very strong correlation between sales and advertising (Figure 11). The model has a fit of 99% and satisfies a battery of model validation diagnostics. This analysis shows that, from relaunch to the end of 1997, advertising has sold 13,088,000 more tubs[9] of Olivio than would otherwise have been the case. Olivio sales were 148% higher than they would have been without advertising.

Furthermore, this modelling exercise was repeated for each and every individual region and in every case the results corroborate the national findings.

Other Contributing Factors

Econometric modelling disentangled the effects of all the primary causal variables in order to calculate an advertising coefficient. What other factors could have caused Olivio's upturn?

The 'olive oil factor'

Did olive oil sales suddenly take off in 1996 and Olivio just get swept along in the slipstream?

Figure 12 (overleaf) shows that this was clearly not the case. Olive oil sales have been rising steadily throughout Olivio's life, displaying only a modest growth rate increase since 1995.[10]

Intuitively, this does not explain why Olivio suddenly emerged from stagnation to record 182% growth in two years, a point that is corroborated by statistical testing.

In any case, a sudden increase in consumer goodwill towards olive oil would not in itself explain Olivio reversing a sales ratio against other olive spreads.

Flora fallout

The brand's *raison d'être* was to act as a mono-unsaturated substitute for Flora. Could Olivio's sudden upturn be a result of Flora haemorrhaging volume on the back of adverse publicity?

Again no. The 'poly-scare' proved to be a drop in the ocean, disappearing long before 1996. In any case, as stated earlier, Flora's principal source of volume loss is to its ROB equivalents.

By contrast, we showed that Olivio's cannibalism of Flora is almost negligible given their relative sizes. The two brands now operate in different worlds, just as consumers told us.

---

7. Standard difficulties in quantifying the effect of press led us to focus on the relationship between TV advertising and sales. TV will thus act as a proxy for all activity, its effect being only as overstated as press effect is understated.
8. Defined as 'any health spread brand'.
9. 500g equivalent tubs.
10. Olive oil sales increased by 12% (1995 versus 1996) and by 16% (1996 versus 1997).

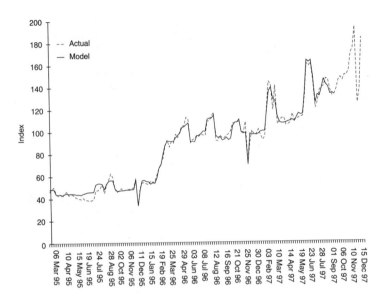

Figure 11: *Olivio volume*
Index Base: Cannot be revealed for reasons of client confidentiality
Source: Nielsen & econometric model

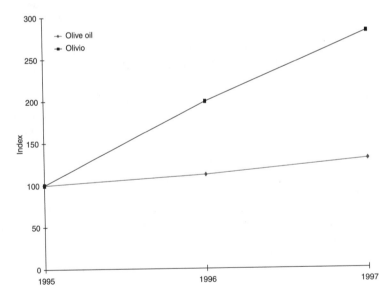

Figure 12: *Olive oil versus Olivio*
Index Base: 1995
Source: Nielsen

Below the line activity

Direct marketing, principally in the form of door-dropped coupons, did not kick off until November 1997. Nevertheless, it could be argued that redemptions would have affected sales in the final month of the study. For this reason steps were taken in econometric analysis to ensure that this short-term additional increase was not spuriously misattributed to advertising.[11]

Thus it can be seen that no other factor could realistically have provided the impetus for Olivio's upturn.

Having proved that advertising was the principal catalyst for Olivio's resurgence, we now seek to quantify its value as an investment.

CALCULATING ADVERTISING PAYBACK

Despite our contention that VdB received more for its marketing pound than a direct sales effect, we will nevertheless focus on sales alone in demonstrating that advertising will prove to be a sound investment.

Payback as a Function of Ad-driven Sales

In total, VdB spent £9,543,000 on advertising over the two-year relaunch. Thirty-three per cent was spent in the 1996 trial run with the remaining 67% spent in 1997 as upfront investment in the brand's future health.

Press expenditure is included in this figure despite the fact that the econometric model is based on TVRs. This is because, as stated earlier, the TV coefficient will be acting as a proxy for all advertising activity. For reasons of client confidentiality we cannot provide profit per unit figures. However, we can give dates when investment paid back based on the number of units sold that are directly attributable to advertising.

We calculate that the company received 83% payback on trial run spend within the year. Such a rapid return on a £3 million investment convinced VdB to plough serious money into a five-year-plan in 1997.

The true test of advertising efficacy thus lies in establishing when the total investment, including the heavy 1997 spend, is recouped. Taking the total amount of Olivio sold as a direct result of advertising between first airing and December 1997, and assuming no further activity, we can forecast the date of payback.

We have observed that Olivio's ad-driven sales display zero decay. Assuming that this degree of retention continues in perpetuity, payback occurs in November 1998 (Figure 13).

---

1. In so doing we are being harsh on ourselves. The econometric model shows that the relationship between advertising and sales is multiplicative. Thus, in effect, advertising would have improved efficacy of the coupon promotion.

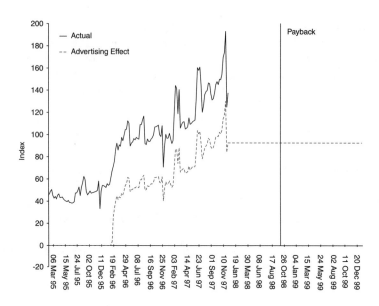

Figure 13: *Olivio volume: actual sales and the contribution of advertising (assume zero decay)*
Index Base: Cannot be revealed for reasons of client confidentiality
Source: Nielsen & Econometric Model

Of course, if, as we contend, this extreme residual effect is at least partly down to the brand's 'kitchen currency' value, it is unlikely that it will continue indefinitely. Conversation is eternal but subject matter comes and goes. We have therefore attached a more standard decay rate to Olivio's ad-driven sales figures and again looked to the future. Assuming a 9% four weekly rate of decay in sales,[12] VdB will receive payback in December 1999.

In reality, the decay rate will not remain uniform over time and will travel between the two parameters set above. So, even when focusing purely on direct brand sales, advertising will make good on a £9.5-million investment within four years of outlay.

Put another way, the heavy 1997 investment used to initiate a five-year brand plan will actually receive payback within three years.

APPLICATIONS OF VdB COMPANY LEARNING

Looking beyond sales, VdB's other principal return on ad investment is the company's acquisition of knowledge, knowledge which, when applied, is already paying further dividends.

---

12. As a gauge, the average four-weekly ad-sales decay rate for health spread brands is 12%. The rate for the low decaying Frizzel Insurance advertising detailed in *Advertising Works 9* was 5%. In observing a zero decay rate for Olivio we felt an estimated rate between these two figures was reasonable.

Trend-catching and International Brand Launch

There are many global food products but few global food brands.

The conventional explanation for this is that in no area is cultural heterogeneity more pronounced than in food. For this reason, the task of transferring brand values into new markets without losing their appeal is said to be particularly difficult.

As a product, VdB had expressed little interest in introducing Olivio to other countries. However, witnessing Olivio's relaunch success as a brand encouraged the company to challenge the conventional wisdom. Understanding that Olivio's success was due to its trend-catching brand benefit, VdB's Innovation Centre undertook a large-scale research exercise to identify emerging health trends across a number of Western countries. Discovering that the picture in those countries mirrored that of the UK, the company decided to launch Olivio internationally.

Crucially, this was seen to be a brand roll-out, not a product roll-out. The UK advertising has been used, and will be used, wherever the brand is launched:

> 'The widespread appeal of the UK advertising has enabled us to launch an international brand, not just an international product.'

> Source: Peter Nota, Marketing Controller for VdB's Health Innovation Centre

Under the name of Bertolli, the brand has already been successfully launched in Australia, New Zealand, Denmark, Finland and Belgium. The intention is to roll out across all Northern European markets in 1998. Interest is also being shown by a number of other non-EC countries.

VdB's belief in the brand benefit rather than just the product format being the catalyst for sales growth is further proved by a controlled market test in Holland.

The Dutch test used every element of the Olivio package except for brand advertising. It used a quality chain of stores, competitive pricing, similar packaging and a product that was identical. They even ran awareness-raising pack shot ads in the store magazine.

Despite all this, demand has been poor and the test deemed unsuccessful. This has led Garance Deelder, the Marketing Manager for Health at VdB Netherlands, to conclude:

> 'These test results are conclusive evidence that the UK advertising is needed if we are to maximise the potential of Bertolli spread.'

By contrast, Belgium used an Olivio TV spot to launch the brand and recorded even better sales results than in the UK. Within one year Bertolli has achieved 7.4% value share of the spreads market and 10% cumulative penetration.[13]

---

3. Having all launched within the last three months it is too early to gauge the performance of Bertolli in other countries at the time of writing. However, the early indications are encouraging.

Thus it can be seen that the increased company knowledge stock is already being applied. A greater understanding of the power of trend-catching in the development of successful brands has led to a latent source of sales opportunity being both recognised and tapped.

In addition to this, buying into a principle of international brand roll-out puts VdB in a position to benefit from significant cost efficiencies going forward. Of these, the most obvious is the increased return on investment in advertising production. However, a further cost reduction is less immediately apparent. Using proven advertising in markets displaying similar conditions reduces risk. Doing so results in VdB incurring lower venture capital costs from their financiers.

Training

The story of Olivio's strategic development is now a case study used in training programmes across the company spanning different disciplines and levels of seniority. BBH have themselves presented to graduate trainees, marketers, the UK sales force and VdB NPD scientists.

Impact Upon New Product Development

The use of agenda-setters and early adopting consumers in the identification of emerging health trends has had a significant impact upon the company's NPD programme.

VdB now runs early adopter qualitative groups continuously throughout Europe in the exploration of new consumer trends. The findings of these trend studies are used to inform the NPD process.

Steps are also being taken to bring quantitative evaluation techniques into line with the consumer triangle. In the future, new product concepts will be tested in ways that reflect consumer trend dynamics ever more sensitively.

CONCLUSION

We have argued that when VdB invested in advertising for Olivio it received two key returns on its investment:

— An increase in Olivio sales from creative work.

— An increase in company knowledge from strategic work.

In terms of payback, we have shown that the direct sales increase alone will cover the investment before the end of the millennium.

At this time it is too early to quantify the additional long-term dividend on an increased knowledge stock. This is a function of how it is applied going forward.

For the moment we can only show that this learning is being used, and have provided examples for this reason. To further this end it seems appropriate to conclude with the views of those who will be doing the applying:

'Olivio's communication strategy developed our understanding of how direct investment in emotional values can help fortify brands and reinvigorate markets. We can therefore envisage a future where brands continue to live happily with ever more advanced retail competition.'

Andy Duncan, Marketing Director

'Olivio is a case example of how big brand ideas can cross national boundaries and work effectively. If the trend is international, then the brand that catches it will work internationally.'

Pieter Nota, Marketing Controller for VdB's Health Innovation Centre

'One could argue that Olivio has helped redefine the market. Consumers' views on Olivio show that butter no longer owns 'natural goodness' in the way it once did. As the dominant force in margarines and low fat spreads, this can only help VdB's cause going forward.'

John Lennon, Marketing Manager

'By selling Olivio on its approach to life we have created a brand that, like Ben and Jerry's, is much bigger than the categories it sits within. Olivio now has powerful and flexible brand equity. Equity that can be leveraged in all manner of ways.'

Lorraine Spence, Senior Brand Manager

My own view is that the best way to value the thinking that went into Olivio's relaunch is to count the number of IPA effectiveness papers submitted by VdB in the future.

Better that than write another one myself ...

★★★★

10

One2Many

How advertising affected a brand's stakeholders

EDITOR'S SUMMARY

This paper looks at how an advertising campaign transformed the fortunes of a company across all its stakeholders and gave a brand a second chance.

Bringing Humanity and Stature to a Complicated Market Place

In October 1996, behind in sales, and faced with falling brand awareness, negative perceptions of One2One extended across all stakeholders. There was an overall lack of confidence in the brand.

An opportunity to stand aside from what was consistently perceived to be an untrustworthy, complicated market was identified. The advertising strategy redefined mobile telephones as conduits for rewarding conversations.

Results and Payback

Over the period in study, One2One's customer base grew by more than any of the other three networks. This dramatic turnaround was accompanied by an increase in brand fame. One2One's campaign format was imitated by other programmes and TV celebrities. As a result disposition to buy increased among new users.

Special analysis of customer satisfaction research showed that the advertising was causally related to an increase in existing customer recommendation and retention. An annual employee study, demonstrated how the change in advertising strategy and execution also contributed to an increase in the pride employees felt in working for One2One.

One2One's existing econometric model was used to relate the increase in sales to the advertising and this produces a total payback figure of £199.3 million from a media spend of £36.7 million. Finally, there was a fundamental change in the perceptions of the City and recognition of the increased credibility of One2One as a contender in the mobile telecoms market was demonstrated by a loan secured in May 1998. One2One raised £1.6 billion to further develop its network. The loan was £1.1 billion oversubscribed.

INTRODUCTION

This paper is not just about how advertising sold more product. It is about a total transformation. It is about a company under threat, and a reversal of fortune.

This paper will show how advertising can be the driving force behind such a reversal. It will encourage a reappraisal of the perceived audience for *any advertising* by showing how its influence can impact on all of a company's stakeholders.

And, of course, it will talk about sales as well. In one year, One2One's customer base went from growing the least of the telecommunications networks to growing the most (Figure 1).

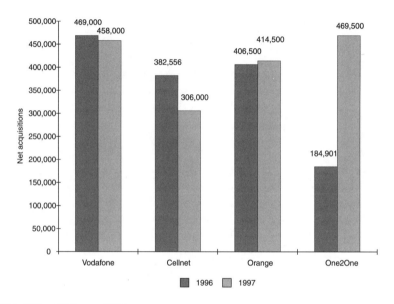

Figure 1: *Net additions 1996 versus 1997*
Source: One2One Competitor Monitor

This paper will chart how such a rapid and immense turnaround was achieved.

IN THE BEGINNING ... MERCURY ONE2ONE

In September 1993, Mercury One2One (MO2O) entered a mobile telecommunications market controlled by only two brands, Cellnet and Vodafone. These giants had had the run of the market since the mid 1980s, building up a substantial business-focused user base (over 1.5 million subscribers). To belong to a network, you had to sign a contract for a minimum of nine months. From the beginning, the emphasis was on attracting new customers (gross additions), because they brought guaranteed revenue.

In September 1993, One2One was launched in London. Adopting a US model of regional roll-out, Central followed. One2One offered a unique deal: free off-peak local calls. In an expensive market, this was a competitive advantage. Mobiles were potentially available to far more customers.

PROBLEMS WITH THE NETWORK

MO2O's initial success and hype were followed by disappointment.

— Customers began using their mobiles as a replacement for their fixed-line phones and were disappointed by the quality of the reception.

— Lines became congested when the free calls began.

The light-hearted launch advertising and local coverage compounded the problem. MO2O was seen as a trivial contender in a market that required technological reliability.

ORANGE ENTERS

In April 1994, a fourth competitor, Orange, launched nationally with a radical per second billing proposition and a wire-free future-proof claim. Recognising the uncertainty that surrounded the whole market, its guarantee centred on technological expertise and it was soon seen as the real innovator in the market.

Orange's entrance into the market affected all aspects of MO2O's business.

FALLING BEHIND ON NEW CUSTOMER RECRUITMENT

For new customers there was no longer such a simple choice when entering the market. Orange offered greater coverage and technological know-how than MO2O, and cost less than Vodafone or Cellnet.

In a market that was viewed as too small for four players, Orange established itself as a real contender and a safer bet for nervous customers.

Figure 2 reveals the speed with which Orange approached One2One. By December 1995, it had more customers than One2One.

The total new customer additions for 1995 showed MO2O running in fourth place. In addition, MO2O brand measures were slipping. Saliency fell; and when the brand was known, it was increasingly described as trivial and low quality (Figures 3 and 4).

'Mercury One2One's appeal to the dependent user is clearly being limited by negative publicity over network performance. It does not really matter if these complaints are valid or not; the image of Mercury One2One as a system in crisis has now been given the authoritative support of the BBC and some newspapers ... the resultant perception is that MO2O is not a particularly serious system.'

Source: John Armstrong Research, December 1995

Fewer people were considering purchasing the brand and more people were rejecting it.

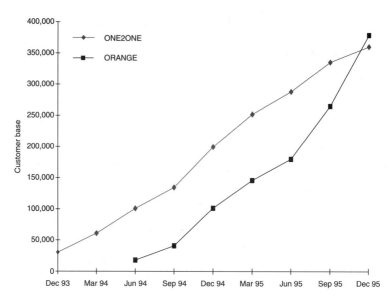

Figure 2: *One2One and Orange customer base*
Source: One2One Competitor Monitor

NEGATIVE EFFECTS ACROSS ALL STAKEHOLDERS

These outward signs of a brand in severe trouble were only part of the story. Evidence of a fundamental problem stretched across all MO2O stakeholders.

Existing Customer Dissatisfaction

Existing customer satisfaction – monitored by MO2O – was also slipping. The likelihood of them retaining their phone or recommending MO2O to someone else was falling as well.

Customers who indicated low satisfaction with MO2O were asked for their reasons. Comments from the Customer Satisfaction Program give a flavour of the concerns:

> 'Because the technical quality of service is dreadful, for example, lost calls, inability to make calls and poor coverage which doesn't match the map.'

> 'A company that promised a lot and delivered a little.'

> 'The service is crap. Mercury One2One hasn't got the coverage. When you pick the phone up you expect to talk to someone not to have to phone again and again to finish the conversation.'

> 'They should take more care of their customers if they want to keep them.'

> Customer Satisfaction Program, CFI Group, January – March 1996

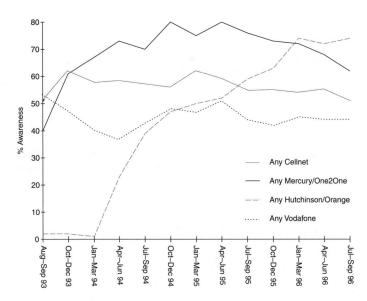

Figure 3: *London total brand awareness to September 1996*
Source: BJM

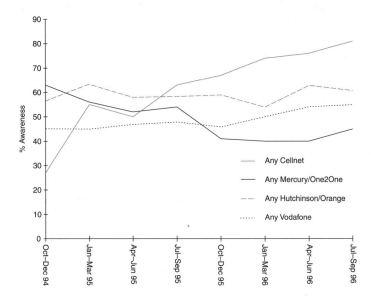

Figure 4: *Central total brand awareness to September 1996*
Source: BJM

Low Employee Morale

One2One employees felt outperformed and outsmarted by Orange. The marketing team, responsible for creating MO2O's public image, felt inadequate compared to the whiz kids at Orange who had created a dynamic brand, rising phoenix-like from the ashes of Hutchinson Rabbit. One2One's annual employee survey is used within the company as an important barometer of staff morale. By May 1996 the situation was severe.

The advertising and marketing was not believed to be on a par with the competitors. This affected employees' perception of their company's ability to compete.

Uncertainty Picked up by Telecoms Commentators

The lack of confidence was reflected in the press:

> 'One2One, the weakest of the four mobile networks.'

> Source: Daily Telegraph City Desk, September 1996

> '(Free calls) have lost them money, clogged up their network and damaged their reputation because people can't get through after 7pm.'

> Source: Daily Mail City pages, September 1996

> '... while One2One has been grappling with the consequences of its marketing hysteria, Orange, the Johnny-come-lately in the mobile phone market, has stolen a march on it ... It is doubtful whether Britain can support four mobile networks in the long run and One2One is looking as if it could end up as the network left standing when the music stops.'

> Source: Times, September 1996

Falling confidence in MO2O was infectious. Orange's market success put off new buyers, and threatened MO2O's existing customers, shook employees' faith, and questioned MO2O's business credibility. Its future looked bleak.

A FUNDAMENTAL REVIEW

Mercury One2One and BBH

BBH was briefed to increase gross customer additions. It was clear that any solution needed to restore confidence to all stakeholders. MO2O's coverage and network capability were improving as it continued to expand, but it did not possess a hardware trump card that would put it ahead of its competitors. In the short term, at least, a change in perceptions was going to have to be delivered from an alternative source.

The business required a fundamental review. We needed the input of current and potential customers to discover whether it was possible to regain their confidence. We also needed to involve other stakeholders, and to understand how advertising could provide context and leadership for the whole company.

A Confused Marketplace

The mobile phone market is composed of many separate elements and a myriad of different brands – handsets, networks and retailers – as Figure 5 shows.

Figure 5: *A confused marketplace*

Research showed that the networks had done little to unravel this complexity. As a result, people:

— were confused and nervous about the purchase process;

— sought help from those they felt close to, for example, friends or business colleagues;

— felt bombarded by hard-sells, product information and small print.

To some extent, Orange had managed to cut through this by building a bond of trust with the customer. One2One needed to build a bond of trust in a way that would be stronger than Orange's.

Orange's Weakness

Qualitative research showed that, while Orange's technological capability was accepted, the brand felt cool and remote. Here, at least, One2One had an advantage. Its history of free calls and social usage had left some positive associations in customers' minds. This suggested a less aloof company and an appreciation of wider consumer needs. Among the brand's weaknesses, this provided a potential platform for positive development.

Understanding people's inherent distrust in the whole category helped the BBH and One2One team to recognise the opportunity to build on these existing human roots and differentiate the brand from its competitors: the *human face of mobile telephony*. The brand would help people to find a way through intimidating technology.

This required us to understand the human relevance of mobile telephony.

The Human Relevance of Mobiles: Learning from the Customer Base

At this point, the existing customer base proved useful. Quantitative analysis showed that while MO2O had many customers attracted by the low cost, higher revenue customers tended to possess an attitude to life that was more exploratory and experience driven than other mobile users. There seemed to be an opportunity to talk about mobile telephony as a conduit for conversations that could enhance your life.

This movement from badge to conversation values had ramifications for the entire market. It broke with existing conventions of technical description and a brisk, prosaic exchange of words and created a new space defined by rewarding conversations.

— Positioning: The human face of mobile telephony.

— Advertising insight: One2One is a tool for self-exploration.

This was not just an advertising thought; it was the reason for the company's existence.

It was an idea that could best be unleashed by liberating the One2One brand name from its Mercury prefix, since research had shown that the Mercury prefix was adding problems because of the visible removal of Mercury-branded phone boxes. It was time for One2One to stand alone.

THE CAMPAIGN

The Advertising Idea ... Having a One2One

The relaunch advertising was not simply about re-expressing One2One to customers in London. It had to work as launch communication in new regions, and present One2One as a plausible contender alongside the three other networks. It had to address all the stakeholders whose confidence in the brand was falling.

Stakeholders	Requirements from advertising
Potential customers	Trust, simplicity, humanity
Existing customers	Satisfaction and confidence in their network
Employees	Ownership and pride, confidence in One2One's ability to compete
Industry commentators	Business credibility, stature

These individual requirements can be best summarised as a need to establish brand fame.

Given the learning from the research, the creative team was briefed with the strategic outline, and asked to devise an integrated idea in which brand fame and humanity took precedence over information.

Among the clutter of telephony-related advertising, there was an opportunity to stand out from the detail of product and deal explanation, and offer a simpler vision of mobiles.

The idea of 'who would you most like to have a one2one with?' was born out of the newly liberated brand name. It suggested exploration via an intimate high-status conversation. This was, importantly, initially between famous people in order to capture interest and confer much needed status upon the brand to all stakeholders.

THE CAMPAIGN GOES PUBLIC

One2One was relaunched in October 1996. Sixty-second conversations between Kate Moss and Elvis Presley, and John McCarthy and Yuri Gagarin were tailed with 20-second simple product messages and supported by information-led press advertising. Later on, product messages were communicated within the brand format; thus 'Derek2Tanya' explained the new Pre-payment option, and 'Mum' communicated One2One's expanded coverage (Figure 6).

Figure 7 shows how the campaign rolled out in regions where One2One already existed. When the campaign launched in Yorkshire in February, this shape was repeated. Once the idea was established, further brand films were shown. Different executions were rotated together.

RESULTS

The Effect on Sales

Between October 1996 and January 1998, One2One's fortunes dramatically changed.

Figure 8 (on page 266) shows how post relaunch additions out performed pre-relaunch additions.

'KATE2ELVIS'

Sound: (SFX) Telephone and Rubber Band by Penguin Café Orchestra.
Kate: Who would I most like to have a One 2 One with?

Kate: Elvis Presley.

Kate: '56 would have been a good year, when he was still a shy country boy from Memphis ... he'd be 21.

Kate: Apparently he really felt lonely at times...

Kate: Even before he was idolised by millions, I'd cheer him up.

Kate: I know he liked cars. It would be great to go for a drive with him, pop round to his mum's for a cup of tea.

Kate: If I had a One 2 One with Elvis, I'd ask him who was his best friend. I'd have been a good friend to him. I think maybe I'd ask him to sing for me. My own Elvis Presley concert.

(FMVO) Who would you most like to have a One 2 One with? Our mobile phone service gets people talking.

'DEREK2TANYA'

Sound: (SFX) Telephone and Rubber Band by Penguin Café Orchestra.
Derek: Who would I most like to have a One 2 One with?

Derek: (Dreamily) Tanya.

Derek: On checkout 21. I'd tell her about my new mobile phone Up 2 You. You can buy one as easily as buying ...

Derek: Bananas.

Derek: I use vouchers for my calls and you're free because there are no bills, or contracts to sign.

Derek: And most of all, if I could have a One 2 One with Tanya, I'd ask her ...

Sound: (SFX) Champagne bottles popping.
Derek: ...Out.

(MVO) Up 2 You. The new pay as you go mobile phone service.

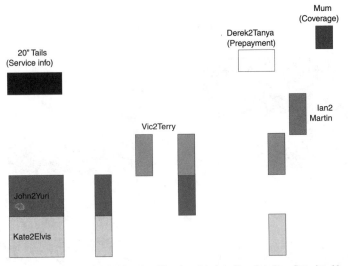

Figure 6: *One2One advertising – October 1996 to January 1998*
Source: Motive

Because gross additions are confidential, they do not reveal One2One's relative performance. In both 1995 and 1996, One2One had gained significantly fewer customers than the other networks. In 1997 *One2One's customer base grew by more than any other network's*. Such results were unimaginable 18 months earlier.

This trend is continuing in 1998. Results from the first three months show that One2One remains in the lead.

HOW THIS TURNAROUND WAS ACHIEVED

This visible change in One2One's sales coincided with the advertising. The remainder of this paper will show how the advertising positively affected each of the stakeholders and delivered a payback figure well in excess of the advertising expenditure.

ENTERING THE VERNACULAR

From October it was clear that the idea of having a One2One had captured the public's imagination. This was manifest in the numerous ways the One2One voice and style entered the vernacular. Terry Wogan and Chris Evans used it. Rory Bremner, Sky Sports and the Cartoon Network copied the visual format for their own shows. *Live&Kicking* and *Blue Peter* asked their audience who they'd like to have a One2One with and the question was set as homework by a headmaster in Cheshire.

ONE2ONE REGIONAL MEDIA WEIGHTS

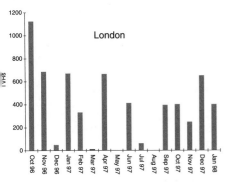

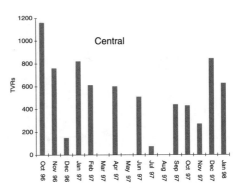

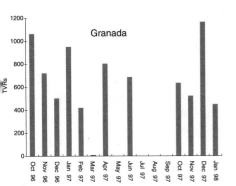

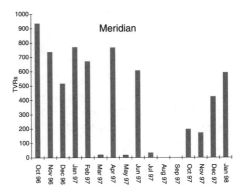

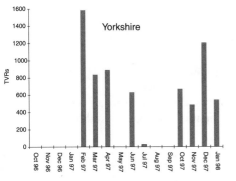

Figure 7: *One2One regional media weights*

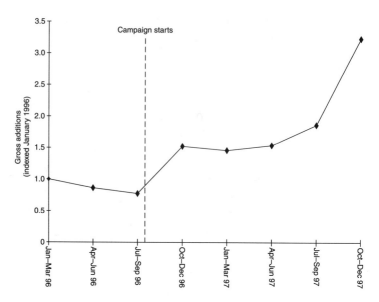

Figure 8: *One2One Gross Additions (indexed for confidentiality)*
Source: One2One Competitor Monitor

BRAND FAME

The campaign worked primarily by helping the customer to believe in One2One's capability as a company. It made One2One famous. Becoming famous was key to One2One's future success. We knew that if customers were interested in buying a mobile phone they would find out details from dealers.

ONE2ONE TV CUT THROUGH BY REGION

Tracking shows how noticeable and memorable the campaign was. TV cut through is the percentage of the target group who manage to describe a TV execution to the extent that it is clear they have seen that particular execution (Figure 9).

TOTAL BRAND AWARENESS BY REGION

By 1998, brand awareness within London had shot up, returning to the heights of the original launch and recapturing first place from Orange.

Outside London, One2One witnessed spectacular growth in all regions. In the majority of them it leapt into second place behind the longer-established Orange (Figure 10).

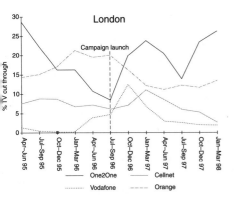

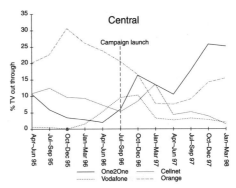

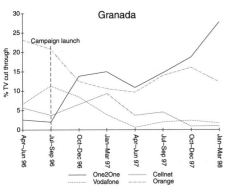

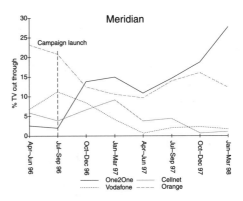

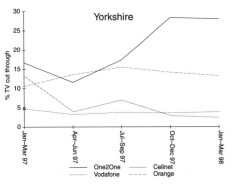

Figure 9: *One2One TV cut through by region*
Source: BJM

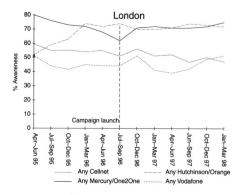

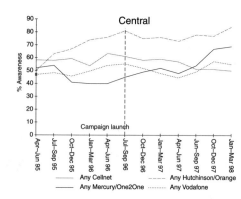

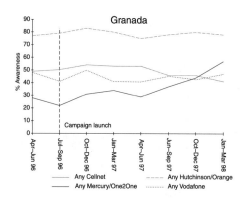

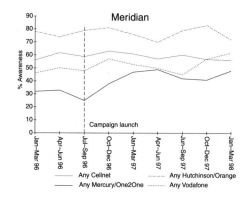

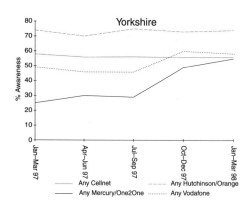

Figure 10: *Total brand awareness by region*
Source: BJM

ADVERTISING AWARENESS AS A PERCENTAGE OF BRAND AWARENESS

Measuring advertising awareness as a component of brand awareness shows that, in all but one region, One2One's advertising is the most effective at driving brand awareness. Because BJM asks for descriptions of advertising before it checks brand awareness, there is no possibility of customers overclaiming advertising awareness simply because they know the brand (Figure 11).

A SHIFT IN PUBLIC PERCEPTIONS

While quantitative tracking is useful for examining general market trends and brand performance, much learning about how the campaign was working came from qualitative research. Between October 1996 and January 1998 we talked in depth, to 596 existing and potential customers, purely about aspects of One2One's communication. Including the people we spoke to about other aspects of mobile telephony, this figure rises to over 1,400. Qualitative research indicated that the increase in awareness was translating through to more positive perceptions of the brand:

'One2One said to suggest personal intimacy ... long calls and even romance ... (due to) the influence of current advertising – personal conversations you want to have.'

'There was widespread liking for the One2One brand values advertisements, which were felt to be noticeful/impactful, entertaining/engaging. All of this seemed to reflect the relevance and accessibility of the advertising's central theme, namely the one-to-one which you would most like to have.'

Source: The Research Practice, June 1997

'The mainstream television campaign, in combination with the brand name in its own right, has clearly given One2One a lively and characterful image, and clear associations with personal calls, social usage, longer calls and an upbeat happy mood.'

Source: The Research Practice, November 1997

'The One2One TV campaign is now sufficiently familiar in order to ensure reliable branding and an understanding that One2One is a mobile phone network. Furthermore, both the question "Who would you like to have a One2One with" and the shared internal structural detail of the individual commercials are now very well established; each film providing a famous person the opportunity to ask searching questions to their own 'hero' figure.'

'The impression is of a brand which is modern, quite fearless, bold and confident and in tune with contemporary issues.'

Source: John Armstrong Research, November 1997

'... for potential private owners in London, this advertising addresses and corrects the perception that One2One is small scale, parochial stuff.'

Source: John Armstrong Research, December 1997

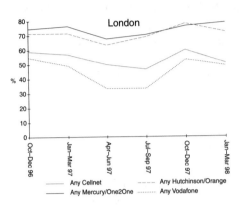

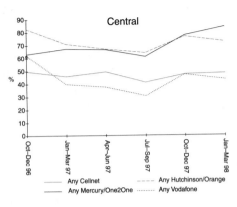

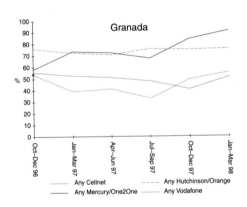

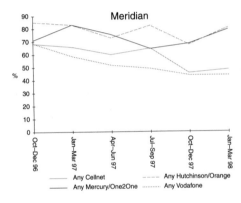

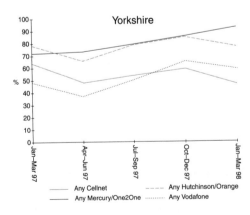

Figure 11: *Advertising awareness as a percentage of brand awareness*
Source: BJM

'One2One television executions were the most widely recalled advertisements for mobiles, and also tended to be recalled in much greater detail than others ... '

'The widespread recall of the One2One commercials, and the enthusiasm and detail with which they were often recalled seemed to reflect the strong entertainment value of the advertisements ... It seemed that the campaign elevated itself above the norms of both network and product-focused advertising in this market, and potentially embraced everyone via its entertainment value and the breadth and universal applicability of some of its themes, such as communications, the inner thoughts of celebrities and so on ...'

'Some of the respondents claimed that the advertising seemed to stimulate a sense of emotional "trust" in the brand, perhaps by exploiting one's relationship with the advertising or the famous celebrities within the commercials.'

Source: The Research Practice, January 1998

POTENTIAL CUSTOMERS: INCREASED DISPOSITION TO BUY

From October 1996, the disposition to consider One2One grew faster than any other network.

EFFECT ON EXISTING CUSTOMERS

Increased Satisfaction

As stated earlier, the advertising had to do more than just attract new customers. It had to reassure existing One2One users that they had made the right choice. In a market where the entry price is artificially lowered and paid for in monthly instalments, true value comes from holding on to customers.

One2One carries out regular customer audits among its own customers and among Vodafone, Cellnet and Orange users. Customer satisfaction is a compound measure made up of responses to questions about all aspects of the brand. Figure 12 shows how One2One's customers' satisfaction has increased. By March 1998, they were happier than the customers on any other network.

The study rates each aspect of the brand in terms of its contribution to overall satisfaction, and advertising has consistently emerged as having had a high impact on the final score.

Increased Recommendation and Retention

The survey also shows a rise in two key measures concerned with future behaviour: retention and recommendation.

Figure 13 shows a strong correlation between One2One's advertising activity and an increase in both of these measures, suggesting that advertising plays a role in influencing them.

By the end of 1997, One2One had increased its lead over Vodafone and Cellnet and had overtaken Orange.

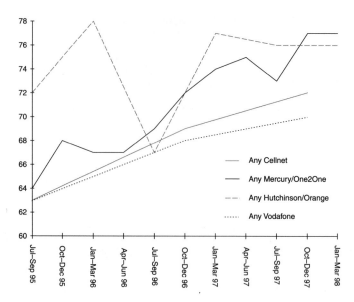

Figure 12: *One2One customer satisfaction versus competition*
Source: CFI Group

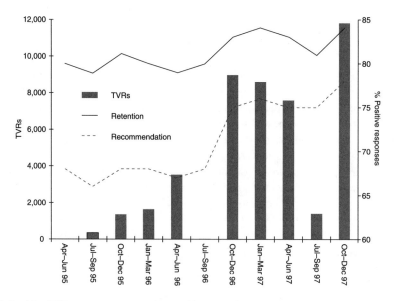

Figure 13: *One2One TVRs versus customer retention and recommendation*
Source: CFI Group

PROUD EMPLOYEES

The effects of the relaunch were also reflected within the company: there was a noticeable change in the attitudes of the employees. You could make a case for the advertising having indirectly increased staff morale and confidence by forming an 'advertising leads to more sales leads to a less insecure workforce' argument. By the end of 1997, staff at One2One had seen something they would not have believed possible 15 months earlier: the underdog of the mobile phone world overtaking a company which claimed to have the future wrapped up.

However, by May, when the 1997 employee survey took place, there were already signs that the advertising was responsible for some dramatic shifts in perceptions, months before such spectacular business results could have been imagined.

In 1996, One2One staff had been involved in both the strategic and creative development of the advertising idea via 60 internal workshops. This had a dual function: not only could the agency learn how the employees viewed themselves and the company's strengths and weaknesses; the employees felt a sense of ownership early on in the process. When Kate went on air imagining a conversation with Elvis in October 1996, it was not a complete surprise to people at One2One.

There is a marked turnaround in some of the key measures related to the advertising. In 1996, fewer than half of all employees believed that the advertising was projecting the right image for the company. By 1997, this figure had nearly doubled.

This identification with the advertising translated through to an increase in the perceived ability to compete (Figure 14).

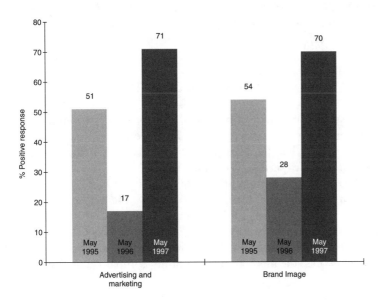

Figure 14: *How does One2One compare with its major competitors?*
Source: One2One Employee Survey

In terms of change relative to 1996, the two biggest shifts within the entire survey came from these statements relating to advertising and brand image.

These shifts suggest that the advertising idea of having a One2One and the executions up to May had, in themselves, restored a degree of confidence to One2One employees.

FROM ADVERTISING APPRECIATION TO PRIDE

It was great that the employees rated the new ads. There is also evidence that the advertising helped to shift deeper feelings towards the company, and this hints at a role for advertising that is rarely touched upon. One of the questions in the survey asks: 'How proud are you to work for One2One?' This figure had remained static between 1995 and 1996. However, 1997 saw an increase from 69% to 87%.

Statistical analysis of the database suggests a link between the increased preference for the advertising, and the increase in pride. In 1996, pride seemed to be largely generated by internal dimensions; for example, relationships with management. 'Our latest advertising, promotional and publicity material projects the right image' is the 74th best predictor of pride, suggesting that in 1996 advertising had little influence on staff pride.

In 1997, the predictors as a whole reflect a greater external confidence. There is a clear relationship between the pride of working for One2One and the advertising. Advertising emerges as the second best predictor of pride. Within a year, advertising has moved from having little or no influence on employee pride to being a key factor in influencing employees' perceptions of their company and its standing in the marketplace.

The Industrial Society, which compiles the employee survey, is able to benchmark One2One results against its database of other companies. One2One's mean score for pride is well above the mean for all other organisations, and even exceeds the high performers' score (top 25% of companies).

THE VALUE OF PRIDE

There is an assumption that it is beneficial for companies to employ people who gain satisfaction from that employment. However, very few studies exist that actually prove this. It has been very difficult to value the increase in pride that One2One's workforce experienced within a year.

Two studies exist which attempt to prove a link between employee satisfaction and productivity/profitability. One, carried out by the Gallup Organisation, has found consistent links between 'soft' measures and staff retention, profitability and productivity, as well as customer satisfaction. Specifically, Gallup has defined 12 areas with a direct correspondence. While none of these mentions pride, one of the measures is defined as 'the mission/purpose of my company makes me feel my job is important'.

'Business units with above average employee perceptions of reward/fulfilment have a 27% higher success rate.'

Source: Gallup Organisation

A second study, carried out by the Institute of Personnel and Development, concludes:

'Job satisfaction explains 5% of the variation between companies in change in profitability.'

Source: Institute of Personnel and Development

IN THE NEWS

Commentary around the campaign stretched from *The Sun* to the *Financial Times*. A selection of quotes demonstrates how the campaign captured journalists' imagination, and how in many cases the advertising was directly linked to a turnaround in the company's fortunes.

'Here is a campaign that mainlines straight into the human condition. It is inspired.'

Trevor Beattie, The *Guardian*, June 1997

'Takings at One2One soared 130% to £230m as wacky telly ads ... brought a surge of new orders ... this surge helped One2One's parent company unveil massive half year profits of £1.2 billion.'

Source: The *Sun*, November 1997

'The One2One ads with Kate Moss are gorgeous, really inspired.'

Jo Whiley, Radio 1 DJ, The *Guardian*, February 1998

Figure 15 shows One2One's share of positive coverage received across the media during the period of advertising, measured against the other three networks.

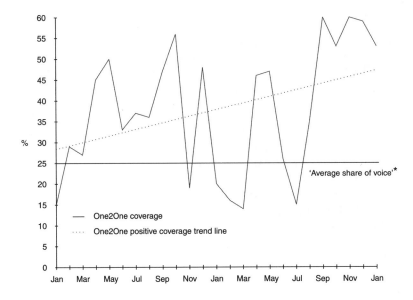

Figure 15: *One2One's share of media coverage*
*Note: Since there are four networks, more than 25% share of voice could be considered as 'above average'
Source: Larkspur

EFFECT IN THE CITY

Such public support is echoed in independent research – carried out by a communications consultancy in January 1998 – among telecom experts, financial analysts, consultants, journalists and user group representatives. In order to develop its network, One2One relies on substantial loans from banks. City confidence in One2One's capability is essential and good advertising is read as a sign of a competent marketing department and clear business direction.

'This is a marketing game, and One2One's marketing has clearly improved.'

Andrew Harrington, Salomon Brothers

'I believe it's seen as a more credible alternative to the other three players.'

Paul Marsh, Morgan Stanley

'I think they are changing. I think analysts are taking them a bit more seriously, expecting them to be more successful than they have been in the past.'

Stuart Jeffrey, Daiwa

'There's much more of a sense that One2One is a fighter. They've been advertising more and have a much higher profile. It used to be Orange that was seen as the up and coming little guy battling against the big guy. Now One2One is moving into that space.'

Shirley Skeel, financial journalist

'It's really since they re-launched their campaign a year or so ago. The "I'll have a One2One with ..." campaign. The perception is no longer that they're cheap, but that they're a value for money proposition. The brand is clearly being changed from a regional one to a national one.'

Andrew Beale, UBS Research

'Advertising is seen as the central plank in all the operators' marketing strategies, with many analysts pointing out how spend has increased. The success of the "who would you like to have a One2One with?" campaign is now seen as one of One2One's strongest cards by the groups. Asked which they believed to be the best advertising campaign, One2One now beats Orange into second place. Vodafone and Cellnet register no support at all.'

Source: Listening In, River Path Associates, January 1998

BBH also carried out its own research into attitudes in the City. Telecom analysts from 20 investment banks replied to a simple questionnaire. We asked them whose business performance had improved most in the last 18 months. One2One was unanimously selected.

We then asked them to rate the importance of different elements of the mobile telephone business:

HOW IMPORTANT HAVE THE FOLLOWING BEEN AS INSTRUMENTS
OF CHANGE IN THE MOBILE TELECOMMUNUCATIONS MARKET?

Element	Very important (Numbers agreeing)	Very important or important (Numbers agreeing)
Coverage	10	18
Network quality	7	16
Advertising	7	12
Customer service	5	11
Price promotions	3	12
Marketing	4	12
Distribution	0	11

Source: BBH house research

After core technological requirements, the analysts rate advertising as the most important driver of change in the industry. When asked about the effectiveness of each network's advertising, One2One was rated by more analysts as having very effective advertising:

HOW EFFECTIVE DO YOU THINK THE ADVERTISING
HAS BEEN FOR EACH COMPANY?

Network	Very effective (Numbers Agreeing)	Very effective or effective (Numbers Agreeing)
One2One	12	18
Orange	8	16
Vodafone	0	2
Cellnet	0	1

Source: BBH house research

SUMMARY OF EFFECTS

The idea of having a One2One, as expressed in the advertising, has captured the minds of three essential stakeholders in the One2One business. Sounding like a more confident, competent brand, it asks them to consider the possibilities of thought-provoking and rewarding conversations. The campaign encourages the three groups to reconsider the One2One company and brand, which in turn affects their particular relationship with it.

For prospective customers, this means that they are more likely to consider One2One when buying a mobile phone; current customers are more likely to recommend One2One to their friends and colleagues; and employees are happier working for One2One.

PROVING IT

While there were no other major step changes in the One2One brand that occurred around the time of the relaunch, there are other factors that may or may not have contributed to the speed and size of the growth in One2One sales.

With the assistance of Billetts Media Consultancy, One2One undertook an econometric analysis to create a predictive model for use in future strategy development. It sought to identify or discount all the factors of influence; and to separate and quantify their individual contributions.

The model focused on London, the most established market, and therefore subject to fewer changes than the other regions. This is likely to give a conservative figure for the advertising effect, since tracking shows that advertising in new regions has had a greater effect.

DISCOUNTED FACTORS

The model diagnostics do not indicate that any important variables are missing from the model.

Dealer

We know that dealer/salesman commission is important in this market, and that the relevant measure is one which looks at the difference between competitor commission. There is little difference between the commission offered by the four networks.

Commission per gross addition has no explanatory power. Not surprisingly, it reflects the brand's market position rather than vice versa. It is the position of the brand that drives commission levels, not commission levels driving the brand.

Network Coverage

This can be explained by the fact that it is perceptions of coverage that are important, not actual coverage. Tracking shows that customer 'mean guesstimates'[1] of coverage moved from just under 60% to 64% across a year. Research among dealers showed that they were less likely to mention coverage as a key differentiator between brands. In terms of coverage, the gap between networks was closing and there were new and interesting products to talk about.

Distribution

Given this is a share model, the measure here is relative distribution. In London, the most established region, relative distribution has remained flat. Consequently distribution could not have contributed to One2One's spectacular success.

---

1. BJM question: 'What percentage of GB population do you think is covered by the One2One network?'

Seasonality

The mobile phone market is seasonal. Our analysis showed that One2One moved in line with the general market seasonality. We therefore modelled One2One by market share, eradicating the relevance of seasonality.

KEY DRIVERS

These factors explain 96% of One2One gross additions.

Handset Prices

One2One's handset price had a significant influence on connections. Since this is the most tangible cost for newcomers to the category, and given the massive discounting that networks have supported, this is not surprising. An effect was identified that correlated a decrease in price with a percentage increase in gross additions.

Credit Control

In 1996 credit control procedures were tightened. This increased rejection rates among applicants and therefore had a negative effect on gross additions.

Promotional Activity

Because the majority of promotional activity is concerned with lowering the initial cost of entry we used handset price as a proxy for promotions.

New Product Introduction

Partners and Up2You were introduced in mid-July and August 1997 respectively. Partners makes it cheaper to own more than one phone, while Up2You lets you pay for airtime before you use it, therefore avoiding a monthly bill. Their introduction has coincided with a step change in gross additions. Between them they have contributed significantly to One2One growth in market share by opening the market to another audience and by making multiple phone ownership easier. Their contribution to new sales has been quantified and is expressed as a proportion.

Advertising

Analysis of the model demonstrates how responsive the market is to advertising. Not only did One2One's advertising prove to be a key driver in increasing gross additions for One2One, but it emerged that when competitors were on air, One2One's gross additions were negatively affected.

All research showed it was the TV advertising which has most successfully communicated the One2One message. The majority of media monies has been TV spend, and it is this that the model has measured. Because only the TV can be satisfactorily quantified (TVRs) it has been used as a proxy for all the advertising activity. The TV was supported by press, outdoor and radio campaigns and is undoubtedly taking some credit for this activity since it is not possible to disentangle simultaneous or continuous activities. (Although the calculation of advertising effect is gross additions per TVR, the final payback calculation will, of course, look at the total amount spent on all media.)

PAYBACK

The Billets model confirmed what we already believed: that there was a direct relationship between One2One's expenditure on advertising and the increase in gross additions (Figure 16).

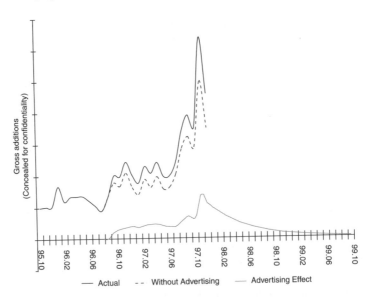

Figure 16: *Modelled advertising effect National gross addition projected from London*
Source: Billetts

The model explains advertising's contribution as a percentage increase in gross additions per 100 TVRs. In London, advertising was responsible for a substantial proportion of the total additions. As stated above, the advertising had greater effect outside London. However, the London figure is used to generate a national advertising effect.

Between October 1996 and January 1998 (16 months), the total number of customer connections attributable to advertising is calculated to be 167,944.

One2One's advertising spend was £36.7 million, distributed nationally, between October 1996 and January 1998. This works out at £219 per new customer. (In Orange's 1996 IPA paper, the figure is £431) Allowing for cost of acquisition, cost of servicing the customer and assuming network average revenue of £40 per month, the value of these additional 167,944 customers comes out as £115.9 million.

The effect of the advertising does not end in January 1998. As Figure 16 shows, One2One advertising has a powerful residual effect. Even if One2One stopped advertising from 1 February onwards, a certain number of gross additions would be attributable to the advertising. If we extrapolate to the end of December 1999, we can attribute a further 120,851 gross customer additions to the advertising that has already been aired. This would result in a further value of £83.4 million.

Therefore the total payback from a £36.7 million advertising spend is £199.3 million.

AND FINALLY ...

One final, resounding vote of confidence from the City occurred in the middle of May 1998.

'One2One, the mobile telephone company jointly owned by Cable & Wireless and US West, has raised £1.6 billion to refinance its existing agreement ... One2One said the debt facility had been £1.1 billion oversubscribed, with £2.7 billion of bank commitments offered.'

Source: *Times*, 15 May 1998

'One2One, the mobile telecommunications group owned by Cable & Wireless and US West, has raised £1.6 billion from a syndicated loan to refinance its existing debt and increase investment capital. The loan shaved 50 basic points off its existing borrowing costs. Bob Koenig, finance director, said the refinancing would generate interest savings of around £7 million or £8 million a year for the group ... "Investors are seeing strong performance, rather than just strong forecasts," Mr Koenig said.'

Source: *Financial Times*, 15 May 1998

As this paper has shown, since October 1996, One2One's advertising has been linked with, and partly responsible for, this 'strong performance'.

The year 1997 was exceptional for One2One, recognised by the Marketing Society as Brand of The Year. It grew in stature and size at a speed unimaginable before October 1996. This was achieved by an advertising campaign that offered a radically different take on mobile telephony and communicated this attitude in a way that not only attracted new users, but also talked to other groups connected with the brand. The increased confidence and capability that the advertising suggested was interpreted by each stakeholder according to their requirements from One2One.

It is always difficult to gain confidence in the minds of your stakeholders: it is even harder to regain it once it is lost. Not many brands get a second chance. One2One took theirs.

11

Meat & Livestock Commission

Pulling round the red meat market

EDITOR'S SUMMARY

This paper is different and we believe unique. There are no brands. Instead we show how advertising supported a market from enormously powerful competition – not in the form of other brands – but from a barrage of negative forces.

The Competition to Meat

Red meat has faced two main problems. First, long-term, 'chronic' forces; social, demographic, ethical, economic, and health related. Second, a shorter-term, 'acute' event; perhaps the biggest health scare to hit any food market – BSE.

We show how a change of advertising succeeded in reducing the impact of these forces and restored the market to year-on-year growth.

Results and Payback

A model shows that the total media spend of £36.2 million spent on red meat advertising between 1994 and 1997 resulted in additional red meat sales of £739 million at retail value – a return of nearly 18:1.

The extra £621 million retail value of GB-produced red meat due to advertising resulted in an additional revenue to farmers of £155 million. Using the average gross margin of 59%, this resulted in an additional £91 million gross margin to farmers (£51 million after subtracting advertising media and production expenditure).

The red meat industry in total is a huge one. Apart from the farmers, there are large numbers of other stakeholders in the carcass red meat market – a chain from auction markets to abattoirs to meat processors to butchers and multiple retailers. All of these businesses' fortunes are harnessed to the fortunes or otherwise of red meat retail sales. Thus, beyond the retail sales benefits, there are huge knock-on effects for retail markets (ready meals, burgers and so on) as well as many other sectors such as catering and fast food, brought on from the advertising effects shown.

INTRODUCTION

We are all familiar with the way advertising can support or grow brands at the expense of competitor brands. Or even how it can help a brand grow a market.[1]

This paper is different and, we believe, unique. There are no brands. Instead we show how advertising from 1994 to 1997 supported a *market* (the red meat market) against enormously powerful competition – not in the form of other brands – but from a barrage of negative forces:

1. Long-term 'chronic' forces – social, demographic, ethical, economic, and health-related.
2. A shorter-term 'acute' event – perhaps the biggest health scare to hit any food market: BSE.

We show how a change of advertising, against all the odds, succeeded in reducing the impact of these forces – slowing the rate of decline in red meat eating and in 1997, restoring the market to year-on-year growth. This, in such a huge market (£2.1 billion in 1997[2]), resulted in significant additional profit to the whole beleaguered farming industry dependent on these sales – not only to the farmers who directly funded the advertising but also to the many other stakeholders (a chain from auction markets to abattoirs to meat processors to meat retailers).

The evaluation task is difficult:

— The market is mature.

— Sales trend lines do not conveniently uplift with advertising bursts.

— Advertising runs virtually year round – ie, no bursts.

— Promotions run simultaneously with advertising.

— Unforeseen 'events' have thrown plans off course.

This paper sets out to show how, despite these challenges, evaluation of the advertising contribution has been achieved.

The Meat & Livestock Commission (MLC)

The MLC is a body set up by the Government in 1967. It is funded by a statutory levy paid by farmers and abattoir owners for each animal slaughtered.

This levy funds all the MLC's activities (covering veterinary research, NPD activities, economic analysis, advertising and promotion and so on). The advertising described in this paper is however funded by the levy paid by farmers.[3]

---

1. BT Grand Prix Paper in 1996 Advertising Effectiveness Awards.
2. Retail red meat carcass sales 1997 (AGB).
3. Abattoirs' levy payments do contribute to the advertising budget, but their proportion of this relative to the farmers' payments is minimal. So for the purposes of this paper, we assume that the advertising is funded solely by the farmers' levy payments.

This paper presents an unusually pure example of advertising effect because the MLC has no direct control over the supply side of the product in question.[4] All it can attempt to influence is the demand.

Focus of the Paper

The primary focus of the MLC's promotional activities (and hence this paper) is in-home consumption of carcass red meat – pork, beef and lamb[5] (which we will call the 'red meat market').

This focus is because:

— This 'market' accounts for the greatest volume of red meat.

— It is where the volume decline has been focused.

— Any uplifts in demand in this area generate greater increases in red meat volume than in other areas such as ready meals.[6]

— Any imagery improvements in this area tend to ripple out into processed meat (but not vice versa) because it is the heart of the 'brand'.

LONG-TERM NEGATIVE PRESSURES

The MLC has a tough job. Red meat suffers from a debilitating range of long-term negative pressures.

Price of Red Meat versus Poultry

Since 1970, red meat prices have steadily increased relative to poultry (Figure 1).

New Poultry Products

Helped by the low cost of raw material, poultry producers have launched an extensive range of value-added convenience food products.[7]

---

4. The Common Agricultural Policy (CAP) and other intervention mechanisms put supply and price outside the MLC's control, and likewise product quality, presentation and distribution are beyond the MLC's direct control.
5. Not game or poultry, and not processed meat – like ready meals.
6. There is more red meat in a portion of roast meat than in a portion of a lasagne ready meal.
7. Child-oriented products like chicken nuggets have been particularly successful.

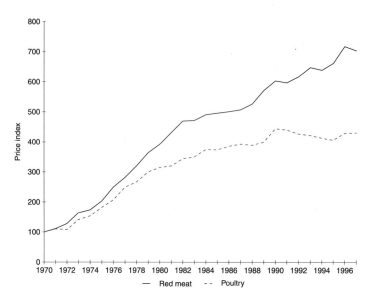

Figure 1: *Prices – red meat versus poultry*
Source: ONS, MLC

Growth in Ready Prepared Food

We are all familiar with the reasons for this.

— More money and less time have fuelled the *demand* for these products, facilitated by the growth of freezers and microwaves.

— Food technology improvements (like chilled processing) and the growth in availability through supermarkets have fuelled the *supply*.

Growth of Supermarkets

The switch to supermarket buying directly depresses red meat sales – due to the juxtaposition of red meat with a vast array of convenient alternatives as well as the loss of the advisory role of the local butcher.[8]

Growth in 'International' Food

Our tastes are broadening. Increasingly we are cooking more 'international' meals.[9] These are more likely to contain little or no red meat compared with 'British' meals.

8. BMP econometric modelling shows that a 1% increase in grocery shopping purchases through supermarkets results in a 1.3% decrease in red meat volume. Sales of red meat through butchers are in decline – having fallen to around 16% of all red meat sales by 1998.
9. Italian, Indian, Chinese, and so on.

Ethical/Health Concerns

Other reasons have encouraged some people to consciously cut down or cut out red meat or even all meat.

— Ethical

Although it is difficult to quantify genuine 'vegetarianism' precisely, *claimed* vegetarianism is increasing, and the rate of growth is also increasing (Figure 2).

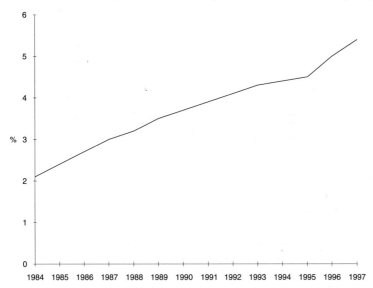

Figure 2: *Claimed vegetarians as a % of population*
Source: Mintel

— Health

Over the past 20 years, a succession of health scares have been associated with red meat: cholesterol levels, animal growth hormones, E Coli, cancer, abattoir procedures, Chernobyl affected sheep, and so on.

BSE

On top of these long-term structural factors affecting all red meat have been the shorter-term problems caused by BSE – affecting beef.

There have been two key phases of media-led BSE consumer concern: the first in 1990 the second in 1996 (Figure 3).

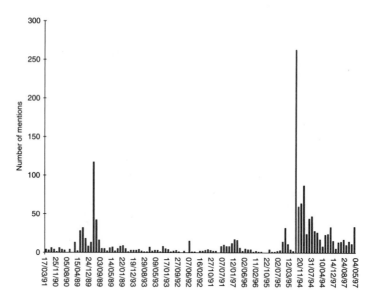

Figure 3: *National press mentions of BSE*
Source: MMD, MLC

1990

Although the cattle disease BSE had been identified a few years before, it was in June 1990 that the first heavy wave of BSE related media coverage occurred. This was prompted by a cat in Bristol dying of the feline equivalent of BSE – raising, for the first time, the terrifying possibility that this type of disease could cross species barriers (and by extension could affect humans).

However, the outbreak of the Gulf War at the end of 1990 wiped BSE off the front pages, although coverage continued at low levels over the next five years.[10]

1996 – The Major BSE Crisis

Catastrophic shock waves were felt after the announcement by Stephen Dorrell in March 1996 that there may after all be a link between BSE and the human equivalent disease, CJD.[11]

---

10. Largely featuring the ongoing debate and conflicting views about the cause and human implications of BSE.
11. This, in fact, only confirmed what the public had suspected all along but had always been denied by politicians/health officials prior to this announcement.

BACKGROUND TO THE NEW CAMPAIGN 1993

Hence, back in 1993 (even before the major 1996 BSE crisis), things looked fairly bleak from the MLC's point of view.

The long-term trends outlined above had resulted in household consumption of red meat declining since the 1960s. In addition, the rate of decline in red meat sales seemed to be accelerating (Table 1).

TABLE 1: HOUSEHOLD CONSUMPTION OF RED MEAT

	Red meat volume (million tonnes)	% change
5 years to 1988	4.3	-11
5 years to 1993	3.3	-22

Source: AGB

In 1993, the MLC appointed BMP to help undertake a major review of strategy. BMP research revealed that behind the accelerating sales decline were worrying attitudinal problems too.

Product Issues

In addition to the discrete health scares mentioned (like E Coli) over the 1980s, red meat had come to acquire an image as more unhealthy (particularly, higher in fat and cholesterol) than chicken, fish or non-meat meals. We often found that there was no real factual basis for these beliefs – just half-remembered scare stories, confusion over types of fat and, most importantly, a lack of effective counter messages from red meat.

User Image Issues

Red meat eaters were consistently portrayed by consumers in research as overweight, old-fashioned and unsophisticated (Les Dawson), while chicken or fish eaters were seen as controlled, virtuous and contemporary (Selina Scott). As a result, people were embarrassed to admit to the extent of their red meat eating – often radically underclaiming in group discussions what their food diaries showed they were actually eating. If actual eating moved in line with these attitudes, then red meat volume would decline even more dramatically in the future.

MLC FIVE-YEAR MARKETING OBJECTIVES 1994 TO 1998

We and the MLC had to be realistic. On an £8 million annual advertising budget, the strength of the forces acting against consumption of red meat at home meant that restoring the market to growth in the short term was unlikely.

Instead we set out to slow down the ongoing rate of decline in red meat in-home volume.[12]

Importantly, this decline was more of *frequency* than penetration – ie, red meat eaters were eating red meat less often at home, but the number of eaters remained relatively static (Figure 4).

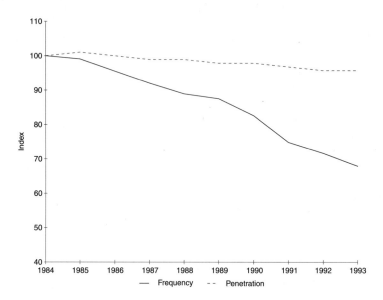

Figure 4: *Red meat – frequency of purchase vs. penetration indexed*
Source: AGB

ADVERTISING STRATEGY DEVELOPMENT 1993

For some years, MLC advertising had been split into four separate campaigns (beef, pork, lamb and red meat) and in fact it was handled by two different agencies.[13]
This resulted in two problems:

— Because of the fragmented spend, awareness of any red meat advertising was low.

— The focus on each species as competing 'brands' (for example, beef – the tasty one, lamb – the easy one, and so on), didn't match the way people thought about and bought red meat – as flavour variants, not separate brands.

'We rotate them – one Sunday we'll have roast pork, the next beef ...'

Source: BMP Qual 1993

We decided to pool the four individual ad budgets and refocus the advertising first and foremost on promoting red meat.

---

12. In a market worth over £2 billion, this could still have huge profit benefits for the farming and related industries.
13. Campaigns like 'Take a Fresh Look at Pork' (talking about pork versatility) and the 'Meat To Live' campaign featuring healthy-looking, active men (talking about the benefits of eating red meat).

People also felt that the previous ads were *tonally* wrong – slapstick humour and clichéd stories were not appropriate. Red meat was thought worthy of respect as it was usually the most expensive part of a meal.

'They're all just a bit naff.'

'You shouldn't really talk about meat like that – it's expensive – not like a bag of crisps.'

Source: BMP Qual, 1993

The Opportunity

Many people were not *actively* avoiding red meat – other meals were often just seen as more convenient.[14] However, research revealed unique rewards when red meat was cooked.

Home-cooked red meat meals were uniquely filling, warming and sustaining. They provided a sense of comfort and well-being – a feeling of being loved and valued. As someone said:

'You wouldn't welcome your long lost son back with a piece of quiche.'

Source: BMP Qual, 1993

Importantly, red meat meals were associated with pleasurable, convivial eating compared with chicken and fish meals (which research discovered were felt to be rather soulless and associated with single-person eating).

These findings helped us to define our advertising strategy.[15]

Advertising Objective

To stem the decline in frequency of people cooking meals with red meat at home.

Advertising Strategy

We believed that advertising could achieve this objective in two main ways.

1. We needed to develop much more popular and impactful advertising.

---

14. Many red meat meals do involve a little more effort in terms of preparation and cooking time (for example, red meat does not microwave well), as do many of the things that people like to eat with red meat (such as gravy and vegetables).
15. NB. At this time (1993) BSE had faded from the press after the initial flurry of media comment in 1990. There was still uncertainty as to the human significance, if any, of BSE and the public it seemed were becoming bored with it. It was therefore agreed that there was no role for advertising at this time regarding BSE.

Thus, advertising needed to be more relevant – we had to bring out the unique feelings that red meat meals provide – and so encourage people to make a little effort and cook them more frequently (instead of ready meals, chicken, and so on) in order to give and share in these rewards. If we could get this relevance right, we hoped to make people feel more comfortable about their red meat eating.

2. We needed to counter some of the mounting negative health misperceptions about red meat eating, with facts which challenged these views.

We had two strong stories based on the fact that red meat is higher in iron levels and lower fat levels than people thought.

Target Audience

We were talking to all buyers and cookers of red meat – no group was unaffected by the trends outlined earlier.

THE PLANNED NEW RED MEAT CAMPAIGN 1994 TO 1997

There were two elements planned in the creative work for red meat over the period 1994 to 1997.

Television: The Recipe For Love (RFL) Campaign

Eleven RFL ads have run over this period. Each features a different meal made with pork, beef or lamb, a different meal situation, and a different personal relationship. Each dramatises the unique pleasures of red meat meals.
Responses to the proposed TV campaign in pre-testing were very positive.[16]

'Overall this has the potential to be a very popular and noticeable campaign which could considerably raise the salience of red meat as a whole.'

Source: Ockwell Associates 1994

The RFL campaign had a total media spend of £28 million between 1994 and 1997. The ads have typically run almost continuously between September and May each year.[17]

---

16. Over the period of the TV campaign we have refined our understanding, and moved the ads away from what research suggested was too much of a focus on posh, dinner party scenarios and romantic situations, to more down-to-earth situations rooted in family relationships.
17. People cook far less red meat meals over the summer months when the weather is warmer and people are out and about.

RECIPE FOR LOVE 'AWKWARD AGE'

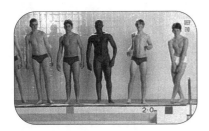 

RECIPE FOR LOVE 'ANNIVERSARY'

The Nutritional Campaign

A series of press and poster campaigns, targeting people concerned about eating healthily have also been run.[18]

Research suggested that people were more likely to be receptive to these factual nutritional messages (which challenged their existing views of red meat quite aggressively) if they were already emotionally on the side of red meat. The nutritional campaign began in 1995 (a year after the new TV strategy).

Nutritional campaigns have been run in press and posters at a total media spend of £4.3 million between 1995 and 1997.

THE MODIFIED CAMPAIGN PLAN 1996 TO 1997 – BEEF REASSURANCE

After the March 1996 Commons bombshell (admitting the probable link between BSE and CJD), the headlines went wild.

Schools and McDonald's banned beef – respondents in groups told how they had cleared their freezers of beef and their cupboards of anything (stock cubes, biscuits, jelly babies) that was likely to contain beef by-products such as gelatin. Collective hysteria at school gates meant that confessing to letting a child eat beef was seen as akin to wilful poisoning. However, as the weeks passed, hysteria gave way to more balanced press coverage, and a further role for advertising emerged.

There were two main groups of people who had given up beef immediately following the 1996 BSE scare.

'Rejectors'

These people claimed they would only return to eating beef when a cast-iron guarantee that BSE had been eradicated could be given (a minority). There was little role for advertising for these people.

'I will never go back to beef until I see guaranteed BSE free on it.'

'They've betrayed my trust so why should I ever eat their beef.'

Source: BMP Qual 1996

'Worriers'

These people wanted to return to eating beef but were just looking for emotional reassurance (the majority).

---

8. In the first year (1995) these consisted of dramatic comparisons of the superior iron or low-fat nature of red meat compared with apparently more healthy alternatives (like cottage cheese or spinach). When we had exhausted relevant comparisons these were replaced with non-comparative facts about red meat.

NUTRITIONAL PRESS

BEEF REASSURANCE PRESS

'It's hard not being able to give them spaghetti bolognese – we love it – but you do worry about the children.'

'You just want to feel you are doing the right thing.'

Source: BMP Qual 1996

As a result, in 1996 and early 1997, the planned red meat campaign was supplemented by a Beef Reassurance campaign on posters, press and TV to communicate emerging facts, the measures put in place to prevent BSE from entering the human food chain and, in particular, to inform people of the new Minced Beef Quality Mark.[19] Total media spend on this Beef Reassurance campaign was £3.9 million over 1996 and 1997.

SUMMARY MEDIA PLAN 1994 to 1997

Total red meat advertising spend over the period 1994 to 1997 was £36.2 million (Figure 5).

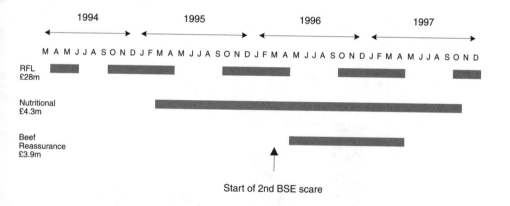

Figure 5: Total red meat ad spend, 1994 to 1997

EVALUATION 1994 to 1997

What happened to red meat sales from 1994 to 1997?

The rate of decline in red meat sales slowed as planned (Figure 6). Unexpectedly, in 1997, red meat sales actually grew year on year (Figure 7).

---

19. This mark was introduced on selected beef mince packs in June 1996 following research which showed that the main BSE-related volume loss for beef was focused on mince rather than on the more 'premium' cuts like roasts and steaks.

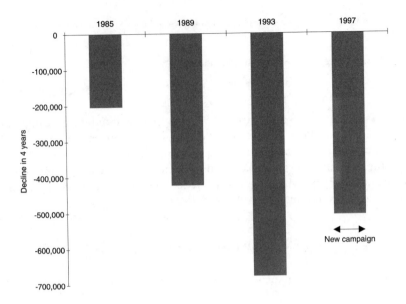

Figure 6: *Rate of decline in red meat sales*
Source: AGB

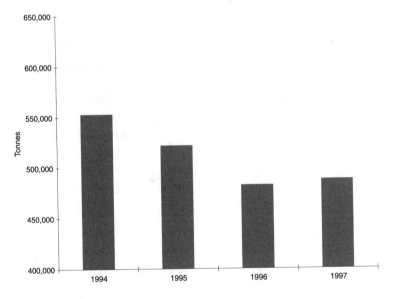

Figure 7: *Red meat volume sales*
Source: AGB

We will now prove the powerful role of advertising in this achievement by considering:

1. The effects of advertising on intermediate data.

2. The effects of advertising on sales.

3. Any other possible factors that could have caused this turnaround.

EFFECT OF ADVERTISING ON INTERMEDIATE DATA 1994 TO 1997

Tracking data and qualitative research show that the new campaign has worked in exactly the way we intended.

ATTITUDES TO ADVERTISING – THE 'RECIPE FOR LOVE' TV ADS

Our new advertising broke into people's consciousness.

TV advertising awareness of red meat (see Figure 8) which had been static for some years at around 20% grew over the period of the new campaign, to over 45% by 1997 (while in real terms advertising spend was constant).[20]

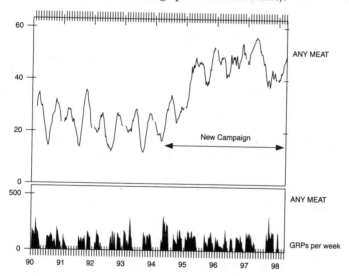

Figure 8: *Claimed TV ad awareness*
Source: Millward Brown

---

20. This is a result of the advertising budget deriving from a statutory levy on animals which changes only to reflect inflationary changes.
   NB. There was a small change in the way this question was asked on the tracking study at the end of January 1995. When asked 'Which of these have you seen advertised on TV recently?' before the change, respondents were shown a list of prompts. After the change, the prompts were read out. However, this effect did not come through well in this data (eight week rolling) until the end of March 1995 and the trend was sharply upwards before this point.

In group discussions,[21] red meat TV advertising is often debated in the 'warm-up' discussion about favourite ads. This popularity is confirmed in tracking data (Table 2).

TABLE 2: PERCENTAGE OF PEAK MEASURES VS. BEST FROM PRECEDING CAMPAIGNS

	New meat ads	Old meat ads
Any positive	95	68
Enjoyed watching it	55	28
Liked the people in it	48	17
Sticks in the mind	51	29

Source: Millward Brown

Qualitatively, the ads are extremely well received and are seen to talk about red meat as planned.

'They're very true to life – life's like that.'

'Some of the best ads on TV.'

'I know it sounds silly but for love is right. That's a meal my gran always used to make for me. She knew it was my special dinner.'

'She shows her appreciation and love for her son by cooking him a proper meal. She loves him enough to take the time.'

'You think – mmm – haven't had a steak for ages.'

Sources: BMP Qual and Ockwell Associates 1994 to 1997

Finally, the ads have generated considerable consumer and industry PR.[22]

ATTITUDES TO ADVERTISING – NUTRITIONAL AND BEEF REASSURANCE CAMPAIGNS

The diverse nature and varied media usage of these campaigns prevents as detailed an analysis of the effects as for the RFL advertising, but we can show the following results:

Nutritional Campaign

The nutritional advertising campaign was challenging people's preconceptions about the healthiness of red meat as planned (Table 3).

21. For food and non-food sectors
22. Most recently for 'Anniversary', an *Evening Standard* article, a feature on London Tonight and The Richard and Judy show. ' House Husband' recently appeared in *Campaign* magazine's People's Jury as a favourite ad. The ads have also received considerable industry recognition – four British TV Advertising Awards in 1998 and four ads have been chosen as *Campaign* magazine's Pick of the Week.

TABLE 3: PROMPTED IMPRESSIONS OF NUTRITIONAL ADS 1995 TO 1996

I found them convincing	59%
The information was relevant to me	53%
They made red meat more appealing	46%

Base: Those aware of nutritional ads 1995–1996
Source: Millward Brown

'Well, to think that all these years on a diet I've been eating cottage cheese and I could have been tucking into pork.'

Source: BMP Qual 1995

Beef Reassurance Campaign

Our target, the 'worried' former beef eaters, reacted in the way intended to our advertising.

'Well, that makes me feel a lot better.'

'It's saying that you can feel reassured.'

Source: Ockwell Associates 1996

So people's attitudes to our advertising were as we had hoped they might be.

ATTITUDES TO RED MEAT

Image of Red Meat

Red meat's image on a number of 'nutritional' dimensions has shown a marked improvement (both absolutely, and relatively to chicken and fish) over the years since the start of the new campaign.[23]

The RFL and nutritional ads appear to have played interesting roles in this turnaround, ie, – the RFL ads, which began in 1994, seem to have helped to get people emotionally on the side of red meat, (so negative feelings about red meat started to decline in 1994)[24] (Figures 9 and 10).

---

23. Although it was the nutritional campaign which was specifically designed to address people's health concerns about red meat, qualitatively we have evidence that many of the RFL ads communicate that 'red meat is good for you' too.
   For example, 'Awkward Age' (schoolboy coming home after disastrous day) 'She's giving him a good meal to build him up after that day.'
   For example, 'Anniversary' (old couple celebrating their silver wedding anniversary with a steak) 'They've lived a long happy and healthy life eating their beef.'
24. NB. Gap in data in image charts in 1997 due to temporary replacing nutritional questions with BSE -related questions.

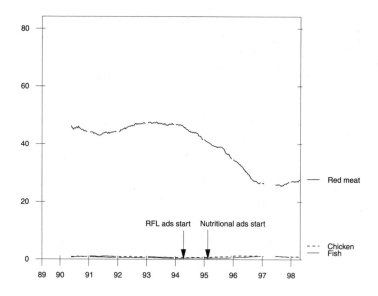

Figure 9: *Percentage agreeing – Not very good for you*
Source: Millward Brown

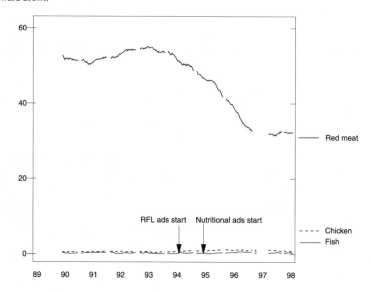

Figure 10: *Percantage agreeing – Can cause high blood pressure*
Source: Millward Brown

Once negative feelings about red meat had started to decline, the nutritional ads beginning in 1995, began to move people's *positive* beliefs (Figures 11 and 12).

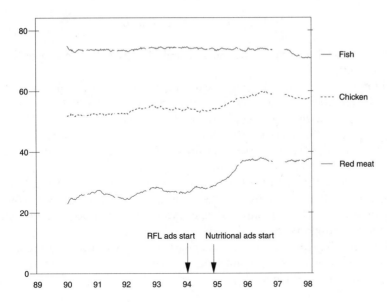

Figure 11: *Percentage agreeing – Important in healthy/balanced diet*
Source: Millward Brown

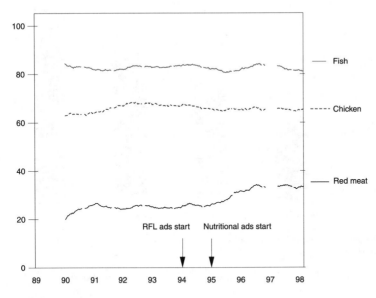

Figure 12: *Percentage agreeing – Good for you*
Source: Millward Brown

Image of Red Meat Eating

As we had planned, people seemed increasingly happy to be and to be seen to be red meat eaters!

Qualitatively, the image of red meat eaters was far more positive. The 'Les Dawson' image was waning and people increasingly described typical red meat eaters as 'people like them' or people like Gary Lineker!

This type of user imagery is difficult to measure *quantitatively* but we believe we can demonstrate this via a question on the tracking study. This asks people 'How often are you buying red meat compared to a year ago?'.

Now we know this is not a true measure of *behaviour* because this started to increase in 1994, but sales were still declining until 1996. Instead we would argue that any increases in this measure indicates improvement in people's *perceptions* of what red meat eating says about themselves.

And this has happened. The percentage of people who say they are buying red meat 'more often or the same compared to a year ago' since the start of the new campaign has *increased* (Figure 13).

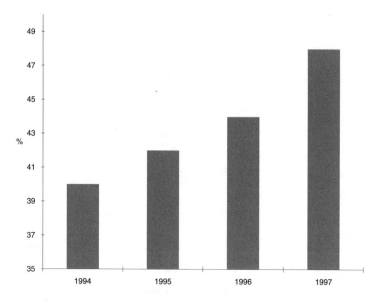

Figure 13: *Percentage claiming to be buying red meat more often or the same compared to a year ago*
Source: Millward Brown

The ads seem to have been remarkably successful in terms of their attitudinal effects.

We now go on to prove that these were translated into *sales* effects.

EFFECTS OF ADVERTISING ON SALES 1994 TO 1997

Before evaluating the effects of advertising on *total* red meat sales as planned, we first address beef separately.

The Effects of Beef Reassurance Advertising on Beef Sales 1994 to 1997

It would be ludicrous to have expected beef sales to have done fantastically well during the period in question. Beef sales were hammered by the publicity surrounding BSE in the immediate aftermath of the 1996 crisis.

Nevertheless we will argue that given the sheer *quantity* of bad publicity,[25]

— Beef sales following the 1996 BSE crisis did better than might have been expected;

— Beef Reassurance advertising played a crucial role in holding up this beef volume.

Beef sales did better than might be expected

To demonstrate this, we compare beef sales after the second BSE scare in 1996 (following which we started Beef Reassurance advertising) with sales after the first BSE scare in 1990 when there was no change to ongoing advertising.

This shows that contrary to expectations, the fall in beef sales during the second and most newsworthy BSE crisis was smaller than that during the first BSE crisis – despite higher levels of bad publicity (Figure 14).

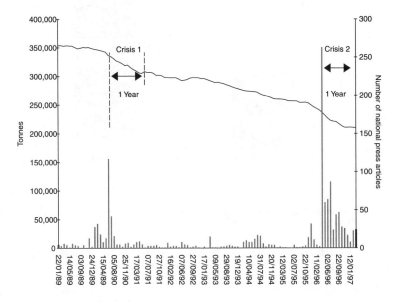

Figure 14: *BSE press mentions vs. beef volume MAT*
Source: AGB, MLC, MMD

---

5. Of course this publicity was far more alarming in 1996 (when the probable link between BSE and CJD was publicly announced) compared with the scare in 1990 which was essentially a more theoretical debate (and rigorously denied by all official bodies) about whether diseases like BSE could potentially jump species.

	BSE crisis 1	BSE crisis 2
Beef volume lost in year post crisis (Start of crisis defined from the week when the major outbreak of publicity occurred)	37,089 tonnes	30,868 tonnes
Number of national press articles in year post crisis	229	715
Beef volume decline per national press article	162 tonnes	43 tonnes

We also know from a special AGB panel analysis, 'pre' and 'post' the second BSE crisis, that by April 1997, 6% of former beef buyers were still not buying beef. But our target for the Beef Reassurance advertising ('the worriers') were buying *more* beef than they had before the second BSE scare (Figure 15).[26]

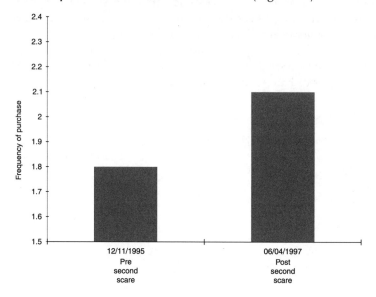

Figure 15: *Frequency of beef purchase of 'worriers' – four weeks ending 12 November 1995 vs. April 1997*
Source: AGB Special Analysis

Beef Reassurance advertising specifically helped to hold up the beef volume during the second BSE crisis
We have two pieces of evidence.

— Regional analysis[27] 1996/1997 (Figure 16).

---

26. NB Obviously, higher income and lower beef prices helped sales in the second BSE crisis but the beef econometric model and regional analysis (see next section) negates these effects.
There is a seasonal difference between November and April red meat sales, but as November sales are higher, ie, without seasonality effects, this difference would be even more pronounced.
27. There was no planned regional 'test'. All regions received Beef Reassurance advertising but, due to media buying share deal arrangements, some regions received more advertising than others.

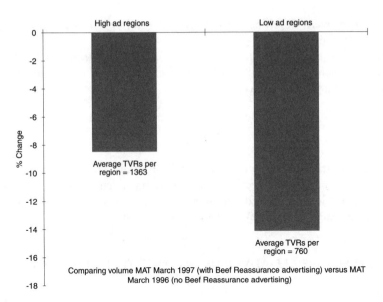

Figure 16: *Decline in annual beef volume during BSE crisis of 1996*
Source: AGB

A regional comparison of beef sales over the period of the second BSE crisis shows that regions with higher levels of Beef Reassurance TV advertising showed *lower* beef volume declines than did regions with less TV advertising.[28]

— A beef econometric model (Figure 17).

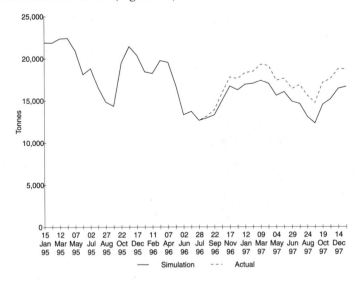

Figure 17: *Beef volume sales – actual vs. simulation: effect of Beef Reassurance advertising in 1996/1997*
Source: AGB, BMP, Model

28. TV advertising accounted for over 60% of the spend on the Beef Reassurance campaign.

Two models were developed (for beef and total red meat) to investigate the effects of advertising.

Modelling of beef sales shows that the Beef Reassurance advertising was responsible for generating £138 million of beef sales over 1996 and 1997 which would otherwise not have occurred.

Summary

There is no way that a scare on the scale of BSE could *not* have had a significant effect on beef volume. In this section however we have demonstrated that this effect was less than would be expected, and have proved the role of the Beef Reassurance advertising campaign in significantly lessening this volume impact.

THE EFFECT OF ALL ADVERTISING ON TOTAL RED MEAT SALES 1994 TO 1997

Now that we have looked at beef, we turn to total red meat sales.

As we have seen, the rate of decline in red meat consumption slowed as planned and was eventually reversed over the period under discussion. We have two pieces of evidence for the contribution of advertising to this:

1. Regions with higher levels of all advertising for red meat performed better than regions with lower levels of advertising over 1994 to 1997 (Figure 18).[29]

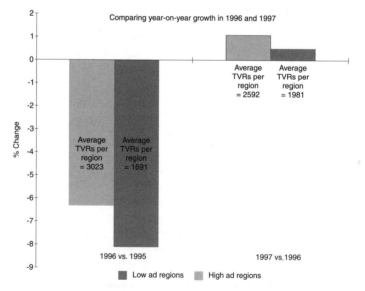

Figure 18: *Red meat volume – regional evidence*

---

29. Unfortunately we only have regional data for three years.

2. The econometric model of total red meat sales proves the direct effect of advertising (Figure 19).

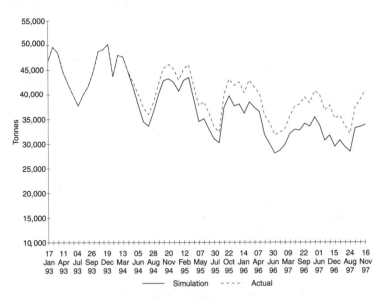

Figure 19: *Red meat volume sales – actual vs. simultation – effect of all MLC advertising*

The model shows that £739 million of red meat sales can be directly attributed to the new campaign over 1994 and 1997.

ELIMINATING OTHER POSSIBLE CONTRIBUTORS TO THIS TURNAROUND SINCE 1994

Red Meat Price Relative to Poultry

This is accounted for in the models but it is also worth noting that red meat prices *grew* relative to poultry over the advertised period 1994 to 1997 (Figure 20).

'Competitor' Advertising

Advertising spend on red meats' main 'competitors' has grown over this period, not declined (Figure 21).

New Zealand Lamb Advertising (NZL)

There has been no increase in the level and no change in the nature of NZL advertising over this period which could explain the effects seen (Figure 22).[30]

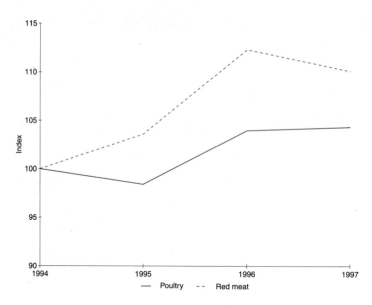

Figure 20: *Red meat and poultry prices – indexed*
Source: MLC, ONS

Expenditure on Promotions by the MLC

In addition to advertising, the MLC ran a promotions programme[31] over 1994 and 1997 – where possible themed and timed around the new campaign. However,

— There has been no change in real terms in the promotional spend over the past ten years.

— Very little change is attributed to promotional activity in the red meat model. What is more, any change that there has been in promotional effect over 1994 to 1997 is really a result of the new campaign, because promotions were themed around the new campaign from 1994.

Demographic Changes

There were no demographic changes over the period 1994 to 1997 which could explain the sales patterns seen.

---

30. On average over the period between 1994 and 1997, NZL adspend has been less than 6% of the total red meat adspend. In addition, advertising recall of New Zealand Lamb advertising was consistently low at around 5% (Millward Brown 1997).
31. Including trade advertising, recipe cards, on-pack promotional tie-ins with products like sauces and so on.

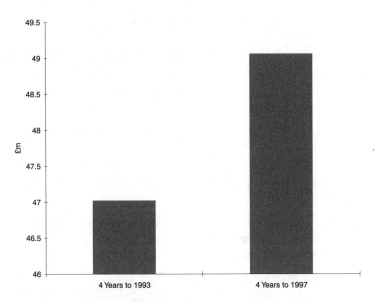

Figure 21: '*Competitor advertising' – average adspend per year*
Source: MEAL

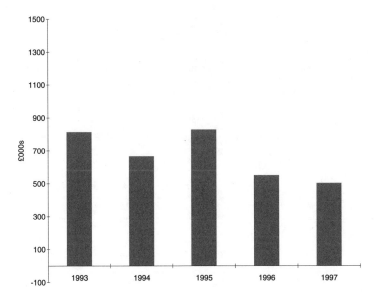

Figure 22: *New Zealand Lamb real adspend (1993 base)*
Source: MEAL

Regional Differences

There were no regional differences in any of the variables considered which could explain the variation in regional volumes seen – apart from regional media weight.[32]

The Introduction of the Minced Beef Quality Mark (MBQM)

A key difference between the first and second BSE crisis was the MBQM. However, we do not believe the introduction of this mark alone would have caused effects seen, because:

— Beef sales were higher in higher Beef Reassurance advertising weight regions than lower weight regions between 1994 and 1997 and there was no difference in regional distribution of the MBQM.

— This fits with qualitative findings that the people whom the MBQM was addressing (those who had temporarily given up beef or at least given up beef mince) were simply not going to the beef section of the meat counter – so they would not have found the new mark on-pack for themselves.

BSE 'Fatigue'

Beef volume did not suffer less in the 1996 crisis because people were less concerned by BSE then. Levels of concern were actually *higher* in 1996 (152%) than in 1990 (100%).[33]

Percentage saying 'very/quite concerned by BSE' Indexed on 1990	
1990	1996
(BSE Crisis 1)	(BSE Crisis 2)
100	152

Source: The National Health Survey

---

32. In fact, the regions making up the high and low advertised regions changed in each of the three years studied so it is even less likely that anything other than the advertising weight differences could explain the regional volume variations seen.
33. Indexed on 1990. As described, the 1990 scare was purely speculation about BSE type diseases crossing species barriers – the 1996 scare was completely different – caused by a government announcement confirming the probable link between BSE and CJD in humans.

PAYBACK

Extra Sales due to Advertising

The scale of return and the financial consequences of the turnaround in red meat sales were dramatic.

'The returns for red meat advertising are much higher than the returns typically found for commodity products of this type (indeed it would be high even for a branded product).'

Source: MMD[34]

The model below shows that the total media spend of £36.2 million spent on red meat advertising between 1994 and 1997 resulted in additional red meat sales of £739 million at retail value, ie, a return of nearly 18:1. This compares with average figures of other generic advertising as follows:

Red meat	18:1
Milk	3.5 – 6.5
Cheese	2:1
Butter	4:1

Source: MMD

Profitability of the Extra Sales to Farmers 1994 to 1997

Farmers' profit margins have varied both by year and by species over the period 1994 to 1997.

To give some indication of advertising payback we therefore use the average gross margin (across the four years and three species). This is 59%.[35]

The extra £621 million retail value of British-produced red meat due to advertising (which includes income for the whole production chain) resulted in an additional revenue to farmers[36] of £155 million. Using the average gross margin of 59%, this resulted in an additional £91 million gross margin to farmers (£51 million after subtracting advertising media and production expenditure).

However, the longer-term profit implications of both the attitudinal improvements regarding red meat, and the damage limitation to beef sales brought about by advertising, are difficult to quantify but will be far, far greater.

---

34. MMD is a company with wide experience of econometric modelling of a range of generic campaigns.
35. Gross margin = farmers' revenue minus variable costs (veterinary/medical costs plus feed and forage costs).
36. Who funded the advertising with their levy payments.

Effects of the 1994 to 1997 Advertising on Other Stakeholders

We have analysed the benefits and profitability of advertising-generated sales for farmers. However, the red meat industry in total is a huge one. Apart from the farmers, there are large numbers of other stakeholders in the carcass red meat market – a chain from auction markets (240 markets) to abattoirs (15,000 employees) to meat processors (60,000 employees) to butchers (50,000) and multiple retailers.[37] All these businesses' fortunes are harnessed to the fortunes or otherwise of red meat retail sales.

All have faced the potentially crippling effects of BSE over the past two years. And all have benefited from the advocacy of the MLC's advertising – a lone voice of support, helping (on a very modest budget) to counter-balance the deluge of hysterical BSE-related media coverage on top of the ongoing long-term problems facing red meat. The following quotes illustrate these stakeholder's views regarding advertising's benefit to them.

> 'In very difficult times, the MLC's campaign provided a reassuring platform on which we can rebuild the market.'

> 'For a market to be hit by the scares we have, without the advertising over the past 4 years – well the effect would have been catastrophic.'

> 'When you're down you've got to fight back and nothing else was doing this on our behalf.'

> Meat Processor 1998

> 'What the MLC have done is excellent – without the advertising over the past 4 years the effects would have been catastrophic for butchers.'

> Family Butcher 1998

> 'The Beef Reassurance campaign dramatically improved sales and limited damage to red meat.'

> 'Supermarket displays are demand-led. Without the advertising, meat space in supermarkets would be much lower than now.'

> Multiple Retailer Meat Buyer 1998

Profitability of the Extra Sales 1994 to 1997 to These Other 'Stakeholders'

It is difficult to calculate precisely the financial contribution to the various elements of the chain but they would all benefit from £584 million of extra sales between 1994 and 1997 (£739 million advertising-generated extra retail sales minus £155 million extra farmer revenue).

Even at 10% gross margin (one-fifth of the level of the farmers' gross margin) this would result in an additional £58 million gross profit along the chain. In reality, the profit would probably well exceed this. And of course, beyond the retail

---

37. MLC 1998.

sales benefits of carcass red meat, there are knock-on profit benefits for other retail markets (ready meals, burgers and so on) as well as other sectors (catering, fast food) from the advertising effects shown.

CONCLUSIONS

Advertising succeeded in transforming attitudes to red meat. This in turn has resulted in a very profitable boost to sales over the four years studied. This increase in sales was beneficial not only to the farmers who directly funded the advertising that caused it but also to other numerous stakeholders in this vast food market. In addition, the effects of the advertising will deliver significant benefits to the industry into the future. We believe that three key conclusions which emerge from this case history are worth reiterating for advertisers contemplating the consequences of advertising investment in other markets.

1. Well-conceived and executed advertising can have tremendously powerful effects even at relatively low levels of expenditure (£8 million p.a. versus £2 billion p.a. market). Advertising can indeed move the seemingly immovable, such as huge long-term structural forces with an unprecedented short-term crisis on top.

2. Truly significant returns from advertising are often the result of 'thinking outside the box' – in this case by looking beyond competitive 'brand' activity (pork vs. beef vs. lamb) and focusing on the total category and its generic, yet powerful, benefits.

3. Effective advertising can not only directly generate large returns for those immediately involved in its funding, but can, and often does, have very significant effects on other stakeholders. These in turn can go on to generate additional benefits for the advertising funders. In this example, increases in profit all along the chain of stakeholders have improved the health and long-term viability of the whole industry, which must in turn protect farmers' long-term prospects.

Impressions of 1998 Shortlisted Papers

Steve Williamson
Smithkline Beecham

There is always the danger that when you are involved or interested in a particular activity it can become the focal point of all your considerations to the detriment of looking at the bigger picture. I believe many Financial Directors see advertising as a big 'expense' on the profit and loss account to be minimised so that more profit can be delivered to the bottom line and ultimately to shareholders. It is to be hoped that this is a view of the fast disappearing past and that times will change in the future. Accountants, marketers, salesmen, production managers, in the traditional sense of those terms, can increasingly be viewed, in successful companies, as 'business managers', individuals who take a much more overall view to their activities than they would have done historically.

A NEW APPROACH TO THE IPA AWARDS

In the past Advertising and Marketing Awards were viewed by some as the industry patting itself on the back for the latest TV creative or campaign. It was therefore rewarding to be asked to sit on the IPA's judging panel for the 1998 Advertising Effectiveness Awards. This was because their brief was not only to reward the ability to talk to multiple targets simultaneously so as to align these groups in a common understanding of the brand's purpose, it was also to address other stakeholders, the city institutions and employees. This to me was a step change in how the industry should consider the impact of advertising.

Reading the short-listed papers was stimulating and rewarding. If you are at the forefront of the finance function today you are much more involved in measurement, not just financially but numerically so more and more companies talk about the balanced scorecard approach and dashboards that give an overview of company progress and direction. In the papers submitted there was a great deal of consistency and similarity in the setting of objectives, how they were going to be achieved, implementation plans, measurement, post appraisal, impact on stakeholders and so on.

By reading and reviewing the contents of the papers with the other panel members it not only did the degree to which there are common measures and methodologies in the industry today become apparent, but also how new techniques were being put forward to support the individual cases concerned. Bringing these together saw the development of some powerful arguments.

Likewise some of the claims and models put forward had to be treated with some caution, not because their claims were not to be believed but more because they needed more time to pass before you could conclude whether or not they could be held up as proven.

From my point of view as a Financial Director those papers which concentrated on share price (Orange), advertising's impact on discounts (North West Water), the effect on residual values and dealer margins (Audi), and savings for industry as a whole (Direct Debit), were the ones I would recommend not only to other members of my discipline but to business practitioners generally.

The more challenging papers were those which attempted to show benefits that were more difficult to substantiate; these would include recruitment (the Army), attacks from a new player (Littlewoods Pools) and the charities and non-profit making organisations. These papers were breaking new ground in the way they attempted to show the effectiveness of their campaigns, a difficult task when you do not have the traditional foundations of sales, profit, market share and so on.

The standard of all the papers was very high and these should all be regarded as the standard from which we should progress in the future. I have had some comments along the lines of 'you only saw the best'. I would respond that this was only a selection of those campaigns which companies decided to submit. There are many other campaigns for which no submissions were made. My honest belief is that there are some truly world-class practices out there and we have to continually try and find ways of teasing them out so that the whole industry can learn and improve.

There can be no doubt that some of the decisions taken by the panel of judges were seen as controversial, this is inevitable when you are trying to move outside traditional boundaries. However, if you look at *Advertising Works 10* alongside *Advertising Works 9* you will see that we have now taken the review of advertising effectiveness one stage further.

Section 3

Three-Star Winners

★★★

12

Audi

*Members only: how advertising helped
Audi join the prestige car club*

EDITOR'S SUMMARY

This paper describes how Audi's progress from probationary to full membership of the 'prestige car club' benefited its three principle stakeholders; Audi UK, Audi dealers and Audi drivers.

Audi Joins the Prestige Car Club

In 1994 brand imagery studies indicated that the 1980's 'Vorsprung Durch Technik' campaign had been successful in moving Audi up from a bland 'Eurocar' to probationary membership of the 'prestige car club'. It was now an unusual alternative to BMW/Mercedes.

Research identified the core Audi values as being Modern, Innovative and, most importantly, Individual. This opened up the opportunity to build prestige credentials around driver imagery to establish full membership of the club.

Results

Research has shown in excess of 50% rises since 1995 in the number of people who rate Audi drivers as being different, intelligent or successful.

By 1997 Audi UK were selling 61% more cars per annum than in 1994, a sales increase well ahead of the other prestige marques. This is despite the fact that distribution has shrunk by 33% and the mix of cars sold has become richer. As a result Audi dealers are making nearly four times as much profit as they were in 1994.

Innovative analysis of second-hand car values shows that the average retained value for the owner of the 1993 Audi range (selected not to include any of the improved product) increased across the advertising period from 71.2% to 84.2%. From this (if we apply basic supply and demand economic theory) we can infer an increased volume demand curve of 33% for the marque, based on image change alone. This 33% increase equates to over £400 million increased revenue.

INTRODUCTION

This paper examines how advertising contributed to the change in status that the Audi brand has undergone since 1995, the year in which Audi introduced its new model range. It demonstrates that Audi achieved membership of what is often called 'the prestige car club', and studies the resultant change in Audi's business and the benefit this brought to the various stakeholders in the Audi brand. It then uses new learning to understand better how we can evaluate advertising's contribution to the fortunes of a car brand.

AUDI AND THE PRESTIGE CAR CLUB

We can split the UK car market into a number of different sectors according to value of product and status of brand. Taking some example car brands, we can draw up the following 'market map' (Table 1).

TABLE 1: UK CAR MARKET

Super prestige	Prestige	Quality	Mainstream	Budget
Porsche	BMW	Volvo	Ford	Kia
Ferrari	Mercedes	Saab	Vauxhall	Proton
	Jaguar		Rover	
			Renault	

The different sectors of this map are characterised by a number of factors.

— Volume tends to increase from left to right until we come to mainstream, which is where the market leaders in volume share terms are located.

— Discounting varies by sector. Prestige status protects from discounting, while mainstream marques are in a weaker bargaining position.

— Premium charged per unit tends to increase from right to left, with super prestige cars retailing as very high value purchases.

— Quality brands share some of the characterstics of prestige brands, but not to a sufficient degree to qualify for membership of the exclusive prestige car club.

The prestige car club is made up of a select group of car marques which are characterised by strong technical credentials and brand desirability. They do not fight over budget and mid-range market share; instead they operate at the high end of the market and account for less than 10% of all new car sales in the UK.

Given the complexity of the car market and the brands within it, moving upwards from one sector to another is very difficult. Consumer views of brands such as Jaguar and Mercedes are built up over years, probably from early childhood. These brands seem to have a birthright that elevates them above the competition; they are the aristocrats of marketing that rarely have to explain themselves.

Indeed, full membership has recently been restricted to Jaguar, Mercedes and BMW. All three have shown the combination of brand image and product strength necessary for membership. These are the criteria that Audi had to meet if it was to assert its rights to be regarded as a class above Saab and Volvo and as a credible peer of Jaguar, Mercedes and BMW.

To graduate to full prestige car club membership might be very difficult, but the advantages of full membership are significant.

The Advantages of Joining the Prestige Car Club

The key benefit of prestige car club membership is consistent with prestige brand behaviour in other markets. Whether we look at the fashion, drinks or car industry, prestige brands operate in the same way. This is characterised by the way these brands drive demand.

In general, demand is a function of hard and soft factors. A combination of the rational and the emotional appeal of a brand and its products determines the level of demand for that brand and those products.

In the case of prestige brands, however, there is an additional element in the equation: their prestige status. Product and image come together so successfully that the brand takes on a 'factor X' prestige that leads to an extraordinary level of demand. Prestige acts as a coefficient on demand.

This point is made in the extreme by Dr Lesley de Chernatony. Even though his example compares a super prestige brand with a mainstream brand, the principle remains relevant. In The Seven Building Blocks of Brands he points to the difference between the functional parity of a Toyota Supra Turbo and a Porsche Carrera and the disparity between their retail price.

Both cars are designed with closely comparable performance characteristics. Both accelerated from zero to 60mph in 6.1 seconds, and have similar top speeds of around 150mph. But the Porsche image meant it was able to charge a premium of around £15,000.

Source: Dr Lesley de Chernatony, *The Seven Building Blocks of Brands*

The high level of demand dramatised by Dr de Chernatony becomes a key determinant in the business success of a brand because it helps the brand to achieve the marketer's ideal: volume growth alongside value growth.

We can represent this as the prestige brand dynamic (Figure 1).

In the case of the car market we can see how the Prestige Brand Dynamic benefits the various stakeholders in the brand. We can define Audi's different stakeholders as the manufacturer, the dealers and the owners.

The Prestige Brand Dynamic in New Cars – The Manufacturer

The benefits to the manufacturer are volume growth accompanied by value growth. This results in increased revenue and income. Value growth can be achieved by both higher margins on equivalent product and by enrichening the product mix, that is, consumers buying more high-end models.

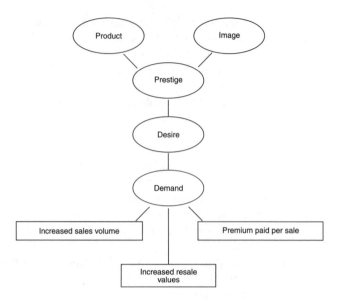

Figure 1: *The prestige brand dynamic*

The Prestige Brand Dynamic in New Cars – The Dealer

The dealer benefits from volume growth and an enrichment of the sales mix for the same reasons as the manufacturer.

He particularly benefits because as demand grows he can harden his selling price and discount less, thereby increasing his profit. He also benefits from the increased parts and service requirements that accompany volume growth.

The Prestige Brand Dynamic in Used Cars – The Owner, Business and Private

The premium brand dynamic brings a benefit to the owner, or purchaser, which distinguishes the car market from many other markets. This is because a huge second-hand car market exists. Products are not purchased, consumed or used and then disposed of; they are sold on. This has sizeable implications for the benefits of prestige car club membership.

Prestige cars drop in value more slowly than do quality or mainstream brands. Because of this, having bought a prestige car the owner stands to lose less money in relative and possibly real terms than if a quality or mainstream brand had been purchased.

If we compare the resale value of a two-year-old Mercedes C Class with a two-year-old Saab 900i and a Ford Mondeo 2.0 Si of the same age and mileage, we can see a definite advantage in Mercedes' favour. The Mercedes retains more of its value (Table 2).

The differences between mainstream and quality and between quality and prestige are significant. This is why it is important for a brand to move up through the various levels.

TABLE 2: CAR BRAND DEPRECIATION

	New price August 1995	Used price September 1997	Retained value %
Mercedes C Class, 95N	£19,248	£16,850	87.5
Saab 900i, 95N	£16,995	£12,925	76.05
Ford Mondeo 2.0Si, 95N	£16,375	£10,000	61.0

Source: Glass's Guide, September 1997

Over two years the Mercedes retains considerably more value than the Saab and the Ford, both in percentage and in absolute terms. As the owner loses less money when the car is sold on the cost of ownership is reduced. Thus the prestige status of a car brand provides material benefit to the often overlooked stakeholder in the brand: the original purchaser.

With membership carrying such significant benefits, it is worth examining the scale of Audi's task in attempting to gain membership.

Audi in the 1980s

In the early 1980s, Audi was seen as a bland 'Eurocar'. Consumers were unsure where the cars were built, had no regard for Audi's technical credentials and, in terms of prestige, Audi were hardly on the map. The Louis Harris Car Image Study groups car brands according to consumer perceptions of a brand's closest competitive set. Figure 2 shows the extent to which Audi lagged behind its German rivals.

This shows that Audi was positioned firmly in the mainstream, bracketed in the minds of consumers with Ford. This belied the engineering excellence of many of Audi's products, and its German heritage, as well as being at odds with the price of a new Audi in 1982 (£6,680 versus a Ford Sierra at £5,071).

For Audi to function successfully in the UK, perceptions had to change. Given that it is so hard to move a car brand from one class to the next, this represented an enormous task.

Nevertheless, with a combination of a world-class product, the Audi quattro, and other important technical innovations such as the UK's first introduction of catalytic converters across all models, together with strong image-based advertising, impressive progress was made.

Audi in the Late 1980s and Early 1990s

By 1987 Audi was a probationary member of the prestige car club. The 'Vorsprung Durch Technik' campaign of the 1980s had encouraged people to think of Audi as an upmarket, technically advanced German manufacturer. Audi was clearly elevated above volume manufacturers such as Ford and Vauxhall.

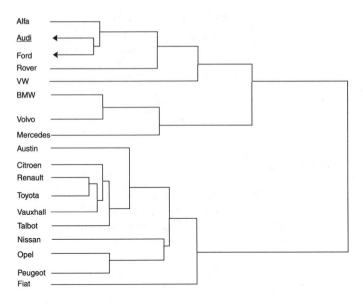

Figure 2: *Car Image Study, 1982*
Source: Louis Harris Car Image Study, 1982

Audi on the 'Waiting List' for Prestige Car Club Membership

However, with the withdrawal of the quattro and the strength of competitive products such as the BMW 3 series, by the time the new 'A' range was introduced, Audi still had some way to go before full membership of the prestige car club could be confirmed. This is evident in the Harris Brand Tracking Study's measurement of prestige from October 1994 (Figure 3):

In short, Audi was by no means certain of achieving full membership to the club.

> 'Audi, a "bridesmaid" in prestige behind Mercedes and BMW.'

> Source: Harris Brand Tracking, July 1994

Remaining on the waiting list ('a bridesmaid') would mean that Audi would never enjoy the benefits of full membership. It would live in the shadows of its illustrious German cousins, existing perhaps as an interesting, oddball alternative but failing to establish itself as an authentic equivalent which demanded consideration in its own right.

To change this situation Audi had to find a way to achieve full membership, but on its own terms. It had to find sufficient differentiation to draw consumers to Audi as a first choice. To achieve prestige status, Audi had to mark out a territory that would give it competitive advantage in image terms. The 1995 advertising brief was built around meeting this objective.

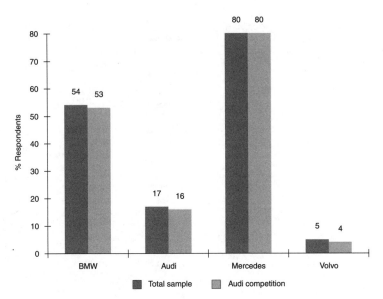

Figure 3: *Manufacturer 'is a prestige make' – October 1994*
Source: Harris Brand Tracking, 1994

Joining the Prestige Car Club on Audi's Terms

The year 1995 was one of opportunity for Audi UK. It was to begin the introduction of its new range of 'A' products, starting with the Audi A8 and the Audi A4, both of which were considerable improvements on previous Audi models. These were warmly received by the press and have gone on to win several awards. However, even with this new range in production, Audi had a broader image job to do.

Building a Model for Audi Advertising

Audi had to define itself in a way which differentiated it from the prestige competition. Our analysis of prestige car advertising showed us that there was a very simple yet effective advertising model at work (Figure 4).

This model had proved successful for Audi's established competitors. Years of technology focus had paid dividends for Audi's rivals, as epitomised by BMW's long-running strapline, 'The Ultimate Driving Machine'. However, for the reasons outlined above, we knew that the technology model could not be adopted wholesale as a model for Audi advertising.

Audi would run the risk of becoming even more of a bridesmaid brand, a 'me-too' contender with no distinguishing features, confirming its waiting list status. We believed there had to be another way.

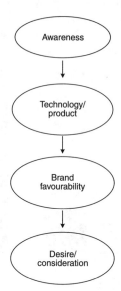

Figure 4: *The prestige car advertising model*

Finding Another Way – Defining and Focusing the Audi Brand

To find a new model of car advertising that would help us to meet our objective of prestige car club membership, we tried to uncover core aspects of the Audi brand. Perhaps here we could identify a set of values to act as a usable and credible brand differentiation for Audi.

To this end, BBH interrogated Audi's product and corporate philosophy, and underlying consumer perceptions of the marque. Research groups were conducted among Audi drivers as well as competitive drivers, Audi evangelists as well as Audi rejectors. BBH interviewed experts from different disciplines within the car industry as well as commentators and opinion leaders from design, music and architecture.

The result of this exercise was a new, clearer articulation of the Audi brand – Modern, Innovative, Individual.

Various qualities and associations of the brand can be distilled into a three-word brand definition.

— Modern: There was a growing sense of Audi as a contempory brand, a brand that was neither traditional nor conservative. This flowed from a sense of Audi having a strong design philosophy which was seen as 'pure' and 'of this time'.

— Innovative: We confirmed that the brand was rich in technology and engineering imagery; not surprising given the success of the 'Vorsprung Durch Technik' campaign.

— Individual: This focused our attention on driver imagery. Particular personality traits such as independence and understatement were associated with the Audi driver. In this context we saw significant areas of differentiation between Audi and its competitors.

The Driver Imagery of Prestige Car Club Members

It was apparent from the research that established members of the prestige set were associated with particular driver imagery (Table 3):

TABLE 3: DRIVER IMAGERY BY BRAND

Jaguar	Mercedes	BMW
Establishment	Established	Ambitious
Successful	Rich	Competitive
British	Successful	Ostentatious
Conservative	Inflexible	Confident
Old School Tie		Successful

Source: BBH Brand Research, 1994

This gave us a landscape to work against. We began to develop a new advertising model that differentiated the Audi brand using driver imagery (Figure 5). If we could portray the Audi driver as a successful (apparently compulsory in this sector), but also intelligent person who likes to be different, we could develop the distinctive brand personality essential to Audi existing on its own terms as a prestige car club member.

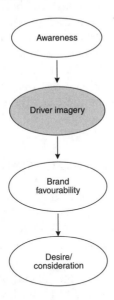

Figure 5: *The Audi advertising model*

Defining the Different Roles for Audi Brand Advertising

Audi's activity in this period included both print and television advertising. Having defined the Audi brand so clearly, it was imperative that we used different media as appropriately and as efficiently as possible. Modern, Innovative, Individual are three levers to be pulled to varying degrees according to whatever message Audi is communicating.

Press advertising

It was decided not to use print advertising to build driver imagery. Instead it was used to underline Audi's technical credentials, a crucial hygiene factor for prestige car club membership. The innovative nature of the Audi brand is brought to the fore as specific product innovations are dramatised in print. Meanwhile the witty, wry tone of voice and the distinctive look of the executions drive Audi's modern and individual values. This provides the basic reassurance of product excellence while contributing to Audi's reputation as a modern, innovative and individual car brand.

Television advertising

It is on television that the main battle is fought. This is the optimum environment for developing the emotional elements required for a driver imagery campaign to be successful. The individual aspect of the brand is the focus of the commercials, while it is left to product reference, executional style and overall tone of voice to demonstrate that Audi is innovative and modern.

The campaign consisted of four television commercials that ran during the period 1995 to 1997.

Each execution communicates the Modern, Innovative, Individual brand values in different ways, but all build the image of the Audi driver as an independently minded individual. In 'No. 1', Freddie, the unreconstituted yuppie and Audi rejector, is positioned as the antithesis of the Audi brand. In 'Mooncar', Sonny Morea's wry observations and NASA credentials help us to understand Audi's personality, as does the Audi A3 driver who turns down the ultimate macho torture-test in 'Gauntlet'. In 'China', the line 'Some consumers, however, are already one step ahead', also communicates the distinctive character of the Audi driver (Figure 6[1]).

THE EFFECT OF THE ADVERTISING ON AUDI'S IMAGE

Has Audi Achieved Membership of the Prestige Car Club?

Using the Audi advertising model as our framework, we will now examine whether advertising and communication have helped to position the brand in the exclusive prestige car club.

We will examine two specific samples; Total Sample (which is made up of all owners of a new car valued above £14,000 who purchased new) and a sample made up of Audi's principal prestige and quality competition (defined as owners of BMW, Mercedes, Jaguar, Saab and Volvo, all to have been purchased new) which we call Audi competition. We believe it is important to look at both samples because to have achieved membership of the prestige car club, Audi must be recognised as such by club members and non-members alike.

---

1. February, March, April TVRs relate to an Audi quattro brand launch and are not considered part of the driver imagery campaign.

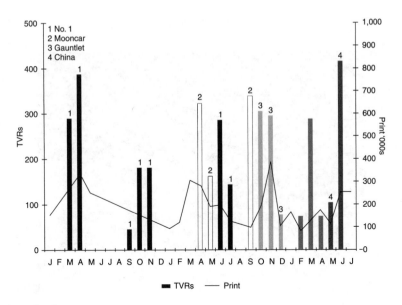

Figure 6: *UK Media plan*
Source: BBJ Media Services

Awareness

The first test for advertising is awareness. Figure 7 shows that the television campaign has been responsible for significant shifts in spontaneous brand awareness among the total sample and Audi's principal competitors.[2]

Driver Imagery

The key objective for the advertising was to start to build the image of the Audi driver. 'Pre' and 'Post' measures across the advertising period for responses to key driver imagery statements show significant positive shifts that are in line with the Audi advertising model (Figure 8).

These responses provide strong evidence that the advertising has started to define the Audi driver. While advertising is not the only communications activity that helps to shape driver imagery, it is by far the most significant.

Other activities like Audi's sponsorship of the Laser 2000 sailing series and motor-sport sponsorship along with advertorials may contribute to Audi's driver imagery, but these are niche activities. They are not broadcast activities that could be expected to register on the tracking study. They are also particularly chosen for their product association. It is therefore reasonable for Audi's television activity to claim the lion's share of the credit for the positive shifts in driver imagery.

2. In 1997, Audi changed tracking study and moved from continuous advertising tracking to a more holistic brand tracking study but on a 'dip' basis. 'China' was the first campaign to be tracked in this way.

PRESS ADS

'No. 1'

Sound: Natural sound throughout – street noises, traffic etc.
Freddy: I've always been very competitive. That's how I got where I am.

Freddy: Money can't buy happiness (laughs) but at the end of the day, you've got to look after number one to survive. It's every man for himself, right?

Freddy: Yeah, the right car is important to me. I think it does impress people.

Freddy: Money, nothing to be ashamed of. If you've got it, flaunt it.

Freddy: The places you go, the clothes you wear, the people you're seen with, the car you drive.

Dealer: Well, what do you think?
Freddy: Nah, it's not really my style. Know what I mean?

The 20 Valve Audi A4.
It won't be appreciated by everyone.
0345 998877

'CHINA'

Sound: Natural sound and dramatic
music throughout.

Sound: Police dialogue in Cantonese.

Sound: (MVO) China is changing fast.
Communism meets consumerism in the
handover of Hong Kong, fuelling the
people's desire for advanced consumer
goods.

Sound: (MVO) There are some consumers,
however, who are already one step ahead.

Sound: (MVO) Vorsprung durch technik, as
they whisper in China.

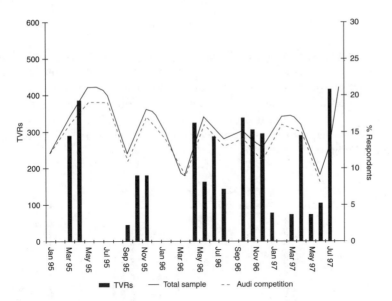

Figure 7: *Spontaneous awareness of Audi advertising*
Source: Harris Brand Tracking/Hall and Partners

The Audi brand now has a set of driver values that clearly differentiates it from its prestige competition. In this way Audi has strengthened its claim on club membership and can avoid being merely an aspirant 'me-too' brand.

If we look at responses to brand measures, we can see that the more defined driver image for Audi is developing in line with other positive shifts in perceptions of the Audi brand.

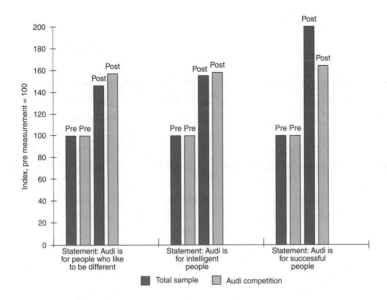

Figure 8: *Driver imagery responses*
Source: Harris Brand Tracking

Brand Favourability

The advertising has also helped to create brand favourability (defined as 'very favourable/mostly favourable'). This measure has shown significant increases over the advertised period among the total sample and Audi competition. This measure is critically important as one would not expect anyone to invest in a prestige car brand without feeling favourably disposed to it.

This and subsequent statements were only measured in the tracking waves indicated in Figure 9.[3]

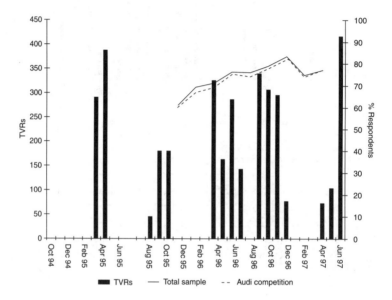

Figure 9: *Audi brand favourability – very favourable + mainly favourable*
Source: Harris Brand Tracking

Brand Desire and Consideration

Increased brand favourability builds desire for the Audi brand, demonstrated in responses to the statement 'Audi is the car I'd like to own' (Figure 10).

As the Audi brand becomes more desirable, consideration levels increase (Figure 11).

The difference between response pattern for the two samples during the period when 'No. 1' played out for the first and then the second time (March 1995 to November 1995) is worth noting. This may be related to the content of the commercial. The execution portrays a driver of an Audi competition marque, and after the initial burst the measurement dips for Audi competition response. Perhaps

---

3. Respondents were asked 'How favourable or unfavourable' is your opinion of the Audi brand? (This and subsequent statements were only measured in the tracking waves indicated on the charts.)

drivers of rival brands did not like the mirror that was held up to them. The sharp incline around the second burst implies they were more convinced at the second time of asking.

Increased consideration is also evident in responses to the statements 'Most likely next car' and 'Other makes would seriously consider'. These are critical measures. The brand is on the consumer's mental shopping list.

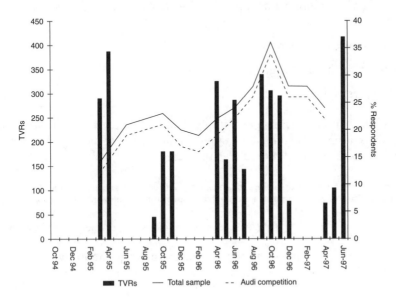

Figure 10: *Statement 'Audi is the car I'd like to own'*
Source: Harris Brand Tracking

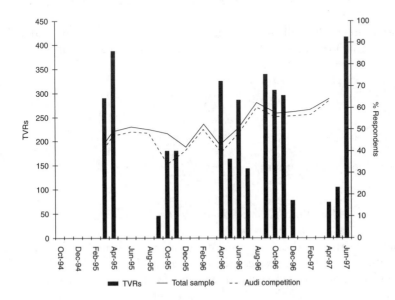

Figure 11: *Statement 'See yourself driving Audi'*
Source: Harris Tracking

Tracking Conclusion

Responses for both our samples are strong evidence that the advertising has been effective. The Audi advertising model has been vindicated.

— Spontaneous awareness moves in line with advertising activity.

— Driver imagery more defined, providing a stronger, more distinctive identity for Audi.

— Brand favourability increases over time.

— Desire for the brand has grown.

— Audi enjoys higher levels of consideration.

These shifts in brand perception imply that Audi is on its way to achieving full prestige car club membership. This implication is strengthened by the summary of the Forrest Associates Audi Brand Healthcheck:

'The primary objective was to explore the consumers' current understanding of the Audi brand. They see it as a prestige car brand on an equal footing with BMW and on a more upward trajectory.'

Source: Forrest Associates Audi Brand Healthcheck 1997

However, a strong image is only half of the prestige brand dynamic. We must look at Audi's business performance and see if that reflects a substantial change in status.

THE EFFECT OF ADVERTISING ON AUDI'S BUSINESS

For Audi to qualify for full club membership, we should be able to see the effects of Audi's increased prestige status on the marque's business performance and how this benefits the various stakeholders:

— Manufacturer.

— Dealer.

— Owner.

We will look at each in turn.

How Prestige Status Delivers for the Manufacturer

Certainly new car sales show a dramatic improvement, with 1997 being Audi UK's fourth consecutive record sales year (Figure 12).

To understand how impressive these sales figures are, it is useful to compare Audi's year-on-year growth with the overall growth in the market. Audi has consistently performed ahead of the market (Figure 13).

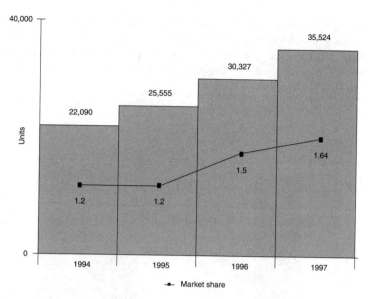

Figure 12 : *Audi new car sales and market share – 1991 to 1997*
Source: SMMT

Another factor which highlights the strength of this sales performance is that changes in the Audi dealer network means it was achieved against shrinking distribution. Since 1994 Audi's annual sales have increased by 60.8% p.a. while distribution has shrunk by 33.3%.

In addition to record volume sales, Audi was enriching its sales mix by selling a greater proportion of high end models.

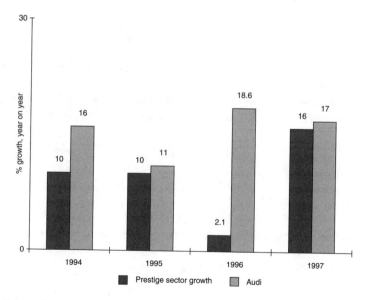

Figure 13: *Audi share sales versus prestige sector sales*
Source: SMMT

The richer sales mix is clearly evident if we look at Audi's performance in the compact executive saloon segment (which has consistently represented 65% to 75% of Audi's sales). We can see how the centre of gravity of the marque has moved upwards as the brand attracts people willing to spend more money on more expensive models (Figure 14).

This is reflected in the gradual increase in average selling price across the Audi brand.

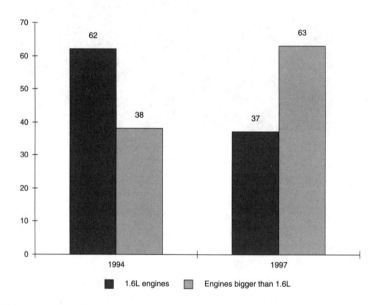

Figure 14: *Higher centre of gravity*
Source: SMMT

How Prestige Status Delivers for the Dealer

Dealers benefit from the business growth shown above, and the clearest indication of specific benefit to the dealer comes if we look at the growth in Audi business coming from the change in Retained Dealer Margin (RDM), ie the amount of profit a dealer makes on each sale. Audi UK have indexed this as follows:

	1994	1995	1996	1997
RDM index per unit	100	127	150	234

Source: Audi UK

This indicates that discounting has been reduced and premium per sale has grown.

By factoring in the increased sales figures, we can see the true extent of the increase in profit being generated in Audi dealerships:

	1994	1995	1996	1997
X Units	22,090	25,555	30,327	35,524
= RDM total index	100	153	206	375

Source: Audi UK

Thus, an average Audi dealer is now making nearly four times as much profit as he was in 1994.

How Prestige Status Delivered for the Owner

We know that the key benefit for the the business or private purchaser concerns resale values.

Taking a selection of cars from across the Audi range, we can calculate the average depreciation rate of a new Audi after one year and see how this has changed over time (Figure 15). There is a dramatic improvement.

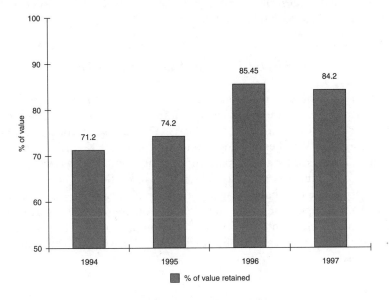

Figure 15: *Audi, average retention of value after twelve months of ownership*
Source: *Glass's Guide*

This shows that since 1994, the relative amount of original investment retained when an owner sells an Audi as a used car has increased. Or, expressed differently, Audi is a better investment.

In conclusion, the prestige brand dynamic is delivering material advantage to the numerous stakeholders of the Audi brand; manufacturer, dealer, business purchaser and private purchaser.

EVALUATING ADVERTISING'S CONTRIBUTION

Advertising Payback

The complexities of the car market mean that proving advertising payback for a car campaign is always difficult. Sales are affected by so many factors, many of which (such as product improvement and pricing) are caused by manufacturers and dealers, that it is hard to establish with absolute accuracy the proportion of new car sales due to advertising.

It would be far preferable to find a purer measure of demand for the brand in question, a measure that is outside the influence of manufacturers and dealers alike, a measure that reflects the way image, rather than hard factors like product and pricing, has helped to build demand for the brand.

In this paper we will use new learning to do just that, and will go on to demonstrate why Audi's advertising can reasonably be considered to have achieved payback.

The new learning involves looking at the changes in resale value (as indicated by changes in residual values) of the Audi brand and its products, in order to estimate the increase in implicit demand for the brand.

Residual Values as a Measure of Demand

Residual values are outside the influence of both manufacturer and dealer because the values they represent are the prices which the open market is willing to pay for used cars, not the prices charged for new cars. They are set according to the prices for which used cars are being bought and sold in the UK and are exhaustively monitored and analysed by an independent organisation, *Glass's Guide*.

Glass's Guide publishes monthly tables that show the residual value of every model of every range of whatever age. For example, it can tell you what a 1994 L registered Audi Coupe 2.0E with 30,000 miles on the clock is worth month by month. By collating the information in the monthly tables, the rise and fall of implicit demand for that car can be tracked by following the fluctuations in its residual values.

Audi and Residual Values

We have seen (Figure 15) that Audi's average residual values improve over the period we are studying. This implies a substantial increase in demand for the Audi brand.

However, the figures shown here could well have been affected by the improvement in product, particularly the introduction of the Audi A4.

The Audi A4 was launched in March 1995 and second-hand models would have returned to the market in 1996. This may account for the step change seen between 1995 and 1996. The Audi A4 is a very strong product and could be expected to command higher second-hand prices than its predecessor. This is likely to be driving up Audi's average residual values.

To factor out the effect of product improvement, we need to find a more senstitive measurement.

Factoring Out Product Effect

To do this we must draw a distinction between 'real' product effect and product 'halo' effect.

The former is the increase in demand for a brand arising from the fact that the products on offer from a manufacturer are of higher quality. They offer a materially superior experience to those purchasing and experiencing them. The latter is the effect of people hearing about improved product, either through PR or word of mouth, without actually having encountered the product.

We can factor out the former; the latter we shall account for later as a constituent part of image effect.

In order to factor out 'real' product effect we have to look at residual values in a slightly different way.

Rather than looking at how an Audi performs after twelve months and comparing it to an equivalent Audi a year later (Figure 15), we track the changes over time of the residual values of exactly the same products, which we can express as retention of value.

By taking five cars from the 1993 model range and seeing how the residual value of those cars[4] changes at six-monthly intervals, we can track how they are becoming more or less in demand.

For example, if a car is bought new for £10,000 and is sold six months later for £9,000 it can be described as having retained 90% of its value. If it is resold six months later for £8,550, its retention of value has risen to 95%. This would imply that the level of demand for the car has increased.

By taking an average of the residual value changes of the five products, we obtain a mean retention of value measurement for the brand.

Figure 16 shows how the average residual value of the Audi cars in this example underwent a step change across the period of advertising, starting when 'No. 1' kicked off the driver imagery campaign.

Exactly the Same Bits of Metal are Depreciating More Slowly

Figure 16 also shows that there is a change in the implicit demand for the Audi brand even where there has been no change in the product.

We have successfully found a way to demonstrate an increase in demand for the brand that factors out the effect of new product.

---

4. Audi 80, Audi Coupe, 3x Audi 100. All 1993 L registered.

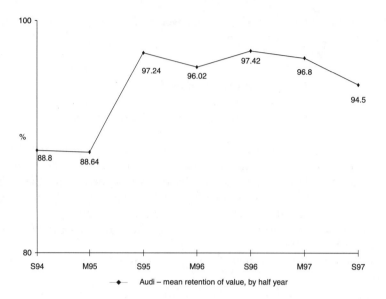

Figure 16: *Audi 1993 product range, mean retention of value, by half year*
Source: *Glass's Guide*

The increase from 88.64% to 97.24% in Figure 16 is significant, especially if we compare it to the changes in mean retention of value in the prestige sector (calculated by taking figures for several models from BMW, Mercedes and Jaguar) (Figure 17).

This comparison also tells us that the change in Audi's retention of value is not a reflection of market trend but an indication of implicit levels of demand brought about by image improvement.

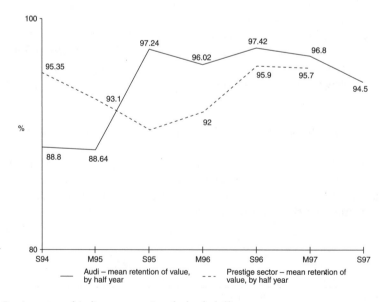

Figure 17: *Prestige sector and Audi – mean retention of value, by half year*
Source: *Glass's Guide*

Putting a Value on the Image Improvement

Audi's improved retention of value represents a price increase; used Audi cars are selling at a higher price in September 1995 than if Audi's retention of value had not increased since March 1995.

To put a value on this price increase we should relate it to changes in the market, that is, to the performance of the prestige sector.

In fact this price increase is at its most extreme if we take the data-points at March 1995 and September 1995, when the step change occurs. To get a more reasonable reading we should average out the 'pre' step change figures and the 'post' step change figures for both Audi and the prestige sector, and calculate the relative price change.

	Average pre	Average post	
Audi	88.72%	96.87%	
			= 10.03%
Prestige	94.23%	93.50%	

The change in relative residual values represents a real price increase of 10.03%.

This price increase is outside the influence of manufacturers or dealers, it is exogenous. It is the amount people are willing to pay for Audi cars.

Basic economic theory says that price and volume sold of a product are linked by demand and supply. By using this basic economic theory, we have been able to directly translate the actual increase in Audi residual values into an implied volume increase (Figure 18).

We have called this an *implied volume* because there are no extraneous factors that would cause the supply curve for Audi in the second-hand market to shift. *Actual* supply along the same curve may or may not have changed when, for example, new models were launched and existing owners may have wanted to trade up. In this instance price would have been reduced as supply increased. This is fully accounted for in our calculations.

By comparing the implied volume to the actual volume we can determine the percentage increase in demand. Our calculations show that there has been a 33.2% increase in demand for Audi. We can now apply this figure to the new car volumes for Audi to determine the percentage attributable to the image improvement.

First, we calculate actual Audi sales and revenue:

	Average selling price	Volume	Revenue
1995	£17,144	25,555	£438.11m
1996	£17,693	30,327	£536.58m
1997	£18,240	35,524	£647.96m
Total:			£1,622.65m

Source: Audi UK

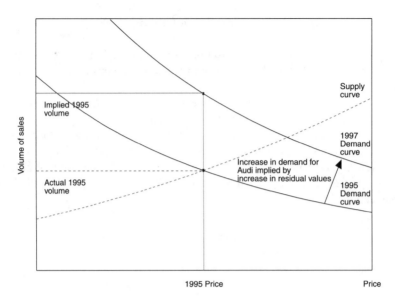

Figure 18: *Increase in demand implied by price increase*

We then take 33.2% of the total revenue to find that the increase in demand driven by improved image accounts for £404.65 million.

That improved image has been brought about by many things as well as advertising. It would be facile for advertising to attempt to claim all the credit for Audi's change of status or the positive effects on Audi's business that the change brings about.

Recognising Other Image Contributors

We have shown that elements other than product which contribute to Audi's improved status, ie image, add revenue of £404.65 million.

The figure relates to all marketing activity such as sponsorship, PR, direct marketing, POS and includes advertising. Any activity, in fact, that contributes to the improvement in Audi's image. We believe it is reasonable to claim that advertising has achieved payback.

Advertising costs in the period 1995 to 1997 were £34.752 million, including fees, production and media. To achieve payback we therefore have to believe that advertising is responsible for 8.6% of the image improvement of the Audi brand.

Given the shift of research findings shown above, we believe that advertising is very likely to have contributed at least 8.6% of the image improvement.

CONCLUSION

In this paper we have told the story of Audi's successful transition from the waiting list to full membership of the prestige car club. This has been achieved by a combination of strong product improvement due to new launches and enhanced image.

These two factors have lifted Audi to prestige status, resulting in impressive business growth for the Audi brand.

We have shown how the various stakeholders in the Audi brand – manufacturer, dealer and owner – have benefited from that prestige status, including its effect not simply on new car sales, but also on used cars.

This gave us new learning with which to demonstrate that the increase in levels of implicit demand for the Audi brand that is attributable to image improvement, as opposed to product improvement, account for a £404.65 million increase in revenue for the brand.

We can therefore state that, provided we believe that advertising is responsible for at least 8.6% of the improvement in Audi's image, advertising can be considered to have paid back the £34.752 million spent by Audi on media, fees and production.

This new learning will help Audi to further differentiate its brand so that it keeps consolidating and developing its position in the prestige car club, occupying a territory which is defined as Modern, Innovative, Individual.

Or 'Vorsprung Durch Technik', as Audi's many stakeholders might say.

★★★

13

Batchelors SuperNoodles
Leading from the front

EDITOR'S SUMMARY

This is a case of how a 20-year-old brand bravely identified a new usage occasion and target audience. As a result the brand is now enjoying an unprecedented step-change in its performance.

Why a Brand Leader Chose to Radically Reposition Itself

For over 20 years, Batchelors SuperNoodles was the children's teatime noodle. But, by 1996 continuous commoditisation from 'me-too' entrants was leading the market to the inevitable saturation point.

The challenge was to find a way of regaining control of the market and leading it as a market leader should. This could only come from growing it, either with new usage occasions or new users – or both.

A U&A analysis revealed a small bunch of young adults consuming a disproportionately large amount of SuperNoodles. They called it 'foody nosh'. Van den Bergh Foods decided to concentrate all resources on targeting these potential new users.

Results

The campaign achieved high awareness, recognition, relevance and enjoyment scores and as a result it generated trial among the new target audience of young adults identified, thus doubling adult eating occasions involving SuperNoodles and creating an additional halo effect on children's usage, which increased by 79%.

Within weeks of the advertising going on-air Nielsen weekly sales rose by 72% against the six-monthly average, rate of sale records were broken and market share lost over a period of years was won back in a period of weeks. All other contributory effects were stripped out by analysing those retailers who opted out of promotions and looking at 200g unit sales, which were totally excluded from any promotional support. This shows that advertising contributed at least 42% to this amazing performance.

INTRODUCTION

This is the story of how an established brand leader identified and single-mindedly targeted a new consumer group to create unprecedented growth for the brand.

With sales far outstripping all forecasts during the advertising, factory supply was simply not able to keep up with consumer demand.

> 'The advertising has had an amazing impact on the factory. There's been something of a 'Dunkirk' spirit with all hands on the pump. People have worked (largely uncomplainingly) for long hours and have really stretched to achieve the output. It has caused us to challenge some of our core assumptions about how we run.'

> Graeme Anderson, SuperNoodles Factory Manager

BACKGROUND

Batchelors SuperNoodles was launched in 1979 and enjoyed considerable success as a mainstream, everyday, side-of-plate alternative to chips for children. It was one of those products which children love because of the taste and play value and which mums endorse as a healthier, more nutritional alternative to the chips.

For a long time SuperNoodles did not have much direct competition. All other noodle products were adult oriented (for example, Sharwoods – the authentic noodle for a proper 'Chinese') or snack oriented (for example, Pot Noodles – the quick fill-up). And retailer own labels gave it a wide berth. As a result the brand went from strength to strength.

By 1996, sales growth, although still strong, began to show signs of slowing. Own label 'me-too' products entered the fray, additional low-priced competitors followed suit and the increasingly commoditised nature of the market benefited the everyday low-price sector at growing expense to SuperNoodles. In 1996, for example, the noodle market grew by 40% year on year – that is 2,000 households entering the market every day – yet the market leader could only manage half that growth rate.

Twenty per cent year-on-year growth is still healthy but Van den Bergh Foods was not comfortable with the fact that its market-leading position was being eroded.

Van den Bergh Foods took the decision to address the problem head-on and look for a way to regain the initiative. It set out to create a step change in the brand's performance by looking elsewhere for growth.

FINDING A NEW MARKET OPPORTUNITY

By looking for growth elsewhere, SuperNoodles needed to find a new market opportunity. This meant either finding new usage occasions or new customers – or ideally both.

A U&A analysis was then commissioned, which confirmed that SuperNoodles was stuck in the traditional children's teatime usage occasion; hardly surprising after 20 years of maintaining that position. The study also identified a potential opportunity for the brand in the form of a small but heavy group of young adult users.

Subsequent qualitative studies (through Sadek Weinberg and Calcraft Buck), focusing on these young users, revealed the motivation behind and the context for this usage. These people led lifestyles where time for 'filling up' was at a premium and throwing together whatever was in the kitchen was a norm rather than an exception. The food had to be quick, tasty and above all substantial – these people were in 'trough' mode, digging in to doorstop sandwiches, munching on bowls of cereal or ripping chicken meat off a carcass (and devouring while standing by the kitchen worktop). Sometimes they even scoffed a plate of SuperNoodles. SuperNoodles were seen as quick, satisfying and 'moreish'. We called this area the substantial snacking sector. Consumers called it 'foody nosh'.

They tended to be men aged between 18 and 35, but not exclusively so. Men, by their nature, eat as often as possible and as much as possible, so naturally they are more inclined to operate in this 'troughing' mode.

This was unprompted usage against all marketing intentions. Now, however, Van den Bergh decided to focus all their efforts on this opportunity, given the scale of the largely untapped young adult audience for SuperNoodles and their heavy snacking propensity.

Thus, SuperNoodles moved away from the nutritional children's meal accompaniment after school to 25-year-olds eating SuperNoodles as a meal at 11 o'clock at night.

DEVELOPING AN ADVERTISING STRATEGY

In anyone's books, this is a radical repositioning from Mum's friendly aid at kids' teatimes. The risk of losing these existing consumers was judged to be slim given that their relationship with the brand was so established. The only way to seriously target this new audience was to do it single-mindedly and exclusively.

The advertising objective was therefore simply defined as follows:

— To generate trial of SuperNoodles among young adults.

This would fulfil the predefined business objective:

— To step change a brand performance and drive market growth.

In order to give the brand credibility among a wider, young adult audience, SuperNoodles needed to win over those most inclined to be substantial snackers – namely men. So the creative target audience chosen was men, who in essence act as gatekeepers to the sector. If they could be convinced that SuperNoodles were foody and substantial enough to be a decent snack, their partners would probably follow. The proposition which the creative work was written to was simply 'Batchelors SuperNoodles – great foody nosh'.

THE CREATIVE IDEA

Owning this foody nosh sector was the creative aim, since there were no brands which had claimed this territory as their own, the creative idea became an exposé of how men behave (not always badly) when preparing or eating in this sector.

Traditional advertising conventions were ignored, in preference to showing how SuperNoodles fits into a hungry bloke's life. In so doing, SuperNoodles would stand out as an original, modern and distinctive brand. Humour was the key ingredient to building empathy with the male viewer but also with his partner sitting alongside him on the sofa.

Creative development research (Sadek Weinberg) indicated that non-users empathised with and warmed to the situation and accepted that the product could fit into their busy, unpredictable lifestyles. The use of men and an adult focus in tone helped to communicate substantiality, which in turn helped to create a greater sense of credibility in the positioning for both men and women.

THE MEDIA STRATEGY

The SuperNoodles TV buying strategy changed to buying against 'foody noshers' as opposed to housewives with children to reflect the new creative strategy. The objective was to expose the foody nosher to the campaign while he was watching with his partner, which allowed them both to enjoy the advertising together.

The first burst started on 6 November 1997, ran for six weeks and was then followed by a drip campaign during February and March 1998. In total, 1,734 network TVRs were invested behind the campaign.

THE TOTAL SALES EFFECT

The advertising far exceeded even the step change hoped for. We can demonstrate an immediate effect on SuperNoodles sales, rate of sale, market share and contribution to total market growth figures.

Sales

Nielsen recorded a 72% improvement in weekly SuperNoodles sales during the advertising: from an average of 65,000 kilos per week in the preceding 6 months to 112,500 kilos per week during the advertised period. During the campaign, every pack of SuperNoodles produced was sold. Production could not keep up with consumer demand, so by the end of the second burst in March 1998 there were significant out-of-stock problems. With demand so far in advance of factory capacity, sales fell back from a peak in March, with all retailers on restricted supply.

'SELFISH'

Julie: So how are your sweet and sour
SuperNoodles then?
David: Mmm.

Julie: ... just a taste.
David: Look, I hate it when you do this, I
offered to make you some.

David: Look, you can finish them off if you
like.

Julie: You really love me, don't you?

(VO) Batchelor's SuperNoodles, because
noodles can be super, can't they?

Rate of Sale

Rate of sale for SuperNoodles jumped from a pre-advertising four-weekly average of 40 packs per store (per day) peaking at 68 packs per store during the advertising – a 70% maximum increase.

Sixty-eight packs per store per day was the highest rate ever achieved in the brand's 18-year history. After the advertising, the rate of sale continued on an uphill climb. As a result, no further marketing support is planned until factory capacity is increased to meet these ongoing levels of consumer demand.

Market Share and Market Growth

In the preceding 12 months, monthly volume market share for SuperNoodles had shown signs of continued erosion, falling from 65% in October 1996 to 59% by October 1997. Own label was the main threat with share gains of five percentage points in the same period, from 12% monthly share to 17%.

When the advertising went on-air in the second week of November, monthly volume share for SuperNoodles rose steadily to 77% forcing own label back below the 10% level. When the second burst followed in February, market share peaked at 84% – a full 25% points gain since October 1996. (The fall-off in March 1998 is a direct result of the out-of-stocks problem.)

Incremental business not only came from stealing own label share. It also came from growing the total savoury noodles market. The market grew by 14% over the four-month advertised period as a direct result of SuperNoodles performance, since SuperNoodles was the only brand growing in this way.

THE TRIAL EFFECT

Since the advertising objective was to generate trial among a new audience, we must substantiate the campaign's effectiveness in more ways than just sales impact and market growth.

The Taylor Nelson AGB Food Index Panel measures number of meal occasions in which a particular product was used and by whom. Although reporting periods are six-monthly, the effects which the campaign has had on both these measures have been dramatic. We can discount the seasonality of the reporting periods, because an analysis of the last five years of SuperNoodles sales, recorded by Nielsen, only shows an 8% maximum shift from quarter to quarter.

In the preceding reporting period (March to August 1997), the number of occasions in household in which SuperNoodles were used were recorded at 4.5 times. In the following period (September 1997 – February 1998), the number of occasions in which the brand was used had risen to 8.8 times: a 95% increase. Importantly, this increase was found to be particularly significant against the new target audience: a 100% increase in adult occasions (Figure 1).

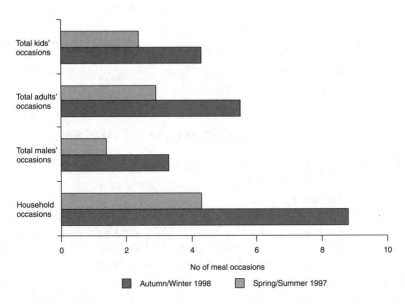

Figure 1: *Meal occasions involving SuperNoodles*
Source: Millward Brown

The bonus was the 'halo effect' which the advertising had on the traditional audience, as children's occasions involving SuperNoodles grew by 79%. Another source for evidence of trial of the brand is Millward Brown tracking data. Van den Bergh Foods conduct continuous tracking on all their savoury brands and one of the questions monitored is that of brand familiarity. The proportion of the sample that claims to have tried SuperNoodles since the advertising broke has risen sharply. Among the core audience of 16 to 34-year-olds, SuperNoodles 'as a brand consumers have tried' has risen from 51% to 65% – a 27% increase in 'ever tried'.

This 27% of new recruits will have contributed a significantly greater proportion to the 72% uplift in weekly sales than this figure suggests, since we already know from the extensive U&A analysis just how heavy a consumer they are when they enter this market.

So, in conclusion, the total effect which the advertising has had on sales and consumption, including any other contributory factors to the brand during the period, has been as follows:

— A Nielsen recorded weekly sales increase of 72% against the 12-month weekly average.

— A four-weekly rate of sales increase of 70% against the long-term average and a new record for SuperNoodles.

— A market share gain of 18% points during the first burst of advertising, climbing to 25% points in the second burst – stealing mainly from own label.

— A clear demonstration of SuperNoodles single-handedly growing the market by 14%.

— An increase in meal occasions involving SuperNoodles of 95%, according to AGB Family Food Index.

— A doubling of usage among adults and males – the new target audience (AGB).

— An increase in 'ever tried' among the core audience of 16 to 34-year-olds of 27%, according to Millward Brown.

EFFECTS ON AWARENESS AND ATTITUDES

Since this new positioning for SuperNoodles is our case for the incremental sales, we need to provide evidence on how consumers' attitudes towards the brand may have changed during the advertising.

The Millward Brown tracking study is a 'syndicated' one for all Van den Bergh Foods' savoury food brands, with a broader than ideal sample definition of the national adult population and no flexibility for fieldwork dates. This may arguably under-represent the real effects of the campaign, which did not benefit from a more suitable and relevant monitoring measure. However, against this limitation, there is a remarkable shift in many critical measures for the SuperNoodles brand.

Three waves of tracking fieldwork were conducted during the period of interest, which may not entirely dovetail with the campaign dates but can for the sake of argument be treated as 'pre' (with one week overlapping into the campaign), 'mid' (all fieldwork during advertising) and 'post' advertising (four weeks still on-air, two weeks off).

Advertising Awareness

TV ad awareness (positive response to the question: 'Which of the brands from this list have you seen TV advertising for recently?') for SuperNoodles rose from 7% in Wave 1 to 20% in Wave 3. Among the core audience of 16 to 34-year-olds, awareness rose from 9% to 25%.

The proportion of the total sample recognising the stills from the SuperNoodles campaign reached 80% by Wave 3, with 56% of those correctly attributing the campaign to the SuperNoodles brand. More than two-thirds of the core audience correctly associated the campaign with SuperNoodles.

Advertising Enjoyment

An explanation for these increases in recognition and correct brand attribution scores may be found in the level of enjoyment gained from watching the SuperNoodles advertising. As was the intention of the campaign, the enjoyment scores shown in Figure 2 demonstrate the level of involvement generated by the advertising. A mean score of 4.06 (out of 5 maximum) sits comfortably in the top 5% of all campaigns tracked by Millward Brown.

This ad awareness, recognition and obvious involvement enhanced the following key dimensions:

— Brand awareness and familiarity.

— Product attribute perceptions.

— Perceived role of SuperNoodles in repertoire.

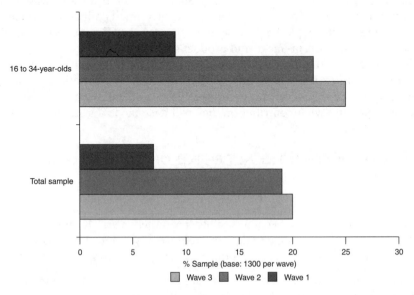

Figure 2: *Enjoyment of watching SuperNoodles ads (November/December 1997)*
Source: Millward Brown

Spontaneous Brand Awareness and Familiarity

In response to the question: 'What brands of savoury noodles or pasta can you think of?', both first and total mentions, have increased significantly throughout the campaign period: from 12% to 17% first mention and from 20% to 26% total mention. Similarly, the proportion of the sample who claim they have 'heard a lot about Super Noodles recently' has doubled both for the total sample and 16 to 34-year-olds.

Brand Product Attributes

The most relevant image statements have seen significant improvements. The greatest shift has been in the statement, which has improved by 40%, clearly confirming that the new positioning is being established in people's minds. Taste credentials have also been enhanced, with a 22% uplift and perceived relevance of the brand for a broader audience has increased by 23%.

Perceived Role of SuperNoodles in the Repertoire

This section demonstrates how the consumer relationship with the SuperNoodles brand has strengthened while the campaign was on-air. A standard series of statements pinpoint a consumer's 'closeness' to the brand. In this case, our core target audience have traded up the 'closeness' scale. Fewer people feel 'It's a brand I'd buy only if it were on offer or I had a coupon' and more people feel 'Of all the brands I'd consider, it's my first choice'. Significant shifts in ad awareness and recognition have been generated during the advertising. The high enjoyment level has guaranteed that people have recognised the new positioning, which is clearly played back in the shifts in image and product statements.

These shifts and the increase in the brand 'closeness' in such a short space of time are not situations which any supporting instore promotions could have realistically created. However, promotions will have definitely contributed to sales, so we must quantify what contribution they will have made during the advertising.

CALCULATING THE NET EFFECT OF THE ADVERTISING

The Effect of Promotions

The category has always been a heavily promoted area. It would have been unrealistic to launch a new campaign and remove any point of purchase incentive. Fortunately, we can isolate the promotional effect in two ways:

— Retailers who were not conducting any instore promotions during the first burst of advertising in November to December 1997.

— The 200g product, which received no promotional support in any of the grocery trade over the entire November to March period (Super Noodles is available in two pack sizes: 100g single pack, which accounts for the majority of sales, and 200g family-sized pack).

TABLE 1: SUPERNOODLES PROMOTIONAL PLAN –
NOVEMBER 1997 TO MARCH 1998*

	Nov	Dec	Jan	Feb	Mar
TV	686	270	85	287	353
Tesco	Trial price	–	–	Trial price	–
Sainsbury	Trial price	–	–	Multibuy	–
Safeway	–	–	–	Trial price	–
Asda	–	–	–	Multibuy	–
Somerfield	Buy 1 get 2	–	–	Trial price	–

*Key five multiples (100g pack only)

Although no major multiples were entirely free of in-store promotions during the campaign, Safeway and Asda had no deals on during the first burst of the advertising in November. For the 100g product, therefore, sales performance in Safeway and Asda can give us an opportunity to isolate the advertising effect.

For Asda, volume increases rose in November from a 1997 pre-advertising weekly average of 10,500 kilos per week to 17,000 kilos per week: a 62% increase, compared with a total grocery weekly increase of 72% in the same period.

The sales peak shown at the beginning of 1997 was due to a 'Buy two get one free' promotion. The peaks during November and December 1997 are a direct result of the advertising.

Although Safeway sales are only available on a four-weekly basis, a similar picture is portrayed: from an average of 35,000 kilos per month in the preceding ten months to 46,000 in the month of November 1997 – a 31% increase (Figure 3).

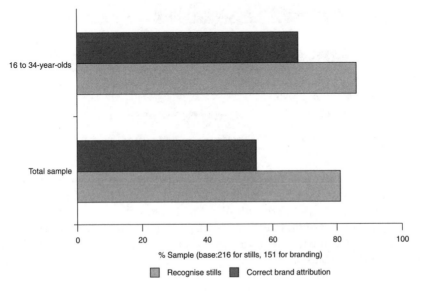

Figure 3: *SuperNoodles four-weekly volume sales in Safeway versus monthly TVRs*
Source: Nielsen

The relative differences in increases between Asda and Safeway can be explained by the relatively greater promotional activity in Safeway during the pre-advertised period. In fact there were twice as many promotions in Safeway in the previous ten months as there were in Asda.

Even so, we can confidently claim the advertising generated as a minimum a 31% incremental uplift in sales (as seen in Safeway) and, at its most optimistic, twice that as witnessed quite clearly in Asda.

Separating out 200g sales tells a similar story. Although the 200g SuperNoodles product is not an ideal format for our foody nosher target audience since the two blocks and one sachet of sauce are designed for family use, it has responded extremely well to the advertising without receiving any promotional support throughout the period (Figure 4).

Average 200g weekly kilo sales increased from the 12-month norm of 1,941 kilos per week to 2,787 in the 23 weeks covering the advertised period: a 42% increase.

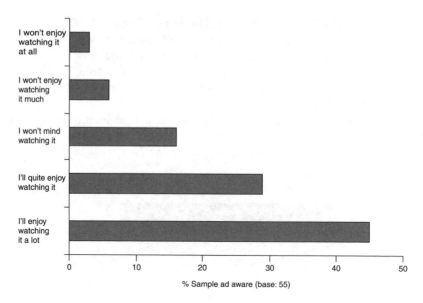

Figure 4: *SuperNoodles total grocery sales of 200g product versus TVRs*
Source: Nielsen

By looking at Asda and Safeway, we concluded that sales growth attributed by the advertising must have been between 31% and 62%. By looking at 200g unit sales the estimate can be more tightly defined, since there was literally no other brand support in the period relevant to the 200g product. With weekly sales of 200g up by 42%, compared with the total brand weekly sales increase of 72%, we can conclude that at least a sales uplift of 42% was generated by advertising alone.

The Effects of Other Possible Factors

Throughout this advertising period there were no distribution gains, since the brand already had 100% distribution. Neither were there any product or product range changes. Apart from the trial price promotion, detailed in the promotional plan, there were no retail price changes before, during or after the re-launch campaign.

We have already discounted seasonality, and competitive influences must also be slight, since there were no product changes or significant activity during the SuperNoodles advertising period (Figure 5).

Summary of the Net Advertising Effect

Apart from the combined promotional activity, which supported the re-launch campaign, there have been no other contributory factors which could have influenced the dramatic sales effect experienced when the new campaign went on-air.

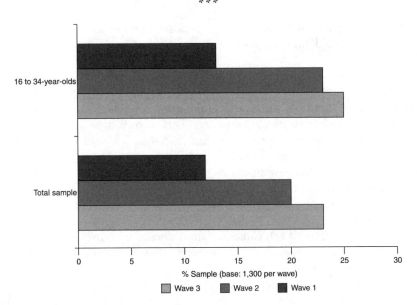

Figure 5: *SuperNoodles and Pot Noodles share of voice 1997/98*
Source: Initiative Media

It has been possible to extrapolate the contribution which advertising made to incremental sales gains by analysing the sales performance of individual retailers who were not promoting the brand instore and by examining sales of the 200g product, which received no promotional support throughout the period.

The sales effect of the re-positioning of SuperNoodles was dramatic, with Nielsen weekly sales against the previous six months growing by 72% during the advertising and instore promotions. We have shown how advertising alone generated at least a 42% weekly volume uplift during the campaign against the previous six to ten months.

SUMMARY – A MARKET LEADER REGAINING TRUE LEADERSHIP

The decision to challenge the direction of the market was a brave one. The resultant ambition to re-position SuperNoodles as 'foody nosh' for young adults was even braver. But both decisions were clearly sanctioned within weeks of the advertising going on-air.

Nielsen weekly sales rose by 72% against the six-monthly average, rate of sale records were broken and market share that had been lost over a period of years was won back in a period of weeks.

The campaign generated trial among the new target audience of young adults identified, doubling adult eating occasions involving SuperNoodles and creating an additional 'halo' effect on children's usage, which increased by 79%. The acid test was the 27% increase in 'ever tried' among the core audience.

The evidence from Millward Brown demonstrated how high advertising awareness and recognition scores created significant shifts in the perceived relevance of SuperNoodles as a product you can eat on its own, along with enhancing taste credentials and the brand's now more universal appeal. It also showed how shifting such key attitudes, closely connected to the advertising communication, could only have come from the campaign as opposed to other possible factors.

We were able to eliminate the only other contributory effect – instore promotional support – by analysing those retailers who opted out of the promotions in the first TV burst and looking at 200g sales, which were totally excluded from any promotional support. This shows that even at the most pragmatic level, advertising must have contributed at least 42% to this amazing performance of the brand – as evidenced by the 200g pack uplift.

In order to deliver this new brand message to our new target audience, we had to entertain them. Against this objective the advertising was extremely successful, scoring one of the highest marks on advertising enjoyment Millward Brown have ever recorded.

The long-term effects of the campaign are impossible to measure, since its very success led to such critical out-of-stock problems that all support after March 1998 had to be cancelled.

Through identifying a new usage occasion and target audience for Super Noodles, the brand is now enjoying an unprecedented step change in its performance. More importantly, SuperNoodles is now leading the market from the front again. And it is quite determined to stay that way.

Until new capacity can be brought on-line however, the next chapter of this brand's success will have to wait. The last word on the effects of the advertising comes from the factory manager again at the Worksop site:

'The message that we can sell every block has got people seeing the value of what they do. Success breeds success and the optimistic outlook helps give confidence around the whole site – benefiting not just the SuperNoodles lines.'

Graeme Anderson, Factory Manager

14

Johnson's Clean & Clear
Global advertising in a local market

EDITOR'S SUMMARY

This paper demonstrates that the global advertising idea can be more effective in a particular country if the advertising in that country is not simply adopted and translated, but instead, that the global advertising is re-interpreted for the local market, using insightful, local consumer understanding.

The Vision for Clean & Clear in the UK

Johnson's Clean & Clear was launched in the US in 1991 and then in the UK in 1992, using both the American positioning and advertising.

While the brand grew, it became alarmingly clear that the brand was not going to meet its objectives. The majority of the brand's growth was due to aggregate distribution gains, due to new product launches, rather than consumer demand. The brand was not establishing a positive relationship with teenage girls and J&J's objective of nurturing young consumers for the future of the Johnson's portfolio was not going to be met.

The problem lay with the translation of the American advertising into English, which UK girls found difficult to relate to. It was clear that we needed to make the promise come alive and become 'real' for UK teenage girls.

Results and Payback

Within just one year of new locally tailored advertising the brand fulfilled all of the objectives set: becoming the No. 1 brand in the medicated skincare market and becoming the most popular brand among female teenagers and forging an empathetic relationship with them.

An econometric model, which accounted for all the factors that could have driven growth, proved that the new advertising was the sole reason for success. The new advertising was far more effective at generating a return – in fact the return was 30 times bigger. Furthermore, Clean & Clear now enjoys over half a million female teenage buyers who are empathetic towards the brand and as such Johnson & Johnson has half a million potential adult Johnson's users.

INTRODUCTION

This paper attempts to show that a global advertising idea can be more effective in a particular country if the advertising in that country is not simply a 'translation' of the global idea, but instead a 'reinterpretation' of the idea based on insightful, local consumer understanding.

This particular story concerns a medicated skincare brand that began life in the USA and was then launched successfully in the UK using 'translations' of the American advertising. The brand's performance was however subsequently significantly improved in the UK, when this advertising was replaced by local 'reinterpretations' of the core American creative idea.

BACKGROUND

The Heritage

By 1990, Johnson & Johnson (J&J) was the proud parent of a healthy brand called Johnson's Baby in both the USA and the UK.[1] As a result, the 'Johnson's' name had a strong reputation for gentleness, care, trust and expertise in babies' skin.

J&J recognised that the name, Johnson's, known for expertise in babies' skin, might have credibility outside the baby market on the basis that the baby market is seen to be the most exacting skincare market.

They therefore decided to develop a series of sub-brands under the Johnson's name, with each sub-brand being specifically targeted at different lifestages.

The Teenage Brand Concept

Because they had a relevant technological lead, J&J first launched a medicated skincare range targeting female teenagers.[2] They launched this under the Clean & Clear name, which they bought from Revlon.[3] Prior to this, Clean & Clear had been a very small and unremarkable adult skincare range, but J&J believed the name was suitable for the medicated market, hence the decision to purchase it. The vision was to make Clean & Clear 'The global leader in female teen skincare'.[4]

Why did they target female teenagers?
Because they:

— have spots;

---

1. Johnson's Baby was launched in the USA at the end of the nineteenth century and in the UK in the 1920s.
2. The medicated skincare market consists of products that help to get rid of existing spots (treatment products) and to a lesser extent products that offer ways to prevent spots (preventive products). Both are used largely by teenagers.
3. Johnson's Consumer Products acquired the worldwide rights to the Clean & Clear name and products in 1991.
4. Clean & Clear Brand Footprint.

— use a lot of medicated products, and;

— more importantly, they would grow up to be potential adult buyers of other Johnson's sub-brands,[5] and by demonstrating understanding and skincare expertise to this audience now, there was the hope that they would carry this belief with them as they grow older.

J&J's Clean & Clear was launched in the UK in 1992, following its successful launch in the USA in 1991.

CLEAN & CLEAR IN THE UK FROM 1992 TO 1996

Despite Clean & Clear's previous existence, in 1992 it was virtually unknown among teenagers.[6] Hence, this was effectively a completely new launch to the female teenage medicated consumer.

The Market

Prior to Clean & Clear's relaunch, the medicated market was dominated by three brands (Table 1).[7]

TABLE 1: THE UK MEDICATED MARKET 1991

	Owned by	Value share	Adspend
Clearasil	P&G	38.2	£2.8m
Biactol	P&G	30.5	£2.0m
Oxy	Smithkline Beecham	12.2	£0.9m
Others	Various	19.1	£0.1m

Source: Nielsen/MEAL

P&G owned both Clearasil and Biactol; both were long-established brands, characterised by angst-ridden advertising: Oxy was launched in the 1980s and was known for its radical, humorous advertising, 'Blitz those zits with Oxy'.[8] All had been heavily supported since 1980 (Table 2).

---

5. J&J launched Johnson's pH5.5 in 1993, targeting adults, and as future mums they were potential buyers of Johnson's Kids, launched in July 1994, and of course, Johnson's Baby.
6. Clean & Clear had existed as an extremely basic skincare range targeted at adult women. It had had little support (MEAL registers only £117,000 between 1978 and 1991).
7. When looking at medicated skincare products in aggregate it is usual to talk in terms of value rather than volume, as some products are high value/low volume (for example, Invisible Treatment Gel) while for other products the reverse is true (for example, Facial Wash).
8. Clearasil and Biactol have historically been advertised and continue to be advertised in a way that plays on teenagers' anxiety about having spots. Oxy, however, broke the mould with a humourous advertising campaign which entered into the 'playground parlance' of teenagers.

TABLE 2: COMPETITIVE MEDICATED BRANDS PRIOR TO CLEAN & CLEAR

Brand	Launch	Target	Benefit	Character	Adpsend since 1980
Clearasil	Pre-1970s	a) Girls and b) boys	Gets rid of spots	Reassuring medical	£20m
Biactol	1970s	a) Boys and b) girls	Facial wash that gets rid of spots	Reassuring medical	£13m
Oxy	1980s	All against spots	Powerful humorous	Streetwise	£5m

Source: MEAL/J&J

Marketing Objectives

Against this tough market background the objectives for Clean & Clear were to:

1. Become the No. 1 medicated skincare brand by value.

2. Become the most popular medicated brand among female teenagers.

3. Establish a relationship with teenage girls that would lead to loyalty to Johnson's for the rest of their lives. This meant getting teenage girls to believe that Johnson's understood them and their needs.

J&J believed this was possible beacause there was a gap in the market. No other brand offered teenage girls their very own skincare range. Clean & Clear's global positioning uniquely filled this gap: a combination of medicated products with adult feminine, skincaring values.[9]

Getting Medicated

Part of the task of transforming Clean & Clear into a medicated brand was launching new products (Table 3).[10]

---

9. Teenage girls want to look after their skin like grown-up women but they need to use medicated products because they have spot-prone skin. They therefore fall between two stools: on the one side there are products offering feminine, caring values but no medicated efficacy, while on the other side there are medicated products that lack the feminine, caring values. Clean & Clear was positioned to fill this gap. Part of this was focusing on the benefits of clean and clear skin, rather than simply getting rid of spots which the competitors did at the time.

10. Includes products launched in 1997 to give the complete picture.

TABLE 3: CLEAN & CLEAR'S PRODUCT RANGE TO 1997

	Pre 1992 (Revlon)	1992	1993	1994 (Johnson & Johnson)	1995	1996	1997
Cleansing Gel 200ml	x D						
Cleansing Lotion 200ml	x D						
Moisturiser 100ml	x D						
Cleansing Bar 100g		x	x	x	x	D	
Facial Wash 150ml		x	x	x	x	x	D
Cleansing Milk 200ml		x	x	x	x	x	D
Cleansing Lotion 200ml		x	x	x	x	x	x
Sensitive Cleansing Lotion 200ml		x	x	x	x	x	x
Deep Cleansing Cream Wash 150ml	x	x	x	x	x	x	
Invisible Treatment Gel Regular 20ml				x	x	x *	
Invisible Treatment Gel Sensitive 20ml				x	x	x †	
Exfoliating Daily Wash 150ml						x	x
Skin Balancing Moisturiser 100ml					x	x	
Clear Skin daily Treatment 40ml						x	
2-in-1 Treatment Stick 4.6ml						x	

D = Discontinued
* Now in Boots only
† Now discontinued
Source: J&J

Advertising

In keeping with Johnson & Johnson's 'Best Practise' policy for global brands,[11] the UK adopted the US advertising. These were translated by BMP DDB into English, using English girls and their colloquialisms.[12]

The television advertising, 'Girls Talking', featured confident 'Girls Talking' about how they did not worry about spots because they used Clean & Clear. The idea had emerged from the observation that teenage girls spend a lot of time talking about spots among themselves. Press advertising also ran. The ads ran in the UK from 1993 to 1996, as shown in Table 4.

TABLE 4: CLEAN & CLEAR MEDIA PLAN 1993 TO 1996

	£000	Jan	Feb	Mar	Apr	May	Jun	Jul	Aug	Sep	Oct	Nov	Dec	Annual Total
1993	TV			438										438
	Press													
1994	TV			600										600
	Press									65	92	90	28	275
1995	TV								128					128
	Press	4	0	44	74	101	32	53	117	107	134	90	81	836
1996	TV		395								125			520
	Press	36					90							126

11. J&J's Best Practice policy results in something that is proven to work in one country being adopted, with minor adaptations, for another country, with the aim of creating a global identity.
12. There were a number of different films, edits and cutdowns.

US 'GIRLS TALKING AD'

Yeah, I use it as an ice-breaker – a conversation piece.

(FVO) Introducing Johnson's Clean & Clear – an oil-controlling astringent.

I'm not going to lose sleep, or not go out over this here today, gone tomorrow, I'm just going to ruin your life today, thing.

(FVO) Deep cleaning with a pharmaceutical ingredient no leading astringent has.

Zit – I mean what's that?

(FVO) It actually helps prevent pimples. Skin is clean, beautifully clear and under control.

Can you handle it, I can handle it.

Clean & Clear and under control.

UK 'GIRLS TALKING AD'

As you get older you definitely feel more in control of your skin.

When your skin is clear and clean ...

... that tends to make you feel healthier.

(VO) Johnson's Clean & Clear is clinically tested to effectively remove everyday dirt and grease.

(VO) Clean skin is the secret of clear skin.

The thing is to get a boyfriend with glasses ...

... and then hide his glasses.

(VO) Johnson's Clean & Clear and under control.

UK PERFORMANCE 1992 TO 1996

Clean & Clear's value share increased significantly over the period of the 'Girls Talking' campaign (Figure 1).

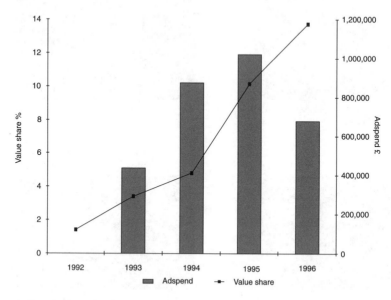

Figure 1: *Clean & Clear value share of the medicated market and adspend*
Source: IRI /MEAL

However, despite this growth there were worrying signals beneath the surface.

WARNING SIGNS

After five years, Clean & Clear had still not achieved its objectives: it was not the No. 1 medicated brand and it was not the most popular brand among teenage girls, which suggested that it was not establishing the depth of relationship that had been hoped for (Tables 5 and 6).

TABLE 5: BRAND VALUE SHARE OF MEDICATED MARKET %

Oxy	23
Clearasil	19
Clean & Clear	14
Biactol	12
Others	33

Source: IRI Infoscan four weeks ending December 1996

TABLE 6: BRAND VALUE SHARE AMONG TEENAGE GIRLS %

Oxy	46
Clearasil	21
Clean & Clear	20
Biactol	7
Others	6

Base: 13 to 18-year-old female buyers
Source: Taylor Nelson year ending 7 April 1996

In addition, there were indications that the future growth needed to meet its objectives would not be forthcoming with the current marketing and advertising strategy. Although sales were rising:

Warning sign 1: Growth was being generated by distribution gains rather than consumer demand
We have already seen that ten new products were launched between 1992 and 1996. The products were high quality and the J&J salesforce was good at selling them into the trade (Figure 2).[13]

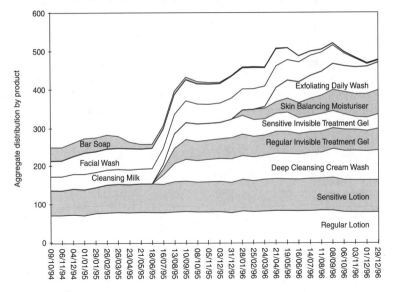

Figure 2: *Clean & Clear distribution by product*
Source: IRI

However, while new products were being launched the stockturn of the brand was slowing down (see Figure 3).[14] (The 1996 uplift is due to a new product promotion, where a free sachet of a new product was attached to a press ad.)

---

13. Figure 2 shows 'aggregate distribution' which is the sum of the distribution facings for each product. So if four products each have 100% distribution, 'aggregate distribution' is 400%. Aggregate distribution can be a more meaningful way of summarising a brand's distribution when it exists in many varieties.
14. Stockturn measures the rate at which the total brand's products are moving off the shelf. It is measured by dividing total value sales by aggregate distribution. It therefore takes into account the breadth (distribution in stores) and the depth (facings) of distribution.

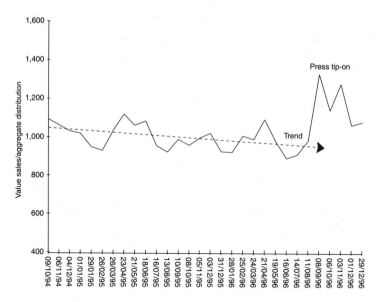

Figure 3: *Clean & Clear stockturn*
Source: IRI

Thus while aggregate distribution increased, stockturn was slowly declining. It appeared that the growth in sales and share was less demand-led than expected. This was worrying because aggregate distribution could not grow forever. Indeed, it had already started to slow down resulting in diminishing sales growth.

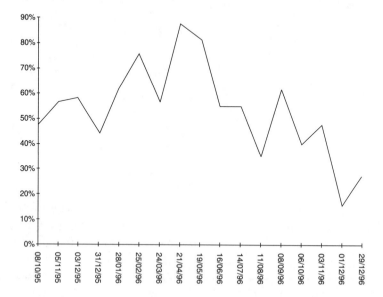

Figure 4: *Clean & Clear year on year growth*
Source: IRI

Furthermore, the rate of sale of the more established products was declining.[15] This suggested that the brand's growth was being driven by new products. This was worrying, because the more established products, particularly the lotion, were more profitable. The new products were more technologically sophisticated and hence less profitable.

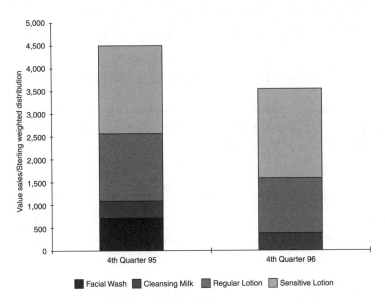

Figure 5: *Clean & Clear – average rate of sale of established products*
Source: IRI

Warning sign 2: Future growth was threatened by the competition becoming increasingly teen-girl targeted

Clean & Clear's unique positioning was increasingly under threat. Oxy launched an Oxy Sensitive range in 1996, offering effective yet gentle products, supported with a stylish new campaign, which would increase the brand's appeal to teenage girls.

There was also an increase in the launch of 'preventive' products, including own label, in direct competition with Clean & Clear.[16]

IMPLICATIONS FOR THE FUTURE OF CLEAN & CLEAR

1. Distribution-led growth, from new products, was unlikely to be sustainable or profitable for much longer.

---

15. Rate of sale can be thought of as how fast a product is selling in the average shop. It is calculated by dividing sales by sterling weighted distribution which, unlike aggregate distribution, can never exceed 100.
16. For example, both Clearasil and Oxy were increasingly offering preventive style products, and T-Zone was launched in 1995.

2. Without stockturn improvements it was unlikely that Clean & Clear would become No. 1 and in a lesser position the brand would become difficult to support and would be potentially untenable.

3. Clean & Clear was not the most popular brand among teenage girls and with the increasing competition it was unlikely that it would be. It looked decreasingly likely that it would generate significant future loyalty to the Johnson's name and act as a springboard into Johnson's products for adults.

BENEATH THE SKIN OF THE PROBLEM

The products were high quality and the salesforce was successful at selling them. So what was causing the problem of declining stockturn and decreasing sales growth? Part of the problem lay with the advertising.

The Advertising Lacked Impact

Clean & Clear's advertising awareness[17] was low in comparison with competitors and the ratio between ad awareness and adspend was lower than for competitors (Table 7).[18]

TABLE 7: ADVERTISING AWARENESS COMPARED TO ADSPEND IN 1996

	Total ad awareness end of 1996 %	Adspend during 1996 £m	Ratio of awareness adspend	Indexed ad awareness
Oxy	72	2.01	36	106
Clearasil	69	1.35	51	150
Biactol	66	0.51	129	379
Clean & Clear	23	0.68	34	100

Sample: Female spot product users
Source: Millward Brown U&A, December 1996
Source: MEAL

Qualitative Research Highlighted the Reasons for the Lack of Empathy Towards the Advertising

Teenagers can be very critical of advertising, especially of what they see as poor creativity, prosaic thinking, lack of style or inappropriate tone and poor production values. They want to see that the 'producers' have made an effort and they don't

---

17. Low advertising awareness had been indicated through qualitative research but was confirmed in a Millward Brown U&A study completed in December 1996.
18. The percentage awareness point per £million spent was lower than its competitors.

make allowances for the medicated advertising sector, judging Clean & Clear against their favourite advertising. As a result, 'Girls Talking' was viewed negatively:

— not realistic enough;

— too perfect;

— slightly patronising;

— not reflecting a picture of life that they could empathise with;

— not displaying enough understanding of them and what they want.

Sample: Females 11–18 years old
Source: Sally Page Qualitative Research/Caroline Oakes BMP Teen Panel, Autmn 1996

Brand Awareness was Relatively Low

Unsurprisingly therefore, brand awareness, particularly spontaneous brand awareness, was also relatively low compared to competitors and in relation to Clean & Clear's value share of the medicated market (Table 8). This suggested that the brand was not at the forefront of buyers' minds[19] and was perhaps a result of low advertising awareness.[20]

TABLE 8: BRAND AWARENESS COMPARED TO VALUE SHARE IN 1996

	Spontaneous brand awareness end 1996 %	Total brand awareness end 1996	Value share end 1996	Spontaneous awareness share %	Total awareness share %
Clearasil	53	98	19.0	2.8	6.2
Biactol	24	94	11.8	2.0	8.0
Oxy	43	93	22.8	1.9	4.1
Clean & Clear	8	51	13.7	0.6	3.7

Sample: Female spot product users
Source: Millward Brown U&A, December 1996
Source: IRI Infoscan value share four weeks ending December 1996

The combination of unimpactful advertising and relatively low brand awareness partially explained the disappointing shifts in stockturn in relation to advertising. Stockturn either decreased at the time of advertising or increased, only to fall shortly afterwards (see Figure 6 overleaf).[21]

---

19. The implication of this is that buyers were simply 'coming across' Clean & Clear in stores rather than making a conscious, pre-planned decision to examine and buy the brand.
20. By comparing the ratio between brand awareness and value share it was clear that Clean & Clear's brand awareness was relatively low in relation to its value share. This was particularly so for spontaneous brand awareness.
21. Figure 6 compares the value of stockturn three months before, during, and three months after bursts of 'Girls Talking'. The first burst refers to 'Girls Talking' in 1995, the second to 'Girls Talking' in early 1996 and the third to 'Girls Talking' later in 1996.

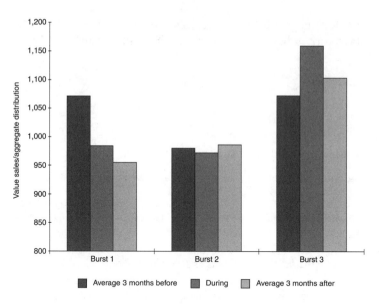

Figure 6: *Clean & Clear stockturn – before, during and after bursts of 'Girls Talking'*
Source: IRI

SUMMARY

It was clear that the translations of the US advertising were not working as well as intended. They lacked impact among teenagers, did not help to generate empathy and led to small or very short-term lifts in stockturn and sales. New advertising was clearly required.

THE NEED FOR NEW ADS

It was essential that the advertising worked harder to:

— Increase brand and advertising awareness among teenage girls.

— Make teenage girls feel that Johnson's understood them more.

— Generate a more sustained sales effect.

If advertising could achieve the above, Clean & Clear might still meet its objectives of:

— Becoming brand leader in the medicated skincare market.

— Becoming the most popular brand among teenage girls.

— Fuelling future loyalty to the Johnson's name.

WHAT NEEDED TO BE DONE

The global advertising idea intended to demonstrate that Clean & Clear had 'a unique understanding of teenage girls' skincare and emotional needs[22] and, because teenage girls talk about spots among themselves, the creative idea was based upon 'Girls Talking' about skincare. In its current form, 'Girls Talking' worked in the USA, but the UK girls found the execution of 'Girls Talking' to be artificial. As such, it was not helping to generate interest or empathy among teenage girls.

It was clear that the insight of 'Girls Talking' was relevant but that we needed to make it 'real' for UK girls. Instead of simply translating the American ads, we needed to understand UK girls and the way they talk about skincare in terms of the language and context of this type of conversation. We therefore developed a new creative brief that focused on 'getting real'.

ADVERTISING SOLUTION

With the help of video diaries, the result of giving video cameras to teenage girls over the Christmas period, we were able to develop new scripts that incorporated shrewd insights into real conversations between UK teenage girls. Two scripts, known as 'Big Bum' and 'Photos', worked best in qualitative research because:

1. Teenage girls recognised themselves in the scripts, which made them feel that Clean & Clear had bothered to find out about them, and therefore would have products they wanted.

2. The scripts were based on universal truths which meant that:

— teenage girls felt they were being treated like grown-up women;

— anyone could empathise with them, whether trendy or square.

Both scripts were made into TV ads, together known as 'Real Girls'. 'Big Bum' featured the long-established lotion product and 'Photos' featured a product to be launched in the Autumn of 1997, Clear Skin Daily Treatment. We also developed a press ad for the existing Deep Cleansing Cream Wash, which ran with an attached sachet.

---

22. Clean & Clear Brand Footprint.

'BIG BUM'

How do they look?
They make my bum look big don't they?

What bum?

Come on it sticks out a mile.

It's a good job you don't have spots to worry about as well – we'd be here all night.

(VO) Clean & Clear's lotion is clinically tested to effectively remove everyday dirt and grease.

(VO) So no matter what, you'll feel confident your skin is beautifully Clean & Clear.

So ... how does this look?
Great!

Are you sure?
Clean & Clear and under control.

'PHOTOS'

Oh no ...

Oh no ...

Oh no!

Well at least we didn't have any spots.

(VO) Clean & Clear New Clear Skin Daily Treatment fights the root cause of spots by controlling oil production.

(VO) So no matter what, you'll feel confident your skin is beautifully Clean & Clear.

Oh no.

Clean & Clear and under control.

MEDIA STRATEGY

BMP Optimum designed the media plan to be very tightly focused on teenage girls' favourite TV programmes such as *The Big Breakfast* (Table 9). In the past, media had been less focused on teenage girls, resulting in wastage and hence a shorter presence among this key target. This tight targeting enabled Clean & Clear to talk to teenage girls for longer.

In keeping with this targeting, we spotted an unusual opportunity: a Boyzone concert in July 1997, where 'Big Bum' appeared on a giant screen in front of screaming fans.

'Big Bum' was the first ad to be shown, aired nationally in two bursts. It was followed by a regional test in Scotland of 'Photos', in October and November of 1997 (Table 9).[23]

The press ad ran in May 1997.[24]

TABLE 9: CLEAN & CLEAR MEDIA PLAN 1997

	£000	Jan	Feb	Mar	Apr	May	Jun	Jul	Aug	Sep	Oct	Nov	Dec	Annual Total
1997	TV				525				227		35			787
	Press					85								85

WHAT HAPPENED?[25]

Increase in Sales

Clean & Clear experienced the largest single increase in value share *ever* in an eight-week period, immediately following the airing of 'Big Bum'; equivalent to two years of the previous distribution-led growth.[26]

The increase was maintained, without falling back to pre-advertising levels, despite a marked increase in competitive spend following 'Big Bum'. Sales increased 26% from year end 1996 to year end 1997, taking the brand to an all-time high.

By April 1998, Clean & Clear had met its objective of becoming the number 1 brand in sales terms only a year after the new advertising had broken (Table 10).

TABLE 10: VALUE SHARE OF MEDICATED SKINCARE MARKET, APRIL 1998 %

Clean & Clear	20
Oxy	17
Clearasil	16
Biactol	10

Source: IRI Infoscan four weeks ending 26 April 1998

---

23. 'Photos' was later aired nationally in March 1998.
24. This was for Deep Cleansing Cream Wash.
25. The majority of our analysis concentrates on the period from March to December 1997, but while writing this paper some data have become available for 1998. The additional data enabled us to carry the analysis forward with reference to some measures. This will be made clear where appropriate.
26. Value share increased 5%. IRI Infoscan.

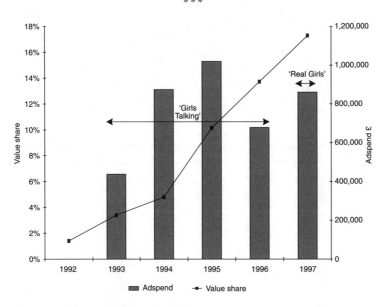

Figure 7: *Clean & Clear value share of medicated market and adspend*
Source: IRI, BARB

Increase in Stockturn and Rate of Sale

Stockturn increased dramatically at the time of the 'Real Girls' advertising (Table 11), demonstrating that growth was now demand-led rather than supply-led and the increase in stockturn was sustained (Figure 8).

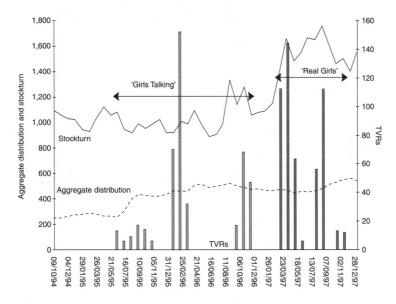

Figure 8: *Clean & Clear stockturn versus TVRs and aggregate distribution*
Source: IRI, BARB

TABLE 11: COMPARISON OF STOCKTURN 1994 TO 1996 VERSUS 1997

Average stockturn (Value sales per aggregate distribution point)	
'Girls Talking' (Oct 1994 to Feb 1997)	'Real Girls' (Mar 1997 to Jan 1998)
1,032	1,558

Source: IRI Infoscan

Practically all the individual products experienced an increase in their rate of sale, including the long-established lotion which was featured in 'Big Bum' and which had previously experienced a decreasing rate of sale.

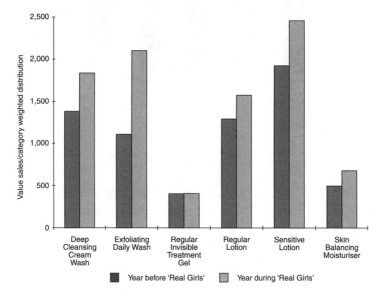

Figure 9: *Clean & Clear average rate of sale by product*
Source: IRI

Increase in the Popularity of the Brand

Clean & Clear became the most popular brand among female teenage buyers[27] of medicated skincare, thereby meeting its objective (Table 12).

This resulted in a dramatic increase in Clean & Clear's brand share among teenage girls (from 20.2% to 28% between April 1996 and April 1998).

---

27. Purchase data is significant because it represents teenagers who actually bought and used the products themselves.

TABLE 12: PENETRATION AMONG TEENAGE GIRLS[28]

	Year to April 1996 'Girls Talking' %	Year to April 1998 'Real Girls' %	% change 1996 to 1998
Clean & Clear	9.6	40.8	+325
Oxy	19.8	18.9	- 5
Clearasil	18.9	18.7	- 1
Biactol	9.4	7.0	- 26

Source: Taylor Nelson Year Ending April 1996/Year Ending April 1998
Sample: Female buyers, 13 to 18 years old

A Dramatic Shift in Teenage Empathy Towards the Brand

Girls now felt that Clean & Clear and Johnson's understood them and what they wanted from skincare.

'There's always something to worry about and one less thing the better – and that's exactly what they're saying.'

15-year-old

You try everything on and then at the last second you get your jeans out and change. That's just like me.'

14-year-old

Sample: Females 13 to 16 years old
Source: Qualitative Research, RDS, August 1997

In fact, teenagers empathised with the brand to the degree that if they could use only one brand, Clean & Clear would be their most preferred choice (Table 13).

TABLE 13: BRAND PREFERENCE

'If you had to use only one of the following medicated brands over a 6 month period, which one would you use?'	
Clean & Clear	35%
Clearasil	32%
Oxy	18%
Biactol	4%
None of these	11%

Sample: Females, 11 to 19 years old
Base: 317
Stimulus: Showcard: Clearasil, Oxy, Clean & Clear, Biactol, None of these
Source: BMP/SNAP Quantitative Survey, April 1998

---

28. We have shown Taylor Nelson data from 1996 and 1998 and not from 1997, because data do not distinguish between the 'Girls Talking' and the 'Real Girls' periods of advertising.

SUMMARY

In short, Clean & Clear had met all of its objectives within one year of the launch of the new advertising. It was now:

1. No. 1 medicated skincare brand.

2. Most popular medicated skincare brand among female teenagers.

3. A brand with which female teenagers could empathise and hence these girls were quite likely to become future adult users of Johnson's other products.

PROVING THE CONTRIBUTION MADE BY ADVERTISING

How do we know that the new advertising had been instrumental in Clean & Clear's accelerated growth? We will prove this by showing:

1. Direct evidence that the new advertising worked as planned.

2. Timing of sales shifts coinciding with advertising.

3. Sales results from a regional advertising upweight.

4. Econometric analysis.

5. Elimination of other variables.

Direct Evidence that the New Advertising Worked as Planned

Impactful advertising and the creation of a famous brand

Advertising awareness improved considerably in relation to competitive brands (Table 14).[29] This occurred even though adspend on Clean & Clear increased only slightly between 1996 and 1997, from £0.68 million in 1996 to £0.87 million in 1997, and share of voice remained stable at 12%. In comparison, Clearasil increased spend from £1.36 million to £3.59 million, accounting for a 50% share of voice in 1997 compared to 25% in 1996.

---

29. While two data sources are used, which could reduce the robustness of the absolute movement, the relative movement in comparison to competitors is meaningful.

TABLE 14: TOTAL ADVERTISING AWARENESS

	Total advertising awareness 1996 %	Total advertising awareness 1998 %	% Change 1996 to 1998
Clean & Clear	23	37	+61%
Clearasil	69	50	-28%
Oxy	72	39	-46%
Biactol	66	21	-68%

Sample: Females, 11 to 19 years old
Base: 317
Source: BMP/SNAP Quantitative Survey April 1998

Source: Millward Brown U&A Study December 1996
Sample: Female spot product user
Source: MEAL

The ratio between ad awareness and share of voice improved in relation to competitive brands (Table 15).

TABLE 15: THE RATIO OF ADVERTISING AWARENESS TO SHARE OF VOICE[30]

	Ratio ad awareness/share of voice		Index of ratio on Clean & Clear	
	1996	1998	1996	1998
Clean & Clear	1.89	3.06	100	100
Clearasil	2.81	0.99	149	32
Oxy	1.98	2.25	105	74

Sample: Females, 11 to 19 years old
Base: 317
Source: BMP/SNAP Quantitative Survey, April 1998

Source: Millward Brown U&A Study, December 1996
Sample: Female spot product users
Source: MEAL

In October 1997 the second execution, 'Photos', was aired exclusively in Scotland, with 275 TVRs, with no other Clean & Clear advertising aired in the rest of the UK at this time. As Table 16 shows, as a result, advertising awareness is higher in Scotland than elsewhere and considerably higher than competitive brands in both Scotland and the rest of the UK.

---

0. We have not included the share of voice of Biactol because it was consolidated under the Clearasil brand name in 1997.

TABLE 16: TOTAL ADVERTISING AWARENESS

	Scotland %	Rest of UK %
Clean& Clear	57	35
Clearasil	50	50
Oxy	47	39
Biactol	30	20

Sample: Females, 11to 19 years old
Base: 317
Source: BMP/SNAP Quantitative Survey, April 1998

Increase in Brand Awareness

As a result of the increase in advertising awareness, brand awareness also increased (Table 17).

TABLE 17: TOTAL BRAND AWARENESS

	Total brand awareness 1996 %	Total brand awareness 1998 %	% change
Clean & Clear	51	76	+49%
Clearasil	98	88	-10%
Oxy	93	78	-16%
Biactol	94	69	-27%

Sample: Females, 11 to 19 years old
Base: 317
Source: BMP/SNAP Quantitative Survey, April 1998
Sample: Female spot product users
Source: Millward Brown U&A, December 1996

Similarly in the Scottish test market, brand awareness was higher in Scotland than in the rest of the UK (Table 18).

TABLE 18: TOTAL BRAND AWARENESS

	Scotland %	Rest of UK %
Clean & Clear	83	76
Clearasil	80	89
Oxy	73	79
Biactol	63	69

Sample: Females, 11 to 19 years old
Base: 317
Source: BMP/SNAP Quantitative Survey

Increase in empathy towards the advertising and the brand

For the first time teenage girls enthused about Clean & Clear's advertising, even laughing about how true it was to their lives and attitudes towards skincare. This was completely different from earlier reactions and was unlike that produced by competitive advertising, which they felt was unnatural and contrived.

'That one's really good.'

13-year-old

'I really like those.'

14-year-old

'They're much better. I can't stand those Clearasil adverts. Really fake. They get on my nerves.'

14-year-old

The advertising depicts, 'A convincing scene which is a major breakthrough where other brands are contrived.' (RDS)

Sample: Females, 13 to16 years old
Source: Qualitative Research, RDS, August 1997

As a result, teenage girls were more likely to use Clean & Clear if they had been exposed to the 'Real Girls' campaign:[31]

TABLE 19: PROPENSITY TO USE CLEAN & CLEAR

	1996 'Girls Talking'	1997 'Real Girls'	% change
Big Breakfast Fans:	110	122	+10.9
Big Breakfast Rejectors:	67	58	-13.4

Question: Of spot creams, lotions and gels, which brand do you use most often?
Sample: Females, 11 to 19 years old
Source: Youth TGI 1996 and 1997

In fact, girls who were aware of the advertising were more likely to claim they would use Johnson's brands when they grew up as well (Table 20). This suggested that this advertising was now helping to establish a long-term relationship with teenage girls.[32]

1. Table 19 compares the likelihood of teenage girls aged 11 to 19 using Clean & Clear according to whether or not they were fans of the Big Breakfast, across 1996 and 1997.
2. While it is virtually impossible to gain an accurate measure of future propensity to purchase a product or brand, we asked teenage girls, both those who were aware and those who were unaware of Johnson's Clean & Clear advertising, 'How likely are you to use a Johnson's brand, such as Johnson's pH5.5 or Johnson's Baby when you are in your twenties?'. Given that we asked female teenagers, regardless of current brand usage, the results showed that teenagers who were aware of the advertising were more likely to say that they were using or were very likely to use Johnson's brand when they were in their twenties.

TABLE 20: LIKELIHOOD OF USING A JOHNSON'S BRAND AS AN ADULT

	Aware of Clean & Clear advertising	Unaware of Clean & Clear advertising	Index of aware/unaware
Very/quite likely	76	51	150
Neither/nor	11	28	39
Quite/very unlikely	13	21	62

Sample: Females, 11 to 19 years old
Base: 317
Source: BMP/SNAP Quantitative Survey, April 1998

Further evidence of the effect of the new advertising came from the J&J salesforce.

' "Big Bum" had a terrific impact on sales across the whole range. It demonstrated to our customers, the trade, both our commitment to support the brand and our ability to communicate to our target consumers.'

Neil Dickenson, Group Controller, J&J Salesforce, May 1998

The feedback didn't stop there. J&J was inundated with letters from teenagers eulogising the advertising, the brand and the products, which had never happened before; plus the advertising was also featured in a television show and a teen magazine.

The Timing of the Sales Shifts in Relation to Advertising

Stockturn increased at precisely the time when 'Big Bum' was aired, a time when there were no increases in distribution and no new product launches (Figure 10).

This led to value share increasing dramatically at precisely the same time when 'Big Bum' was aired, again suggesting advertising's key role (Figure 11).

The Sales Results from a Regional Advertising Upweight

As already discussed 'Photos' was aired only in Scotland in October 1997. Scotland's performance, relative to the rest of the country, improved significantly exactly when these extra TVRs were screened (Figure 12).[33]

---

33. Figure 12 shows Clean & Clear's value share in Scotland versus the rest of the UK, which increased at the time of 'Photos'.

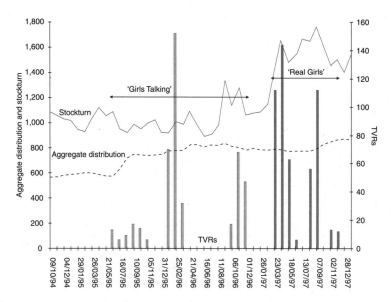

Figure 10: *Clean & Clear stockturn versus TVRs and aggregate distribution*
Source: IRI, BARB

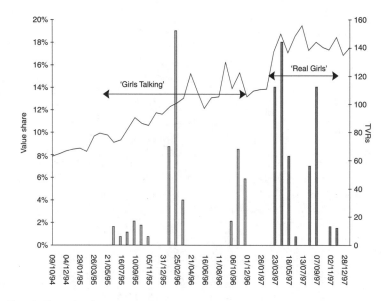

Figure 11: *Clean & Clear value share versus TVRs*
Source: IRI, BARB

Econometrics

An econometric model, which takes account of the different factors that might affect sales growth, provides further evidence of the effect of the 'Real Girls' campaign. The model shows that without 'Real Girls', value share would have been markedly lower and growth would indeed have petered out (Figure 13).[34]

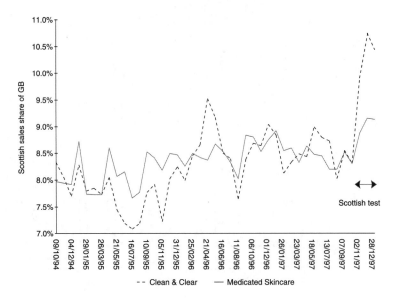

Figure 12: *Scottish share of GB sales*
Source: IRI

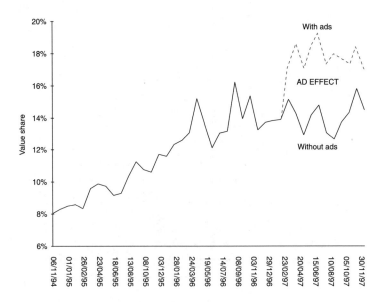

Figure 13: *Clean & Clear value share effect of 'Real Girls'*
Source: IRI, BMP Model

---

34. The exact revenue generated from 'Real Girls' is discussed in the Payback section.

Eliminating Other Factors

Although Clean & Clear's rapid and sustained increase in sales, share, stockturn, rate of sale and the positive movements in intermediary measures all reflect the campaign's effectiveness, we need to eliminate the possible effects of some other factors in order to be certain.

New products

New products cannot have caused the bulk of Clean & Clear's growth during 1997, because this occurred immediately after the start of the 'Real Girls' campaign and during this time no new products were launched

Furthermore, as we have already seen, rate of sale increased across practically all of the product range, so growth cannot be attributed only to new product launches. We have also shown that stockturn, which accounts for the number of facings, increased (Figure 10).[35]

Product improvements or reformulations

No products were reformulated or repackaged in 1997.

Distribution

The initial increase in sales could not have been driven by an increase in distribution, as Clean & Clear's distribution across all the products was static at the start of the 'Real Girls' campaign (Figure 14).

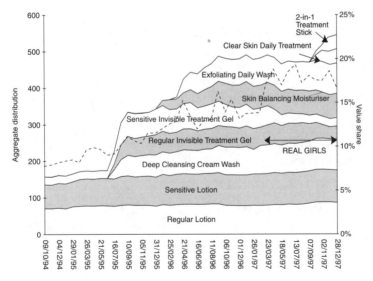

Figure 14: *Clean & Clear value share and aggregate distribution*
Source: IRI

---

35. Two new products were eventually launched in Autumn 1997 – Clear Skin Daily Treatment and 2-in-1 Treatment Stick – but this occurred six months after the initial increase in sales.

In addition, the market became tougher in terms of new launches and distribution. The aggregate distribution of Clearasil, Biactol and Oxy actually increased after the start of the 'Real Girls' campaign, both in the short term and in the long term, so Clean & Clear's relative distribution actually fell.

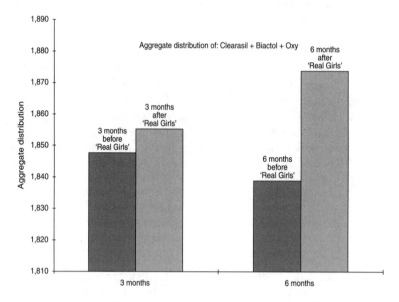

Figure 15: *Average aggregate distribution of competition – before and after start of 'Real Girls' campaign*
Source: IRI

There was no change in Clean & Clear's instore siting.

Promotions/sampling

Promotional samples could not have effected the initial and largest increases in sales because there were no sampling promotions during this period. A sampling promotion only occurred later (see Figure 16).

There was no point-of-sale promotional material at the time of the 'Real Girls' campaign. Price promotions are captured in the price variable which is discussed in the pricing section below.[36]

Pricing

Because we are concentrating on sales value, it might be argued that the uplift we have seen was an artefact of rising prices, or volume increases might be a result of price cutting. Neither is true. Prices did rise a little (absolutely and relative to competition). See Figures 17 and 18.

---

36. Price promotions are captured in the definition of price (value/volume).

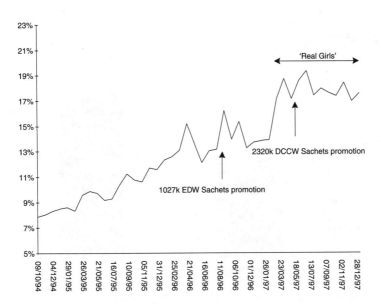

Figure 16: *Value share and promotions*
Source: IRI, J&J

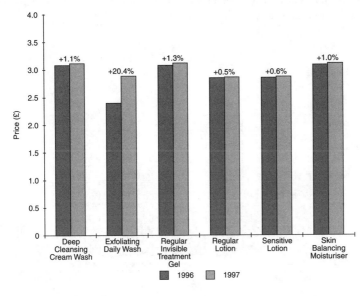

Figure 17: *Clean & Clear price by product*
Source: IRI

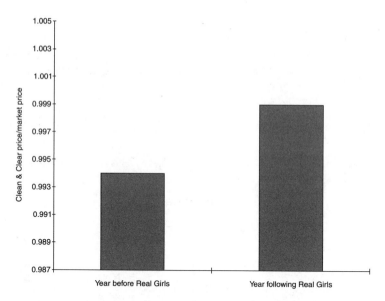

Figure 18: *Clean & Clear average price relative to medicated market average price*
Source: IRI

Thus price could not have driven volume. In addition, volume, not just value, grew substantially (see Figure 19). Hence price rises cannot account for the (much larger) growth in value sales.

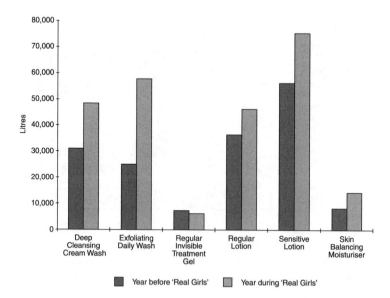

Figure 19: *Clean & Clear volume by product*
Source: IRI

Competitive adspend

Competitive adspend increased in 1997, especially for Clearasil, making Clean & Clear's performance more remarkable and proving that Clean & Clear did not benefit from any decrease in competitive adspend (Figure 20).

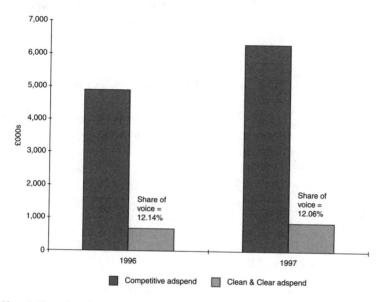

Figure 20: *Clean & Clear adspend versus competition*
Source: MEAL

Competitive product changes

The medicated market became more competitive in 1997. Clearasil launched a totally new product, Clearasil Complete, Boots relaunched their medicated range, giving it a more up-to-date image, and Clean & Clear's product positioning was further threatened by the introduction of similar products.

Despite the launch of competitive products, new brands and the blurring of Clean & Clear's unique positioning, Clean & Clear's value share grew.

Consumer factors

Other factors, such as an increase in the population of teenage girls, an increase in the number of teenage girls suffering from spots or an increase in teenage girls' disposable income, can be eliminated as factors affecting Clean & Clear's success because the brand's share increased. If the above factors had played a part they would have affected the total medicated market.

Momentum of previous advertising, 'Girls Talking'

It is possible that the previous four years of 'Girls Talking' advertising might have generated sufficient momentum to drive the initial increase in sales after 'Girls Talking' was taken off air. However, this cannot be the case because there was a gap of three months between the 'Girls Talking' advertising and the 'Real Girls' campaign. If 'Girls Talking' had generated a head of steam, sales would have increased before the airing of 'Real Girls'.

SUMMARY

It was clear that the new advertising had a momentous effect. Brand and advertising awareness was boosted and now on a par with competitive brands, sales and value share had increased, stockturn had increased and teenage girls could empathise with the advertising, the brand and with Johnson's, and no other factors could explain such improvements.

THE FINANCIAL CONTRIBUTION OF ADVERTISING

The econometric model has helped us to assess the financial contribution of advertising. We will show that the advertising running in 1997 (ie, the 'Real Girls' campaign) has had two financial consequences:

1. A profitable return within the first year, ie, from March to December 1997.

2. An even more profitable forecasted return within two years, from March 1997 to December 1998 based on estimated adstocks.

We will also provide the estimated returns had 'Girls Talking' continued to be aired instead (Tables 21 and 22).

TABLE 21: THE RETURN IN THE PERIOD MARCH TO DECEMBER 1997

THE RETURN FROM 'REAL GIRLS' Return within one year of airing 'Real Girls'	
Revenue from 'Real Girls'	£1.75m
Adspend on 'Real Girls'	£0.87m
Short-term return from 'Real Girls'	£0.88m
THE RETURN THAT WOULD HAVE BEEN GENERATED HAD 'GIRLS TALKING' BEEN AIRED INSTEAD OF 'REAL GIRLS' Return within one year of airing 'Girls Talking' (if it had been aired at the same weight)	
Revenue from 'Girls Talking'	£0.78m
Adspend	£0.87m
'Girls Talking' would not have covered adspend	-£0.09m

Note: Based on IRI Infoscan value

Had 'Girls Talking' been aired instead of 'Real Girls' there would have been a negative return from advertising within one year.

TABLE 22: FORECASTED RETURNS IN THE PERIOD
FROM MARCH 1997 TO DECEMBER 1998

From the model we estimate that the adstock is 75%. This means that the direct effect of airing ads in 1997 will have reached almost zero by the end of 1998.

THE RETURN FROM 'REAL GIRLS'

Return within two years of airing 'Real Girls'

Revenue from 'Real Girls'	£2.04m
Adspend on 'Real Girls'	£0.87m
Short-to medium-term return from 'Real Girls'	£1.17m

THE RETURN THAT WOULD HAVE BEEN GENERATED IF 'GIRLS TALKING' HAD BEEN AIRED INSTEAD OF 'REAL GIRLS' (if it had been aired at the same weight)

Revenue from 'Girls Talking'	£0.91m
Adspend during this period	£0.87m
Short + medium-term return from 'Girls Talking'	£0.04m

Note: Based on IRI Infoscan value

In summary, because 'Real Girls' was aired instead of 'Girls Talking', an extra £1.13 million return has been forecasted after adspend has been deducted.

Figure 21 shows the difference in sales generated by: (a) What actually happened; the airing of 'Real Girls'; (b) What would have happened if 'Girls Talking' had continued to be aired, and (c) What would have happened if no advertising had been aired at all.

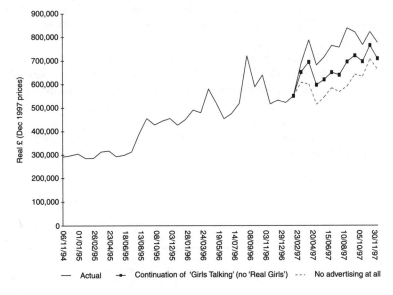

Figure 21: *Clean & Clear value sales: actual versus different advertising scenarios*
Source: IRI, BMP Model

Profit

In terms of profit in the short-to-medium term, 'Girls Talking' would require a break-even profit margin of at least 95.6% for the advertising to have been profitable.[37] By comparison, 'Real Girls', requires a break-even profit margin of 43% for the advertising to be profitable. The industry average profit margin lies between 50% and 70%.[38] Therefore it is not unreasonable to suggest that 'Real Girls' will be making a profit for J&J which would not have been the case if 'Girls Talking' had been aired in its place. Based on these margins we can calculate a return on investment (Table 23):

TABLE 23: RETURN ON INVESTMENT CALCULATION

	Profit generated from extra revenue due to advertising	Minus advertising expenditure of £0.87m	Return on investment %
50% profit margin	£1.02m	£0.15m	17.2
70% profit margin	£1.22m	£0.35m	40.2

Longer Term Payback

The new advertising has helped both Clean & Clear and the Johnson's brand portfolio for the future. Until the airing of the new advertising, Clean & Clear's growth was substantially driven by distribution and economic growth, together accounting for approximately 60% of the growth in the previous three years. Given that distribution growth is unsustainable and given that economic growth is forecasted to slow down in the future, Clean & Clear was on borrowed time.

The new advertising has addressed this problem, reducing Clean & Clear's reliance on the economy and aggregate distribution. Without such a change, the brand was at risk of losing a significant proportion of sales and ultimately would have become untenable (Figure 22).

Instead, the new advertising has generated consumer demand, has enabled Clean & Clear to become the No. 1 medicated skincare brand by value share and has helped to forge a relationship with teenage girls. J&J now has over half a million existing teenage Clean & Clear buyers who are likely to convert into half a million adult Johnson's buyers. This is not included in the payback calculation because it is difficult to quantify, but this must make the payback a gross underestimate of total return.

---

37. Break-even profit margins are measured by dividing adspend by revenue generated form advertising. Therefore to make a profit, the margin on the products needs to be above this percentage.
38. This includes the more sophisticated, technological products which are at the lower end of the profit margin.

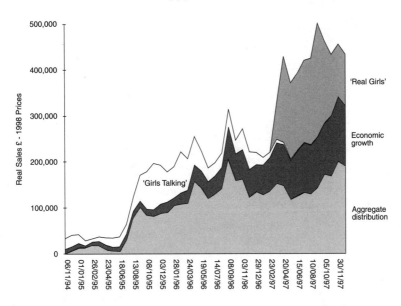

Figure 22: *Clean & Clear growth (November 1994 – December 1997) and main conributors to growth*
Source: IRI, BMP Model

CONCLUSION

Prior to the 'Real Girls' campaign, the brand was not on track to meet its objectives. By maintaining the theme of a global advertising idea but changing the UK advertising from translations of the US ads into ads based on genuine insights gained from local consumers, the situation was dramatically reversed. The brand's stockturn increased and the brand was able to become the No. 1 medicated skincare brand by value share. At the same time the advertising developed strong brand values which forged a relationship with teenage girls. This has increased Johnson's chances of building a lifelong relationship with them.

As a result of the new advertising, Clean & Clear became a star in J&J's portfolio. J&J was thrilled with the performance and became increasingly confident about rolling out the brand into 14 countries across Europe and the Middle East, doing so with advertising that suited each country's local needs.

★★★

15

Ford Galaxy
Building brand value for Ford

EDITOR'S SUMMARY

This case shows how highly differentiated advertising can redefine a category. Ford Galaxy has shifted perceptions of 'people movers' from the functional, to the aspirational and stylish.

Changing How a Category is Perceived

The success of the advertising owes much to the consumer insight that the space around the driver can be seen as more than just room to carry other people or cargo. Space can also make people feel important, relaxed, and can even convey a sense of luxury. This insight led to a different way of positioning Galaxy and the proposition; 'the luxury of unused space'. The airline analogy of travelling in First Class provided the creative breakthrough.

Results and Payback

Galaxy became a brand leader almost immediately. Advertising achieved the highest levels of awareness and efficiency of communication and created a brand that is regarded as stylish and different, as well as outperforming the competition on the rational aspects. This imagery and communication is linked to levels of purchase consideration, which, in turn, is closely correlated with sales.

Galaxy's sales in the first year were approaching the size of the total market in the previous year. This was achieved by bringing in new users to the category. Furthermore, they were not just new to this category, they were also new to Ford.

The concurrent launch of a near identical product – VW Sharan – enabled product performance to be separated away from advertising effects. Using this as a benchmark, and accounting for the effect of other variables such as distribution, has isolated the sales increment directly attributable to advertising.

An initial advertising investment of £7.2 million created an additional £25.5 million within 18 months of launch. The long-term significance is a valuable brand that is contributing to Ford's overall corporate and image objectives.

INTRODUCTION

This case study shows the value of advertising in creating a strong brand. It is about the success of Ford Galaxy in becoming the brand leader in the MPV ('people movers') segment. Advertising not only helped Galaxy achieve short-term sales objectives, but it also built enduring brand values that have maintained its brand leadership over the last three years. Galaxy succeeded over the established category leader of ten years' standing – Renault Espace, and over new competitive threats, without significant product advantage.

We show how advertising has driven sales by examining its relationship to brand imagery and purchase consideration. We link the following elements:

This provides the model for the way Galaxy advertising has worked. The model goes further than many other IPA car case studies by also estimating the value of the Galaxy brand (not simply the revenues earned).

We assess how the Galaxy brand contributed to the overall Ford brand, and created an incremental £25.5 million from an initial advertising investment of £7.2 million.

Perhaps the case study can be best introduced by Ian McAllister, Chairman of Ford of Britain, who was quoted by Campaign as saying, 'We know creativity sells, look at Galaxy'.

THE PROBLEM

The Renault Espace created the MPV segment in 1985, and had been brand leader ever since. Other strong brands in this segment included Toyota Previa, Nissan Serena and Mitsubishi Space Wagon, but the Renault Espace still maintained brand leadership with a 50% share in 1994.

Ford believed the category could grow substantially. However, Ford was not the only company with that view, as VW was launching the Sharan at the same time, swiftly followed by MPVs from Citroën, Fiat, Peugeot and Seat.

An unusual circumstance for Ford's launch of the Galaxy was that the Volkswagen Sharan (and indeed later the Seat Alhambra) was a near identical product. Built on the same production line, the chassis, body panels, transmission and even some of the engines were identical. While there was variation in interior fittings and specifications, they were essentially the same vehicle. Our major challenge was to use advertising as the primary tool in creating consumer preference for a near identical product. This was particularly difficult when the image strength of the overall VW brand was compared to Ford's. VW was known for its safety and product quality – key attributes for a high-priced family car.

Galaxy's launch also had a wider strategic significance for Ford. Over previous years the car market had started to fragment, which was reducing the share of the mass market segments where Ford was traditionally strong. This is illustrated by the fact that Ford now have ten models competing in different segments, whereas a decade earlier they had only four. Ford wanted to become a brand leader in these new segments in order to maintain volume.

The MPV buyers were more likely to have professional occupations, be better educated and to have higher incomes than the average Ford customer. Attitudinally, they were independent and less likely to choose a mainstream brand. Ford wanted to reach this new type of consumer and give the Galaxy values which were attractive to them.

The launch objectives were daunting:

— Brand leadership within the first year.

— Volume target over 7,500 units (Espace's 1994 sales).

— Build enduring brand values.

— Appeal to an upmarket, discerning audience.

— Contribute to Ford overall brand values.

THE STRATEGIC BREAKTHROUGH

When Galaxy was shown to consumers in product clinics, the disappointing result was that the product, in isolation, was not going to change opinions of the segment. Although the product was seen as good, and offered significant refinements on many functions already available with MPVs, it was not seen as revolutionary. We needed a new way of presenting this vehicle.

The breakthrough came from one of the largest research programmes conducted for a single car line for Ford of Britain. It involved mailing 49,000 new-car buyers in a quantitative study, supplemented by qualitative group discussions.

The research revealed that there were two key groups of potential purchasers. 'MPV lovers' were those who understood the functional benefits of an MPV, who may have had some experience of one (such as having driven or been driven in one), and who liked the idea of purchasing an MPV. This group was most likely to gravitate towards the Renault Espace. The second group, 'MPV doubters', were those who understood the concept of an MPV, but rejected the image. They referred to MPVs as 'Mum's taxis' and were scathing about them. MPVs were unaspirational, functional vehicles, weighed down by associations of family obligation.

Despite the seemingly difficult task of appealing to 'MPV doubters', they provided the breakthrough for the Galaxy strategy. We recognised that only by targeting 'doubters' (three times the size of 'lovers') would we be able to gain the necessary volume.

We knew that 'doubters' were the key to growing the market, and to being highly differentiated.

Galaxy needed to reframe the battleground to appeal to this new customer group. The task of changing the image expectations of the category was neatly illustrated by a motoring journalist who wrote, 'driving an MPV says I need a vasectomy'. An advertising budget was set that would lead the market in the launch year (advertising expenditure in 1995 was reported at £7.2 million by MMS[1]). This was seen as critical, given VW's launch and the need to establish leadership quickly. It meant that advertising needed to pay back within 18 months of launch.

The breakthrough strategy was:

— To grow the market by bringing in new users.

— To appeal to 'MPV doubters' who have a functional need, but who are image adverse.

— To position Galaxy as a stylish and aspirational car.

CREATIVE BRIEF

All other MPV advertising talked about the benefits of the size of the vehicle in functional and practical terms. They showed how many people or lifestyle products you could pack into an MPV. We needed to appeal to 'MPV doubters' with an emotional message. Having more space than is needed for physical needs is a sign of social status; a bigger house or office is a form of 'conspicuous consumption' that is recognised as a status symbol. A different way of looking at the benefits of space is not how much you can pack in, but how it makes you feel. Empty space is valued by people because it makes them feel important and special. This insight led to a new way of positioning Galaxy. The proposition on the creative brief was:

'The luxury of unused space.'

The notion of luxury coming from the space around you was entirely different for the category and allowed the advertising to be aspirational. Luxury was not a word normally associated with MPVs. We were persuading people to think of the Galaxy more as a luxury car than as an MPV.

The requirement was *not* to show families or fully occupied seats as a means of further breaking away from the category conventions.

---

1.   All budgets quoted are from independent monitoring sources in order to protect confidentiality and ensure comparablilty.

CREATIVE BREAKTHROUGH

Where are you made to feel important and special with more space around you? The creative solution of travelling first class on an aeroplane created an immediate analogy. The 'Travel First Class' campaign broke on TV, posters and in print.

The TV made the viewer feel they were watching an airline advertisement, with all the appropriate sophisticated and relaxed imagery, only then to reveal it was for the Galaxy. The use of the British Airways music (Delibes – Lakme) was an important part of creating this feeling (thanks to British Airways for permission to use).

This creative platform formed the basis for the entire brand launch including brochures, dealer showroom materials, direct marketing materials and PR.

SUCCESS STORY

The sales results far exceeded expectations. Galaxy became brand leader within two months and has maintained brand leadership every year since.

In an 18-month launch period, Galaxy sold over 16,000 units. The volume target to beat Espace sales of 7,500 units in 1994 was easily exceeded (Figure 1).

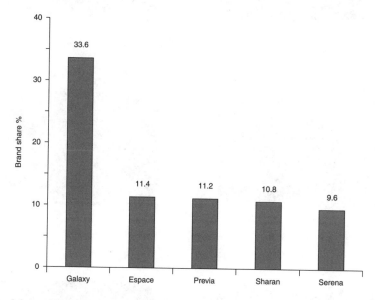

Figure 1: *Brand shares – MPV segment (July 1995 to December 1996)*
Source: SMMT

Galaxy succeeded in growing the market by bringing in new customers: 90% of Galaxy's sales came from people who had not previously owned an MPV (compared with Espace at 50%).

Galaxy also succeeded in bringing 73% new customers to Ford. This is in contrast with the average for Ford cars where 75% of Ford buyers had previously owned a Ford.

'TRAVEL FIRST CLASS' CAMPAIGN

Music: Lakme – Delibes.

PRESS ADS

THERE'S ALWAYS MORE ROOM IN FIRST CLASS.

ENJOY THE RAREFIED ATMOSPHERE OF FIRST CLASS.

YES, WE DO HAVE SEATS AVAILABLE IN FIRST CLASS.

These new customers were upmarket, better educated and more professional:

	Ford Galaxy owners	MPV segment (excluding Ford)	Ford overall brand
Average Income	£46,000	£38,000	£28,000
Professional	22%	17%	6%
Higher education/University	54%	49%	39%

Source: NCBS 1996

These results show that Galaxy met its objectives in terms of brand leadership, sales volume, growing the market, and bringing new, more valuable customers to Ford.

In addition, Galaxy advertising contributed to dealers' businesses. It generated an unprecedented high level of enquiries that were fed through to dealers. The conversion of enquiries to sales was 30% higher than that for the Ka launch. This increment was worth an additional £10,000 for every Ford dealer.

ADVERTISING AND BRAND IMAGERY

There is a clear relationship between the advertising and the brand image of Galaxy.

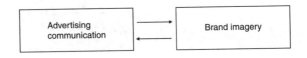

Millward Brown monitored advertising communication and brand imagery in six monthly dipsticks amongst MPV considerers. Results from the first dipstick after the 18-month launch period (April 1997) showed that people's perceptions of the brand were closely matched by their impressions of the advertising.

	Advertising impression	Image dimension
Highest scoring emotional attribute	Classy/chic/upmarket/ luxury/elegant	Has a more stylish design
Highest scoring rational attribute	Comfortable/lovely to drive	Better road-holding and handling

Base: MPV considerers/non-owners
Source: Millward Brown

The advertising created the brand imagery rather than reflected it.

While brand image was naturally strong among owners of a particular model, it was also leading among non-owners.

TABLE 1: IMAGE STRENGTH AMONG NON-OWNERS OF
GALAXY/ESPACE/SHARAN (AUTUMN 1997)[2]

	Ford Galaxy	Renault Espace	VW Sharan
Has a more stylish design	28	18	10
Better road-holding and handling	26	12	11
Is the car to be seen driving	18	10	12

Base: MPV considerers/non-owners
Source: Millward Brown

Comparing Galaxy's strength with the VW Sharan is particularly significant given the product similarity.

Looking at an image map of all dimensions (Figure 2) we can see that Galaxy has a closer association with the attributes of stylish, professional and intelligent, than the average MPV brand.

Figure 2: *Image of models (April 1997)*
Base: MPV considerers/non-owners
Source: Millward Brown

The role of advertising in achieving the imagery is seen not just in the communication, but also in how powerfully these messages were put across. Galaxy achieved over twice the level of ad awareness than its nearest competitor.

We know that Galaxy's expenditure was not just effective, but also efficient. Millward Brown calculated that Galaxy had an Awareness Index of seven, which is almost twice the average efficiency of four for car brands in generating ad awareness per TV rating point. It was stated above that an important additional objective of launching Galaxy was to maximise the contribution to the overall Ford brand. Figure 3 (overleaf) shows how Ford's overall brand is regarded as stylish among considerers of MPVs. This contrasts with Ford's image among considerers of all cars, where Ford is closely associated with better value.

---

2. Data not available in this form for April 1997.

Figure 3: *Image of manufacturers (April 1997)*
Base: MPV considerers/non-owners
Source: Millward Brown

Overall, the brand image created through advertising was highly distinctive and clearly related to the advertising content.

ADVERTISING AND PURCHASE CONSIDERATION

Having demonstrated that advertising, rather than product, was the key influence on brand imagery, we can now see the relationship to purchase consideration.[3]

Galaxy has led the segment consistently on consideration (see Figure 4). An analysis by Millward Brown identifies those image dimensions that correlate most strongly with purchase consideration.[3] Galaxy scores higher than its competitors on both the rational and emotional dimensions that most relate to purchase intent (see Figure 5). The effect has been so marked that it has changed the rules for the category.

Millward Brown comments in its report that 'stylish design' has become one of the most important drivers of consideration in the category, due to the 'Galaxy Effect'.

---

3.   Derived importance by Jacquard analysis.

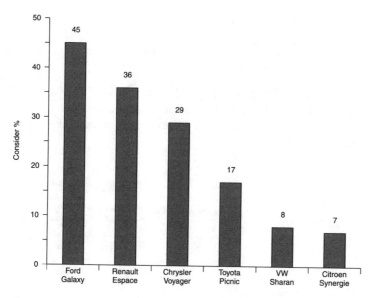

Figure 4: *Will strongly consider as next car (April 1997)*
Base: MPV considerers/non-owners
Source: Millward Brown

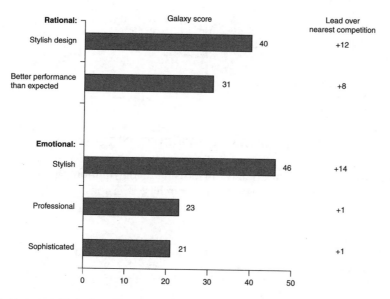

Figure 5: *Most important drivers of consideration (April 1997)*
Base: Considerers/owners
Source: Millward Brown

Millward Brown's summary was:

'Galaxy, as the sector's standard bearer, is in an enviable position. It leads the field in nearly all rational and emotional attributes, including those that correlate with sales.'

The link between the familiarity of the Galaxy brand and purchase consideration is shown in Figure 6. We can see that increasing familiarity through advertising will increase consideration. Galaxy advertising has created leading scores on familiarity and consideration.

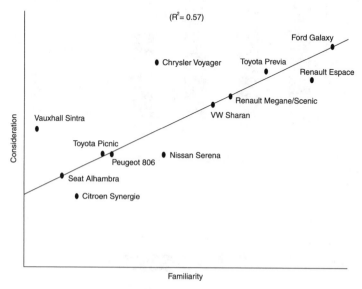

Figure 6: *Consideration and familiarity*
Base: MPV considerers
Source: Millward Brown

ADVERTISING'S CONTRIBUTION TO SALES

It is 'devilishly difficult' to isolate advertising's contribution to sales in the car market since sales are highly seasonal and purchase decisions are long.

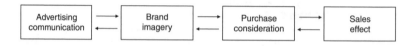

To take account of seasonal effects we can index Galaxy sales against industry monthly sales. The advertising investment can be lagged in its effect to take account of the decision-making period for new-car purchase. Other industry studies show the decision period at three to six months. The 'best fit' is using seasonally adjusted sales with a lagged effect of five months, together with a 'decay rate' of 25% on advertising investment (Figure 7). This shows a good correlation ($r = 0.66$) between ad investment and sales.

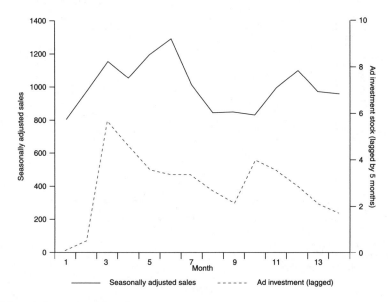

Figure 7: *Sales and ad investment (adjusted)*
Source: SMMT/MMS/Adjusted data

Other evidence of the relationship between advertising and sales comes from consumers' stated 'reasons for buying'. This shows that the principal image dimension communicated in the advertising, that is, 'stylish', was the principal reason for purchase. Thirty-eight per cent of people stated that the reason for buying a Ford Galaxy was that it was 'stylish' versus 13% for the segment average.

Additional validation can be provided by the Corporate Image Survey which shows that consideration is correlated with segment share ($R^2 = 0.64$; see Figure 8 overleaf).

This provides the final evidence needed to assert the link from advertising through to sales.

PROVING THE CASE

With any launch campaign study, the onus is on demonstrating what might have happened if the campaign had been less successful and quantifying the difference between the expected sales level and the actual results. We have used three different methods to calculate 'expected sales'.

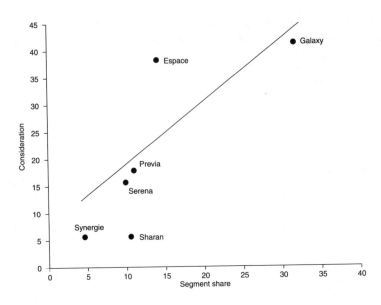

Figure 8: *Consideration and segment share*
Base: MPV considerers
Source: Corporate Image Survey 1996

Method 1

In this case, the expected sales level is provided by a near identical product – the VW Sharan. It is unusual to have this opportunity to compare sales with essentially the same product.

Galaxy sold 16,556 units compared with 5,575 for VW Sharan over an 18-month period from launch. Galaxy outsold the VW Sharan by a factor of three – 10,981 additional units (see Figure 9).

In making this comparison we need to examine whether the VW Sharan represents a valid basis for expected sales.

What other factors could account for the sales difference?

Distribution

Although Ford has many more dealers (787) than VW (344), it seems reasonable to suggest that distribution would not be a limiting factor for such an infrequent high value purchase, provided that the catchment area for purchasing and servicing was reasonable. With 344 VW dealers, it is estimated that the majority of the population would be within a 20-minute drive of a dealer.[4]

To make this case more robust, we are able to make a comparison with another launch where the distribution effects are fully taken into account.

---

4.   Reference: 87% of the population are within 20 minutes' drive of one of M&S's 370 stores.

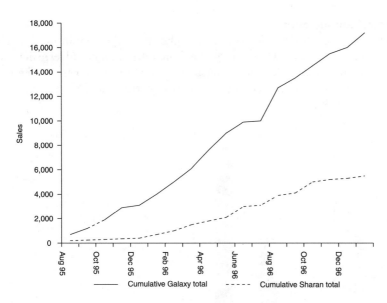

Figure 9: *Galaxy cumulative monthly volume sales – comparison with VW Sharan (expected sales)*
Source: SMMT

The launch of the Ford Maverick in 1993 paralleled that of Galaxy in that a near identical competitive product was launched at the same time – the Nissan Terrano. Again, these two products were built on the same production line with the majority of key components being identical. The Nissan dealer network is a similar size to that of VW.

In the 18 months following the launch, Maverick sold only 55% more than the Terrano, with a slightly higher level of advertising support (while Galaxy sold three times more than the Sharan). The key point is that the distribution network cannot have accounted for the *scale* of Galaxy's success. We have, however, made an allowance for its effect in the final calculation of increment.

Availability
There were no reported problems with the availability of either model – given the same production facilities, any difficulties would affect both models.

Previous buyers base
The majority of Galaxy buyers did not previously own a Ford (73% of buyers of Galaxy previously owned competitive brand. Source: NCBS 1996).

Fleet strength
The fleet component of Galaxy's sales was at a very similar level to that of Sharan (Galaxy 59%, Sharan 52%).

Price or sales promotion
The entry price of both models was at a similar level and there were no sales promotions that offered significant advantage.

Initial brand consideration

Consideration levels for the Galaxy were higher than the Sharan pre launch – due to early press reports. However, after the September launch advertising, Galaxy's consideration almost doubled while Sharan's stayed at a similar level (Figure 10).

This shows that the advertising launch was the major factor in increasing consideration levels.

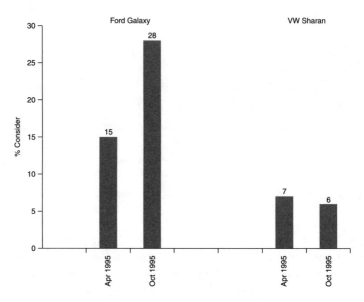

Figure 10: *Percentage who would consider buying a Ford Galaxy or VW Sharan*

Having discounted availability, price, current owner base, fleet sales and initial brand consideration as reasons for Galaxy's disproportionate success, the conclusion is that the advertising launch was the major contributor.

We need, however, to make an allowance for the distribution advantage. The fairest way of doing this is to examine the advantage that Ford's dealer network gives in terms of share of the total market. We have calculated total market share points per hundred dealers for both Ford and VW and found that it gives Ford overall a 19% sales advantage. Increasing expected sales (that is, VW Sharan's) by 19% reduces the figure for incremental sales.

Compared with a near identical product launch, Galaxy exceeded expectations by 9,922 units.

Method 2

A more common method of deriving expected sales is a comparison with previous launches within the company. This takes account of Ford's distribution, brand and business strengths. Galaxy achieved a much higher segment share than previous launches (see Figure 11).

Each launch was into a different segment with varying numbers of competitors and market maturity. In order to make a fair comparison we have taken the average.

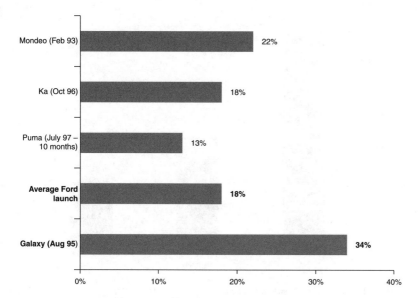

Figure 11: *Comparison of Ford Galaxy launch with previous launches*

Again, to make this comparison we need to investigate factors which could mean that Galaxy might do better than other Ford launches:

Target audience
The MPV segment is significantly more upmarket than the other segments in to which Ford has launched. Among this upmarket audience, Ford's brand imagery is relatively weak.

Product superiority
Satisfaction ratings show that Galaxy achieved a similar rating to other Ford launch products. Within its sector, the Galaxy product cannot be regarded as superior, due to the existence of the Sharan which offers functional parity.

Compared with previous Ford launches, Galaxy exceeded expectations by 7,800 units.

Method 3

The third benchmark for greater than expected sales is other European markets. Galaxy was launched in Germany and France, followed by other EU countries. Different advertising was used in Germany and France.

In making this comparison we need to assess whether there are other factors in these markets which would have affected Galaxy sales.

We have taken Germany as the principal comparison due to the concurrent launch of the VW Sharan (see Figure 12).

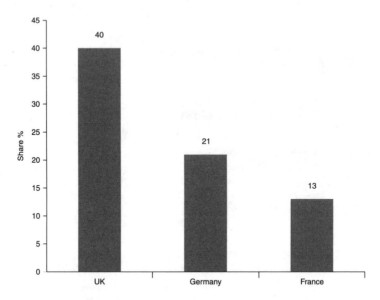

Figure 12: *Share of segment (%) three months after launch*
Source: M&M European Case Study

Market growth
The growth in 1996 over 1995 was nearly identical to the UK.

Ad investment
The total ad spend was a similarly high level.

Pricing
The pricing was at similar levels.

Domestic market strength
Significantly, the Sharan only achieved 29% share in its domestic market.

In France a similar analysis shows that factors such as market growth, price and investment levels are not the primary explanation.

Galaxy in the UK achieved a 23% share advantage over the average of Germany and France. Even allowing for a domestic market effect (8% share points) this shows that Galaxy in the UK had a 15% share lead.

Compared with share performance in other markets, Galaxy exceeded expectations by 9,197 units.

Taking an average of the three methods, we can say that the expected sales level was exceeded by at least 9,000 units.

RETURN ON ADVERTISING INVESTMENT

Based on the advertising investment generating an additional 9,000 units, the total incremental revenue generated is £131 million (taking an average selling price of £19,000 and deducting VAT and an assumed 10% dealer margin). At first sight, the advertising investment of £7.2 million compares very favourably with this figure.

However, the critical analysis is in calculating the payback in terms of gross margin. The gross margin is the difference between the net revenue gained from selling the vehicle to the dealer and the cost of purchasing the vehicle from the manufacturing company. It takes account of all the variable manufacturing costs, shipping and warranty. This margin then needs to cover fixed costs such as distribution company overheads and advertising.

This margin is a closely guarded statistic for individual models. What can be disclosed, however, is that Galaxy's gross margin per unit is greater than the average of all Ford cars in Britain.

Automotive industry investment analysts have estimated an average industry gross margin of between 15% and 35% worldwide.[5] Assuming a figure of 25%, Galaxy would produce a margin per unit of £3,638 excluding VAT and dealer margin. At this level, the incremental margin from Galaxy would be £32.7 million. Deducting the advertising investment of £7.2 million shows that an additional £25.5 million has been created.

While Ford does not wish to publicly declare that these figures are representative of any financial aspects of its business, it is prepared to endorse a statement that the Galaxy has been a success in Britain both in terms of the launch marketing and advertising programmes and in terms of its financial contribution to Ford's business.

Analysis of Past IPA Car Brand Case Studies

To put this into context, we have analysed all past IPA entries for car brands since 1990 which give financial figures. The results show that Galaxy has the highest level of efficiency at generating incremental sales revenue.

	BMW	Vauxhall Astra	Toyota RAV 4	Range Rover	Cherokee Jeep	Galaxy
Ad spend (£m)	91.0	17	0.7	1.6	3.0	7.2
Total sales revenue at RSP (£m)	6,521	19,040	121	30	93	241
Incremental sales revenue at RSP (£m)	3,000	246	36	9	13	131
Incremental sales revenue(%)	43	13	30	30	15	54

---

5. The FT reported 25% gross margin for Nissan and 30.6% for Honda (21 May 1998).

In summary, this shows the financial performance of Galaxy in a very positive light.

	Galaxy
Incremental sales revenue	54%
Ad spend	£7.2m
Incremental margin (after deducting ad spend)	£25.5m

We hope that this case study furthers the understanding of effectiveness in the car market, by being the first study to use estimated gross margin as a means of getting closer to the real economics of the business.

BRAND VALUATION

'Brand value' is a term that is often used loosely. Here we use it in terms of its financial value; the value of the brand as opposed to the value of the business. What would an acquirer pay for the brand? To calculate Galaxy's brand value we need to start with Ford Motor Company – the only entity with a public value.

How much is the Ford brand worth? Brand value can be described as the total value of a company less the tangible value (such as bricks and mortar) and less other intangible values (such as goodwill). Although there are many ways of calculating brand value, a simple approach is to take existing data about the auto sector and apply it to Ford. Estimates provided by Brand Finance Limited show the following breakdown of market capitalisation.

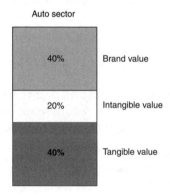

Figure 13: *Percentage of market capitalisation*

The market capitalisation of Ford Motor Company worldwide was $58 billion in 1997 (1,195 million shares at a share price of $48.56). If we use this as a starting point, we can calculate Galaxy's brand value assuming a pro rata sales basis:

— Ford worldwide brand value of $23.2 billion at 40% of market capitalisation.

— Ford of Britain brand value of $1.55 billion at 6.7% of worldwide sales.

— Galaxy brand value of $47 million at 3% of Ford of Britain sales.

— This estimates Galaxy brand value at £28 million (at $1.65 to £1).

This makes a number of assumptions. First, is Ford's brand value likely to be in line with the auto industry average? As a major player in the industry, it seems reasonable to use this average. Second, is it reasonable to proportion a brand value worldwide to Galaxy on the basis of sales? Galaxy's strength as a brand has been demonstrated in earlier sections to be greater than the average Ford brand in the UK, so this again seems reasonable. Similarly the strength of Ford of Britain as a brand, relative to worldwide, is evidenced by market leadership in Britain. We regard the above brand value as a minimum.

While the calculations are somewhat basic, they do provide a valuable starting point for comparing the financial value of a brand with advertising investment levels.

This provides the last link in the chain.

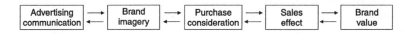

LEARNING FROM THIS CASE STUDY

1. Differentiated advertising can create substantial business gains even for parity products.

2. Investing for brand leadership can pay long term dividends.

3. Firmly established category conventions can be overturned.

4. Finding an emotional point of difference can be more powerful than rational communication of the same benefit.

5. Purchase consideration is a key variable and needs to be linked to other variables such as sales and brand imagery.

6. Calculation of brand value and a closer understanding of financial aspects of a business represent a better test of effectiveness.

Overall, the Galaxy case seems to prove the adage that investing in a good idea will pay back.

SUMMARY

The launch of the Ford Galaxy has changed the way people think about 'people movers'. It has shifted perceptions from the functional, to the aspirational and stylish. No longer can this type of vehicle simply be regarded as 'mum's taxi', now that Galaxy has redefined the category.

The case study demonstrates the value of highly differentiated advertising in building a strong brand.

Galaxy became brand leader almost immediately, and has maintained that position ever since. This is all the more remarkable when the historical dominance of Renault Espace is considered, along with the fact that four other manufacturers were launching new products into the category.

The success of the advertising owes much to the consumer insight that the space around the driver can be seen as more than just room to carry other people or cargo. Space can also make people feel important, relaxed, and can even convey a sense of luxury. This insight led to a different way of positioning Galaxy and the proposition; 'the luxury of unused space'. The airline analogy of travelling in First Class provided the creative breakthrough.

The resulting advertising achieved the highest levels of awareness and efficiency of communication. It can be directly related to the brand imagery, and created a brand that is regarded as stylish and different, as well as outperforming the competition on the rational aspects. This imagery and communication is linked to levels of purchase consideration.

The advertising effect is closely correlated with sales. Galaxy's sales in the first year were approaching the size of the total market in the previous year. This was achieved by bringing in new users to the category. They were not just new to this category but also new to Ford.

What is unusual about this case, is that the effect of advertising can be isolated more clearly than most other studies. The concurrent launch of a near identical product – VW Sharan – enabled product performance to be separated away from advertising effects. Using this as a benchmark, and accounting for the effect of other variables such as distribution, has isolated the sales increment directly attributable to advertising.

The financial impact of advertising is assessed not only in terms of revenues but also in terms of margin. The case, then, goes further than other case studies in the car market by estimating the financial value of the Galaxy brand (as distinct from the revenues it earns).

An initial advertising investment of £7.2 million created an additional £25.5 million within 18 months of launch. The long-term significance is a valuable brand that is contributing to Ford's overall corporate and image objectives.

16

Pizza Hut

Turning around the way you look at Pizza Hut

EDITOR'S SUMMARY

This case shows how advertising helped Pizza Hut successfully move away from a self and category destructive spiral of price-cutting, indicating that the new restaurant sector can be highly advertising responsive.

The Need for a New Direction Other Than Price-cutting

In 1992 Pizza Hut responded to recessionary pressure by implementing a short-term promotional marketing strategy aimed at driving volume sales. This was initially hugely successful, producing revenue gains in 1992 and 1993. However, price-cutting eventually led the business into a revenue spiral, impacting negatively on quality credentials for the brand, and as category leader, for pizza.

In mid 1995 a new advertising campaign featuring celebrity 'Friends' undertook to meet the objectives of raising brand saliency, increasing traffic by regaining lapsed users and adding contemporary value to the now old-fashioned chain. Product launches (for example, Stuffed Crust) were employed to inject 'news value' into the advertising message. The creative idea was built on a core product truth; Pizza is shared food, which breaks down social barriers.

Results and Payback

The paper demonstrates effects in five areas; the campaign created an upturn in saliency, acheived its communications objectives, increased frequency and recency of visits, caused a decline in 'lapsed' usership, and improved food quality and occasion values.

As a result sustained and significant revenue growth was realised across both Eat-In and Delivery sectors. An econometric model of sales across the whole product portfolio demonstrates the link between advertising and revenue uplift and calculates a 3:1 pay back on advertising investment. Compared to earlier advertising the relative uplift on each 'Friends' execution demonstrate the enhanced efficiency of this creative work.

INTRODUCTION

Pizza Hut is the leading UK Pizza restaurant chain, holding over 50% of the market. It sits in an interesting but squeezable position, sandwiched between high interest 'proper eating out' and true fast food (for example, burgers). Its core users are adults aged between 16 and 34, who face an increasingly wide range of options in a fast growing market.

This paper sets out to demonstrate three things:

1. That the Pizza Hut brand has proved to be highly advertising responsive, building revenue impressively and producing a three to one payback on investment. (This is a first for the Eating Out category in the IPA *Advertising Works* series and the return outperforms most service and FMCG cases recorded.)

2. That Pizza Hut has been able to successfully move away from a self – and category – destructive spiral of price cutting, into a positive cycle in which new product news is used to fuel brand advertising.

3. That in undertaking this task, Pizza Hut has succeeded in fighting the squeeze on the product category, achieving;

— Increased brand saliency (spontaneous awareness).

— Increased restaurant traffic (transactions).

— Reducing lapsed users.

— Consistently increasing absolute visiting and frequency.

— Raising food and quality values.

Overall, the 'Friends' campaign has succeeded in contributing fame and saliency to the brand and positioning Pizza Hut against a clear eating occasion.

BUSINESS BACKGROUND

A joint venture between Whitbread and Tricon (formerly PepsiCo), Pizza Hut UK was launched in 1973. Mid-way between 'proper', 'knife and fork' restaurants and fast food, Pizza Hut was a pioneer in carving out a new sector in the market – casual dining.

Through the late 1970s and 1980s growth was fuelled by the increase in disposable income and occasions when consumers wanted to eat out. But by mid-1995, when the Pizza Hut account was aligned into Abbott Mead Vickers.BBDO, a number of factors had conspired to squeeze the business opportunity.

Changing Tastes Encourage Competition

Spurred on by growth in foreign holidays and a fascination with cooking programmes, British consumers began to develop an increasingly sophisticated palate. Interesting new cuisines arose to meet this challenge and many of these entrants – Balti, Thai, Tapas – blurred the boundaries between traditional and casual restaurants.

Brewers Invest in Their Assets

There were improvements in pub catering as the 1986 MMC ruling on vertical integration fostered new independent chains of pub retailers. They realised there was profit potential in fulfilling consumer demand for good quality food. As a result, particularly at lunch-time, Pizza Hut increasingly competed with pubs as a venue for casual dining.

Fast Food Continues to Grow

Meanwhile, the burger and chicken sector of the market continued its inexorable rise (Figure 1), buoyed up by the trend towards eating on the move and less formal meal occasions.

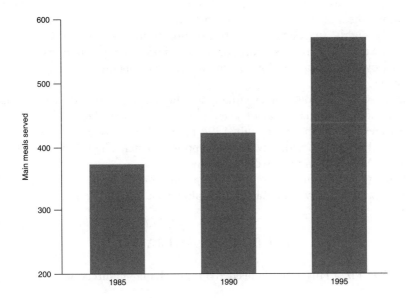

Figure 1: *Growth in the fast food sector*
Source: Marketpower Catering Industry Population File

Home Delivery Growth Stretches the Brand

There was also a significant structural change within the Pizza sector. Growth of home delivery (Table 1) served to change the dynamics of the business, putting more pressure on the brand.

TABLE 1 : GROWTH OF PIZZA HOME DELIVERY

	1992	1996	1992/1996
Total (Mn Pizza Meals)	97	112	+15%
On Premises	33	34	+3%
Delivery/take away	64	78	+22%

Source: Taylor Nelson Eating Out Monitor

Thus, not only was the sector caught in a pincer movement, under pressure from above and below, but also the Pizza Hut brand, built in (and dominant in) the on-premise segment, was having to fight very hard to compete in the home delivery market (where it was just one of many players).

Pizza Hut Adopts Aggressive Marketing Strategy

In 1992, to combat these pressures, Pizza Hut implemented a short-term promotional marketing strategy, aimed at driving volume and sales. Offers included 'special' pizzas available for limited periods, lunch time buffets and finally discounting (meal deals or 'two for one' offers).

Initially highly successful, the strategy produced revenue gains in 1992 and 1993. However, the tactics wore out over time. The promotions were easily replicated by competitors and it was the many small operators which reacted most aggressively.

The move into discounting eventually led the business into a downward revenue spiral. A moving annual total of average sales per store (Figure 2) dramatically demonstrates the decline. From July 1994 to July 1995 revenue fell by 6% despite promotional attempts (with advertising support) to stem the tide in July, October, March and May and an improving economy.

Against the undermining tide of price promotion the previously successful 'Hit the Hut' campaign proved unable to add value back into the brand.

THE BUSINESS IMPERATIVE

By mid-1995 Pizza Hut urgently needed a rapid change in direction.

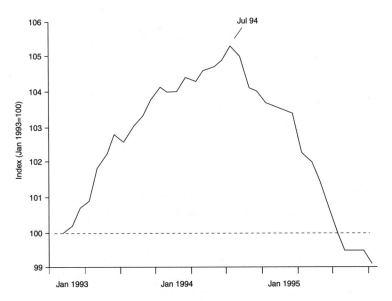

Figure 2: *MAT of average revenue per store. Index January 1993 to September 1995*
Source: Pizza Hut sales data

Identifying the Problem

Analysis of TGI and tracking (Table 2) revealed very high levels of ever used, at, or near, saturation point for a chain that serves one type of food; it also highlighted significant lapsed usage. Comparison with other sectors indicated a category malaise.

TABLE 2: 1995 RESTAURANT PENETRATION (ADULTS AGED 15+)

	Fast food *	Pizza	Pizza Hut
Ever	90	72	59
In the last week	15	5	3
In the last 3 months	75	22	13
Lapsed	15	50	46

Note: * Burger and Chicken outlets
Source: TGI GB (weighted by population)/Conquest

Analysis of average guest spend against store revenue (Table 3) reinforced the fact that the key issue was a decline in footfall.

TABLE 3 : AVERAGE SPEND PER CHEQUE VERSUS STORE REVENUE

	January 1994	September 1995
Average store turnover	100	95
Average size of guest cheque	100	107

Source: Pizza Hut sales data

Worse still, TGI indicated that many of the lapsers were heavy users of casual diners. Qualitative research uncovered the underlying reasons for this decline.

Pizza stripped of value

Price cutting had undermined quality credentials. Pizza had caught 'kebab syndrome'; it had become the sort of food you only eat when you cannot get, or cannot be bothered to get, something else – a 'face stuffer'.

> 'I wouldn't bother to cross the road unless there was an offer.'

> 'It can't be that great if they're going to give you an extra one free.'

Source: AMV Qualitative

Pizza was seen as passé

Pizza was boring, fatal in a sector where spend is discretionary. The Pizza Hut experience was redolent of the 1970s and had no contemporary values.

Pizza occasion was debased

Respondents defined the pizza experience by negatives; they were not as convenient as burger outlets; not as special as 'proper' restaurants; not as novel or entertaining as theme restaurants or the new generation of pubs.

Pizza restaurants had become commoditised

Finally, consumers were unable to differentiate one brand from another; there was no loyalty.

> 'You wouldn't say let's go to Pizza Hut or Pizzaland, you'd go out for a pizza ... you wouldn't prefer one over the other.'

Source: AMV Qualitative

Quite simply, pizza and Pizza Hut had fallen from grace.

To recap, casual dining was under pressure from above and below. Growth in the pizza market was in the area of home delivery, a segment in which Pizza Hut were not dominant and traded at a premium. Price cutting had devalued pizza *per se*, which, combined with declining relevance, had eroded the customer base and eventually led to a downward revenue spiral.

The Role for Advertising

The priority for marketing was to rebuild absolute visiting and frequency and hence return the business to consistent growth.

Analysis of the customer base (Figure 3) indicated that, although the delivery side of the business was growing, over 90% of consumers had experience of the brand in restaurant.

Given the category value issue we have outlined and Pizza Hut's dominance of on-premise (over 50% of market volume and value), we believed it was important to build value back into the restaurant experience on the assumption that this would transfer to the delivery market.

Target audience

The primary target audience was lapsers – those who had drifted away from Pizza Hut into an increasingly wide range of alternatives.

Since nearly two-thirds of the British population has used Pizza Hut at some point, this is a very broad target but the key age brackets were young singles and new families.

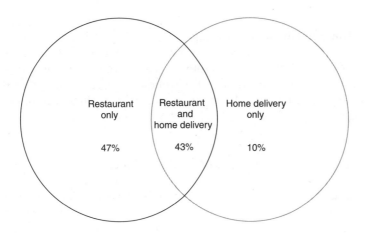

Figure 3: *Pizza Hut cross-customer usage*
Base: All users – 500
Source: Pizza Hut U&A – The Value Engineers 1994

How consumers choose restaurants

Eating out in this sector of the market is essentially an impulse decision founded on two criteria: top-of-mind saliency and a positioning that is relevant to the occasion you have in mind (a quick lunch, a night out with the girls, and so on).

The role of advertising was therefore, first, to replace the brand solidly front of mind and second to generate traffic. To do this we had to resecure relevance by creating a clear pizza occasion. Back to qualitative ...

The product truth

Pizza introduces an aura of 'relaxed familiarity'. It is shared food – naturally bringing people together. This was most visibly demonstrated in research, when on arrival of a take-away pizza, barriers were immediately dropped as respondents shared the food.

'We all dig-in, everyone for themselves, that's the way we are, very casual ...'

'You can't be posh with sticky fingers and a foot of stringy cheese dangling from your mouth.'

Source: AMV Qualitative

We wanted Pizza Hut's advertising to amplify this latent product truth, 'owning' relaxed fun, and meals among friends or close family.

Adding interest
But defining and securing an occasion was a long-term task. To kick-start sales growth, and demonstrate a change, we needed to quickly grab consumer attention with something newsworthy. Stuffed Crust, a unique pizza that has cheese wrapped into the crust, had been successful in the US and was earmarked as the spearhead in the UK.

The importance of famous advertising
The strap-line of the previous campaign 'Hit the Hut' had become a familiar mantra inextricably linked with the brand. But it also encapsulated the deal-driven strategy. If we were to successfully turn around perceptions and add value into the brand we would need to quickly strike out any residual memories of the old advertising.

Summary of the Advertising Brief

The task for the advertising was to begin to build traffic for Pizza Hut by increasing salience and in the long term, making the brand more appropriate for relaxed, convivial meal occasions. To catalyse the brand reappraisal, Pizza Hut would be introducing a unique, new pizza: Cheese Stuffed Crust.

THE CAMPAIGN 1995 TO 1998

The Creative Solution

At the core of the creative idea is social interaction. It uses celebrity 'friends', giving them an imaginary life off-duty, enjoying a pizza in Pizza Hut.

Twelve ads have been written for the campaign; all but two (pan-European executions[1]) feature a famous, if unexpected grouping: 'Clunes and Quentin', 'Lomu and Underwood', 'Hill and Walker', 'Crawford and Evangelista', 'Southgate, Pearce and Waddle', 'Pamela Anderson (x 2)', 'Ross and Caprice (x 2)', 'Luke Perry (x 2)', and finally 'Ruud Gullit and his agent'.

PR – maximising saliency
Freud Communications were briefed to create news value and hype around the launch and throughout the campaign, by leveraging the celebrities and relationships in the advertising.

---

1.   It is almost impossible to find celebrities of sufficient stature and topicality across all Pizza Hut's European markets within budget.

TV ADS

Media

Because of the imperative that we quickly step-change sales, at launch we concentrated all our media money on TV.

Between September 1995 and March 1998 £15.4 million[2] has been spent on the campaign, a total of 22,125 TVRs. While the majority of this was in three core advertising regions (London, North and Scotland), the campaign in one form or another did actually run everywhere bar HTV, Border and West.[3]

Since launch, we have experimented at various stages with adapting the TV campaign for regional radio and cinema. However, essentially, the vast majority of our budget still goes to TV. As we will show below, this has proved to be a highly effective deployment of spend.

PIZZA HUT'S PERFORMANCE SINCE 1995

Issues with Intermediate Data

We have been unusually unlucky in the quantity and continuity of our intermediate data.[4]

But what we can demonstrate is that since the start of the campaign there has been:

— significant and sustained revenue growth across both business sectors;

— a shift in the key intermediate consumer and image dimensions;

— exceptionally well received advertising;

— substantial pay back on advertising investment as indicated by econometric modelling.

Revenue Growth

Since the start of the campaign business results have been impressive (Figure 4) and Pizza Hut has achieved the desired turnaround in fortune.

---

2. Media register costs at ratecard.
3. These three TV regions only represent 14 stores, less than 3% of the Pizza Hut estate. Because of this, patterns of awareness and visiting by loyalty are very different and hence they were not intended or used as a matched control region. This is one of the key reasons why we had to use econometrics to identify the contribution of advertising.
4. The Pizza Hut tracking study switched supplier to Conquest to align with its sister brand KFC during the launch period (the BJM study was cancelled in October 1995 – as advertising began. The new study did not start until February 1996). The methodologies are completely incomparable. Where we can we have used back data from the KFC study but only a few measures are available. In addition, there is a long-term U&A study (6 April 1992) but the questionnaire and sample sizes are inconsistent. Also, there is no accurate market share data for pizza outlets.

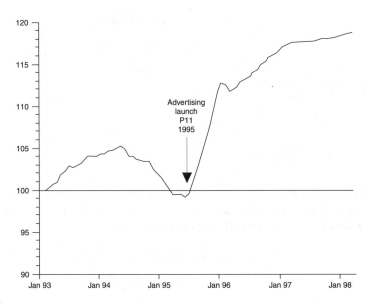

Figure 4: *MAT of average revenue per store (Index January 1993 to March 1998)*
Source: Pizza Hut sales data

Despite the fact that initially there was no price premium attached to Stuffed Crust, revenue increased immediately, indicating increased traffic. The business continues to go from strength to strength. Since September 1995 average revenue per store has increased by over 21%. This has been achieved by sustained uplifts in both the restaurant and the highly competitive home delivery business sectors.

Traffic data backs up the argument that a key part of the turnaround has been due to a significant increase in customers coming through the door (Table 4).

TABLE 4: PIZZA HUT CUSTOMER TRAFFIC

(Index on 1995)	1995	1996	1997
Out of town	100	111	113
High street	100	107	103
Metro 100	100	110	111
Delivery	100	109	102
Total	100	110	108

Source: Pizza Hut sales data

Intermediate Measures

Advertising set out to rebuild sales value by encouraging lapsers back into Pizza Hut and increasing frequency. As Table 5 shows, saliency has improved, lapsing declined and, following the expected huge initial hike (influenced by novelty), the average number of visits among current users has settled down at a significantly higher level.

TABLE 5: AWARENESS AND USAGE OF PIZZA HUT

	Sep 95 %	Sep 96 %	Sep 97 %	Mar 98 %
Spontaneous brand awareness	36	52	49	53
Visited in last 3 months	19	27	28	26
Lapsed users	51	40	38	41
Average no of visits*	1.7	3.1	2.3	2.5
Base:	624	558	860	917

Note* Among those who have claimed to visit in the last 3 months
Source: Conquest

Stuffed Crust acted as we had hoped; it was the focal point of the advertising and, as the most recent usage and attitude study demonstrates (Table 6), it provided the catalyst for shifting perceptions of Pizza Hut's product.

TABLE 6: PIZZA HUT BRAND IMAGE – FOOD VALUES

	June 94 %	August 96 %	
Good quality	31	39	+ 8
Interesting menu	16	20	+ 4
Base	1000*	150*	

*Note: Quota sample, split: half users, half non-users
Source: Pizza Hut U&A – The Value Engineers

We have also seen shifts in 'occasion values' (Table 7), a clear indication that Pizza Hut is beginning to carve out a meaningful and relevant occasion. For an established and highly trialed brand this is obviously a significant achievement.

TABLE 7: PIZZA HUT BRAND IMAGE – OCCASION VALUES

	June 94 %	August 96 %	
Sociable	26	32	+ 6
Friendly	30	34	+ 4
Fun	14	22	+ 7
Modern	33	37	+ 4
Base	1000*	150*	

*Note – Quota sample, split: half users, half non-users
Source: Pizza Hut U&A – The Value Engineers

Response to the Advertising

Comparison with the other major sector advertisers shows how efficient Pizza Hut's advertising has been in generating awareness (Table 8).

TABLE 8: ADVERTISING EFFICIENCY 1997
– RATIO OF AWARENESS TO SPEND* IN TVRs

Pizza Hut	2.0
McDonald's	0.6
KFC	1.0

*Note: Measured in adult equivalent TVRs
Source: Conquest /MEAL

Qualitative research over the period of the campaign demonstrates how the advertising has strongly connected with its target audience and evoked the sociable nature of pizza.

'Pizza Hut would appear to have built a recognisable and much loved 'advertising property' for itself.'

'There would seem to be plenty of fuel remaining in several of the old commercials (Clunes & Quentin, Lomu & Underwood, Hill & Walker, Ross & Caprice) expressed not only by a verbal chorus of approval but also the genuine animation on respondents' faces.'

Source: Zinkin Planning & Research Partners, March 1998

'The advertising is well remembered and liked. Mentioned spontaneously, it is universally seen as entertaining, involving and relevant.'

'The humour is very British – cynical, sarcastic humour ... that's how you are when you're out with your mates, taking the mick – that's how we bond.'

'The advertising taps into common cultural experience and the characters' ability to laugh at themselves raises their esteem in the eyes of the British public.'

'The product message is clearly communicated, Stuffed Crust was well received, as the featured product and subsequent trial claimed.'

Source: Fusion Research – April 1996

The advertising sets up a very appropriate characterisation. In line with the experience it is outgoing, sociable and carefree – people become involved and identify with it very easily indeed.

Source: The Marketing Clinic, March 1998

Identifying Growth Due to Advertising

In June 1997, as part of an ongoing exercise to determine optimum media weights, The Billetts Consultancy was commissioned to establish sales effects relative to media spend. The models it produced (for London and the Midlands) have since been refined and extended to include the national restaurant business and, since the dynamics of the business and advertising effects are logically different,[5] a separate model for home delivery.

---

5. We hypothesised that there would be a greater short-term effect from advertising. In order to make the delivery model as robust as possible it is based on sales in the London region, covering over 85% of Pizza Hut's delivery business.

The Econometric Analysis

The two models examine total weekly sales for all product lines over the Pizza Hut estate from December 1994 to mid-April 1998. In order to strip out the influence of distribution increases, Billetts measured average sales per store (a simple calculation of revenue divided by the number of stores). In actual fact, distribution increases have been minimal, and the majority of new stores have been conversions from Pizzaland (also owned by Whitbread) into the stronger performing Pizza Hut brand.

The Variables Included in the Models

Advertising
As we have already mentioned, there have been 12 executions in the campaign to date. Analysis (and logic) tells us that each stimulates short-term sales to differing extents. The advertising variable has therefore been broken down by execution.

New product effect
Billetts found that there was an identifiable step change in sales as new products are introduced. Novelty and curiosity of course encouraged take up.[6] A new product variable has therefore been included and this effect quantified.

Seasonality
There are some seasonal variations that impact on the magnitude of a week's sales and therefore need to be explained. Five variations were found to have a meaningful effect on sales and have been included as variables.

Other variables
A number of other variables were examined and excluded. The final stage in the construction of the model was to allow for one-off events that had a significant effect on business (for example, the week of Princess Diana's funeral).

Calculating the Payback of Turning Around Pizza

The models indicated that over the period of the Stuffed Crust campaign, advertising generated incremental revenue in the order of £54.9 million.[7]

---

6. Subsequent work by Billets, outside the scope of this paper, modelling guest cheque data against store revenue indicates that new product introductions have an identifiable effect on value per cheque as exisiting users discover the product, but that it is advertising that drives new users into the store.
7. This includes a contribution allowed for an adstock effect of past TVRs on future business at the advertising decay rate identified in the model.

If we take away the cost of media and production[8] at £17.8 million this leaves a return on investment of over three to one.

Given that the incremental costs to the business are marginal, the majority of this can be taken straight to the bottom line.

Other Possible Factors in Revenue Growth

Market growth

Would Pizza Hut's revenue have grown anyway? We do not believe so.

First, as we have previously outlined, the brand was mature, tired and undifferentiated in a sector that had become devalued.

Second, the competitive squeeze from other sectors continues to intensify. As evidence of this, meals served in pubs grew in volume by 13% MAT 1998 over 1997, likewise Chinese restaurants grew by 21% (largely through an increase in number of outlets).

Over the same period Taylor Nelson estimate that volume accounted for by pizza restaurants grew by only 3%. Given that Pizza Hut is over half of this market and sales are growing at around 10 to 12% per annum, it demonstrates the positive contribution which advertising investment has had in securing growth.

Finally on a technical note, there is no evidence of any unexplained underlying trend in the data.

Discounting a regional effect

Eighty-five per cent of Pizza Hut's delivery business is concentrated in London. Could a disparate regional effect have contributed to growth attributed to advertising? Again we do not believe so. If anything, Pizza is least popular in the south.

Discounting PR

There continues to be a big PR response to the campaign.

Freud estimates the extra publicity over the course of the campaign to be worth £5.2 million in media terms – making a strong case for PR effectiveness. This has undoubtedly had an effect but it was part of the strategy, and the publicity was driven by the advertising rather than the product.[9]

Discounting price

In stark contrast to the days before Stuffed Crust, there have been no price promotions. Indeed, a strong case could be made for the role of advertising in supporting a premium over other pizza brands, particularly in delivery.

---

8. For Pan-European executions production costs are amortised across a number of countries. This has been allowed for in the calculation.
9. However, even if we add the media value of PR to the costs of the campaign we still see a huge return on investment of 2.4 to 1.

Any changes in price that have occurred have coincided with new product introductions. The new product variable therefore extracts this as an influence.

Is the Effect due to Sheer Weight of Advertising?

We have been able to demonstrate that advertising is a sound investment for Pizza Hut (ie media effectiveness) but we did not leave it there. There was a nagging doubt that *any* advertising describing the product would have achieved the effect that we have shown. We had after all benefited from increased spend once Pizza Hut saw the huge potential of the campaign.

Our first port of call was to compare uplift in advertised versus non-advertised areas against similar new product news in the last campaign – 'Hit the Hut'.

For new product introductions (nine in total) the average uplift in advertised areas with 'Hit the Hut' was 5.2%. Typically, these pizzas were in restaurants for limited periods of anything up to four months. Over the first four months of the 'Friends' campaign the increase in advertised areas was 7.4%. However, tracking indicates that there was a lag effect between the initial burst of advertising and the trial of Stuffed Crust really taking off. Possibly this was because the concept was so different from standard pizza. There was a difference, but it was far from conclusive.

To provide categorical proof, we asked Billetts to extend the models backwards through time to make a comparison of uplift in turnover between the 'Friends' campaign and 'Hit the Hut'. This covers the last two bursts of 'Hit the Hut' (and an estimation on adstock by examining TVRs back to 1992).

The results indicated that while 'Hit the Hut' was very effective for the business, it did not address the key underlying issues for the brand which we identified earlier and hence the 'Friends' campaign was roughly 2.5 times as efficient per 100 TVRs in restaurants and 1.5 times for delivery.

Interestingly, both campaigns compare very favourably with other published service and FMCG campaigns, a sure indication that given the right advertising the restaurant market is highly advertising responsive.

CONCLUSION

We have demonstrated that Pizza Hut, a mature brand in the eating-out market, has been able to move away from a destructive spiral of price-cutting. The brand has proved to be advertising responsive and since 1995 the advertising has produced a healthy three to one return on investment. The 'Friends' campaign through Abbott Mead Vickers.BBDO has helped Pizza Hut carve out a clear eating occasion and added contemporary values, fame and saliency to the brand.

17

Polaroid

How living for a moment gave Polaroid a future

EDITOR'S SUMMARY

This is a case of how advertising can help lead and direct a complete change of positioning for a brand by redefining its competitive set.

Rediscovering Polaroid's Magic

Polaroid's USP – instant pictures – was being eroded as 35mm processing became faster and cheaper and cameras became more simple to use. By the late 1980s Polaroid sales were flat or declining. In 1994, Polaroid undertook a fundamental brand rethink.

Research showed that Polaroid's instantness had a role. The spontaneity of the instant camera made people lose their inhibitions. Polaroid was not a camera – it was a social lubricant.

Results and Payback

Since the relaunch of the brand, Polaroid's decline has reversed: by 1997, annual sales of film were up 37% compared with 1995 and camera sales up 102%.

An econometric model revealed that advertising had been the single greatest contributor to volume growth and generated total short-term payback of 61%.

Further analysis of lifetime value of cameras sold showed that Polaroid can expect additional long term payback. This increased the total payback from advertising to 176%.

While this is a strong performance by any standards, it misses the wider impact of the strategy, which also gave Polaroid a direction that could lead every aspect of the marketing mix. This is exemplified by the Spice Girls project which involved a special edition camera and new distribution as well as a TV ad, PR and Spice Girls promotions. As a result of this total integration, payback on the Spice Girls project was 263%. This is the value that an idea big enough to stretch through the mix can add.

INTRODUCTION

This paper will describe how a big idea turned a brand around.
It will cover:

— How Polaroid had a USP, but one that had lost its relevance.

— How the process of advertising development found Polaroid a new, emotional relevance that fundamentally repositioned the brand.[1]

— The effects of advertising that resulted.

— How the success of the advertising propelled the big idea to the heart of the company, where it has stimulated a range of other changes.

Most of all, this paper gives an account of how that big idea has become a profitable reality.

This paper focuses on the UK, where the data are most comprehensive. The strategy, however, has spread beyond this market. In 1995 it was in place in four markets, by 1997 in 18 across Polaroid's Europe and Export region, and had even reached Australia.

BACKGROUND

1937 to 1977: The 'Magic Camera'

In 1937 Dr Edwin Land founded Polaroid, making Polarising filters. In 1948 the first Instant Camera was launched.

In 1972 *Life* magazine proclaimed on its cover: 'A Genius and his Magic Camera', as Dr Land launched the first easy-to-use Instant Camera, the SX-70. It was followed in 1977 by the first inexpensive mass-market Polaroid camera.

These were wonder products, in a very different world from today's.

— Cameras were often complicated and difficult to use. Polaroid offered point and shoot, with easy film loading.

— Colour prints were expensive and had to be sent away for developing, taking days or even weeks. Polaroid offered prints on the spot.

More than this, the technology was amazing! Polaroid became an icon of its times.

1977 to 1992: Losing its Relevance

By the early 1990s, Polaroid's advantages had evaporated.

---

1. For further details, see the Polaroid paper published by the Account Planning Group, 1995.

— Cameras had become simpler and smaller, with automatic focus, exposure and film loading.

— Developments in processing had eroded the value of the instant camera. Minilabs, introduced in 1979, had 'revolutionised the photographic market world-wide'[2] with one-hour processing on the high street.

— The cost gap with 35mm had widened. This left Polaroid, whose pictures had once been twice the cost of a 35mm print,[3] at something closer to six times the cost.

— Polaroid cameras had stayed the same size, when every other piece of technology had shrunk.

It had become a white elephant, left behind by 35mm's innovations.

1992: Sales Reflected the Loss of Relevance

Sales of both cameras and film fell.

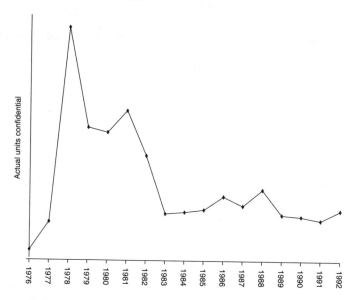

Figure 1: *Shipments of Polaroid cameras to the UK, 1976–1992*
Source: Polaroid UK

2.   A 1995 Key Note report on photographic services.
3.   *Which?* Instant Picture cameras, February 1978.

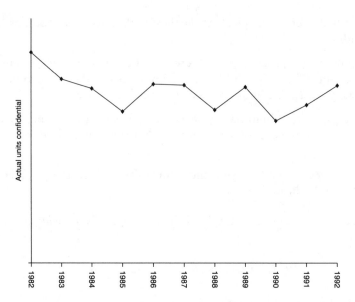

Figure 2: *Shipments of Polaroid film to the UK, 1982–1992*
Source: TGI

Every year, fewer people could *recall* owning a Polaroid, regardless of whether or not they actually did.

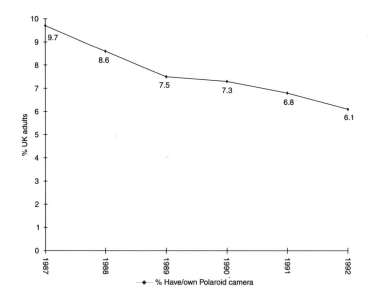

Figure 3: *Percentage of UK adults owning a Polaroid, 1987–1992*
Source: TGI

Subsequent research confirmed the 'back of mind/back of cupboard' syndrome:

'I'd actually forgotten I had [a Polaroid] until someone asked me a few weeks ago.'

Source: Fusion Research, 1994

1992: Polaroid's Response – A New Generation of Products

In 1992, Polaroid responded. Every piece of research had pointed to problems with the equipment. In particular, the cameras were not portable: 35mm compact cameras were the norm.

Polaroid developed a more portable camera, the Vision, which measured up to the 35mm's technical standards:

— Single Lens Reflex.

— Autofocus.

— Built-in flash.

— Sleek design.

While they reacted well in development research, the public failed to respond in real life, and sales did not meet expectations.

Innovating within the rules of the photographic market had not worked. Polaroid's sales showed no improvement (Figures 4 and 5).

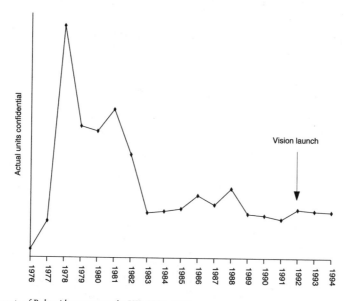

Figure 4: *Shipments of Polaroid cameras to the UK, 1976–1994*
Source: Polaroid UK

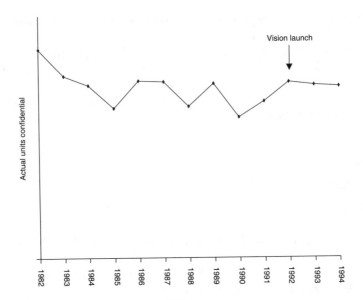

Figure 5: *Shipments of Polaroid films to the UK, 1982–1994*
Source: *Polaroid UK*

Claimed penetration continued to decline (see Figure 6).

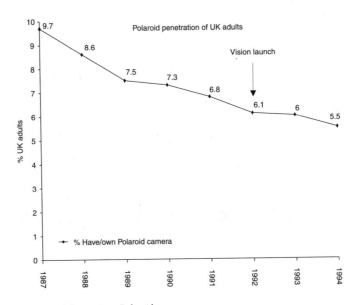

Figure 6: *Percentage of UK adults owning a Polaroid,*
Source: TGI

1994: REFRAMING THE BRAND

Looking for a New Role

In 1994, Polaroid came to BBH with the question: 'Can you make advertising that will galvanise our business?' Their objectives were:

— To recruit new users (selling cameras);

— To re-recruit lapsed users (using old cameras or buying new ones);

— To stimulate film purchase among existing users.

It quickly became apparent that Polaroid had problems so fundamental that it needed a brand rethink as much as an advertising solution.

Conventional research techniques told us what they had told Polaroid: 'The film's too expensive'; 'The picture quality is terrible'; 'The camera's too big and bulky – it's a pain to carry around'; 'The technology's outmoded'. At the root of it all lay one problem: Polaroid no longer had a role in people's lives.

So we turned to less conventional research, using social experiments to explore how Polaroid might be used. Pictures taken at the same event with 35mm and Polaroid were revealing.

In the 35mm pictures people are posed, stiff and formal, while in the Polaroids they are expressive and sociable. The instantness of Polaroid had a social effect – it encouraged people to let their hair down.

This was an opportunity to position Polaroid differently:

Polaroid is not a camera

It is a social lubricant.

This gave Polaroid a new way of seeing itself. Its set of peer brands had changed. It could be imagined alongside Bacardi, Coke and Nike instead of Canon, Nikon and Minolta.

However, further research revealed a major barrier to unleashing the potential of the positioning: Polaroid was an embarrassment.

The Role for Advertising

The role for advertising became to overcome that social embarrassment by drawing on Polaroid's role as a social lubricant.

To do this, we highlighted the unpredictability of instant photography. With Polaroid you never know quite what will happen. Polaroid is for people who are spontaneous and risk-taking, and provides a distinct emotional benefit:

'Polaroid gives you the opportunity to live life on the edge.'

Target audience
To build social credibility, we had to target sociability leaders – people who are open-minded enough to experiment and outgoing enough to pass on trends. Their confidence would be our first milestone.

The Media Strategy

The media strategy was devised to communicate with these people at the right time, when they were in an appropriate mood. Media research by the media agency, Motive, showed that there was a time which ideally fitted this: just before they go out; the 'Friday/Saturday night feeling'.

TV was the best medium, as it showed public confidence; important in giving people 'permission' to use Polaroid socially, and it had the best creative potential to communicate an aspirational end user.

This precise targeting allowed maximum impact from low media budgets:

	1995	1996	1997
Media spend £m	0.48[4]	2.21	2.48

Source: Motive

The Advertising

The advertising strapline is 'Live for the Moment'. We have shortened it to 'LFTM' in this paper, and use it to refer to both advertising and strategy.

Brand advertising
The TV executions, – 'Rock Star', 'Cure All', 'Resignation' and 'Scissors' – present aspirational users whose Polaroids help them engineer changes in their situations.

In all executions since 'Rock Star', the contents of the picture are not shown. This allows viewers to imagine their own image, creating additional intrigue.

Spice Girls
During 1997, Polaroid sponsored the Spice Girls. We will look at the effects in detail later, as an example of how the LFTM strategy has stretched beyond advertising.

Part of this sponsorship involved a TV advertisement for the special edition 'Spice Cam'.

---

4.   This lower figure was for Christmas spend only, 1996 and 1997 were year round.

'ROCK STAR'

Sound: (SFX) Heavy rock music, screaming
and the sound of flashing cameras throughout.

Sound: (SFX) We hear the Polaroid click-
whir sound.

Sound: (SFX) We hear the familiar click-whir
of a Polaroid.

'SPICE GIRLS SCHOOL'

Sound: (SFX) Dramatic music.

Mel B: Well, what are we going to do now then?

(MVO) The Spice Cam from Polaroid.

'ICE CREAM'

(MVO) Beware, Polaroid film under £10!

'MIRROR'

(MVO) Beware, Polaroid cameras under £30!

'GIFT'

(MVO) Beware, Polaroid cameras under £30!

Brand and Spice executions were run as follows:

Timing	Title	Total National/30" equivalent 16 to 34 adults TVRs	Coverage
1996	Rock Star	175	Carlton, LWT, Granada/Border, Yorkshire/Tyne Tees; Ulster, MTV
1996	Cure All	149	Carlton, LWT, Granada/Border, Yorkshire/Tyne Tees, Ulster
1996/1997	Resignation	234	1996 regional as above 1997 regional as above plus National Channel 4, Channel 5 and Satellite, plus Cinema *estimated at equivalent to 45 TVRs, included left.
1996/1997	Scissors	287	As above
1997	Spice Girls School	180	National ITV, MTV

Source: Motive

Promotional advertising

These were altered from information-led creative to reflect the new strategy.
Promotional campaigns ran nationally in groups of two or three 10" executions.

Execution	Timing	National 30" equivalent 16–34 adult TVRs
Mirror / Ice Cream / Gift	1995	264
Mirror / Ice Cream	1996	489
Club / Contort / Eject	1997	461

Source: Motive

REFRAMING THE BRAND: EFFECTS OF BRAND ADVERTISING ON CONSUMERS

Effects on Positioning

In qualitative research in 1996, the research company RDSI looked at three of the executions: 'Rock Star', 'Cure All' and 'Resignation'. This confirmed that the advertising was working to strategy:

Overall effects

'Response to the advertising executions 'Rock Star, 'Cure All' and 'Resignation' was extremely encouraging and contributed to a shift in perceptions of Polaroid Instant.'

Source: RDSI 1996

Developing aspirational user imagery

[Rock Star] 'This invests the brand with a young, trendy image. It credibly positions the product in an out-of-home context. This execution also communicates powerfully in terms of user imagery.'

[Cure All] 'The Polaroid is converted into the young hedonist's partner in crime.'

[Resignation] 'This appeals more to a mature target with relevant user imagery: turning your back on the establishment; taking control of your own destiny.'

In respondents' words:

[Rock Star] 'It could be you.'

[Rock Star] 'She's the cool one who is always one step ahead.'

Source: RDSI

Communicating the role as social lubricant

We feel 'Cure All' occupies the heartland of the Polaroid social lubricant territory... Polaroid is at the heart of having a good time.'

[Cure All] 'The camera itself receives a much needed injection of coolness in this execution. It appears here as a viable accessory at any party.'

In respondents words:

[Cure All] 'It's like the picture was really alive.'

'If you see this ad, you think it'd be a laugh to have a Polaroid.'

Source: RDSI

Breaking down social embarrassment
In respondents' words:

[Resignation] 'I can relate to that – sticking two fingers up to the establishment.'

'I'd love to have done something like that'

[Summary of all ads] '[The advertising] begins to break down prejudices and inhibitions about the conspicuousness of the camera, in short the social embarrassment.'

Source: RDSI

Effects on Purchase Intention

These were examined in quantitative work in 1998. Consumers were shown three brand ads and their purchase intentions compared with a control sample (see table overleaf).

	Control sample not shown ads	Sample shown ads
Extremely likely to buy a Polaroid camera	1%	11%

Base size: All respondents 108/107
Source: IM Apel Wegner[5] for Polaroid, UK 1998

Effects on Consumer Penetration and Profile

The repositioning drew in claimed new users. Within two years decline had stabilised, then turned into growth (Figure 2). The growth was strongest among the creative and media target; 16 to 34-year-olds.

Age	1992	1995	Rolling 1998	1998/1995 change (%)
15–24	4.7	3.4	4.0	+17.6
25–34	5.8	3.4	5.0	+47.0
35+	6.6	4.9	5.1	+4.0

Source: TGI

Comparison with actual Polaroid sales figures suggests that this has come from a combination of recruiting new users and lapsed users remembering their Polaroids again.

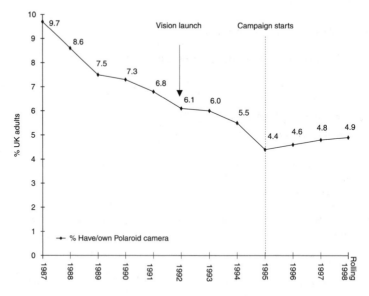

Figure 7: *Percentage of UK adults owning a Polaroid*
Source: TGI

---

5. Polaroid's pan-European research co-ordinators.

Recruitment has drawn in people who are more 'LFTM' in their attitudes (Figures 8 and 9).

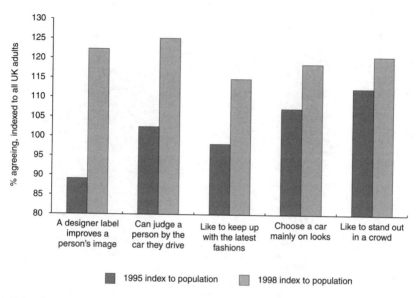

Figure 8: *Polaroid owners – becoming more outer directed and aware of trends*
Source: TGI

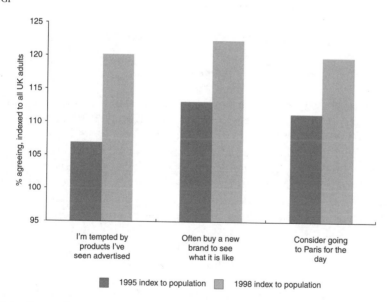

Figure 9: *Polaroid owners becoming more spontaneous and prepared to try new things*
Source: TGI

They are also less likely to be affected by Polaroid's lack of technical credentials.

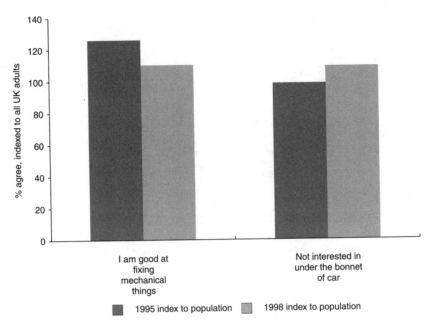

Figure 10: *Polaroid owners – becoming less technically minded*
Source: TGI

SALES GROWTH AND SOME POSSIBLE CAUSES

Topline Results

Business followed the growing consumer base. Imports of cameras were particularly strong, growing by 168% between 1995 and 1997 (Figure 11). Imports of film also grew by 35% between 1995 and 1997 (Figure 12).

At retail level, we can see the same increases. Annual camera sales have grown by 91% since 1995. This has been driven by both increased Christmas sales and a higher base level during the year (Figure 13). Annual film sales have grown by 46% since 1995, again with increased sales at Christmas and throughout the year. The higher Christmas sales reflect the social usage patterns of Polaroid (Figure 14).

Possible Causes of Growth

The Polaroid business is driven by a combination of factors. The sales upturn came with changes in some but not all of these. Retail audit data let us look at these factors individually.

Macro-economic factors

Macro-economic factors could have improved sales, in particular at the end of the recession. However, using category sales (total still film) as a proxy, we can see that Polaroid has grown faster than we would expect from these alone (Figure 15).

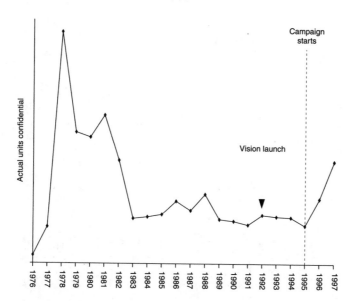

Figure 11: *Shipments of Polaroid cameras to the UK, 1976–1997*
Source: Polaroid UK

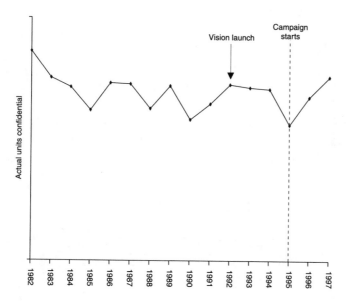

Figure 12: *Shipments of Polaroid films to the UK, 1982–1997*
Source: Polaroid UK

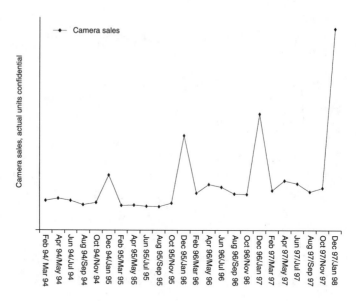

Figure 13: *Total Polaroid T-600 film sales*
Source: GfK

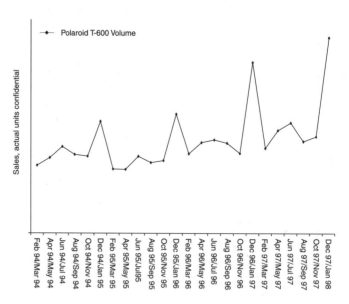

Figure 14: *Total Polaroid camera sales*
Source: GfK

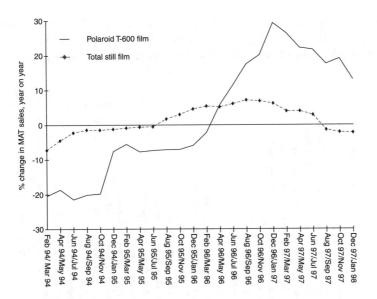

Figure 15: *Polaroid T-600 film year-on-year volume changes versus category*
Source: GfK

What changes throughout the marketing mix might have affected sales?

Distribution

Changes in GfK's total distribution would not have driven the growth. At a micro level, the only extra camera listing was in Currys' for Christmas 1997, stocking one model only (the Spice Cam).

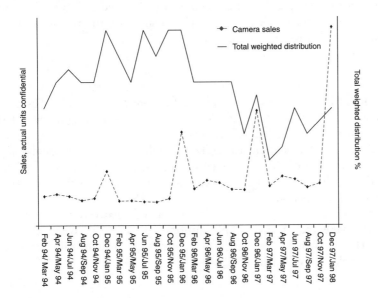

Figure 16: *Total Polaroid camera sales and distribution*
Source: GfK

Film distribution did not increase between 1995 and 1997. The Currys' listing did not include film. Store layout and facings have not changed significantly. Yet sales have grown consistently. Distribution changes do not appear to have driven film sales increases.

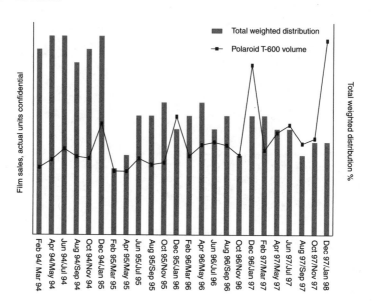

Figure 17: *Polaroid T-600 film sales and distribution*
Source: GfK

Promotions

Since the strategy change, there has been a three for two film offer in Boots and a film rebate offer in independents. These are possible contributors at fixed times and channels, but not across the board.

Price

The upturn in sales coincided with price changes. Camera prices were cut in the repositioning, from over £40 to just above £30. Sales rose visibly. The price cut of approximately 25% produced a 100% volume gain, suggesting a price elasticity of four, which would be very high. Christmas 1997 saw camera sales up 73% year on year, with a cut of less than 10%. This would be an exceptionally high price sensitivity. Further, since the first step change in price, prices have been broadly stable and growth has continued. It seems reasonable to infer that the price is part, but not all, of the explanation for growth (Figure 18).

Film prices support this view, having remained relatively stable over the long term. There were reductions for promotions and in 1997 when exchange rates changed. This may have had an effect; however, growth still occurred during periods of stable or rising prices (Figure 19).

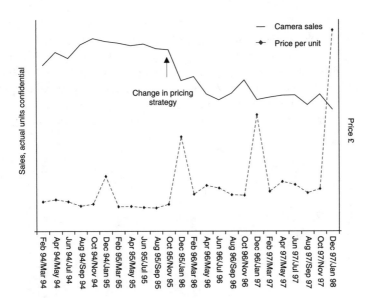

Figure 18: *Total Polaroid camera sales and price*
Source: GfK

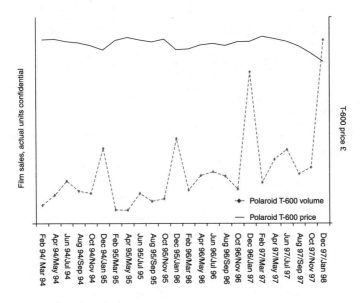

Figure 19: *Polaroid T-600 film sales and price*s
Source: GfK

Advertising

The upturns in both camera and film sales occurred simultaneously – coinciding with the introduction of advertising.

Christmas peaks have been successively higher, corresponding to the greater weight of advertising accumulated before each. After each Christmas peak, sales have returned to a higher level than before, and experienced a peak in April/May which did not occur in 1994/1995. This matches the media timing.

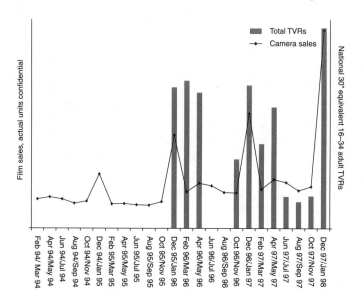

Figure 20: *Total Polaroid camera sales and TVRs*
Source: Sales, GfK; TVRs, Motive

For film, the growth trend is clearer and begins with the introduction of advertising (Figure 21).

As there was no advertising during 1994 and the majority of 1995, it is possible that the growth was due to the presence of advertising *per se*, and not this advertising in particular. However, prior to 1994 advertising had run without any turnaround (Figure 22).

Short-term Effects of Advertising and Payback

To quantify the contribution made by advertising, we need an econometric analysis. This was commissioned by Polaroid as part of its ongoing evaluation of activity.

Econometric models tend to give a short-term view of the effects.

'Econometric modelling helps to clarify understanding of the reasons why sales may have moved as they did during a recent period ... econometrics has little to say about the effects of advertising over long periods of time.'

Source: Colin McDonald *'How Advertising Works'*; 1992, pp.67–8

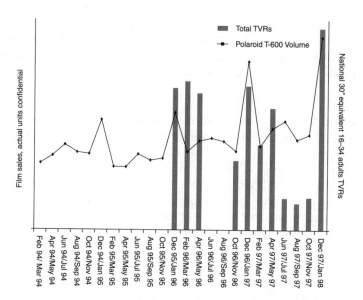

Figure 21: *Total T-600 film sales and TVRs*
Source: GfK/Motive

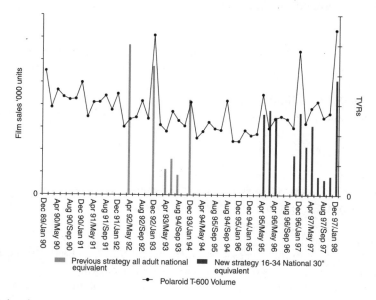

Figure 22: *Polaroid T-600 film sales and TVRs by strategy*
Source: GfK; TVRs Motive/MediaVest

We have therefore supplemented this with a long-term view in a later section. The model was commissioned by Polaroid from the Hudson River Group[6] of the USA, which over the last two years has completed marketing mix models for Polaroid's business in the United States and the United Kingdom.

The model

The analysis focuses on film sales, which are Polaroid's main source of profit. Their business model is comparable to razor manufacturers, for whom blades are the main source of profit.

The focus is T-600 film sales – the main consumer line. This accounts for the majority of Polaroid's total film volume.

Six separate models were constructed, covering three distribution channels and two film pack sizes in each, for the period Christmas 1990 to Christmas 1997.

The following factors were incorporated:

Advertising

Brand advertising and promotional advertising were considered separately. Within brand advertising, individual campaigns were also isolated.

Hudson River has applied a 13-week cut-off to advertising effects – its standard methodology, which allows Polaroid to compare with its US studies. We have looked at long-term effects separately.

Pricing

Taken into account: single pack, twin pack, and the price gap between them to assess switching.

Category volume (still film)

Representing macro-economic factors, found to have an effect on Polaroid's performance.

Seasonality

Polaroid also has a strong sales uplift at Christmas. As the category volume does not have this peak, a seasonal factor was introduced.

Consumer promotions

Two consumer promotions were run in 1996 and 1997: a Boots 'three for two' offer and a cash-back rebate offer valued at £1.50 per pack.

The three for two offer was found to be a strong volume driver, but not the rebate offer.

6. The Hudson River Group of Valhalla, New York, is the leading third-party supplier of analytical services in the United States, Canada and the United Kingdom. The company was founded in 1989 to provide customised advanced analytics to consumer goods and services companies and is best known as the leading supplier of customised marketing mix models.

Camera sales

While the focus of the analysis was film sales, camera sales are also important because they affect film sales – most visibly in the period when the camera is sold, suggesting that camera purchasers also buy film to go with it.

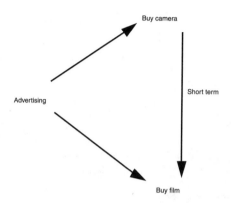

The Hudson River Group found that 42% of cameras sold between 1996 and 1997 were sold due to advertising activity. This was 22% in 1996 when the price cut took place and rose to 60% in 1997 when the Spice Girls project pushed Christmas sales to a record high. These are high figures, but reasonable, given that sales nearly doubled over the same period.

From this, the Hudson River Group have been able to calculate the contribution of advertising to film sales via camera sales.

Short-term Volume Contribution

The degree of fit and statistical tests give us confidence in the accurate measurement of the various drivers (Figure 23).

The incremental contribution of advertising can be seen over time, in Figure 24. This amounts to a yearly volume contribution of:

	1996	1997
% of annual volume driven by advertising	7.44	20.92

The growth between 1996 and 1997 reflects two factors:

— The switch from Regional to National broadcast of Brand TV. Promotional TV remained National throughout.

— The higher contribution of Spice advertising in 1997 (see last section for details).

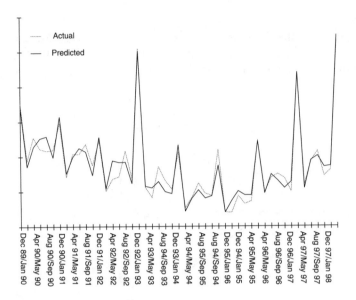

Figure 23: *Actual T–600 film sales versus modelled*
Source: The Hudson River Group (composite of all models)

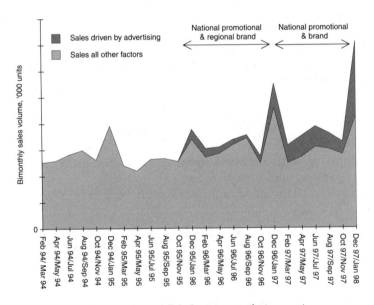

Figure 24: *Polaroid T–600 film sales. Composite modelled advertising contribution over time*
Source: The Hudson River Group

Advertising was also the largest single contributor to film volume in both years. In 1997, its contribution was five times that of price reductions and ten times that of promotions (Figure 25).

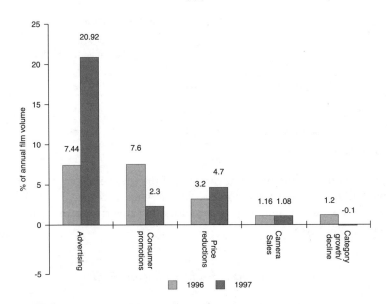

Figure 25: *Percentage of annual film volume contributed by each driver*
Source: The Hudson River Group

Short-term Payback from Advertising

Polaroid cannot reveal profit per film; being unique in its category, the information is highly sensitive. The paybacks that follow are presented as percentage returns on investment. Investment is defined as cost of media, production and agency fees. For the Spice Girls sponsorship, we have added sponsorship and PR fees.

As production and agency fees are billed to Polaroid Europe, there is no actual production cost or fee for the UK. An estimate has been used, based on the UK's percentage of total Europe/Export media spend. This gives the impact of advertising directly on film (Table 1).

TABLE 1: SHORT-TERM ADVERTISING PAYBACKS

		Direct impact of advertising on film sales
Promotional advertising 1995–97	Payback[7]	12%
Brand advertising 1996–97	Payback	80%
Total advertising 1995–97	Payback	44%

As described above, camera sales affect film sales, and camera sales are driven by advertising. The effect of this, in addition to the above, is given in Table 2 overleaf.

---

7. Paybacks are calculated on the basis of actual market volumes, not the GfK ones shown here.

TABLE 2: SHORT-TERM ADVERTISING PAYBACKS

		Impact of advertising via selling film with each camera sold
Promotional advertising 1995–7	Payback	13%
Brand advertising 1996–7	Payback	21%
Total advertising 1995–7	Payback	17%

Source: The Hudson River Group

This suggests that while brand advertising is the most effective way to sell film, promotional advertising is much closer to brand when it comes to selling cameras. This makes sense, as the majority of promotional advertising in 1996/1997 was promoting camera prices.

Long-term Effects of Advertising and Payback

However, cameras use more films in their lifetime than are bought initially. The contribution of film over the lifetime of the camera is a long-term effect of the advertising which sold that camera.

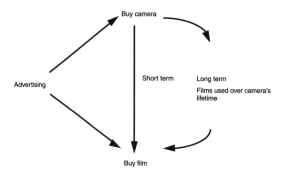

To quantify this, we have supplemented the econometric model with further analysis. This is based around a standard Polaroid business model, called the 'film burn model', which estimates the number of films sold over a camera's lifetime.

The film burn model
The film burn model was built by Polaroid, using data from consumer diaries and surveys, matched to actual sales. The version currently in use at Polaroid was reviewed in 1994. Its accuracy between 1984 and 1993 was +/-7% of actual sales. The model is felt to be accurate enough to give a broad indication of long-term payback for the period 1995 to 1997.

Basic parameters of the model

Different kinds of users have different usage patterns. The model estimates lifetime usage of film according to the way the camera was acquired:

Camera purchase type	Lifetime average film usage
Bought for self	*
Received as a gift	*

*Figures have been removed to preserve confidentiality

The one new variable is the Spice Cam. In 1997, Polaroid sponsored the Spice Girls and produced a special edition camera, the 'Spice Cam', positioned as a Christmas gift against a younger target than usual. We have given this camera a lower figure than the 'received as a gift' figure, as we expect the users to be shorter term consumers. We have used the average first-year film burn:

Camera purchase type	Lifetime average film usage
Bought for self	*
Received as a gift	*
Spice Cam	*

*Figures have been removed to preserve confidentiality

Some of these film sales will be generated by marketing activity, for example, price promotions, which must be discounted from the model in order to find the real value of the camera sale to Polaroid. We will call the resulting value the 'base film usage' of the camera.

During 1996 and 1997, 23% of films were sold by marketing activity, which leaves 77% of films sold as the base usage:

Camera purchase type	Lifetime average film usage	Base film usage of camera over its lifetime, excluding marketing effects
Bought for self	*	*
Received as a gift	*	*
Spice Cam	*	*

*Figures have been removed to preserve confidentiality

By looking at the relative numbers[8] of each type of camera sold, we can calculate number of films used by an average camera (see table overleaf).

---

8. We have estimated numbers by taking all Christmas sales as being 'gift', all others as 'self-purchase'. For Spice, we have actual audited numbers as it was a separately measured item.

Camera purchase type	Base film usage of camera over its lifetime, excluding marketing effects	Cameras sold 1996–1997 %
Bought for self (non-Christmas volume)	*	*
Received as a gift (Christmas volume)	*	*
Spice Cam (Retail audit)	*	*

*Figures have been removed to preserve confidentiality

This gives a weighted average lifetime film usage per camera.

Long-term Payback of Advertising

The Hudson River model calculates the payback of advertising on the basis of initial films sold per camera. We now know that the figure over the lifetime of the camera is much higher than this, it is actually 6.75 times higher.

This means that lifetime paybacks from camera sales are 6.75 times higher than the short-term paybacks calculated by the econometric model (Table 3).

TABLE 3: LIFETIME ADVERTISING PAYBACKS

		Short term Impact of advertising via selling film with each camera sold	Long term Lifetime value of cameras sold by advertising
Promotional advertising 1995–97	Payback	13%	88%
Brand advertising 1996–97	Payback	21%	142%
Total advertising 1995–97	Payback	17%	115%

Total Advertising Payback

We now have two figures which we can use to calculate total advertising payback:

— Direct short-term impact of advertising on film sales

— Lifetime value of cameras sold by advertising

The results of this calculation are given in Table 4.

TABLE 4: TOTAL ADVERTISING PAYBACKS

		Short term Direct impact of advertising on film sales	Long term Lifetime value of cameras sold by advertising	Total impact of advertising
Promotional advertising 1995–97	Payback	12%	88%	100%
Brand advertising 1996–97	Payback	91%	142%	233%
Total advertising 1995–97	Payback	61%	115%	176%

HOW THE STRATEGY HAS REACHED BEYOND ADVERTISING

As we said at the beginning of this paper, the big idea was more than an advertising idea. The strategy and its success have driven changes which will affect the future of the business.

LFTM has given key multiple retailers increased confidence in Polaroid, allowing closer relations.

— Argos has put Polaroid film in its top 500 products, committing never to be out of stock, and is planning a full page for Polaroid in the catalogue, with LFTM styling.

— Knowledge sharing and NPD. Boots is giving input on NPD and R&D at Polaroid's global headquarters.

— The Spice Cam was listed in Currys as a one-off, for Christmas only. This was so successful that in 1998 Currys will stock the standard range of Polaroid products on an ongoing basis in 220 stores.

— Tesco has just agreed to list Polaroid products, in 450 stores. Another major supermarket chain is interested.

Product and packaging:

— New camera launches now reflect the positioning, being style rather than function based. The latest version is the 'Extreme' with this season's colours.

— Polaroid has developed a new visual identity, where a 'Pulse' has been added to what was very functional packaging.

Promotions:

— The UK had previously run promotions such as one with Abbey National, giving a camera and film to people opening Instant Saver accounts.

— Since LFTM it has run a sampling programme with Lynx (also called 'Axe' in other markets), the male toiletries brand targeted at style-leading 18 to 19-year-olds. The promotion is now being extended into the Scandinavia region.

— More obvious 'social lubricant' partners have included The Ministry of Sound, the UK's leading youth nightclub, Cuervo Tequila and Diamond White cider.

The Spice Girls – Living 'Live for the Moment'

This is a project that put the LFTM strategy at the heart of the marketing mix for the first time. The payback from this project has been included in the modelling; however, when broken out of the total, the relatively high contribution shows the power of an idea which can go beyond advertising.

The Spice Girls offered Polaroid a number of benefits:

— They were a powerful embodiment of the LFTM positioning.

— They were able to reach a new audience in a new way.

— They were able to make brands famous, something which Polaroid had lacked since the late 1970s.

'It was the Rock Star ad that made the Spice Girls get in touch – Geri in particular had always loved Polaroid, but it wasn't until they saw what we were doing that they thought we were right for them.'

Mark Bernard, Consumer Marketing Manager, Polaroid UK

'The Spice Girls came to us because they loved our advertising ... it was the perfect fit for both sides.'

Tim Palmer, European Marketing Director

Polaroid was able to accept the offer because it matched the LFTM strategy.
The project reached across the marketing mix:

— A special edition camera, Spice Cam, was designed, in new colours and positioned as a Christmas gift.

— Pricing: the Spice Cam, gift-packed with a film, was sold at a higher price.

— Advertising: a 30-second execution featuring the Spice Girls and Spice Cam.

— Brand fame: news of the sponsorship and advertising reached an estimated 74.6%[9] of the UK population. PR elsewhere in Europe has been valued at US$4 million.[10]

The effects of the Spice Girl project

As we saw above, Christmas 1997 had record sales, due to the exceptional contribution of Spice.

If we benchmark the project against the next best performing advertising in the campaign, the power of total integration is clear. Even assuming that cameras sold by Spice contribute half the film sales that normal brand advertising does, payback is 50% better.

---

9. Inskip PR.
10. Motive.

	Payback of advertising on film sales	Lifetime value of film sales	Total payback
Scissors/Resignation	101%	101%[11]	202%
Spice Girls 'School'	94%	169%[12]	263%

CONCLUSIONS

The process of advertising development found a new role for Polaroid, where its instantness had a powerful benefit: social lubrication. Advertising brought the role to life by overcoming the embarrassment people felt about using Polaroid in public.

In doing so, a sales decline of around 20 years was turned around.

— Films sales are up 46% and cameras sales up 91% since the launch of the strategy.

— Advertising has contributed up to 20% of annual film sales.

— Total payback on advertising is 176%.

The strategy has reached 18 markets in the region for which it was intended, and is already impacting on Australia. That is a statement of faith of enormous proportions from Polaroid.

More than this, the strategy has offered Polaroid something that other marketing tools could not: a new vision of its future. The Spice project is one example of how that future can unfold.

11. Payback calculated at standard rate of 8.8 films per camera over its lifetime.
12. Payback calculated at lower rate of 77% of 5 films per camera over its lifetime.

The Growing Importance of Brand Valuation

David Haigh
Brand Finance

The IPA Advertising Effectiveness Awards 1998 were judged against a background of increasing shareholder interest in the contribution that marketing in general and advertising in particular can make to business success.

There is no doubt that the City is now fully aware of the impact strong brands can have on investment performance. For example, the *Brand Finance Report 1998* demonstrated that City analysts have a strong interest in the level of marketing investment and the measures of brand performance. They want to know how and why brands work and what results can be expected from them in the future. Out of the 100 analysts interviewed 80% thought that more information should be published about marketing expenditure and 66% thought that more information should be published about brand values. It seems that there is a clamour for such information and a genuine interest in long-term brand strategy.

CURRENT TREND IN BRAND VALUATION

In the words of Sir George Bull, Ex-Chairman of Diageo; 'A new recognition is emerging in company boardrooms and the City that brands add intangible value to products and businesses and redefine the value of their company owners.'

There are increasing instances of City analysts putting explicit values on brands, most notably the Orange brand, which ABN AMRO valued at £200 million in early 1997, at a time when the company was still making heavy losses and sustaining highly negative cash flows. It did this because of the expected future returns over the following ten years, value driven by advertising-induced sales.

The City's interest in brand values is not just passive. A number of brand-rich companies have come to market or out-performed the market. Two examples of this phenomenon are Britt Alcroft and Hay & Robertson. These two companies respectively own the trademark rights to Thomas the Tank Engine and Admiral football shirts, the brand in which England's 1966 squad won the world cup. Both have grown at phenomenal rates and both have seen their share prices rocket. These are just two examples of a re-rating process that is going on in many sectors where brands have been hiding their lights under a bushel.

In more traditionally advertised sectors some analysts are now openly critical of managers who underinvest in their brands.

There is also plenty of evidence that the shares of strongly branded companies perform better over the long term than unbranded companies. For example, Citibank has correlated share price performance over nearly 20 years with investment in brands. Total Research has demonstrated a link between share price performance and its own perceived brand quality index, Equitrend.

And when the City is convinced, CEO's increasingly want to know more about the value of their brand portfolios, where the brand values are being created and what contributes most to that growth. This is part of a wider trend towards shareholder-value growth and an understanding of the levers which create such growth. In a business environment where costs have been squeezed, profits growth through marketing investment is one of the few avenues left open.

There is therefore an increasing trend in companies towards the establishment of marketing finance departments and brand value tracking models, which allow management to get a better handle on which brands are worth most. They are being used to monitor which brands will generate the highest return in the event of increased investment. Companies such as Cadbury, BAT and Diageo have sophisticated tracking mechanisms of this sort.

Such investment is clearly not just about advertising but in many markets advertising is a major part of the mix. It is therefore natural that the IPA Advertising Effectiveness awards should have seen a marked increase in references to profit and shareholder-value growth.

David Bell, Chairman of the *Financial Times*, and keynote speaker at the awards dinner, set the tone. He pointed out that there is now an inexorable drive to establish the 'measures and links' between 'advertising and creativity and the long term health of the profit and loss account and the balance sheet'. The financial quality of many papers submitted to the judging panel revealed that the search for such measures and links is in full swing within the advertising business.

EXAMPLES FROM THE IPA CASE STUDIES

The One2One case from BBH included research with financial analysts which demonstrated that they felt the brand's fortunes had revived principally because of improvements in marketing and advertising. The Orange case from WCRS, coincidentally in the same sector, had an even more impressive analysis of financial returns from the campaign, based on a Lehman share valuation model.

In previous years cases have pointed to incremental sales and profits arising out of advertising campaigns. The Cooperative Bank case from BDDH from a couple of years ago provided a clear exposition of how a brilliant advertising campaign can build business very quickly and effectively.

The notable change which has occurred since The Cooperative Bank case study won an award is that agencies now seem much more comfortable hobnobbing with financial accountants and equity analysts to explicitly prove a return on investment. Admittedly only a couple of cases went the whole hog in 1998. However, I suspect that many more will go this way in future years.

In addition to those papers which explicitly drew in the investment community, or the investment argument, many others gave very clear and well reasoned financial appraisals of the returns from the advertising budgets used. The Colgate case from Y&R demonstrated a 15% margin improvement, the Polaroid case from BBH demonstrated sales growth of one third and a long-term payback of nearly double the spend. The Impulse case from O&M demonstrated over £9 million of short term sales increase and £18 million of long-term shareholder-value growth. The Marmoleum case from the Morgan Partnership demonstrated that an advertising budget below £50,000 produced a return of £150,000 in the test phase and £1.3 million for a £300,000 investment in the roll out, producing an overall payback of 427%. The Ford Galaxy campaign produced £25 million of incremental revenue and so the financial evidence piled up.

Many of the case studies used econometric models to demonstrate incremental sales uplifts. However, in many ways this only told half the story; in the final analysis we all know that sales of themselves may not produce a profitable long term outcome. Those case studies which used econometrics and other measures as inputs to a more rigorous financial valuation model got the highest marks from me.

These are the kind of cases with which CEOs and financial analysts will feel instantly at home. These are the kind of case studies which could slot straight into a boardroom discussion to justify higher budgets. They should be strongly encouraged.

Interestingly enough, I do not believe that putting the econometric analysis, the sales figures and other similar data into a full-blown financial appraisal or brand valuation means the death of more subtle benefits from advertising. Some have suggested that all this financial stuff is deeply serious, deeply boring and totally antithetical to great advertising. The numbers will drive out the 'creative' and sensitive.

One of the instructions to the judges was to judge the entries on the basis of their manifold effects. These range from the impact of advertising on personnel motivation to social benefit. In my view there was no contradiction between a balanced approach to the manifold effects of advertising and a rigorous, hardnosed financial appraisal of the cases.

In this regard I believe that the 1998 Advertising Effectiveness Awards were a watershed in the evolution of the Awards. Perhaps more importantly I believe that they represent a paradigm of the way the whole advertising industry is developing. Yes, advertising must be creative, it must be subtle and it must have manifold effects. But equally it must justify itself in the probing world of the accountants. The awards merely highlight a rapidly developing trend which is long overdue. Making a good financial case will not only justify higher media budgets but will also earn agencies higher respect for their contribution to the clients' business objectives and ultimately to higher agency earnings for a job well done.

Section 4

Two-Star Winners

Bacardi Breezer

SUMMARY

This is the story of how a brand with no role, insightfully repositioned, created a category and transformed a company. It is about the opportunity that can flow from tapping an unmet consumer need. This was a case of asking the fundamental question 'what market are we in?'.

The Repositioning of Breezer

Breezer was developed by Bacardi-Martini in the US, and tested market in the UK by the local company. The test market, while hardly spectacular, was sufficiently encouraging to persuade Bacardi-Martini UK to launch Breezer nationally, positioned as 'relaxing refreshment from the Caribbean'.

Sales grew with distribution, but research into advertising provoked management concerns about the brand's femininity and raised fundamental questions about the strategy. The problem was that Breezer had no role. It was not a product that consumers were familiar with, consumers did not know what to do with it and the advertising did not tell them.

The strategic breakthrough was that there are occasions when drinkers, particularly, though not exclusively, in the on-trade, do not fancy a beer, they fancy a change, but cannot find anything suitable (because before Breezer there wasn't anything).

The vision was to reposition it as a 'refreshing alternative' to beer. The resulting campaign, 'True Stories' was in stark contrast to any preceding Bacardi advertising – no palm trees, no sand; instead gritty, witty films with plenty of cool guys as well as girls, set in a trendy urban bar.

Results

Some of the most compelling evidence of advertising effect is the step change in sales whenever it comes on air. Access to very precise weekly sales data allows us to model the advertising econometrically, isolating advertising effect from other variables. This shows a very strong correlation.

In trying to understand how advertising is working, we observed strong correlations between advertising and awareness, awareness and trial and trial and recent consumption.

Pre-testing and other research vindicates both the strategic approach and the creative direction. The advertising is making the brand more unisex, more sophisticated and emphasising its spirit, as opposed to its fruit content.

Indeed, the whole Premium Packaged Spirit category, which Breezer founded, has been profitably developed by Bacardi-Martini, who have gone on to dominate it.

Payback

Beyond the creation of a profitable brand, the most dramatic evidence of advertising effectiveness is found in the impact that Breezer's success has had on the company.

It has acted as the catalyst in a cultural revolution, which can be felt right through the organisation.

— Production has struggled to keep pace with relentless consumer demand and the operations' people have had to think on their feet and with their wallets, revolutionising working practices and investing in a huge new plant.

— Marketing has been totally restructured to handle a multi-brand portfolio.

— Sales have had to adapt to focusing in the on-trade, previously little-known territory.

— New product development has been put at the epicentre of brand management.

Moreover, the value of the investment and new jobs is multiplied two to three times when one looks at the economic impact on the local community.

Bud Ice

SUMMARY

This paper demonstrates the considerable role advertising has played in making Bud Ice arguably the most successful ppl launch of the 1990s. Without the advertising or with more averagely effective advertising, Bud Ice would have not have met its ambitious marketing objectives. In a world where much of the literature on brand stretching pessimistically concentrates on the dilution of the parent brand – either in sales or image terms – there are significant conclusions to be drawn here. In fact, we have shown that the opposite is possible.

Ambitious Obectives for the Brand to Market

Anheuser-Busch launched Bud Ice in the summer of 1996, making Budweiser, for the first time in the UK a stretched brand. By the time Bud Ice entered in 1996, the market consisted of Labatt Ice, Carlsberg Ice, and Fosters Ice (the market leader).

Marketing Objectives

The ambitious marketing objectives, however, were to increase overall Anheuser-Busch market share by:

— In the off-trade becoming the number one Ice beer in share within two years.

— In the on-trade becoming the number one Ice beer in ROS within two years.

— Keeping Budweiser cannibalisation to a minimum.

Results

The ads were among the most popular lager ads ever among our male, 18 to 24-year-old target. In terms of appeal, they were in the top 2% of ads that Millward Brown ever LINK[TM] tested. Further they were famous: qualitatively recalled more than any other lager ads, and spawning a hit Bud Ice branded single.

Bud Ice fulfilled all its ambitious marketing objectives, in a year and a half – well ahead of schedule. It became number one in the off-trade in share, and number one in the on-trade in terms of ROS. Further, Budweiser did not appear to be cannibalised. This was despite being the fourth brand into the market, and launching two years after the other main Ice brands. With such results, Bud Ice has arguably been the most successful ppl launch of the 1990s.

Advertising strongly influenced both ROS and distribution of Bud Ice – and hence its market share. This was shown through the correlation between uplifts and advertising bursts; and the relative strengths of the advertised over the non-advertised regions. An econometric model shows that, at its peak, the advertising caused a 40% uplift in Bud Ice share.

As this all suggests, Bud Ice advertising was very efficient in terms of generating both awareness and sales, compared with other advertising. The Awareness Index of 12 is, according to Millward Brown, 'among the highest ever recorded in the category'. Moreover, Bud Ice generated more Bud Ice share and ROS per advertising pound spent than other Ice brands at their launches.

Rather than cannibilism, the advertising also benefited Budweiser – the parent. It shifted both spontaneous awareness and sales. By constructing a model of Budweiser's market share over the last five years, we have shown that the effect is quite large. At one point, the Bud Ice ads boosted Bud's share by 14%.

Payback

Anheuser-Busch only spent £3.2 million during 1996/97, so the advertising would have paid for itself if the gross margin were 5.5% or more. We cannot disclose the margin of Anheuser-Busch. However, average margins in the industry as a whole are around 10% (Sources: CAMRA, Mintel). Hence, if Anheuser-Busch margins are in line with industry margins, the advertising has paid for itself very comfortably indeed.

As importantly, we have shown that Bud Ice advertising has increased sales of the parent brand.

The Famous Grouse

SUMMARY

'A new stage is reached when the market enters a period where volume looks set for permanent decline ... The usual recommendation from advocates of product life cycle theory or portfolio concepts such as the Boston Consulting Group's matrix, is to divest from the market. Such a view can be a costly oversimplification.'

Peter Doyle, *Marketing Management & Strategy*, 1994

Our paper demonstrates how costly this oversimplification can be.

The Need for Famous Grouse to Bridge the Old and the New

In the early 1990s, The Famous Grouse experienced a 'triple whammy' of market pressures. Declining volumes in spirits, blended Scotch whisky and the premium blended sector in which our brand sits, resulted in a decline in the brand's sales volumes.

As is the case in many post mature markets, whisky brands are very reliant on a small number of heavy, and increasingly ageing consumers, to provide the majority of volume. The Famous Grouse was no exception.

Our first advertising task was to protect and build this core drinker base by persuading existing consumers and drinkers of competitive blends to choose The Famous Grouse more often. In the longer term we had to attract more younger drinkers – the heavy-using loyalists of tomorrow.

The potentially disastrous implications of losing heavy drinkers had locked whisky advertising into a creative paradigm defined by past executions, the so called 'whisky cage'. To achieve our objectives, we needed to break out of this cage. We had to retain the brand's authority while making it more relevant and accessible. The 'Grouse Icon' campaign – was launched in December 1995 to meet these challenges.

Results

The 'Icon' campaign achieved the highest levels of spontaneous awareness, memorability and advertising uniqueness scores in the category while maintaining the brand's authority.

TGI shows a 2% increase in the number of 'most often' drinkers while Bell's and Teacher's, our main competitors, lost 8% each. Our 55+ drinkers, disproportionately important in volume terms, increased by 144,000 between 1995 and 1997. Despite relative price movements in their favour, Bell's and Teacher's lost 42,000 and 155,000 55+ drinkers respectively.

During the same period, the number of 18 to 24-year-olds 'ever drinking' TFG has risen by over 10%, despite a 12% drop in penetration among this age group within Scotch whisky as a whole.

The resultant 3% rise in The Famous Grouse share of premium blends volume, contrasted with Teacher's and Bell's major losses, was the first indication that two years of the 'Icon' campaign was reversing the brand's fortunes.

To isolate the effects of advertising on volume and share an econometric model of multiple grocer sales, the fiercest and largest arena of competition enabled us to strip out the effect of price, promotions and distribution (product and packaging have been roughly constant since 1896!).

Eliminating seasonality was challenging. There is a very large seasonal peak in sales around the two Christmas/New Year periods modelled. To estimate how much of the rise in sales was due to the advertising, we used year-on-year comparisons of the 'net base' level of sales that ACNielsen had isolated.

Payback

Several major econometric studies provide compelling evidence that long-term advertising effects, will have longer term sales effects. The exact scale of these effects depend on the assumed decay rate of the advertising effect.

Accepting both the worst, and best, decay rate scenarios of two such studies (Lodish and Simon), we calculate the *net* three year payback of 'Icon' advertising, to be between £700,000 and £2,300,000.

The 'Icon' campaign has reversed the decline in the brand's fortunes and, in so doing, has broken the rules of marketing in a post mature market.

Imodium

SUMMARY

This case shows how Johnson and Johnson MSD's Imodium brand was able to turn leadership into dominance, building dramatic share increases due to the marketing team's refusal to be satisfied with number one position.

A Hidden Opportunity in the Market

Imodium is able to stop diarrhoea in a single dose. It is not unique in this. It has been in pharmacy since 1993, and on prescription before that. The first TV advertising in the UK – the 'Wedding' execution – was run in 1995. Developed by the previous agency it was extremely successful – growing the market and Imodium's value share within that market to take leadership position within a year. The success of 'Wedding' made further growth appear difficult.

Furthermore, a market analysis uncovered hidden weaknesses of the brand. Market growth was slowing down – it had declined from +26% in 1995 to +10% in 1996. Imodium share of the market had peaked – at around 42%. The own label threat became more apparent – there was the possibility of own label products applying for a GSL licence, which would widen their distribution. Imodium was underdeveloped – other remedies were seen as soothing and approachable, Imodium was described as a German Doctor – people felt that it was effective but far removed from them. Consumer attitudes appeared entrenched. Competitive remedy users saw it as a 'super cork' only to be used when absolutely necessary. Non-treaters viewed the remedy as potentially dangerous – trapping toxins in the body. Although successful the previous 'torture test' execution contributed to the notion that Imodium should be kept in reserve and was limiting us as a 'once a year' remedy.

This meant there were, even as market leader, hidden opportunities in the market:

— The frequent sufferer represented a huge market opportunity. Only a small proportion were Imodium users and a large proportion were not treating at all.

— Our target audience – the 'comfort seekers' and the 'non treaters' wanted more of an emotional benefit to switch brands or try Imodium.

The solution was to introduce an emotional benefit to the brand and to own the category high ground of confidence which sufferers otherwise lacked due to their loss of control. The creative solution lay in advertising, which showed the confidence that Imodium could give to the sufferer and sought to show how Imodium would allow them to get on with their lives, without giving diarrhoea second thought.

Results and Payback

— Imodium share of the market grew from 42% before the advertising to 57%.

— The category experienced a 12.5% growth compared to 10% for the previous year.

— Awareness of Imodium and its 'one dose' efficacy was increased.

— Attitudes to treating diarrhoea were changing and the product was becoming more 'everyday' to the sufferer.

— The advertising investment was recouped with an incremental profit attributable to the change in strategy.

— The success of the campaign encouraged J&J MSD to develop new products and categories in partnership with pharmacy and consumers and set the scene for the launch of a line extension – Imodium Plus, in April of 1998.

— 'Eyes' cemented relations with the pharmacy trade, who voted for 'Eyes' as their favourite advertising campaign of 1997. This positive feedback from pharmacies increased sales force morale.

North West Water

SUMMARY

This paper demonstrates the benefits of advertising in managing perceptions of value and hence customers' satisfaction, in a market under fierce attack from the media.

An Industry Under Siege

For many, water was one privatisation too far. A target of extreme hostility, the industry was a political football from the outset. The media adopted the moral highground and as reports of excess profits and high executive remuneration gave way to serious questions about the management of the 1995/96 drought and the leakage crisis, public satisfaction hit rock bottom.

North West Water found that support among all key stakeholders was at an all time low. Despite the fact that customers and the media attacked the company for high costs, research revealed extreme ignorance of actual prices.

Advertising therefore provided customers with yardsticks against which to measure the company's performance by educating them as to both how much they pay and also the range of services provided.

Distinctive, unbranded '60p' advertisements intrigued customers in order to force them to take notice of our message and reappraise the offer. Having commanded attention, communication gave customers a context in which to judge costs and encouraged an appreciation of the wide range of services and benefits the company bring to the customer, community and wider environment.

Results

Advertising generated awareness of the focus of the business and forced customers to re-evaluate their perceptions of North West Water in the following key dimensions:

— value for money which increased by 22 percentage points;

— over a third of customers became aware of the 60p figure itself and increasingly appreciated that water is cheaper than they had previously believed;

— customers became more aware of services provided and increasingly recognised the company's contribution to the community and its role as custodian of our environment;

— customer satisfaction increased to 78%, its highest level ever;

— by the end of the advertising three quarters of customers were loyal to North West Water up from just over half.

The campaign also had significant impact across other stakeholder groups. Three quarters of all stakeholders came to view North West Water as a socially responsible company – in the same category as BT – and agreement that North West Water meets or exceeds community expectations increased from 54% to 70%.

The advertising even appeared to quieten the company's most hostile critics and beneficial media coverage was double that of negative and consistently exceeded adverse publicity throughout the campaign.

Most importantly, liberated from the negative press that had publicly berated the company for so long, employees became increasingly optimistic and twice as many staff believed public perceptions of the company would improve. Ultimately, employees rated North West Water more positively as a place to work and job satisfaction increased by 10 percentage points at the end of the advertising.

Payback

It is almost a decade since privatisation and attitudes towards NWW have turned full circle. As the end of the Millennium approaches, OFWAT is carrying out its regulatory review of costs and services – a process which will determine the price limits for customers' bills and the extent of service improvements that will take place from the year 2000.

To draw a link between improved value for money perceptions and long term pricing would be inappropriate. However, flash results of customer research as part of the Periodic Review is demonstrating that there is only minority support for bills to fall in preference to a programme of environmental and service improvement. On the contrary, 87% of customers have stated a preference for bills to remain the same or rise.

Advertising has transformed stakeholder perceptions of one of the most reviled companies in the region, empowering North West Water to take control of its own future.

Wallis

SUMMARY

This paper is not simply an illustration of advertising's contribution to the magnitude of Wallis' sales growth. It is a testament to advertising's contribution to the quality of business growth, demonstrating as it does, not only how advertising attracted existing customers, also new, and therefore future users.

Uniting Wallis Customers Inside and Outside the Club

Wallis is over 60 years old and has over 210 outlets nationwide. Unlike its key competitors, Wallis had never advertised, but was still reliant upon the seasonal trappings of fashion and the need to predict it correctly.

Wallis required the advertising to pay back in the short term and in this context, could have resorted to retail conventions; increase short-term sales by using product advertising as a glorified shop window.

However, on analysing Wallis' user base closely, it was recognised that there was a different challenge advertising could overcome. Wallis' user base was relatively small, and 77.9% were shopping infrequently. It also had a static average 5% buying penetration in previous years. There was therefore untapped potential in non-users who considered Wallis as outdated and something of a 'closed shop'.

A double opportunity existed: to increase users and increase frequency. Mostly, traditional investments tended towards trying to increase frequency by attracting from existing users.

Rather than focusing on product, there was an opportunity to target attitude. Through TGI, one shared value was identified across both Wallis users and Wallis non-users: they all like to look smart. We drew a pen-portrait of our target woman and called her 'Forever 30'.

Wallis' heritage was true to 'smartness', and so a credible proposition could be expressed:

'Wallis, because dressing up is important to you.'

The campaign idea asserted the benefit of dressing up, and while the product featured, it did not dominate. Each execution was a dramatisation of smartness and how that affected onlookers.

Results

— In 1997, Wallis sales increased 10% year on year.

— During the latter half of 1997, sales were up 13% when compared to the last half of 1996.

— Wallis' market share had grown from 0.7% to 1.1% year on year.

— The advertising could be shown to achieve a 62% rate of return on investment within 6 months of launch.

   In order to isolate the effect of advertising all variables were eliminated.

— Like-for-like stores (LFL – unchanged store environment) accounted for store refits and new stores.

— A test and control analysis compared with LFL stores eliminated clothes and price differentials.

Payback

Ulster was used as the control (no advertising). We identified a strong correlation (0.976) between the UK and Ulster in order to predict UK sales *with* advertising and *without* advertising.

— Earlier, during the advertising period, Wallis increased its frequent shopper base by 13,939. These people bought over twice yearly.

— Wallis also attracted 121,253 new shoppers who bought once.

— The advertising got attention. PR generated an additional media value of £324,610.

— Dipstick tracking showed that attitudes moved significantly forwards. Equally, it proved that the advertising achieved greater shifts than competitors with significant historic adstock.

— Furthermore, the results promised long-term growth through new users. They would consider Wallis before they shopped. Indeed, the early months of 1998 indicate that this is the case.

   The difference was that 5.1% of Wallis' half year sales are equivalent to a profit of £511,000.

The Use of Econometrics in the Papers

Louise Cook
Holmes & Cook

Approximately 40% of papers and almost 60% of four and five-star papers included one or more econometric models (though models were most prevalent in the four stars). But, as 40% of four and five-star papers had no econometric models, this does not mean a model has to be included in order to produce a high-ranking paper. In reality, not all evaluation problems require this degree or type of complexity. The 1998 Grand Prix paper had no model, nor did slightly more than half of the star-rated papers.

From a development perspective, what was most encouraging was the variety of markets for which models had been developed. Where once the majority might have been for FMCGs or financial services, some very laudable attempts were made to model other types of services including fast food and mobile telephones.

It was also very promising to see variety, both in the types of models being employed and in the practitioners constructing them, because this in itself introduces a range of approaches and insights. Of those papers where the source of the modelling was stated, slightly more than half were produced by consultants or research companies with the remainder being produced by advertising agencies themselves.

Many of the models quoted were clearly used on an ongoing basis as part of the brand-management process. This is always good to see, as it implies that a model has had to prove itself in the real world. However, this is not to imply that models constructed specifically for the awards are second-class citizens. They may be better able to push the technical ball forward, being developed specifically to address current evaluation issues and to test the hypotheses which have been developed about the way a campaign is working.

From the current set of papers, Olivio and First Direct stand out as particularly good examples of something new being done or found and comprehensively validated. In the case of Olivio, a fairly traditional econometric framework produced some quite startling results. Olivio's adstock did not decay as would normally be expected but effectively caused step-changes in sales. What is more, these occurred at a diminishing rate as the campaign progressed. In the case of First Direct, a very interesting analytical approach was used to measure the magnifying effect that television advertising had on other media.

WHY EMPLOY ECONOMETRIC ANALYSIS?

Econometric analysis has three functions it can offer to advertising evaluation:

— It can disentangle and quantify the separate effects of the many influences on a brand's sales.

— It can be used as a means of testing hypotheses about the way a particular campaign works (for example in the long term).

— It can help to beat a path through the forest data now becoming the norm in many markets.

By identifying the underlying structures within data, models help to turn a sea of numbers into usable information and assist more generally in developing and testing hypotheses about various aspects of a brand's behaviour.

In many instances, as marketing activity diversifies, it becomes increasingly difficult to assess the contribution of any one particular component without resorting to advanced statistical techniques. As a general research tool, econometric analysis is also much more widely used and understood than was the case even five years ago, and so possibly both these trends have contributed to the quite extensive use of econometric modelling in papers submitted for the awards.

THE IMPORTANCE OF MODEL VALIDATION

For the 1998 Awards a big emphasis was put on the importance of rigorous model validation. It is now very easy for any computer-literate person to throw some data into a spreadsheet, run a regression, find a relationship, call it a model and interpret it as he or she sees fit. He may be lucky and produce something which is correct, even without being aware of the vast body of statistical theory underlying regression and other modelling techniques. However, because many data relationships are multi-dimensional and may occur over a period of time (that is, a factor may affect sales with a lag), producing the right relationship on a regular basis requires considerably more than luck! It is thus very important that any models claiming to produce a realistic quantification of advertising (or any other) effects are put through their statistical paces and shown to be sound. There is no British justice system here. Econometric models are 'guilty until proved innocent'!

THE PROPERTIES OF AN ADMISSABLE MODEL

There are three key phases involved in constructing any model: a theoretical stage; model estimation based on both this theory and the available data; and finally the process of testing the model to ensure that it has appropriate statistical properties, thereby making it likely that the relationship it implies between sales and advertising (or sales and any other factor) is valid. In statistical terms this generally means the properties listed opposite must be taken into account.

— The residuals (the difference between actual sales and the model's estimate of sales at each data point) must be normally distributed (bell-shaped when plotted on a histogram).

— There must not be a relationship across time between these residuals. If there is, this typically implies a factor is missing from the model, or that one (or more) of the variables in the model is incorrectly specified.

— Parameters should generally be stable over time (this may mean finding the correct functional form which allows a particular elasticity to vary under certain conditions).

However, even before putting a model through its statistical paces, there are a number of features it should have that can be checked by a non-technician:

— All relevant factors should have been considered at the outset of the modelling (even if not included in the final model).

— The model should be theoretically sensible. Parameter values (the model's quantification of how the various factors impact on sales) should appear reasonable. Can a 1% increase in a particular factor really be expected to cause a 5% (say) increase in sales? This often requires particular vigilance where there are trends in distribution.

— It should capture the turning points in sales.

— It should have no tendency to under or over-predict sales at high or low points or for any more than a few data points in succession.

— It should not be obvious that the model fits the sales data much better over one part of the sample period than the remainder.

There are thus a great many things to check, which inevitably takes time. It can take longer to build and validate the models for a paper than to write the main body of the paper itself.

THE LEVEL OF STATISTICAL VALIDATION INCLUDED IN THE 1998 PAPERS

The level of statistical validation submitted with the models was generally much improved, though not all models included the requisite detail. As a group, the agency models had a higher average level of documentation, though where the consultant/research company models were well-documented a high standard was provided.

Not supplying technical detail can only count against a model. On the basis of an actual and fitted graph it is generally straightforward for an experienced practitioner to spot potential problems. Without a proper technical appendix there is nothing to explain any unusual features of the model or justify a particular course of action. There is thus nothing to counteract any resulting suspicions with respect to the model's validity.

Technical problems do not necessarily mean an automatic 'fail' for a model. It is appreciated that some markets are inherently much more difficult to model than others, due to their underlying movements or competitive structures or for reasons of data paucity. Where this is the case, it must be demonstrated that any statistical problems are not the source of material inaccuracies in the estimation of advertising's effects. The Pizza Hut paper deals with this situation well. Competitive data was limited and the results of some statistical tests were potentially consistent with a missing variable situation. However, an explanation of how this was checked and ruled out was provided.

There were numerical mistakes in the main body of a number of papers. It goes without saying that numerical accuracy is vital. Although proofreading a technical appendix is vile, getting a number wrong is not the same as a spelling error. A spell-checker will not pick it up and readers cannot unconsciously correct it. It will therefore be taken at face-value, whatever it says.

THEORETICAL VALIDATION

The construction of a few of the models did not accord immediately with theoretical intuition. Some were fairly standard least-squares regression models, while others relied on more obscure modelling, approaches which were not always well explained. If non-standard approaches or data manipulations are used and believed to be superior to more standard ones, it is advisable to provide an adequate explanation as to why this was done and the means by which the model has been validated. It may even be helpful to include references for the methodology.

Every effort was made to obtain a good understanding of the different types of analysis which were presented, and to determine whether each produced sensible estimates of advertising's effects. In some instances this involved algebraically determining either the exact functional form and interpretation of a model or its long-run steady-state solution (or the equilibrium conditions implied by the model). In others it involved mounting the model's mathematical structure on a spreadsheet in order to check the advertising response path it implied. One model, for example, included two lagged dependent variables. A curious technical reader wants to understand how these work together, but most crucially what they infer for the way advertising works. These theoretical checks complement the formal statistical checks and may lead to improvements in a model. They are things every modeller is urged to do for themselves.

THE 'STATE OF THE UNION'

The best econometric models submitted for previous Awards have always been rigorous, employing 'best practice' methods. However the general standard in the past was very variable. What has been achieved in 1998 is that this general standard has been considerably improved, while the documentation of models is also much better. In the wider world, econometrics has made great strides over the life of the awards. The reporting of a standard battery of model validation diagnostics is now routine rather than the exception and it is right that the awards follow this example. It would be nice in the next awards to see a few unit root tests applied where data is obviously trending.

In the past, many papers which supplied detailed technical appendices for the econometric analyses have tended to lose them at publication principally for reasons of space. (Technical appendices can be longer than the body of a paper itself.) This has meant that much of the technical development, derived from using econometric methods to quantify advertising effects, has reached only a very limited audience. Although publishing space may still be an issue and the technical details still a minority interest, by extending the proportion of papers which include detailed explanation of models, there is now a much better chance that ideas can be shared and built on via the IPA's database of papers.

There are still many opportunities to push the evaluation ball forward using econometrics. The area pursued by First Direct, investigating the way that different media work together, is a compelling one. Long-term effects still present the analyst with a substantial, although not intractable, challenge. Econometric methods are still only routinely used to quantify short and medium-term advertising effects (up to five years). Perhaps with the exception of Olivio, econometric analysis was not really used to pursue long-term effects in the 1998 competition. Maybe everyone's sights were on the 'beyond sales' ball.

With respect to long-term effects, there are undoubtedly obstacles to overcome. However, oddly enough, it is not the inability of econometric techniques but often the lack of a precise enough hypothesis of how advertising influences the consumer over the very long term which prevents long-term effects being measured.

There is another area which is becoming increasingly interesting. Models are now constructed using many different data sources and different data frequencies. Can different frequency datasets tell us different things about advertising or are the results which they generate a function of the nature of the data used?

Innovation requires creativity so perhaps we should reinterpret a comment made by Charles Channon in one of the early volumes of Advertising Works as a spur to greater artistry. Namely: 'econometrics is art in the domain of science'. After all, we have the tools to validate our creations.

Section 5

One-Star Winners

Boots Advantage Card

SUMMARY

This case demonstrates the benefits of using advertising in conjunction with the new form of retail competition – the loyalty card – to create an emotional relationship with its users.

Differentiating Boots Advantage Card

The mid 1990s saw the explosion of a 'new' retail marketing tool – the loyalty card. About 150 retailers now have one and, like a price war, it is a difficult game to win, and an even tougher one to stay out of.

Such has been their expansion, and subsequent penetration, that the City view such retailer schemes as a 'zero sum game'. Not everyone thinks that they work, seeing them simply as a discounting device or defensive mechanism.

Boots The Chemists disagreed, seeing the potential of a loyalty card as an intelligent marketing tool that could contribute to profitable growth, strengthen their relationship with important customers, enhance brand values and help further distinguish them from competition.

There were, however, three major handicaps to overcome when they decided to enter the loyalty stakes:

— being effectively last to the starting gate;

— slower points accumulation compared to grocery shopping (due to smaller trip frequency and basket size – £6 versus £40);

— a huge potential card base – as 60% of Britons shop at Boots every month and almost everybody does at Christmas – what if everyone applied?

The fact that the launch date of the card coincided precisely with the death of the Princess of Wales, which resulted in one of the most massively debilitating weeks in British retailing, might make you think the project was jinxed from the outset.

However, this case demonstrates how an advertising-led, emotionally differentiated 'indulgence' positioning for the Boots Advantage Card, communicated through a focused national campaign to get the new service off to a flying start.

Results

The Boots Advantage Card, far from jumping on the bandwagon, has been able to break the 'loyalty cycle' whereby programmes are launched, reviled (remember 'electronic green shield stamps'?) copied, become commonplace and, finally, simply the cost of doing business. It has achieved this via:

— Higher than average AI scores and increased intention to get a card.

— Selective recruitment of card holders, avoiding simply deal seekers.

— Faster card sign up and usage.

— Reactivation of card use even after dropping the reward levels.

— Sales increase worth over £100 million in the targeted categories.

Payback

Since the launch of the Advantage Card the market capitalisation of Boots has grown by 19% to £8.48 billion. This performance is broadly in line with the FT All-Share Index, over the period. The strong incremental BTC sales growth attributable directly to the Advantage Card has more than compensated for certain less positive factors (such as low medicine sales due to a mild winter and the largest industrial fire in post-war Britain).

Chicago Town Pizza

SUMMARY

This case study sets out to demonstrate the contribution made by advertising in transforming the fortunes of a relatively unknown, but ambitious, young brand, the impact of which helped carry it from fourth position within the main meal frozen pizza market, to brand leadership within a remarkably short space of time.

A Tough Market in which to Become a Leader

The opportunity for what was a relatively new manufacturer with a previously unknown and unsupported American pizza brand, at first, seemed limited.

Own label already accounted for 60% of the market. The remaining 40% was dominated by brands from four major, well established manufacturers, all of which received advertising support.

The brand was initially launched in 1992 without advertising support and achieved reasonable success through aggressive trade marketing, product development and pricing. By the end of 1994, due to competitive pressure, growth had reached a plateau.

The decision was made to support the brand in earnest for 1996. This recognised the necessity for advertising, if the brand was to achieve its long-term objective of brand leadership.

The role for advertising was clearly evident. For the brand to gain in saliency and trial, the brand's positioning and personality would need to be communicated in such a way as to gain distinction and differentiation in a heavily supported marketplace.

The brand's original positioning of 'The Authentic American Pizza', combined with the fact that the brand was also 'America's Best Selling Frozen Pizza', form the bedrock of the advertising direction.

Results

The brand not only recaptured its place as the leading American pizza brand, but achieved the primary objective of total main meal market leadership during this time.

At the time of this entry being submitted, the Chicago Town Pizza is still the brand's leader, with the highest level of loyalty in the market.

Payback

Advertising's contribution to Chicago Town's resurgence has been outstanding. Despite immense competitive pressure, total sales attributable to advertising activity were £12.5 million at RSP.

This compared with a total expenditure level, including media, production and research of under £2 million.

Even though we are unable to divulge detail on margins and profitability, we can confidently state that its contribution is far in excess of the investment made.

Direct Debit

SUMMARY

In 1985, Direct Debit was a pretty unpopular way to pay regular bills. Today it is actively used by 79% of the adult population. Direct Debit has come a long way, and the advertising strategy has evolved as the service has matured. This case evaluates the effect not of one campaign but of several, and shows that the consistent use of advertising has helped to drive Direct Debit to a level of popularity that was previously thought impossible.

Advertising's Role in Supporting Direct Debit

This is the story of a financial service that since 1985 has saved British industry £3.6 billion. In 1997 alone, it saved bill paying consumers 640 million hours. We will show that advertising for Direct Debit was responsible for £700 million of these financial savings.

This is an unusual case in other ways too. While the impact of advertising on consumer attitudes is a key part of the tale, advertising originally arose from the need to support direct marketing and this role has continued ever since. Advertising Direct Debit has always been part of a comprehensive media campaign, the main components of which are advertising, direct marketing and public relations; campaigns that have involved hundreds of organisations and millions of mailing. In 1997, for example, consumers were presented with 146 million opportunities to sign a Direct Debit from 478 organisations.

The other effects of advertising are less obvious but no less important. Direct Debit is a mass-market consumer product, but the structure that supports it is far from straightforward. It is offered by companies and the banking industry, who work together to support the service. BACS (formerly Bankers Automated Clearing Services) is the UK's automated clearing house and acts on behalf of the banking industry to not only process Direct Debits but also to co-ordinate marketing. However, along with its shareholders and members (the UK banks and building societies), it can only influence the Direct Debit marketing of other organisations by gaining their co-operation.

Yet a series of successful advertising campaigns has provided a platform for persuasion, enabling a co-ordination of communications and the provision of advice in a way that would not otherwise have been possible.

Advertising has driven the climate in which a range of marketing activities have been able to flourish, compounding its impact on Direct Debit volumes. Its catalytic effects have been substantial.

Results

In sum, the effects of advertising have been manifold. Apart from saving enormous costs, 12 years of advertising has:

— helped to win over the hearts and minds of a sceptical British public;

— increased the effectiveness of mailings by 30%;

— increased distribution campaign periods by over 50%;

— improved the quality of Direct Debit mailings and supporting literature;

— created a climate of positive opinion for the launch of new marketing initiatives.

Payback

Despite modest budgets and focused periods of activity, the savings to British industry have been enormous, quite apart from savings to the banking industry itself. Advertising has paid for itself more than 40 times over.

Impulse

SUMMARY

In 1995 Impulse was in long-term decline; its target audience no longer considered it relevant. But within two years it reversed its slump. By restoring relevance to the brand, advertising has been instrumental in revitalising Impulse.

This case shows advertising's contribution to short and long-term sales upturn. Also, for the first time, we show a new method of quantifying the way many intuitively believe advertising works, using financial options.

Why Impulse Needed to Rediscover its Relevance

Impulse bodyspray is a dual-function deodorant and fragrance. Its core audience is young women. In its 1980s heyday, Impulse had a 12% share of deodorants and 50% share of bodysprays.

Improvements over time in both the deodorant and fine fragrance sectors put bodysprays under pressure. Inactive against the threat, Impulse lost relevance. By 1995 it had a 6.4% share of deodorants.

Improving the product
New, higher quality fragrances and packaging were developed for a 1996 relaunch.

Managing the variants
In order to launch variants successfully, the brand needed to be able to capitalise on current trends. The new 1996 variant O$_2$ did this successfully.

Repositioning the brand
The ability to exploit trends demands a strong brand base. We needed consumers to feel ownership of the brand again, through rebuilding the key measure of closeness.

Closeness to the brand was low; for years advertising had offered no reason to re-appraise it. However research showed that an underlying consumer relationship still endured.

The key insight for advertising was the persevering validity of the message: 'Men can't help acting on Impulse'.

However we needed to create advertising different and motivating enough to provoke consumers to reappraise the brand.

Results

Two new executions, 'Cars' and 'Artschool', improved brand perceptions significantly. At 80%, enjoyment of 'Artschool' was double Impulse's previous average. Claimed usage by the core 16 to 24 target has grown to an all-time high of 80%.

Against the key measure, 'closeness', Impulse more than doubled, from 20% to 45% (more than twice the closeness of its nearest competitor).

Payback

Ogilvy & Mather's advertising has created incremental value for Impulse worth at least £17.6 million since 1995. Value has been created in three ways:

— Econometric modelling shows the new campaign has increased short-term sales both directly and through launching new variants.

— Revitalising the brand was critical to its success. We have estimated the additional brand value of £4.4 million created by the advertising through its effect on recent successful new variant launches.

— By re-establishing the brand's relevance, the advertising has widened the strategic options open to the Impulse brand, particularly to launch future variants. The value of this additional brand flexibility is quantified at £3.8 million by making innovative use of the methods used to price financial options.

Littlewoods Pools

SUMMARY

This paper demonstrates the importance of focus and in particular focus on a brand's roots when faced with growing and massive competitive threat.

Facing a Vicious Circle of Decline

The launch of the National Lottery in November 1994 had a dramatic impact on Littlewoods Pools' revenue. By December 1995, weekly remittances had declined form £16 million to £9 million.

The forecast pointed to a terminal decline for Littlewoods:

— It was losing valuable regular players.

— As players left, the prize pool diminished, rendering the game less attractive.

— As players stopped playing, coupon collectors (paid on commission) stopped collecting; hence the very means of entry was disappearing.

To stimulate involvement, advertising needed to reverse this vicious circle and both reawaken a desire to play among players, and to give collectors the impression that players had a renewed interest in the game.

To breathe life into Littlewoods Pools, we decided to revisit its roots, and bring back a dimension to the game that had been largely ignored for years – football.

Results

There was clear evidence of an uplift in brand involvement after the advertising, particularly among our primary target of weekly players.

Changes in claimed behaviour were also encouraging: The decline in claimed participation slowed, and the average claimed stake grew.

An analysis of weekly remittance data provided a preliminary indication of an advertising effect. We could demonstrate that advertising was saving the company £70,000 per week.

We then fitted a trendline to remittance figure to project what would have been expected to happen without the advertising. Comparing this projection to actual remittances from when the advertising began, showed an apparent saving of £49 million.

Although this was encouraging, we know that this analysis greatly underestimated advertising's contribution, as the projections were inflated by data which included the August uplift in business generated by the start of the 1995 football season.

Econometric modelling was then used to calculate advertising's actual contribution, and to factor out the influence of other possible elements that might be having an effect.

Payback

This econometric analysis demonstrated that the 'Get a Result' campaign saved Littlewoods £120 million in remittances. This represented a return on funds invested of over 1000%.

By apportioning these 'savings', we could show that it yielded specific financial benefits to individual stakeholders (for example, the collector network – £15.2 million; the Football Trust – £3.6 million).

The paper also demonstrates that the saving made by the advertising protected jobs for Littlewoods Leisure. The funds also contributed a significant amount to the division's operating cashflow. We calculated that the advertising protected £104.9m in cashflow for the company. These funds represented approximately 17% of the division's total turnover over the period of evaluation and created an investment fund for the future, for example, a full-scale telephone Pools betting system and a new fixed-odds sports telephone betting service.

Finally, the football repositioning for the brand provided a renewed focus to Littlewoods, so that the company can now approach new football-related gambling ventures outside the Pools franchise with a feeling of greater confidence.

Marmoleum

SUMMARY

This paper demonstrates how Forbo-Nairn, the last remaining UK manufacturer of Linoleum, asked advertising to revive interest in a product that had all but disappeared off the consumer map by creating a new brand around the old product promise.

Relaunching an Old Product as a New Brand

The company have manufactured Linoleum since 1850 and are the last remaining UK manufacturer. With 90% UK market share they 'are' the market. Since the 1950s, sales of Linoleum in the UK have declined steadily, losing share to both vinyl and carpet.

In the face of this decline, Forbo-Nairn successfully relaunched Linoleum to the contract market with a new brand called 'Marmoleum'. This success led Forbo-Nairn to consider relaunching Linoleum to the consumer.

Research identified that there was a gap in the market for a resilient floorcovering that was both stylish and durable; not just attractive but also easy to maintain. For this 'new promise', women would be prepared to pay a premium.

Despite the brand name 'Marmoleum' and its similarity to Linoleum, the advertising was designed to dissociate Marmoleum from Linoleum's unhelpful baggage, yet at the same time give new life to pre-existing product truths.

Results and Payback

In 1996 Linoleum was relaunched via a three-month test market on a spend in press of £48,676. The advertising generated a retail sales value of £150,000, which is a 50% excess on target and represents a payback of 308% on the advertising investment.

The campaign was rolled out nationally on a press spend of £320,773, resulting in 8,103 telephone enquiries and over 16,000 direct enquiries, and £1,369,550 retail sales. Payback on the second stage of the advertising investment was 427%.

In addition to sales effects, the consumer advertising has had a significant impact on the contract market, contributing estimated sales in excess of £200,000.

In response to the interest in Marmoleum, Forbo-Nairn have also developed a brand extension of Marmoleum in the form of a lower spec product with a value for money positioning. Forbo Group also plans to launch Marmoleum in the USA, Australia and Switzerland on the back of its UK success.

All in all, a product that was in long-term decline is now in growth and facing a bright future. It is almost impossible to imagine that this reversal of fortune would have occurred without belief and investment in advertising, which laid the past to rest and reinvented Linoleum.

Health Education Board for Scotland

SUMMARY

This case shows how real information can be used to motivate real changes in attitude and behaviour and so demonstrates advertising's value in saving people's lives and government money.

Overcoming the Barriers to Regular Exercise

In 1995, the Health Education Board for Scotland (HEBS) identified the need to increase adult participation in physical exercise.

Research had identified that regular moderate activity (not just vigorous exercise) could offer enormous health benefits.

Unfortunately, the Scottish Health Survey identified that 53% of men and 62% of women acknowledged that they did not get sufficient regular exercise. And 23% of men and 26% of women undertook no moderate physical activity in an average week.

Qualitative research suggested that key barriers to physical activity lay in the received wisdom that physical exercise is:

— For the young.

— Only does you good if it is vigorous exercise (the 'no pain; no gain' mentality).

— Involves too much time and money (gyms and so on).

It was important to find a way of re-positioning physical exercise as easy to do and as something that does not require money.

Qualitative research was used to examine a range of propositions. The proposition that emerged was:

> 'Walking a mile uses as many calories as running a mile.'

The creative task was to find a credible way of communicating that walking a mile was a 'real' form of exercise.

Gavin Hastings was, at the time, captain of the Scottish rugby team and a popular TV personality. In pre-testing he was seen to be an appropriate spokesman who provided the necessary credibility to the 'new news' facts.

Results

— Advertising awareness levels rose to 70%.

— The commercial challenged the target group's perception that exercise was for 'others' and showed that walking was a 'real' form of exercise. After the campaign 56% were convinced that walking was a genuine form of exercise compared to 20% before.

— It stimulated significant changes in knowledge and attitudes about the health related benefits of walking among adults in Scotland.

— It generated 4, 036 calls to *Fitline* over a five-week period.

— At the ten-week follow up, 50% of respondents stated that they were more physically active than they had been before the campaign. Of this group 94% reported increasing their frequency of walking.

— The General Household Survey shows that while other forms of exercise do not show an increase in claimed four-weekly participation, walking increased from 41% to 45%.

— TGI information suggests that there was a difference before and after the campaign in Scotland that was not demonstrated in England.

Payback

Even at the most conservative estimate, it would appear that there was a return on investment in excess of 500%, and an incalculable human value in preventing premature deaths.

Learning from 20 Years of Effectiveness Cases

Peter Field
IPA Data Bank

This is the tenth biennial IPA Advertising Effectiveness Awards competition. The 54 cases submitted in 1998 now take their place alongside the previous 638 cases in the IPA hall of fame – the Data Bank. With 20 years of advertising evaluation covering just about every market you can think of, this is the most comprehensive and valuable database of advertising effectiveness anywhere in the world. Happily, it is not gathering dust in the vaults of 44 Belgrave Square – it is a hardworking Data Bank, regularly accessed by practitioners, their clients and academics. In 1998 the IPA received around 800 search enquiries and subsequently sold 420 copies of past effectiveness papers – a record on both counts. In addition, the IPA has licensed the entire Data Bank to the World Advertising Research Center, whose subscribers may search and download papers via the Internet. Never before has the Data Bank been so useful or so well used.

The Data Bank reflects an important aspect of the spirit of the 1998 Awards. It was a concern that, while the Awards are, quite rightly, a celebration of success for the best papers entered, they have appeared to downplay the valuable contribution to learning played by the less successful papers. The new star system of awards in 1998 was an attempt to put this right. The Data Bank goes a step further by giving equal prominence and access to all papers, whether Grand Prix winners or non-awarded papers. All have great value, so all have a place. In so doing, we particularly hope to encourage entrants to submit papers regardless of whether or not they have sufficient evidence to win a major prize. In intellectual as well as meritorious terms, the Awards are not a 'winner takes all' competition.

This year, for the new papers, the IPA has dramatically improved the classification and search fields available. This will not only enable more precise searching of the papers, but also it will allow us, for the first time, to look quantitatively for patterns in the details of the case studies. The IPA will therefore possess an unbeatable research tool to examine the validity of the numerous models and theories of advertising effectiveness. Hopefully the Data Bank will spawn an ever better theoretical understanding, among practitioners, academics and clients alike, of how advertising works.

The improvements to the Data Bank also reflect the new emphasis in the Awards on assessing the manifold effects of advertising. So researchers will be able to search for papers that explore effects on employee productivity and satisfaction, investor confidence, supplier commitment and so on. These kinds of measures are not absent from earlier papers, but they are more rare – prior to 1998 there were, for instance, only 13 papers that looked at staff productivity and morale. The British Airways paper (1994) pioneered the use of brand valuation in the Awards and demonstrated just how powerful, at the corporate and shareholder level, the payback from advertising can be. This tool was developed further in the Orange paper (1996) and elegantly refined yet further in the 1998 sequel paper. Arguably the AA paper (1996) pioneered the exploration of the qualitative effect of advertising on staff morale, although credit is due to TSB (1986/88) for its study of staff productivity and Allied Dunbar (1990) for staff retention. The GLC paper (1986) remains, a dozen years on, the definitive guide to monitoring the PR impact of advertising on press coverage and content.

As intended, the 1998 Awards prompted a flurry of innovation in the measurement of the manifold effects of advertising beyond sales-related profits – inevitably with varying degrees of success. However, I would recommend all would-be manifold effects measurers to study the following papers, starred winners and nonwinners, from the 1998 Awards.

— **Christian Aid**: explored the effect of advertising on collector productivity and morale.

— **Ford Galaxy and Orange**: examined in new depth the effect of advertising on the market capitalisation and added shareholder value of the company.

— **KFC**: shed valuable light on advertising's effect on franchisee support and investment.

— **Littlewoods Pools**: demonstrated advertising's effect on employment, Government tax revenues and donations to good causes.

— **One2One**: made use of staff surveys to demonstrate advertising value.

— **Bacardi Breezer**: looked at sales-force loyalty and the economic benefit of the advertising to the local community around the bottling plant.

— **The Meat and Livestock Commission**: revealed the effect of advertising right along the value chain.

— **Impulse**: broke new ground using a technique borrowed from the financial options market to value the effect of advertising on reducing the risk of new variant launches.

— **VW and Audi**: both examined the effect of advertising on second-hand prices and hence retained value to owners – a less obvious, but important driver of company profits in the long term, given the customer loyalty to the two marques. VW also assessed the value of advertising on dealer motivation while Audi demonstrated a significant impact on dealer profitability.

Taken together, the 1998 papers demonstrate very successfully the multitude of ways in which advertising can add value to companies. I hope that this will encourage greater interest in the Data Bank and that the Millennium awards will add even more to this new body of knowledge.

KEY LESSONS FROM THE DATA BANK

The Data Bank has already provided much source material for training courses and seminars and has contributed greatly to the science of effectiveness evaluation. It is worth looking back over the Data Bank as a whole to see what lessons can be learnt about evaluation.

An obvious and increasingly important lesson is the need to demonstrate that advertising boosts profits, not merely sales or other non-financial measures. As the marketing and advertising communities strive to build the case for advertising investment to increasingly accountancy-orientated senior client management, such demonstration becomes ever more important. Small wonder, then, that the level of prize awarded appears to reflect whether papers can show a profit impact (see Table 1).

TABLE 1: PERCENTAGE OF PAPERS DEMONSTRATING PROFIT IMPACT

Prize won	Papers demonstrating profit impact (%)
Grand Prix	56
Gold/First	45
Silver/Second	41
Bronze/Third	35
All awarded	39
Non-awarded	26

Another conclusion that can be drawn is that while it is desirable to demonstrate advertising standout as a means of asserting effectiveness, it is neither necessary nor sufficient as proof of effectiveness (see Table 2).

TABLE 2: PERCENTAGE OF PAPERS DEMONSTRATING
ADVERTISING STANDOUT

Prize won	Papers demonstrating advertising standout (%)
Grand Prix	67
Gold/First	48
Silver/Second	61
Bronze/Third	74
All awarded	54
Non-awarded	23

This will hopefully encourage agencies and clients alike to look beyond simplistic tracking study measures of advertising impact as a proxy for effectiveness. From the IPA perspective, the use of advertising tracking alone does not qualify as creating an effectiveness culture.

In lieu of the more sophisticated analyses of the Data Bank that are going to become possible, a crude analysis of award winners already implies something very interesting about the way advertising most powerfully influences consumer behaviour. By reading the award-winning papers or by inspection of the advertising (where necessary) they can be categorised in three ways: by whether the advertising principally used rational persuasion (that is, changing knowledge), non-rational persuasion (that is, changing feelings) or both equally. The results confirm the views of many practitioners, and offer a tantalising glimpse of the riches that will be available in the Data Bank.

TABLE 3: TYPE OF PERSUASION USED IN PAPERS

Persuasion used	Papers (%)
Largely rational	18
Rational and non-rational	23
Largely non-rational	59

The Data Bank clearly suggests that non-rational persuasion is more likely to be linked to demonstrably effective advertising than rational persuasion (see Table 3). It does not suggest that using both is inadvisable, merely that it is rare to have the luxury of both. Many top prizewinners fall in the middle category. In the future, with the new improvements in the classification of papers, it will be possible to take this analysis still further.

The Data Bank also teaches us something about the limitations of research. It perhaps suggests that quantitative advertising testing falls far short of being a guarantee of effectiveness: not only because its use does not appear to correlate with demonstrable effectiveness, but also because it appears to correlate negatively with a paper's ability to demonstrate effectiveness (see Table 4).

TABLE 4: PERCENTAGE OF PAPERS USING QUANTATIVE TESTING

Prize won	Papers using quantative testing (%)
Grand Prix	11
Gold/First	26
Silver/Second	34
Bronze/Third	45
All awarded	32
Non-awarded	33

Perhaps this is not surprising given the earlier finding of the importance of non-rational persuasion in advertising effectiveness. Quantitative research, whether pre-testing, post-testing or tracking, still appears to struggle to measure the status and communication of non-rational persuasion messages. There are more examples in the Data Bank of authors 'making do' with inadequate quantitative research measures than there are examples of the use of elegant measures. Quantitative research is commonly still asking respondents to think (rationally) about whether they associate a brand with a non-rational purchase motivation. At best the resulting data is likely to be a blunt instrument; at worst it may be misleading. Perhaps that is why there appears to be a tendency in papers where non-rational persuasion has predominated, for overall predisposition shifts alone to be reported: there is less illustration of softer intermediary measures of advertising effect in these papers. This outcome neither helps us to learn how advertising works nor how better to demonstrate that it does. This is regrettable. Yet, between 1980 and 1996 the incidence of quantitative testing of advertising in IPA papers more than doubled. Hopefully the research industry will in future rise to the challenge of the knowledge emerging from the Data Bank.

Analysis of the most successful papers demonstrates that to prove effectiveness beyond doubt, you need multiple measures of effect. Our aim should be to achieve what Simon Broadbent, the father of the awards, referred to as 'spotlights on a statue from different angles'. Thus, Grand Prix winners on average use 40% more measures of effect than non-winners; an observation nicely demonstrated by the resourceful winner of the 1998 Grand Prix.

PROMISING SIGNS FROM THE PAPERS

Encouragingly, the awards entrants *have* been rising to the challenge set by Simon Broadbent: the average number of 'standard' measures used in papers approximately tripled between 1980 and 1996, and the measurement of manifold effects is likely to push this still higher. This trend towards more sophisticated metrics is good for agencies and their clients who need to justify communications investment to sceptical financial managers.

Perhaps what is most encouraging is the way that, over the years, econometric modelling has been embraced by agencies. In 1980 it was a misunderstood and feared 'black art', used only by 9% of papers. By 1996 it was a familiar friend to many planners, used in 38% of papers. More importantly, it has helped to drive more sophisticated analysis of the impact of advertising. In 1980 only 5% of papers demonstrated the value of advertising in supporting price. This rose to 24% in 1996. Commensurately, the proportion of papers demonstrating profitable payback rose from 15% to 62%. No one can now fairly criticise the papers for lack of profit focus. The challenge for future papers will be to extend this rigour to the manifold effects of advertising, for which profit impact can be very difficult to evaluate.

The 1998 papers used a greater variety of measures of advertising effect than we have seen before; employee surveys, customer satisfaction surveys, city analysts' shareholder value measures and so on. The papers have also made greater use of academic research and theory for models and norms. I hope this continues and that planners end their self-imposed exile from the wealth of learning residing in our academic institutions. But most of all I hope that the IPA Data Bank continues to consolidate its position as the pre-eminent authority on how advertising *really* works. Many papers have used the Data Bank itself as a normative reference point for evaluation and to substantiate their arguments. The Data Bank is there to be used to support and generate beliefs – I urge you to do so.

How to Access the IPA Data Bank

The IPA Advertising Effectiveness Data Bank represents the most rigorous and comprehensive examination of advertising working in the marketplace, in the world. Over the 18 years of the IPA Advertising Effectiveness Awards Competition (1980 to 1998), the IPA has collected over 650 examples of best practice in advertising development and results across a wide spectrum of marketing sectors and expenditures. Each example contains 4,000 words of text and is illustrated in full by market, research, sales and profit data. Now the IPA is giving access to this material via a new IPA computer system.

HOW IT WORKS

Using a sophisticated PC database, every case history is comprehensively indexed according to an evolving classification. The classification interrogates each case history against a set of pre-selected criteria. For example, the case material can be can crossreferenced on the criteria of target audience, medium, marketing objective, marketing measures of effectiveness, advertising strategy and so on. Any number of variables can be used.

Once these are chosen, you will be sent an accurate, timesaving printout of the case history titles most relevant to your needs. From this, you will be able to choose those you would be most interested in seeing in full. A more limited version of this database is located on the IPA Internet site at http://www.ipa.co.uk. Again, case histories can be cross referenced against broader criteria such as author, agency, client, brand name and product category. An order form can be filled in as different case histories are selected, and e-mailed, on lesley@ipa.co.uk, directly to the IPA.

WHAT IT COSTS

We will happily do searches on the Data Bank free of charge but, if you decide to purchase, the individual case histories cost £20.00 each (inclusive of postage and packaging in the UK only). Please note that pre-payment is required, either by sterling cheque made payable to the IPA and drawn on a UK bank, or by the full range of credit cards.

For IPA member agencies only, we offer a 'virtual money' scheme whereby the agency has its own account at the IPA, which can be debited to purchase case histories, IPA Publications or IPA Appraisals, or to cover the cost of events organised by the IPA Society or the Information Forum. The agency can credit its account at any time and also receive statements on request. For further details of the virtual money scheme contact Mark Rasdall at mark@ipa.co.uk.

HOW TO INTERROGATE THE DATA BANK

You can choose from any number of the following variables: brand, advertiser, agency, target market (by age, sex, class, and so on), medium (primary and secondary), category (new products, small budgets, longer and broader effects, and so on), market segment, other marketing activity, market measure used for evaluation, length of activity, type of advertising strategy change and marketing objective.

For further information, please contact Lesley Scott at the Institute of Practitioners in Advertising, 44 Belgrave Square, London SWIX 8QS. Telephone: +44 (0)171 235 7020. Fax: 0171 245 9904. Internet: http://www.ipa.co.uk, or email: lesley@ipa.co.uk

AN ALTERNATIVE ROUTE TO THE DATABANK

The IPA Case Histories Data Bank can also be accessed through the World Advertising Research Center (WARC). Reached by logging on to www.WARC.com, the world's most comprehensive database enables readers to search the IPA Case Histories and thousands of other essential reference works by subject matter, author, date or virtually any other selection criteria. Sources include the Advertising Research Foundation, Canadian Congress of Advertising, *Admap*, and the American Assocation of Advertising Agencies as well as the IPA. WARC is being continually developed and expanded and will soon feature papers from ESOMAR, the Direct Marketing Association (US) and the Association des Agences Conseils en Communication.

Further information on the World Advertising Research Center can be obtained from editor@warc.com, by writing to WARC, Farm Road, Henley-on-Thames, Oxfordshire RG9 1EJ, UK, or by telephoning +44 (0)1491 418 639.

IPA Data Bank Case Availability

B

1988	Baby Fresh
1988	Babycham
1996	Bacardi Breezer
1992	Bailey's
1988	Barbican
1990	Barbican Health & Fitness Centre
1996	Barclaycard*
1992	Barclaycard
1994	Batchelors
1986	Benylin*
1990	Billy Graham's Mission 89
1986	Birds Eye Alphabites*
1992	Birds Eye Country Club Cuisine
1994	Birds Eye Crispy Chicken
1982	Birds Eye Oven Crispy Cod Steaks in Batter*
1988	Birmingham Executive Airways
1990	Black Tower
1996	Blockbuster Video
1982	Blue Riband
1994	BMW*
1994	Boddington's*
1990	Bodyform
1994	Book Club Associates
1988	Boots Brand Medicines
1994	Boursin
1986	Bovril
1990	Bradford & Bingley Building Society
1986	Bradford & Bingley Building Society*
1980	Braun Shavers
1982	Bread Advisory Council*
1982	Breville Toasted Sandwichmaker
1996	British Airways
1994	British Airways*
1984	British Airways Shuttle Service
1994	British Diabetic Association*
1980	British Film Institute*
1994	British Gas Central Heating
1988	British Gas Flotation*
1988	British Nuclear Fuels
1988	British Rail Young Persons' Railcard
1982	British Sugar Corporation
1980	British Turkey Federation
1992	BT
1986	BT Consumer*
1996	BT Business*
1994	BT Business
1992	BT Call Waiting*
1986	BT Privatisation*
1988	Budweiser
1980	BUPA
1996	Butter Council

C

1996	Cable Television
1994	Cadbury's Boost*
1992	Cadbury's Caramel

1988	Cadbury's Creme Eggs
1984	Cadbury's Creme Eggs
1992	Cadbury's Crunchie
1984	Cadbury's Curly Wurly*
1980	Cadbury's Dairy Box
1982	Cadbury's Flake
1984	Cadbury's Fudge*
1994	Cadbury's Highlights
1990	Cadbury's Mini Eggs
1994	Cadbury's Roses*
1986	Cadbury's Wispa
1988	Cafe Hag
1996	Californian Raisins
1980	Campari*
1988	Campbell's Meatballs*
1992	Campbell's Condensed Soup
1994	Campbell's Soup
1996	Cancer Relief Macmillan Fund
1984	Canderel
1994	Car Crime Prevention
1992	Caramac
1996	Carling Black Label
1994	Carling Black Label
1984	Carousel
1986	Castlemaine xxxx*
1992	Cellnet Callback
1992	Central Television Licence Renewal
1988	Center-Parcs
1990	Champagne Lanson*
1990	Charlton Athletic Supporters Club*
1996	Cheltenham & Gloucester Building Society
1980	Cheese Information Service
1988	Chessington World of Adventures
1994	Chicken Tonight
1994	Child Road Safety
1992	Childhood Diseases Immunisation
1990	Children'sWorld
1984	Chip Pan Fires Prevention*
1990	Choosy Catfood*
1992	Christian Aid
1994	CICA*
1992	Citroen Diesel Range
1988	Clairol Nice n' Easy
1988	Clarks Desert Boots*
1996	Classic Combination Catalogue
1994	Clerical Medical
1992	Clorets
1988	Clover
1984	Clover
1990	Colman's Wholegrain Mustard
1996	The Cooperative Bank
1994	The Cooperative Bank*
1980	Cointreau
1990	Copperhead Cider
1986	Country Manor (Cakes)
1982	Country Manor (Alcoholic Drink)
1984	Cow & Gate Babymeals*

1982	Cracottes*
1992	Le Creuset
1990	Croft Original*
1982	Croft Original
1980	Croft Original
1990	Crown Solo*
1982	Le Crunch
1984	Cuprinol*
1986	Cyclamon*

D

1996	Daewoo*
1982	Daily Mail*
1992	Danish Bacon & Meat Council
1980	Danum Taps
1990	Data Protection Registrar
1980	Day Nurse
1994	Daz
1996	De Beers Diamonds*
1980	Deep Clean*
1980	Dettol*
1984	DHL Worldwide Carrier
1992	Direct Line Insurance*
1990	Dog Registration
1980	Dream Topping
1988	Drinking & Driving
1994	Dunfermline Building Society
1980	Dunlop Floor Tiles
1990	Duracell Batteries
1980	Dynatron Music Suite

E

1988	E & P Loans*
1992	The Economist*
1994	The Edinburgh Club*
1990	Edinburgh Zoo
1980	Eggs Authority
1992	Electricity Privatisation
1980	Ellerman Travel & Leisure
1996	Emergency Contraception
1986	EMI Virgin (records)*
1980	English Butter Marketing Company
1986	English Country Cottages
1992	The Enterprise Initiative
1992	Equity & Law
1990	Eurax
1994	Evening Standard Classified Recruitment
1984	Exbury Gardens

F

1990	Family Credit
1982	Farmer's Table Chicken
1996	Felix*
1980	Ferranti CETEC
1990	The Fertilizer Manufacturers' Association

1982	Fiat Auto UK
1980	Findus Crispy Pancakes
1988	Findus French Bread Pizza & Crispy Pancakes*
1992	Findus Lasagne
1984	Fine Fare
1982	Fine Fare*
1994	Fona Dansk Elektrik
1996	First Choice Holidays
1992	First Direct
1992	Flowers and Plants Association
1980	Ford Fiesta
1986	Ford Granada*
1982	Ford Model Range
1980	Foster Grant
1984	Foster's
1982	Frish*
1996	Frizzell Insurance*
1994	Fruit-tella

G

1986	General Accident
1992	Gini*
1986	Glasgow's Lord Provost
1986	GLC's Anti 'Paving Bill' Campaign*
1996	Glow-worm Central Heating
1996	Gold Blend*
1988	Gold Spot
1984	Golden Wonder Instant Pot Snacks*
1980	Goodyear Grandprix
1984	Grant's Whisky
1992	Green Giant
1988	Green Science
1988	Greene King IPA
1990	Greenpeace
1982	The Guardian
1996	Guinness Book of Records
1990	Guinness (Draught) in Cans

H

1990	H. Samuel
1992	Haagen-Dazs*
1994	Halifax Building Society
1992	Halifax Building Society
1982	Halifax Building Society
1980	Halifax Building Society Convertible Term Shares
1994	Halls Soothers*
1982	Hansa Lager
1994	Heineken Export
1980	Heinz Coleslaw
1980	Heinz Curried Beans
1984	Hellman's Mayonnaise*
1982	Henri Winterman's Special Mild
1996	Hep30
1992	Herta
1990	Herta
1980	Hoechst

1992 Hofels Garlic Pearles
1984 Hofmeister*
1984 Home Protection
1982 Home Protection
1990 Honda
1994 Horlicks
1986 Horlicks
1986 Hoverspeed
1996 Hovis
1992 Hovis
1984 Hudson Payne & Iddiols
1996 Huggies Nappies
1994 Hush Puppies

I

1996 I Can't Believe It's Not Butter!*
1992 Iceland Frozen Foods
1980 ICI
1984 ICI Dulux Natural Whites*
1992 IFAW*
1990 Imperial War Museum
1988 The Independent
1988 Insignia
1992 IPA Society
1992 Irn Bru
1982 International Business Show 1981
1990 International Wool Secretariat
1994 Israel Tourist Board

J

1994 Jeep Cherokee
1992 Jif
1988 Job Clubs
1982 John Smith's Bitter*
1994 John Smith's Bitter*

K

1992 K Shoes*
1992 Kaliber
1996 Kaliber
1990 Karvol
1980 Kays Catalogue
1992 Kellogg's All Bran*
1984 Kellogg's Bran Flakes*
1994 Kellogg's Coco Pops
1984 Kellogg's Coco Pops*
1982 Kellogg's Cornflakes
1980 Kellogg's Frozen Waffles
1980 Kellogg's Rice Crispies*
1982 Kellogg's Super Noodles*
1986 Kensington Palace*
1984 KFC
1988 Kia Ora*
1984 Kleenex Velvet
1990 Knorr Stock Cubes*
1988 Kodak Colour Print Film
1994 Kraft Dairylea

1984 Kraft Dairylea*
1980 Krona Margarine*
1986 Kronenbourg 1664

L

1990 Lada
1992 Ladybird
1980 Lea & Perrin's Worcestershire Sauce
1990 Lea & Perrin's Worcestershire Sauce*
1988 Leeds Permanent Building Society
1988 Lego
1984 Leicester Building Society
1992 Levi Strauss UK*
1980 Levi Strauss UK
1988 Levi's 501s*
1996 Lenor
1996 Lil-lets
1990 Lil-lets*
1996 Lilt
1992 Limelite*
1980 Limmits
1980 Lion Bar
1992 Liquorice Allsorts
1988 Liquorice Allsorts
1988 Listerine*
1980 Listerine
1992 Lloyds Bank
1984 Lloyds Bank*
1990 London Buses Driver Recruitment
1984 London Docklands*
1982 London Docklands
1990 London Philharmonic
1992 LonclonTransport Fare Evasion
1986 London Weekend Television
1980 Lucas Aerospace*
1992 Lucozade
1980 Lucozade*
1996 Lucky Lottery
1988 Lurpak
1994 Lyon's Maid Fab
1988 Lyon's Maid Favourite Centres

M

1988 Maclaren Prams
1990 Malibu
1988 Manpower Services Commission
1982 Manger's Sugar Soap*
1994 Marks & Spencer
1988 Marshall Cavendish Discovery
1994 Marston Pedigree*
1986 Mazda*
1986 Mazola*
1996 McDonald's
1980 McDougall's Saucy Sponge
1990 Mcpherson's Paints
1988 Mcpherson's Paints
1992 Mercury Communications
1988 Metropolitan Police Recruitment*

1990   Midland Bank
1988   Midland Bank
1992   Miele
1988   Miller Lite*
1988   The Mortgage Corporation*
1994   The Multiple Sclerosis Society
1984   Mr Muscle
1996   Murphy's Irish Stout*

N

1996   National Dairy Council – Milk*
1992   National Dairy Council – Milk
1980   National Dairy Council – Milk
1992   National Dairy Council – Milkman*
1996   National Lottery (Camelot)
1996   National Savings
1982   National Savings: Save by Post*
1984   National Savings: Income Bonds
1986   National Westminster Bank Loans
1982   Nationwide Building Society
1990   Nationwide Flex Account
1988   Nationwide Flex Account
1990   Navy Recruitment
1988   Nefax
1982   Negas Cookers
1982   Nescafé
1992   Neutrogena
1982   New Man Clothes
1980   New Zealand Meat Producers Board
1994   New Zealand Lamb
1996   Nike
1994   Nike
1994   Nissan Micra*
1986   No.7
1988   Norsk Data
1990   Nouvelle Toilet Paper
1990   Nurofen
1986   Nursing Recruitment
1994   Nytol

0

1980   The Observer French Cookery School
       Campaign
1988   Oddbins*
1982   Omega Chewing Gum
1992   Optrex*
1996   Orange*
1984   Oranjeboom
1990   Otrivine
1992   Oxo*
1990   Oxo
1988   Oxo
1988   Oxy 10

P

1986   Paignton Zoo
1988   Paracodol*

1984   Paul Masson California Carafes
1982   Pedal Cycle Casualties*
1994   Peperami*
1994   Pepsi Max
1990   Perrier
1986   Perrier
1990   PG Tips*
1996   Philadelphia*
1994   Philadelphia
1994   Phileas Fogg
1988   Phileas Fogg
1988   Phileas Fogg
1980   Philips Cooktronic
1980   Philips Video
1990   Le Piat D'or
1986   Le Piat D'or
1990   Pilkington Glass
1992   Pilsner
1986   Pink Lady
1996   Pirelli
1990   Pirelli
1986   Pirelli
1984   Pirelli
1996   Pizza Hut
1994   Pizza Hut
1990   Plax
1980   Plessey Communications & Data
       Systems
1994   The Police Federation of England and
       Wales
1996   Polo Mints
1984   Polyfoam
1986   Portsmouth News
1980   Post Office Mis-sorts
1986   Post Office Special Issue Stamps
1996   Potato Marketing Board
1984   Presto
1980   Pretty Polly*
1990   Price Waterhouse
1992   Prudential

Q

1984   QE2
1982   Qualcast Concorde Lawn Mower*
1984   Qualcast Mow-n-trim and Rotasafe
1986   Quatro
1986   Quickstart
1996   Quorn Burgers
1988   Quaker Harvest Chewy Bars*

R

1982   Racal Redec Cadet
1994   Radio Rentals
1990   Radio Rentals
1990   Radion Automatic*
1996   RAF Recruitment
1980   RAF Recruitment*
1994   Range Rover

1992	Real McCoys
1984	Red Meat Consumption
1988	Red Mountain*
1996	Reebok*
1992	Reebok
1990	Reliant Metrocabs
1994	Remegel
1990	Renault 19*
1986	Renault 5
1996	Renault Clio*
1992	Renault Clio*
1984	Renault Trafic & Master
1996	Ribena
1982	Ribena*
1986	Rimmel Cosmetics
1996	Rocky
1988	Rolls Royce Privatisation*
1996	Ross Harper*
1988	Rover 200
1982	Rowenta
1990	Rowntree's Fruit Gums
1992	Royal Bank of Scotland
1986	Royal College of Nursing
1986	Royal Mail Business Economy
1990	Royal National Institute for the Deaf
1996	RSPCA
1988	Rumbelows

S

1994	S4C
1988	Saab*
1996	Safeway
1996	Samaritans
1986	Sanatogen
1980	Sanatogen
1988	Sandplate*
1986	Sapur
1992	Save the Children*
1988	Schering Greene Science
1980	Scotcade
1984	Scotch Video Cassettes
1992	Scotrail
1992	Scottish Amicable*
1980	Seiko
1992	Sellafield Visitors Centre
1980	Shake 'n' Vac
1984	Shakers Cocktails*
1980	Shloer*
1986	Shredded Wheat
1996	Le Shuttle
1990	Silent Night Beds*
1992	Skol
1982	Skol
1980	Slumberdown Quilts
1990	Smarties
1980	Smirnoff Vodka
1980	Smith's Monster Munch
1982	Smith's Square Crisps

1992	Smith's Tudor Specials
1994	Smoke Alarms*
1992	Smoke Alarms
1996	So ...?
1986	Soft & Gentle
1996	Soldier Recruitment
1994	Solvent Abuse
1996	Solvite
1992	Sony
1988	Sony
1992	Sony Camcorders
1996	Springers by K
1984	St Ivel Gold*
1996	Stella Artois*
1992	Stella Artois*
1994	Strepsils*
1990	Strongbow
1982	Summers the Plumbers
1980	Sunblest Sunbran
1990	Supasnaps
1980	Swan Vestas*
1984	SWEB Security Systems
1992	Swinton Insurance
1996	Switch

T

1992	Tandon Computers
1990	Tango
1986	TCP*
1986	Teletext
1986	Territorial Army Recruitment
1980	Tesco
1990	Tetley Tea Bags
1984	Thomas Cook
1992	Tia Maria
1990	Tia Maria
1990	TheTimes
1994	Tizer
1980	Tjaereborg Rejser*
1980	Tolly's Original
1984	Torbay Tourist Board*
1986	Toshiba*
1986	Touche Remnant Unit Trusts
1992	Tower of London
1996	Toyota RAV4
1982	Trans World Airlines
1984	Tri-ac
1980	Triumph Dolomite
1994	TSB
1988	TSB*
1986	TSB*
1982	Turkish Delight*
1986	TV Licence Evasion*

U

1984	UK Canned Salmon
1986	Umbongo Tropical juice Drink
1990	Uvistat*

V

1988	Varilux lenses
1994	Vauxhall Astra.
1996	Vauxhall Cavalier
1990	Vauxhall Cavalier
1996	Vegetarian Society
1986	Virgin Atlantic
1994	Visa
1986	Vodafone
1992	VW Golf*

W

1980	Waistline
1992	Wales Tourist Board
1980	Wall's Cornetto
1996	Wall's Viennetta
1984	Wall's Viennetta*
1996	Walker's Crisps*
1984	Walnut Whips
1990	Warburtons Bread*
1984	Websters Yorkshire Bitter
1988	Weight Watchers Slimming Clubs
1990	Westwood Tractors
1992	Whipsnade Wild Animal Park*
1980	Whitegate's Estate Agents*
1990	Wilson's Ultra Golf Balls
1988	Winalot Prime*
1994	Wonderbra*

Y

1980	Yeoman Pie Fillings
1980	Yorkie
1982	Yorkshire Bank

Z

| 1984 | Zanussi* |
| 1994 | Zovirax |

* Denotes publication in the relevant *Advertising Works* volume

Index